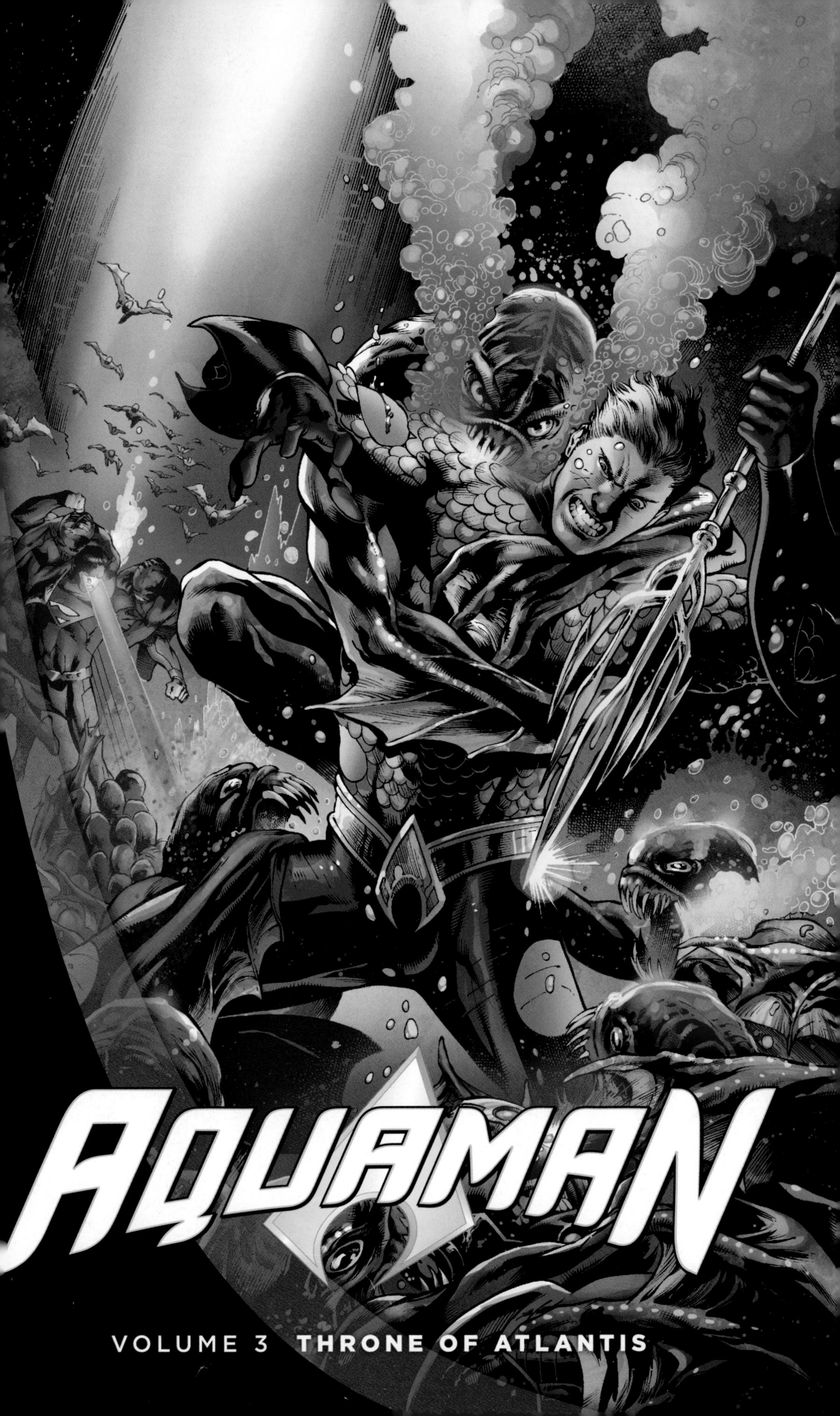
AQUAMAN
VOLUME 3 THRONE OF ATLANTIS

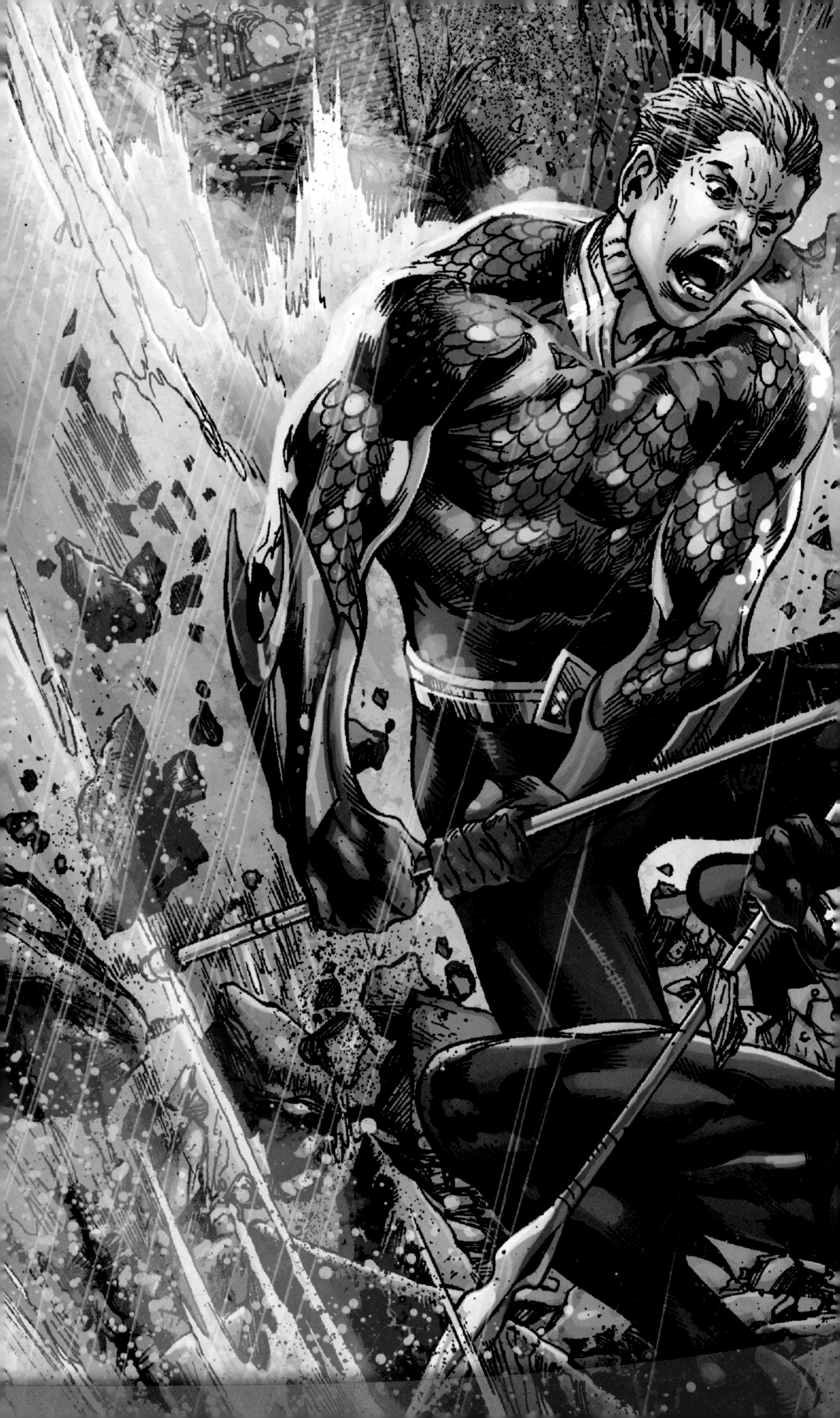

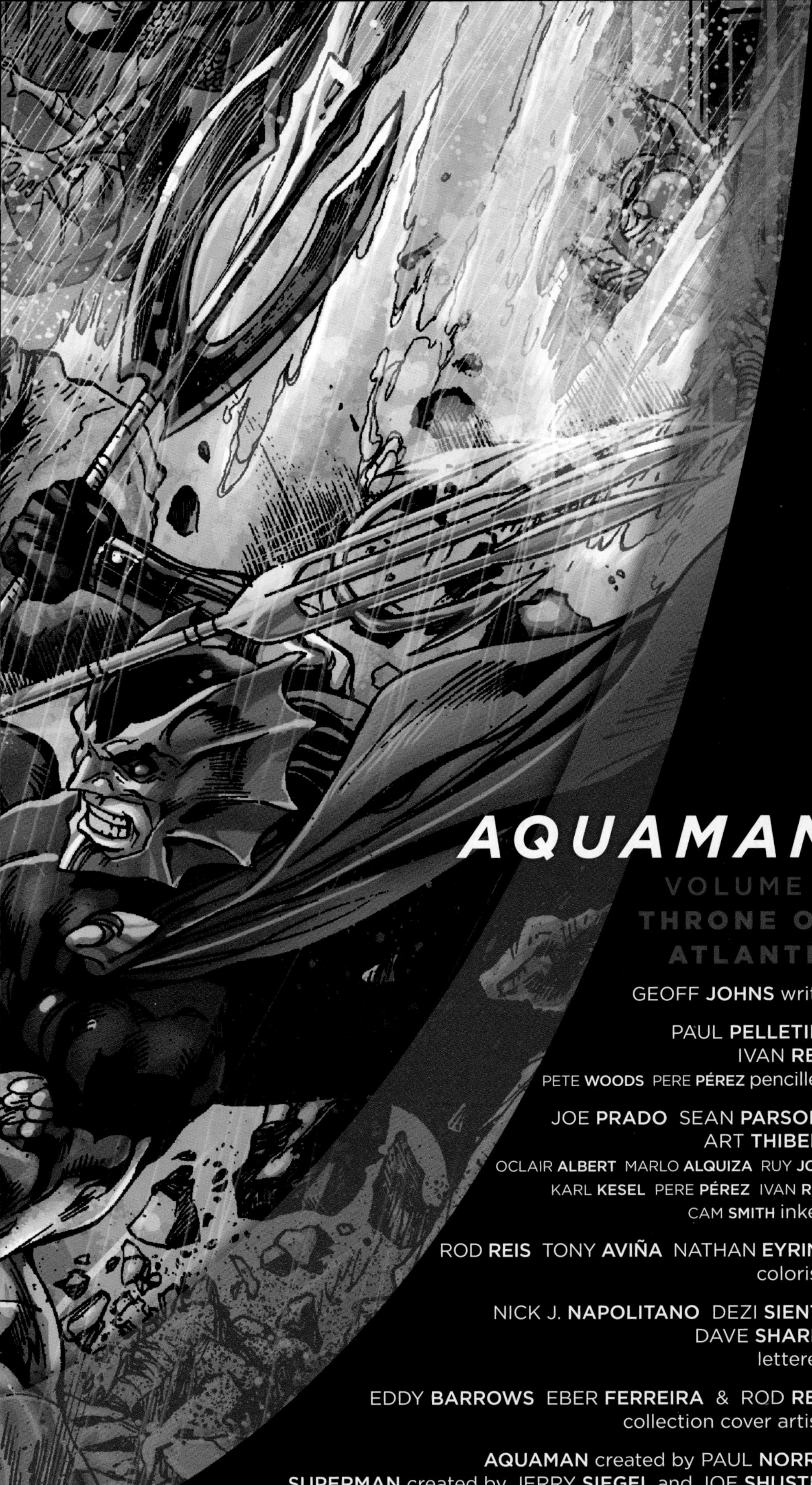

AQUAMAN

VOLUME 3
THRONE OF ATLANTIS

GEOFF **JOHNS** writer

PAUL **PELLETIER**
IVAN **REIS**
PETE **WOODS** PERE **PÉREZ** pencillers

JOE **PRADO** SEAN **PARSONS**
ART **THIBERT**
OCLAIR **ALBERT** MARLO **ALQUIZA** RUY **JOSE**
KARL **KESEL** PERE **PÉREZ** IVAN **REIS**
CAM **SMITH** inkers

ROD **REIS** TONY **AVIÑA** NATHAN **EYRING**
colorists

NICK J. **NAPOLITANO** DEZI **SIENTY**
DAVE **SHARPE**
letterers

EDDY **BARROWS** EBER **FERREIRA** & ROD **REIS**
collection cover artists

AQUAMAN created by PAUL **NORRIS**
SUPERMAN created by JERRY **SIEGEL** and JOE **SHUSTER**
By special arrangement with the Jerry Siegel family

BRIAN CUNNINGHAM PAT McCALLUM Editors – Original Series KATIE KUBERT CHRIS CONROY Associate Editors – Original Series
KATE STEWART Assistant Editor – Original Series ROBIN WILDMAN Editor
ROBBIN BROSTERMAN Design Director – Books ROBBIE BIEDERMAN Publication Design

BOB HARRAS Senior VP – Editor-in-Chief, DC Comics

DIANE NELSON President DAN DIDIO and JIM LEE Co-Publishers GEOFF JOHNS Chief Creative Officer
JOHN ROOD Executive VP – Sales, Marketing and Business Development
AMY GENKINS Senior VP – Business and Legal Affairs NAIRI GARDINER Senior VP – Finance
JEFF BOISON VP – Publishing Planning MARK CHIARELLO VP – Art Direction and Design
JOHN CUNNINGHAM VP – Marketing TERRI CUNNINGHAM VP – Editorial Administration
ALISON GILL Senior VP – Manufacturing and Operations HANK KANALZ Senior VP – Vertigo and Integrated Publishing
JAY KOGAN VP – Business and Legal Affairs, Publishing JACK MAHAN VP – Business Affairs, Talent
NICK NAPOLITANO VP – Manufacturing Administration SUE POHJA VP – Book Sales
COURTNEY SIMMONS Senior VP – Publicity BOB WAYNE Senior VP – Sales

AQUAMAN VOLUME 3: THRONE OF ATLANTIS

DC Comics, 1700 Broadway, New York, NY 10019
A Warner Bros. Entertainment Company.
Printed by RR Donnelley, Salem, VA, USA. 10/11/13. First Printing.

HC ISBN: 978-1-4012-4309-8
SC ISBN: 978-1-4012-4695-2

Library of Congress Cataloging-in-Publication Data

Johns, Geoff, 1973- author.
Aquaman. Volume 3, Throne of Atlantis / Geoff Johns, Paul Pelletier, Ivan Reis.
pages cm
"Originally published in single magazine form as AQUAMAN 0, 14-16, JUSTICE LEAGUE 15-17."
ISBN 978-1-4012-4309-8
1. Graphic novels. I. Pelletier, Paul, 1970- illustrator. II. Reis, Ivan, illustrator. III. Title. IV. Title: Throne of Atlantis.
PN6728.A68J66 2013
741.5'973—dc23
2013026273

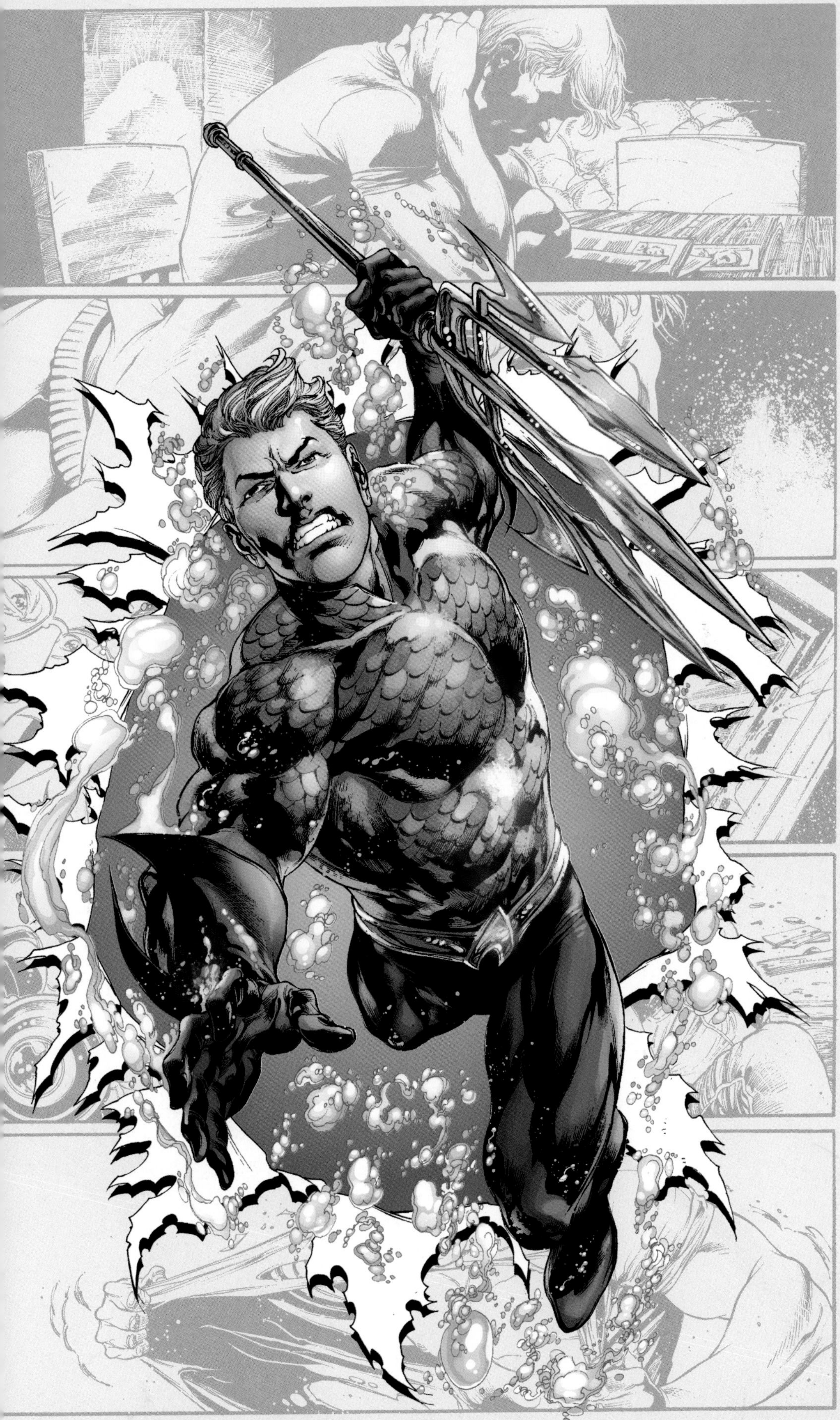

GEOFF JOHNS writer **IVAN REIS** penciller **JOE PRADO** inker cover by **IVAN REIS, JOE PRADO & ROD REIS**

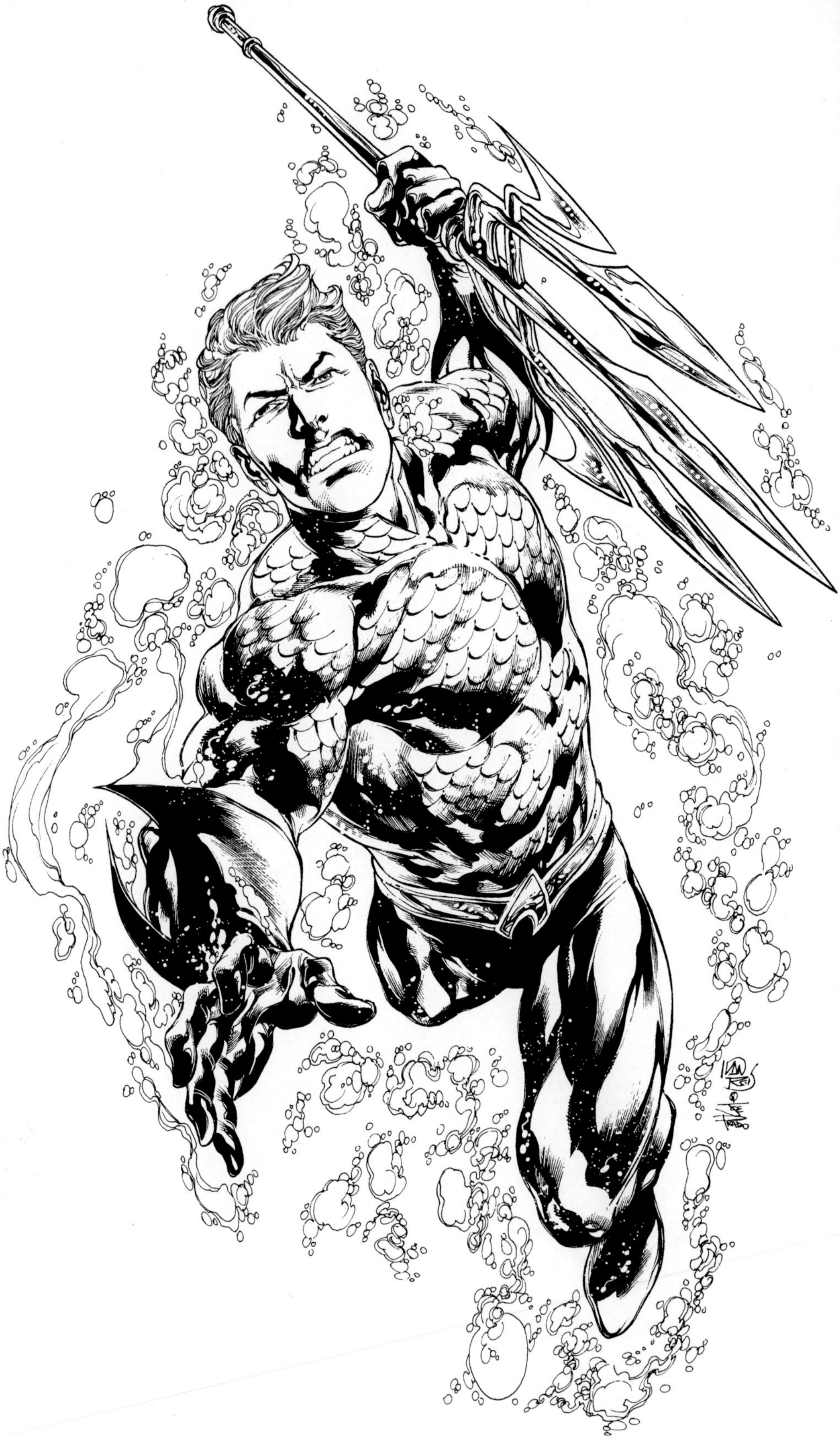

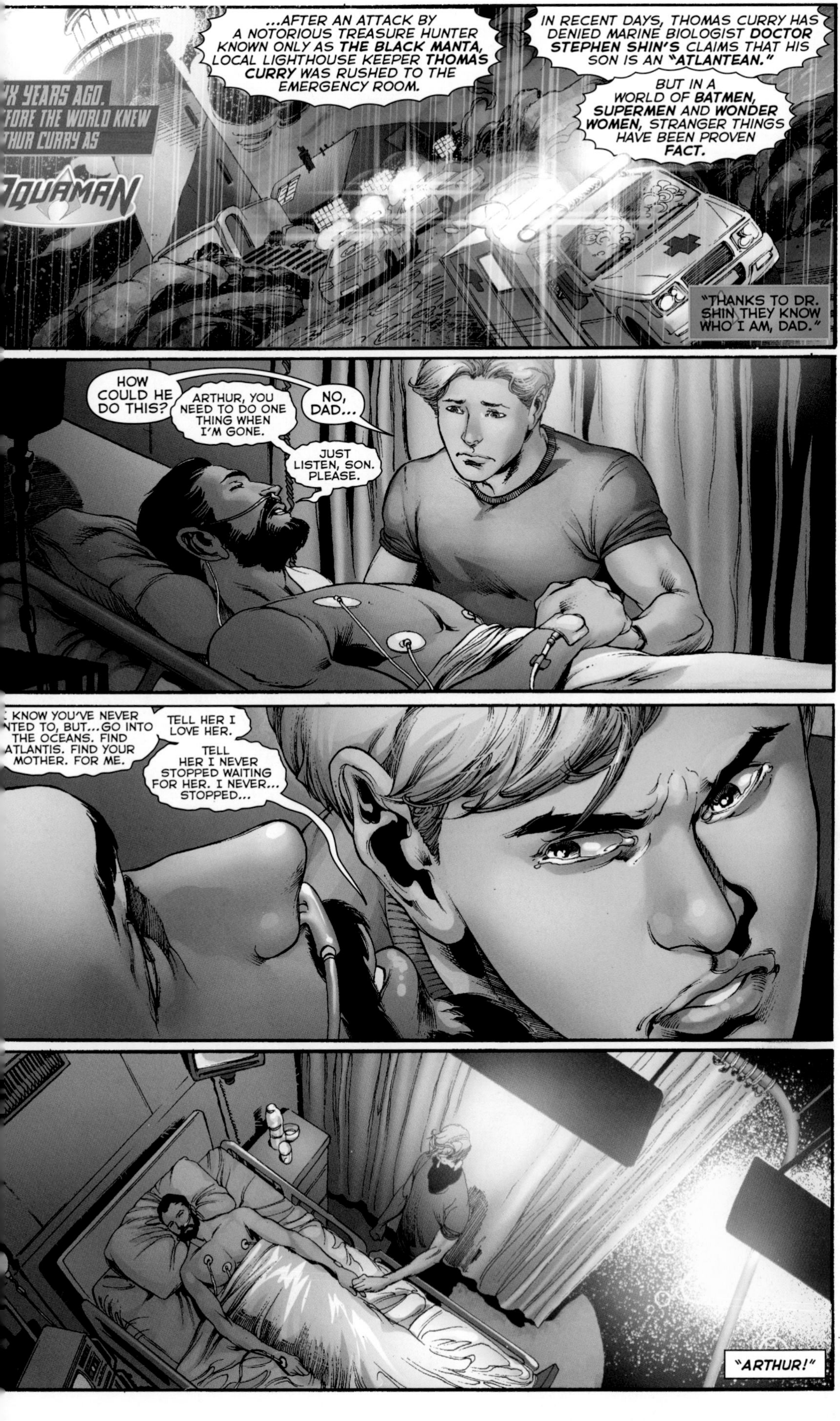
...AFTER AN ATTACK BY A NOTORIOUS TREASURE HUNTER KNOWN ONLY AS THE BLACK MANTA, LOCAL LIGHTHOUSE KEEPER THOMAS CURRY WAS RUSHED TO THE EMERGENCY ROOM.
IN RECENT DAYS, THOMAS CURRY HAS DENIED MARINE BIOLOGIST DOCTOR STEPHEN SHIN'S CLAIMS THAT HIS SON IS AN "ATLANTEAN."
BUT IN A WORLD OF BATMEN, SUPERMEN AND WONDER WOMEN, STRANGER THINGS HAVE BEEN PROVEN FACT.
"THANKS TO DR. SHIN THEY KNOW WHO I AM, DAD."
HOW COULD HE DO THIS?
ARTHUR, YOU NEED TO DO ONE THING WHEN I'M GONE.
NO, DAD...
JUST LISTEN, SON. PLEASE.
TELL HER I LOVE HER.
TELL HER I NEVER STOPPED WAITING FOR HER. I NEVER... STOPPED...
"ARTHUR!"

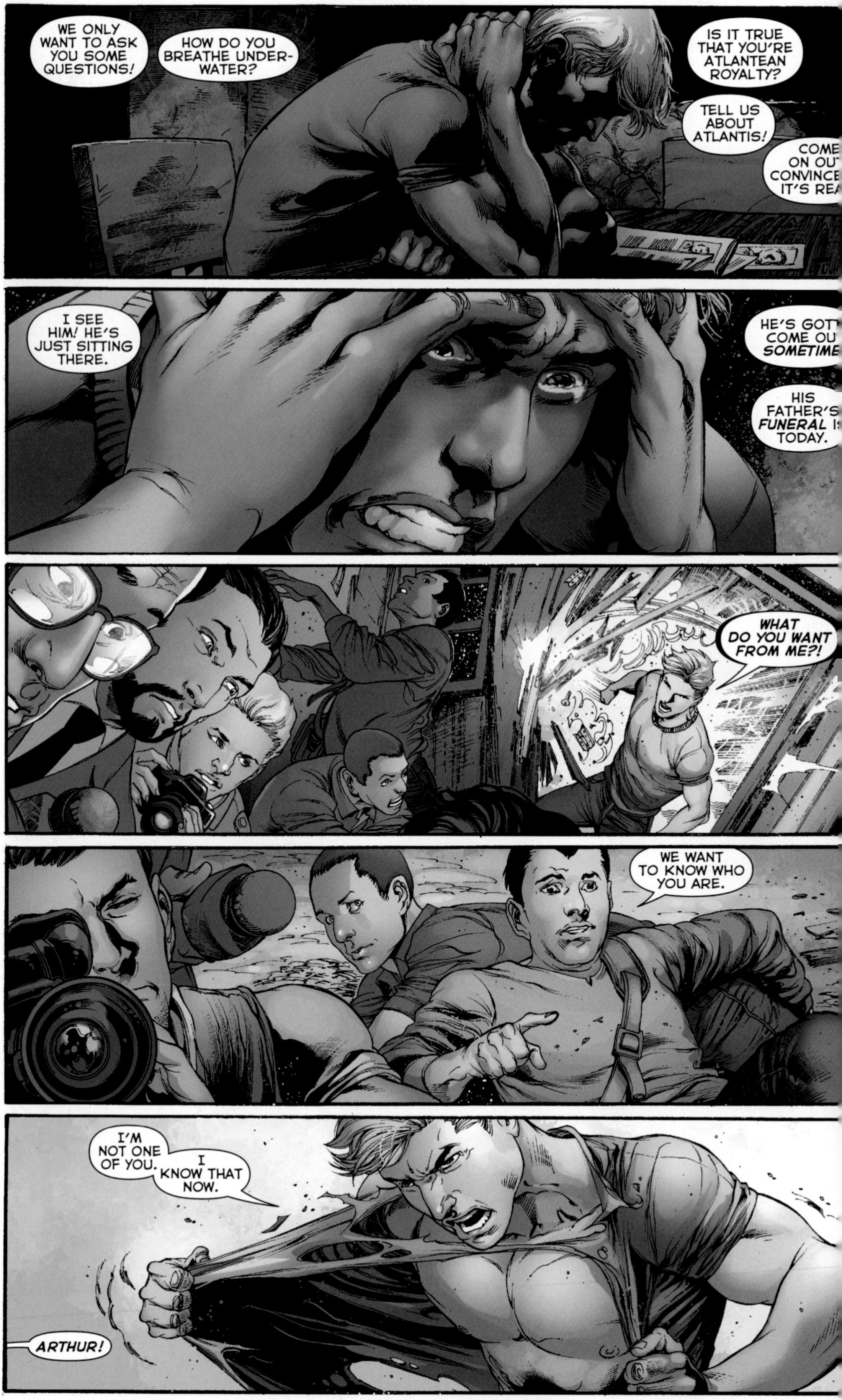
WE ONLY WANT TO ASK YOU SOME QUESTIONS!
HOW DO YOU BREATHE UNDER-WATER?
IS IT TRUE THAT YOU'RE ATLANTEAN ROYALTY?
TELL US ABOUT ATLANTIS!
I SEE HIM! HE'S JUST SITTING THERE.
WHAT DO YOU WANT FROM ME?!
WE WANT TO KNOW WHO YOU ARE.
I'M NOT ONE OF YOU.
I KNOW THAT NOW.
ARTHUR!

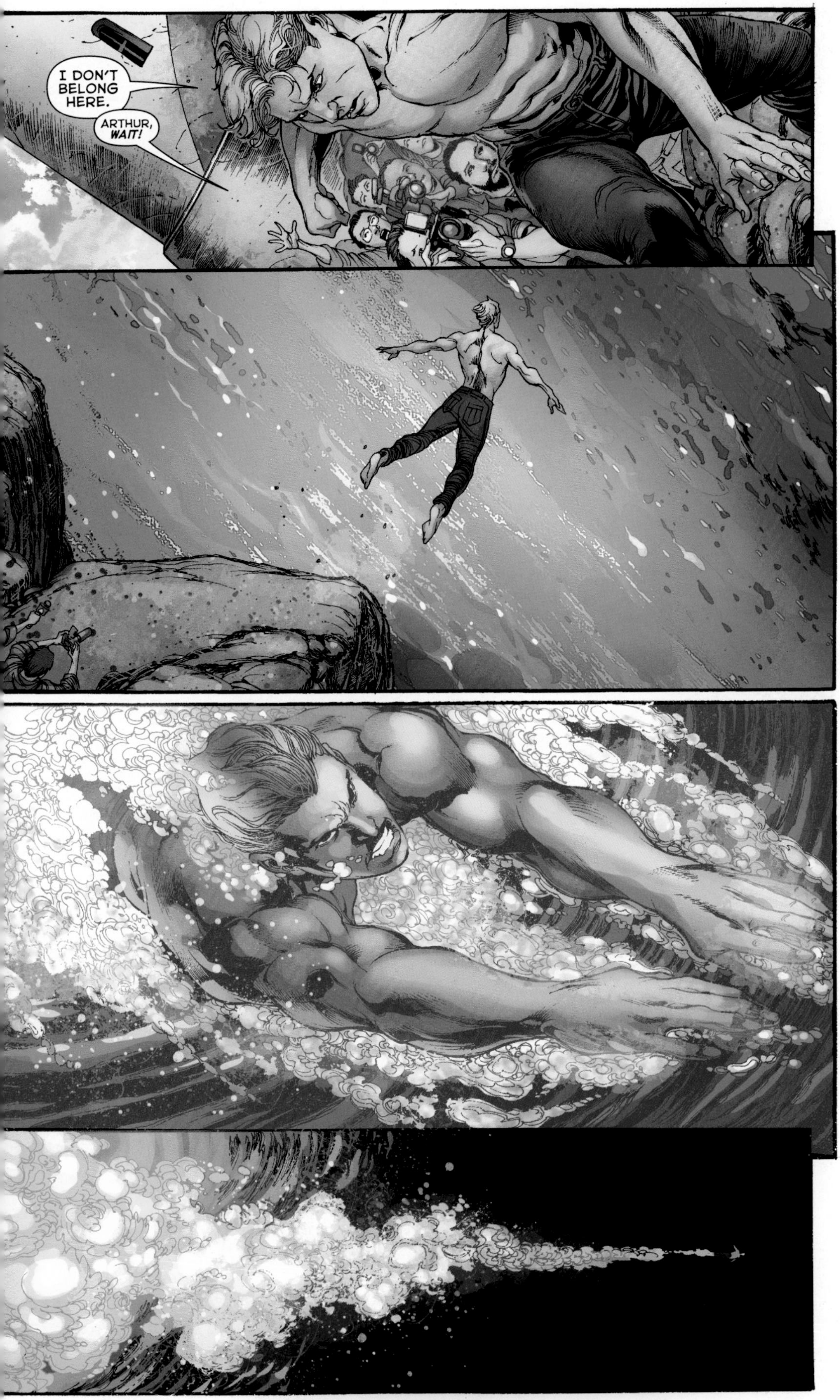
I DON'T BELONG HERE.
ARTHUR, WAIT!

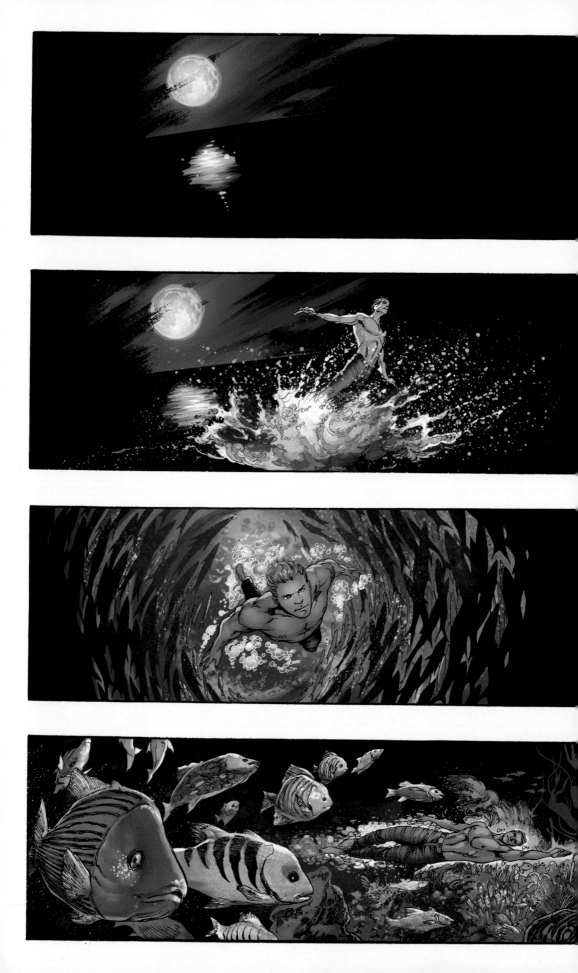

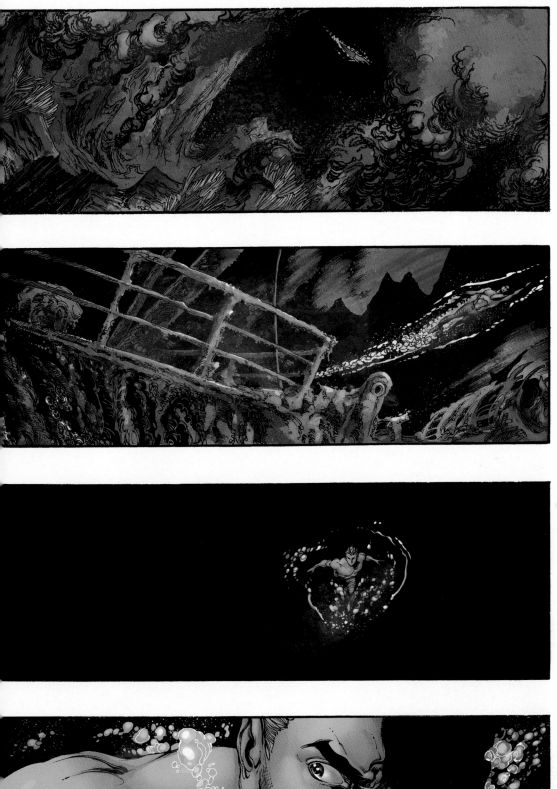

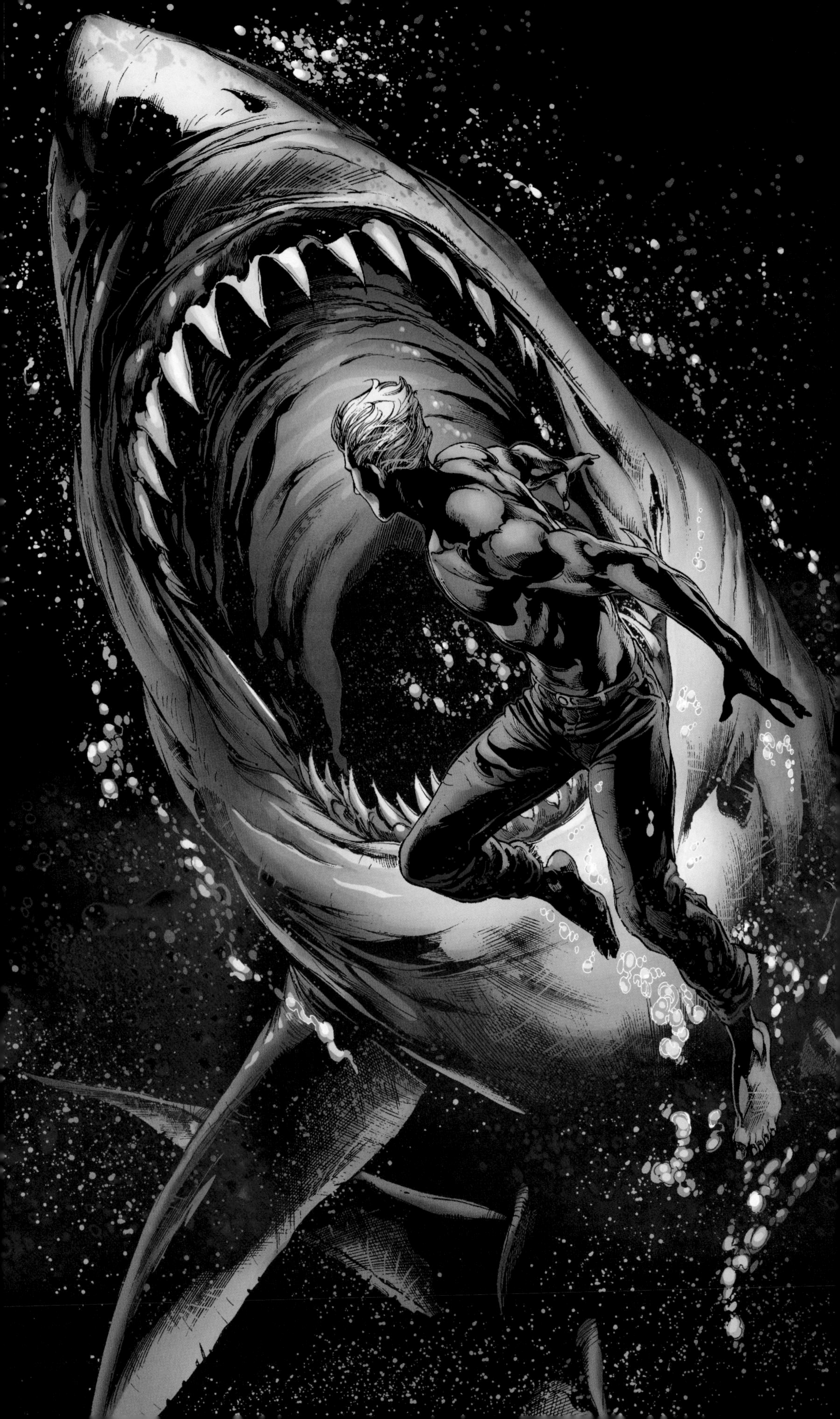

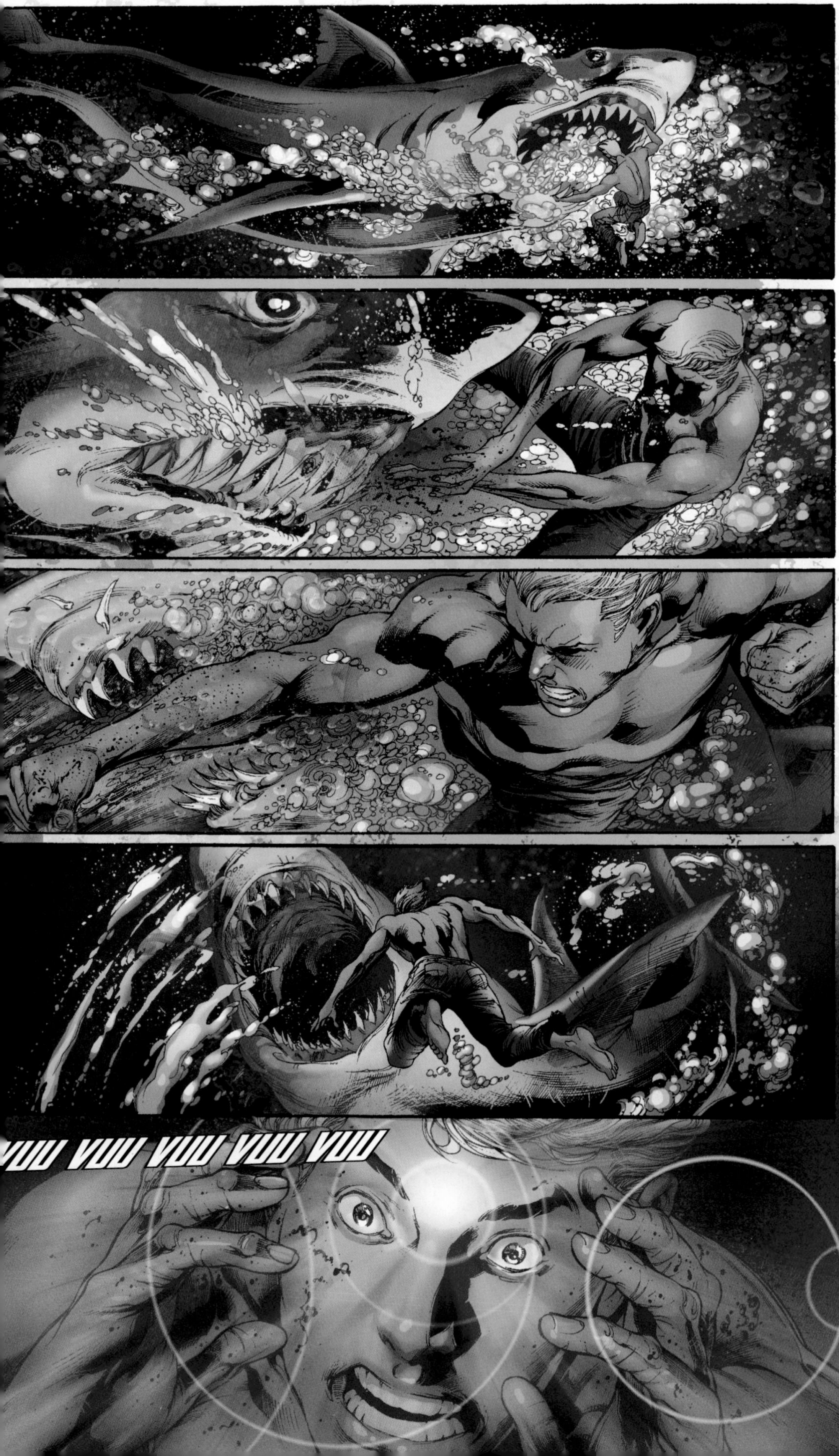
VUU VUU VUU VUU VUU

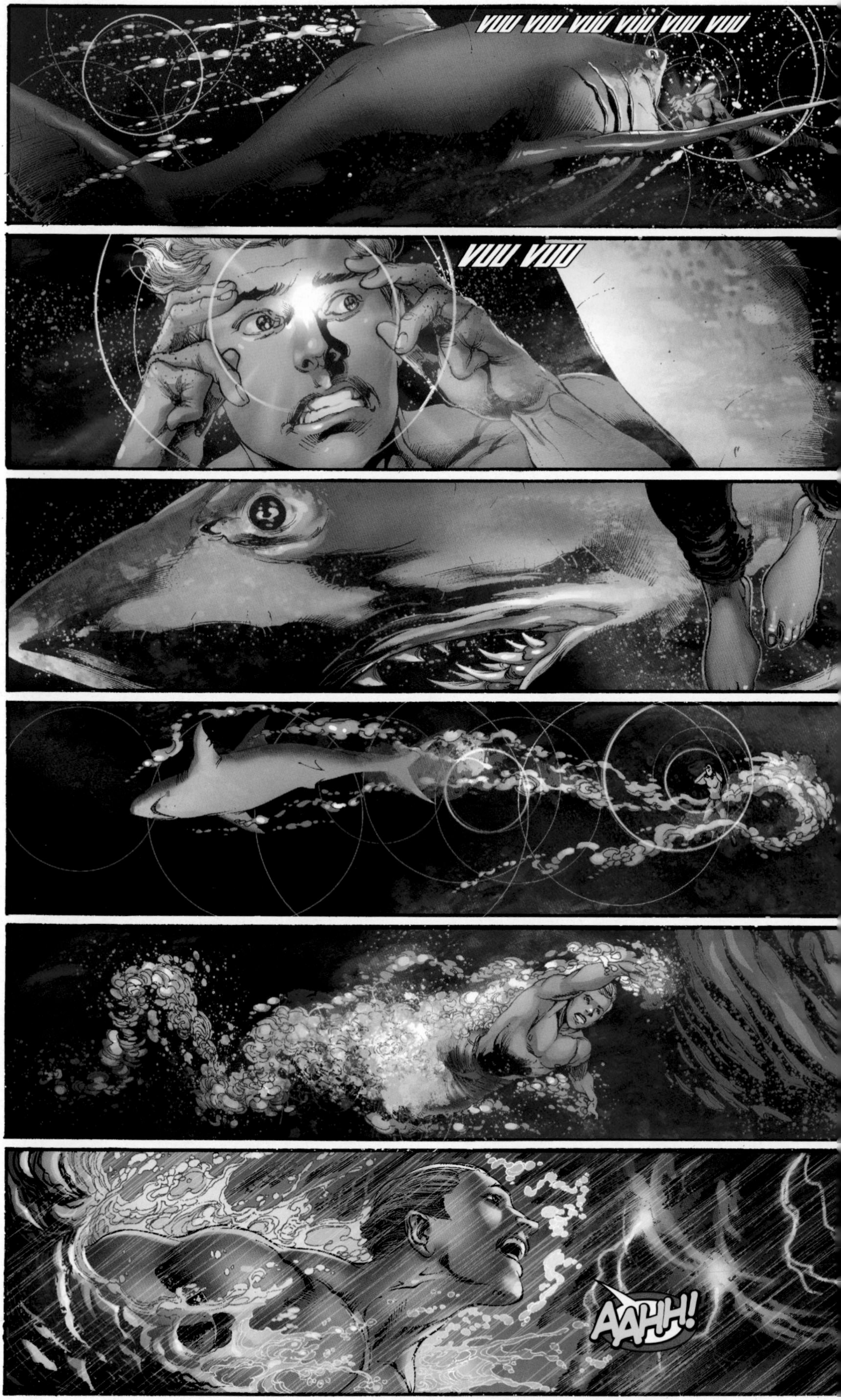
VUU VUU VUU VUU VUU VUU
VUU VUU
AAHH!

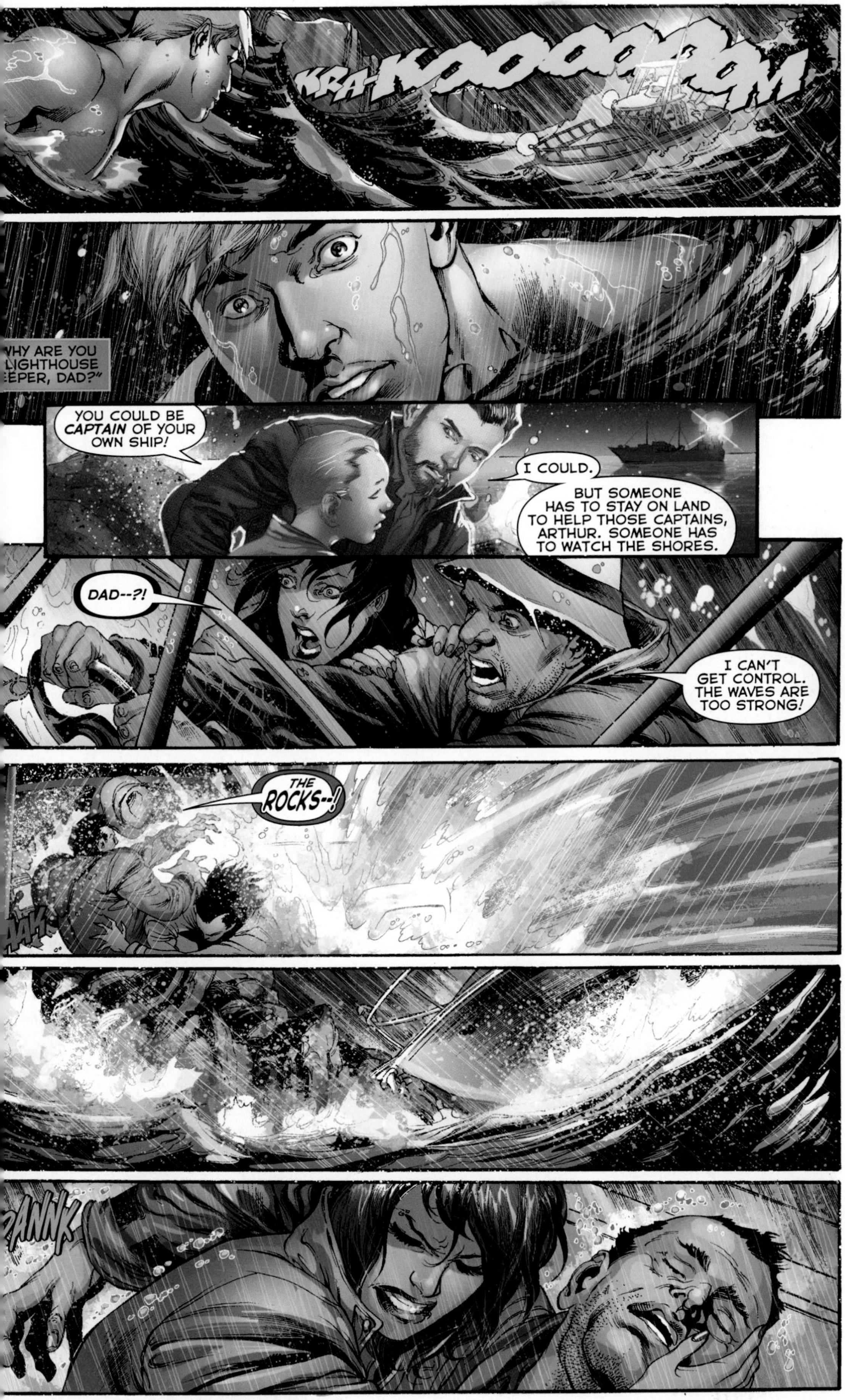
KRA-KOOOOOOM
"WHY ARE YOU A LIGHTHOUSE KEEPER, DAD?"
YOU COULD BE CAPTAIN OF YOUR OWN SHIP!
I COULD.
BUT SOMEONE HAS TO STAY ON LAND TO HELP THOSE CAPTAINS, ARTHUR. SOMEONE HAS TO WATCH THE SHORES.
DAD--?!
I CAN'T GET CONTROL. THE WAVES ARE TOO STRONG!
THE ROCKS--!
AAK
ANNK

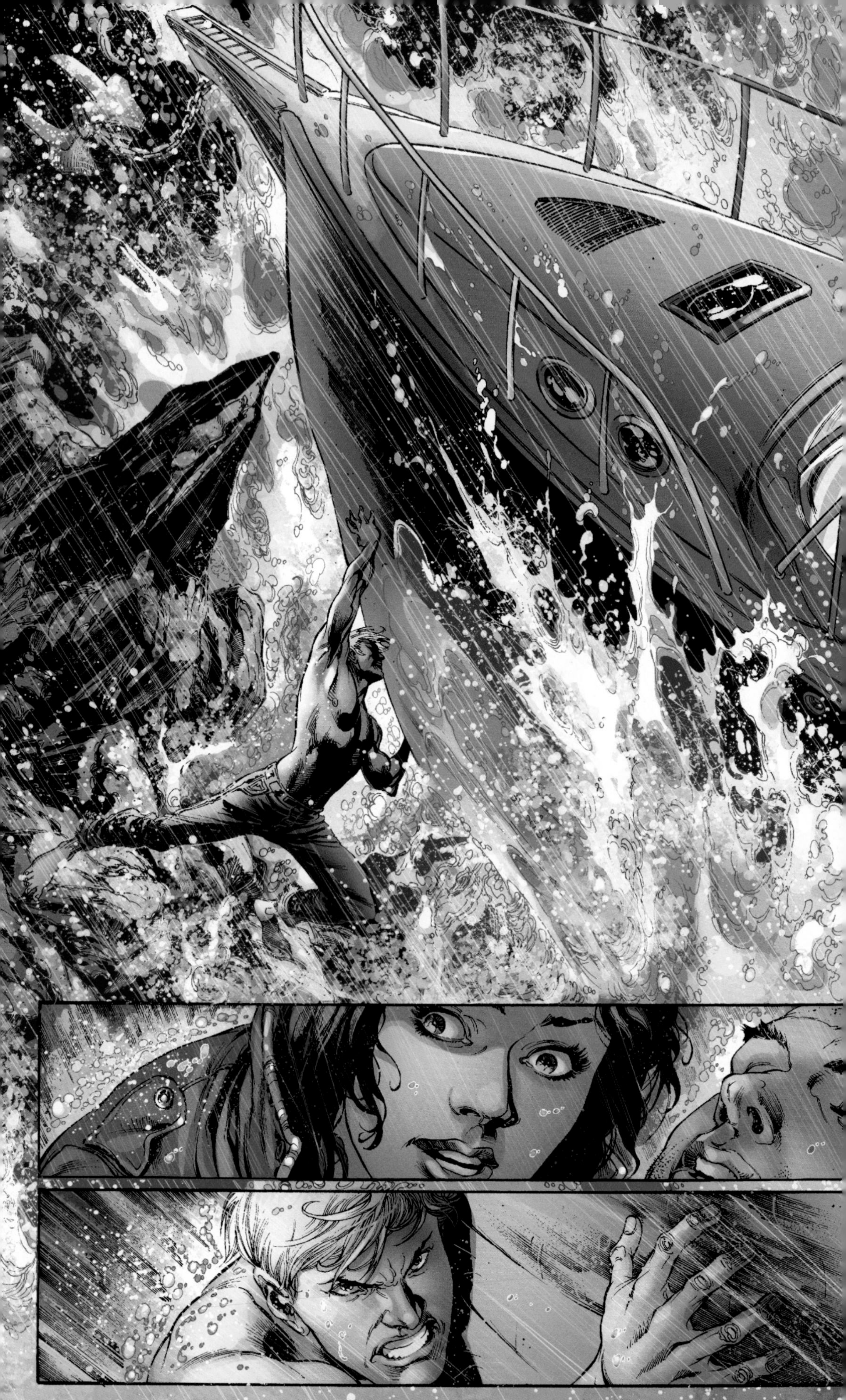

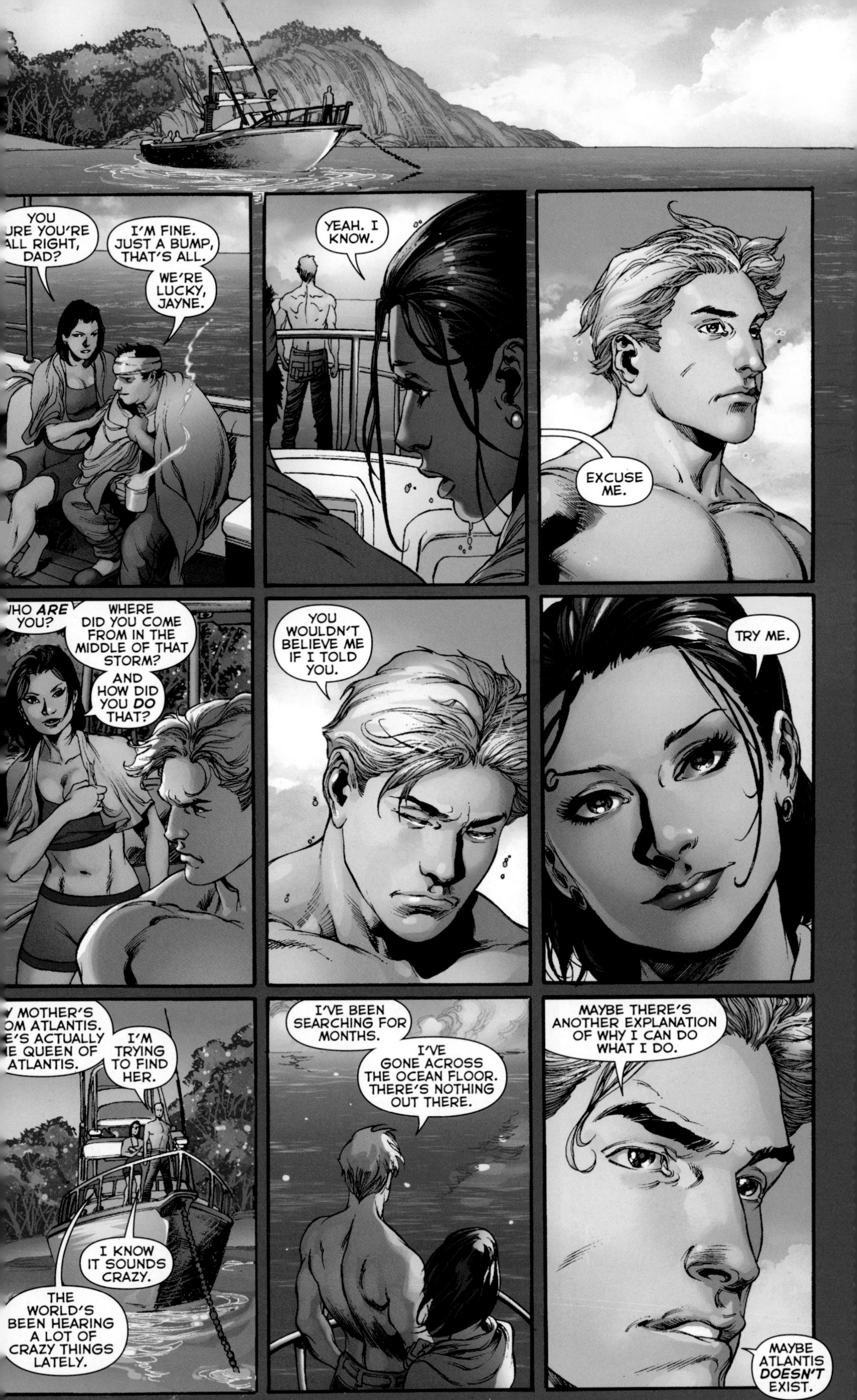
YOU
URE YOU'RE
ALL RIGHT,
DAD?
I'M FINE.
JUST A BUMP,
THAT'S ALL.
WE'RE
LUCKY,
JAYNE.
YEAH. I
KNOW.
EXCUSE
ME.
WHO ARE
YOU?
WHERE
DID YOU COME
FROM IN THE
MIDDLE OF THAT
STORM?
AND
HOW DID
YOU DO
THAT?
YOU
WOULDN'T
BELIEVE ME
IF I TOLD
YOU.
TRY ME.
Y MOTHER'S
OM ATLANTIS.
E'S ACTUALLY
E QUEEN OF
ATLANTIS.
I'M
TRYING
TO FIND
HER.
I KNOW
IT SOUNDS
CRAZY.
THE
WORLD'S
BEEN HEARING
A LOT OF
CRAZY THINGS
LATELY.
I'VE BEEN
SEARCHING FOR
MONTHS.
I'VE
GONE ACROSS
THE OCEAN FLOOR.
THERE'S NOTHING
OUT THERE.
MAYBE THERE'S
ANOTHER EXPLANATION
OF WHY I CAN DO
WHAT I DO.
MAYBE
ATLANTIS
DOESN'T
EXIST.

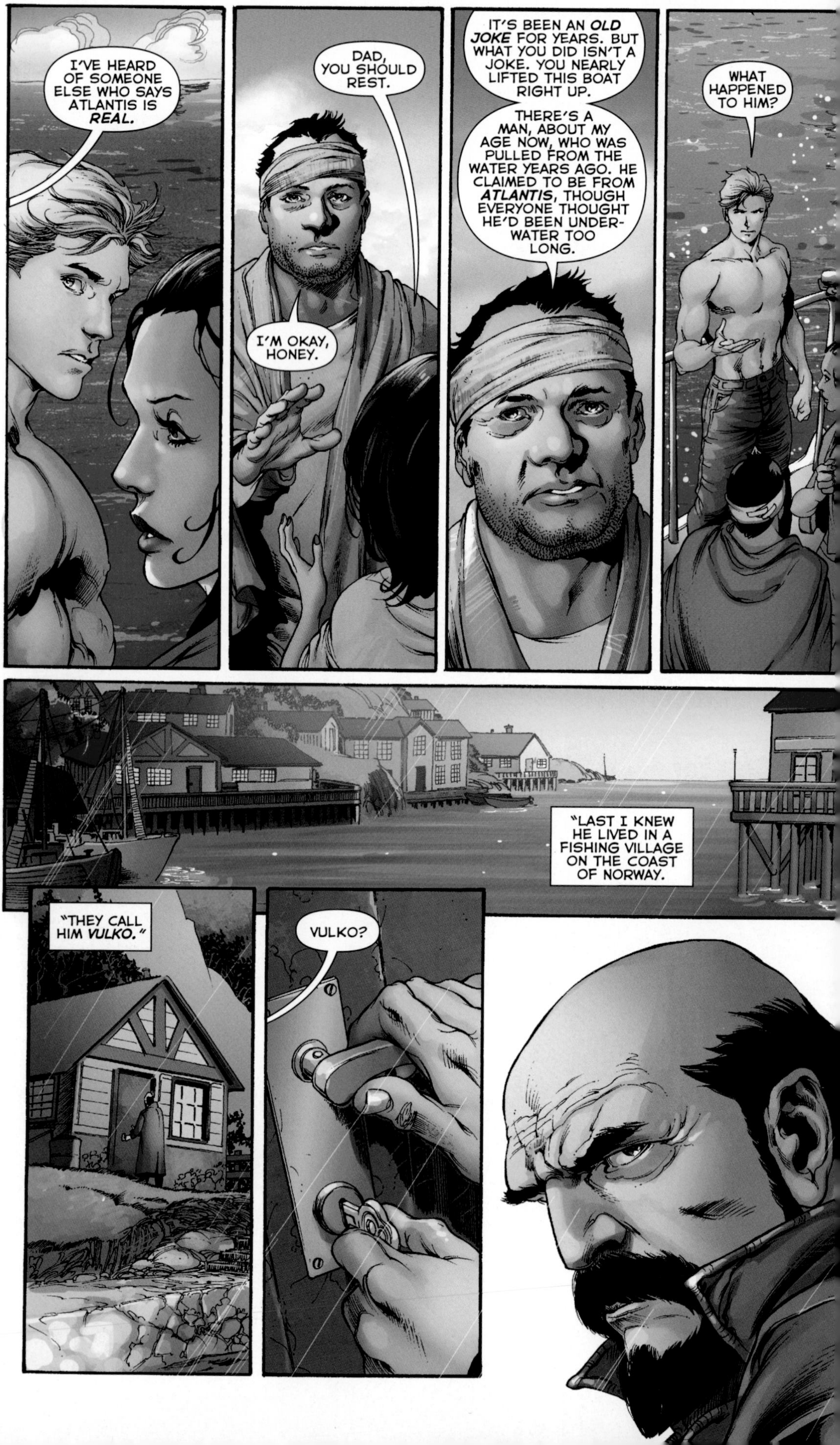
I'VE HEARD OF SOMEONE ELSE WHO SAYS ATLANTIS IS *REAL.*
DAD, YOU SHOULD REST.
I'M OKAY, HONEY.
IT'S BEEN AN *OLD JOKE* FOR YEARS. BUT WHAT YOU DID ISN'T A JOKE. YOU NEARLY LIFTED THIS BOAT RIGHT UP.
THERE'S A MAN, ABOUT MY AGE NOW, WHO WAS PULLED FROM THE WATER YEARS AGO. HE CLAIMED TO BE FROM *ATLANTIS*, THOUGH EVERYONE THOUGHT HE'D BEEN UNDER-WATER TOO LONG.
WHAT HAPPENED TO HIM?
"LAST I KNEW HE LIVED IN A FISHING VILLAGE ON THE COAST OF NORWAY.
"THEY CALL HIM *VULKO.*"
VULKO?

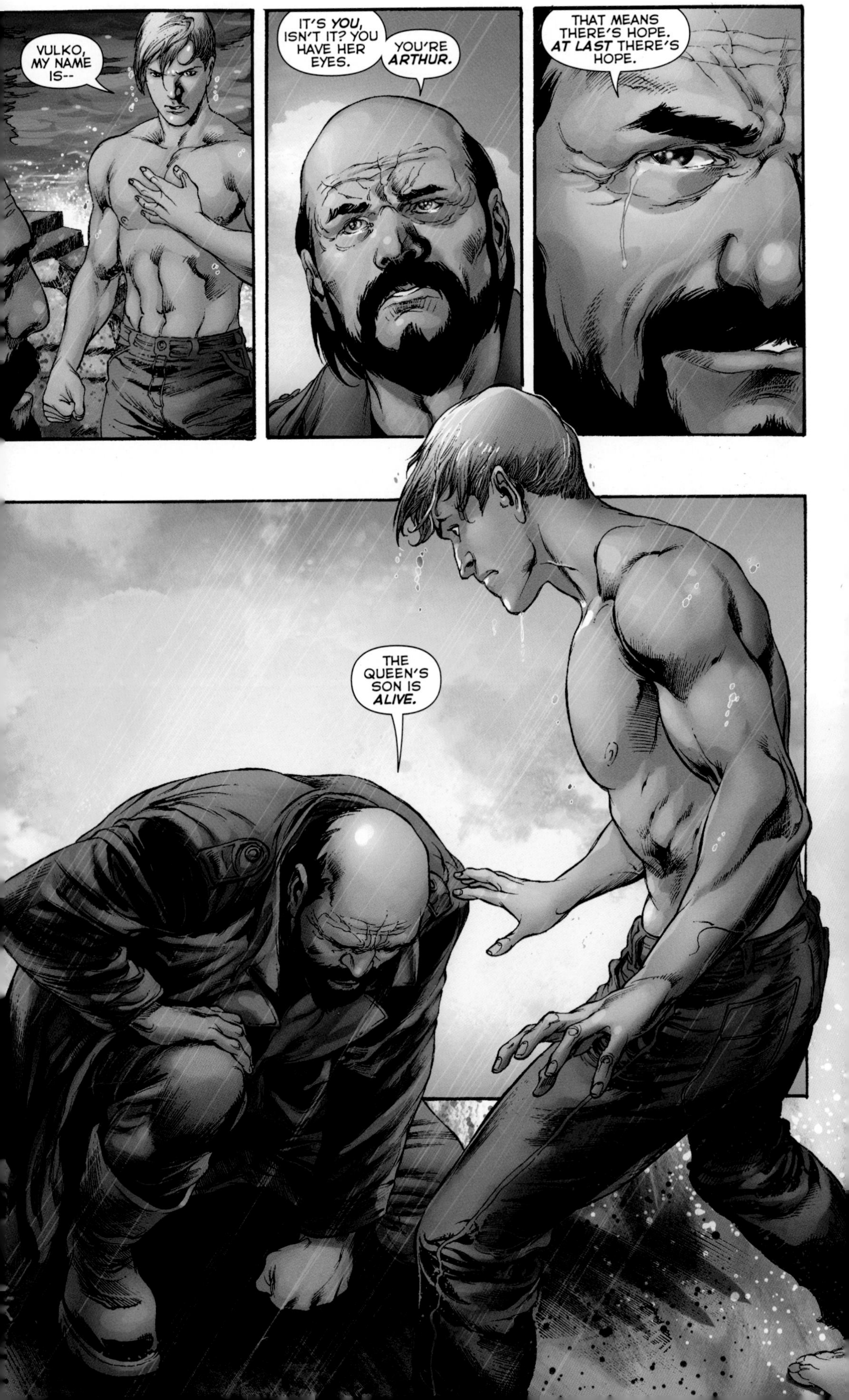
VULKO, MY NAME IS--
IT'S YOU, ISN'T IT? YOU HAVE HER EYES.
YOU'RE ARTHUR.
THAT MEANS THERE'S HOPE. AT LAST THERE'S HOPE.
THE QUEEN'S SON IS ALIVE.

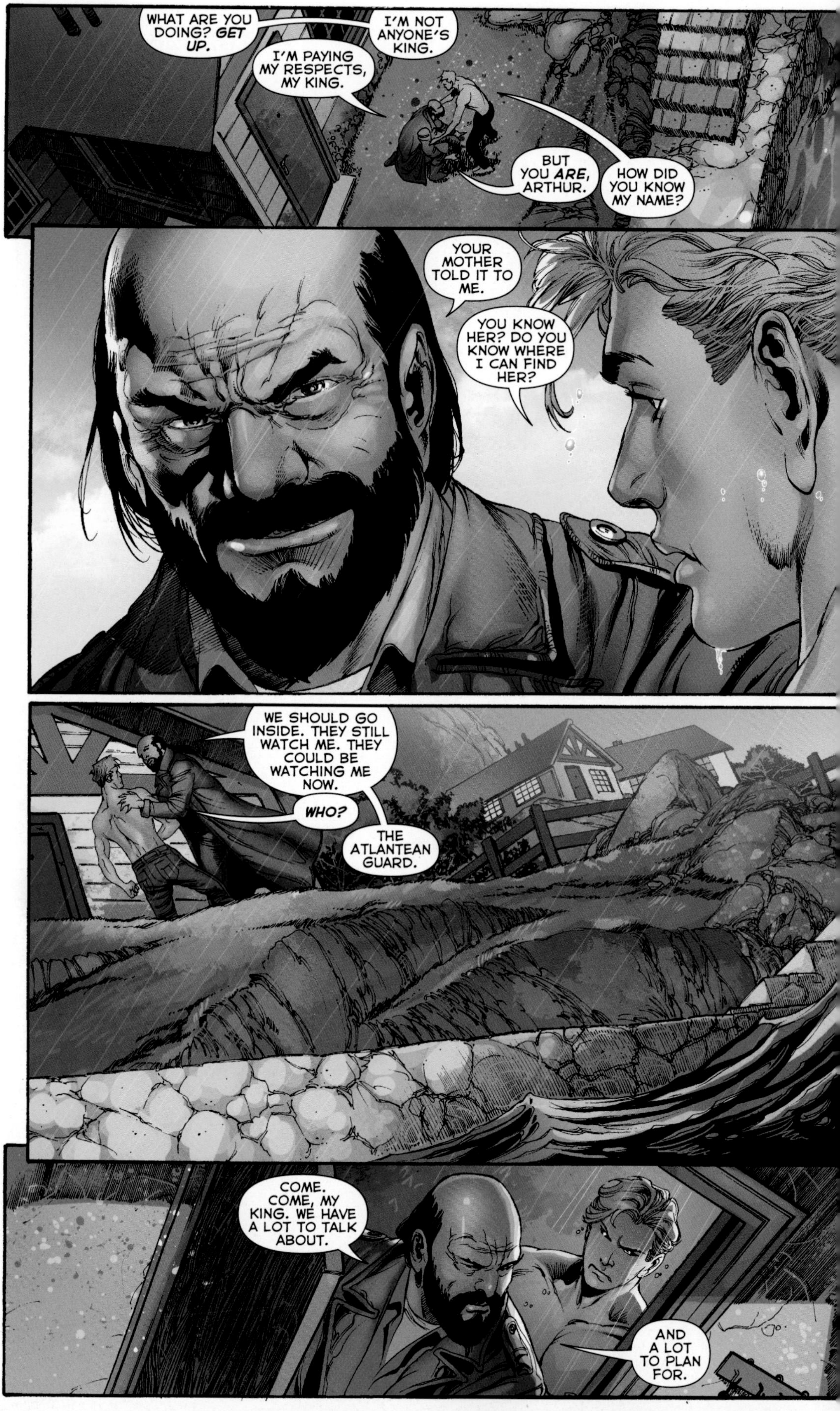
WHAT ARE YOU DOING? *GET UP.*
I'M PAYING MY RESPECTS, MY KING.
I'M NOT ANYONE'S KING.
BUT YOU *ARE*, ARTHUR.
HOW DID YOU KNOW MY NAME?
YOUR MOTHER TOLD IT TO ME.
YOU KNOW HER? DO YOU KNOW WHERE I CAN FIND HER?
WE SHOULD GO INSIDE. THEY STILL WATCH ME. THEY COULD BE WATCHING ME NOW.
WHO?
THE ATLANTEAN GUARD.
COME. COME, MY KING. WE HAVE A LOT TO TALK ABOUT.
AND A LOT TO PLAN FOR.

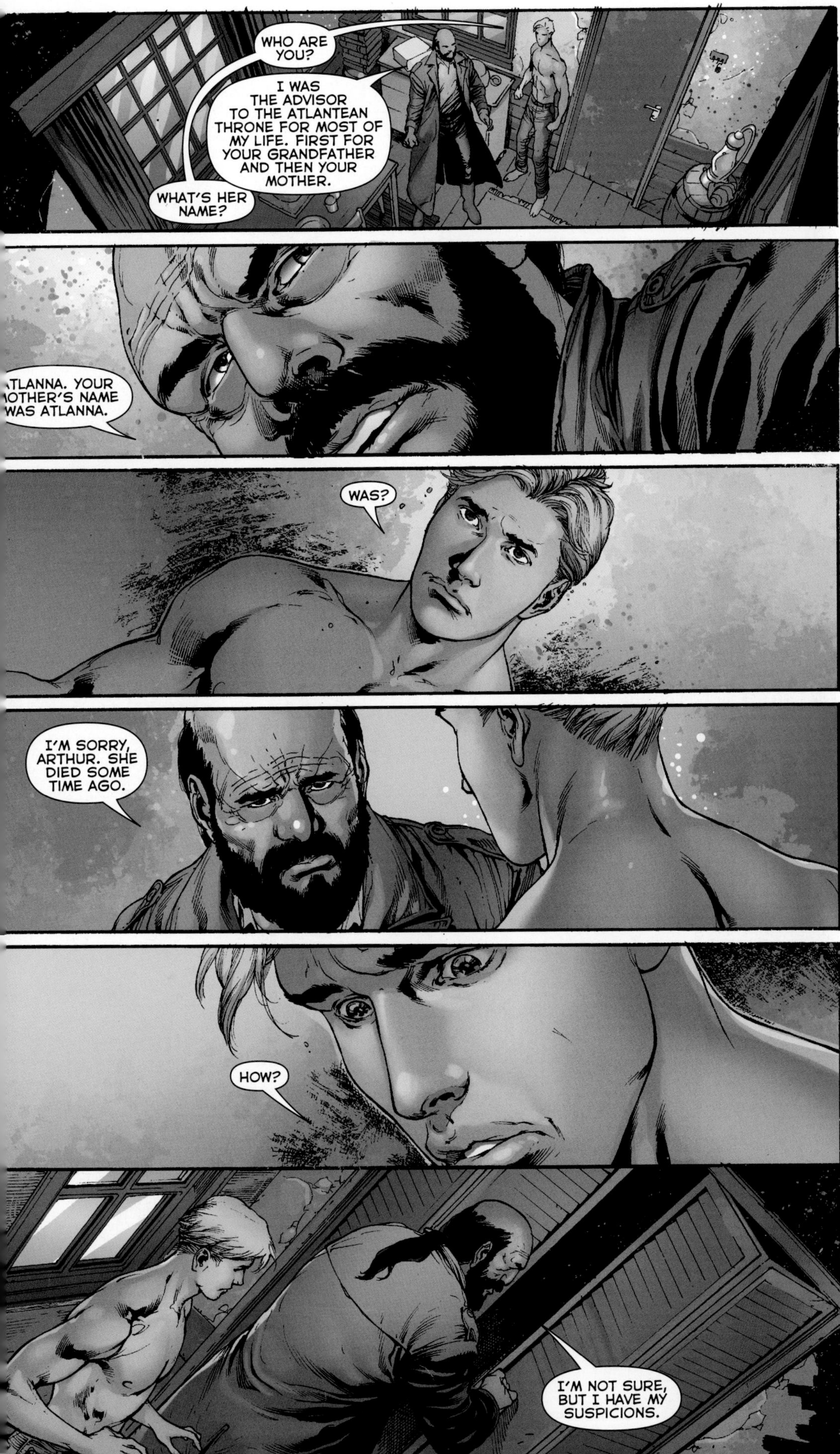
WHO ARE YOU?
I WAS THE ADVISOR TO THE ATLANTEAN THRONE FOR MOST OF MY LIFE. FIRST FOR YOUR GRANDFATHER AND THEN YOUR MOTHER.
WHAT'S HER NAME?
ATLANNA. YOUR MOTHER'S NAME WAS ATLANNA.
WAS?
I'M SORRY, ARTHUR. SHE DIED SOME TIME AGO.
HOW?
I'M NOT SURE, BUT I HAVE MY SUSPICIONS.

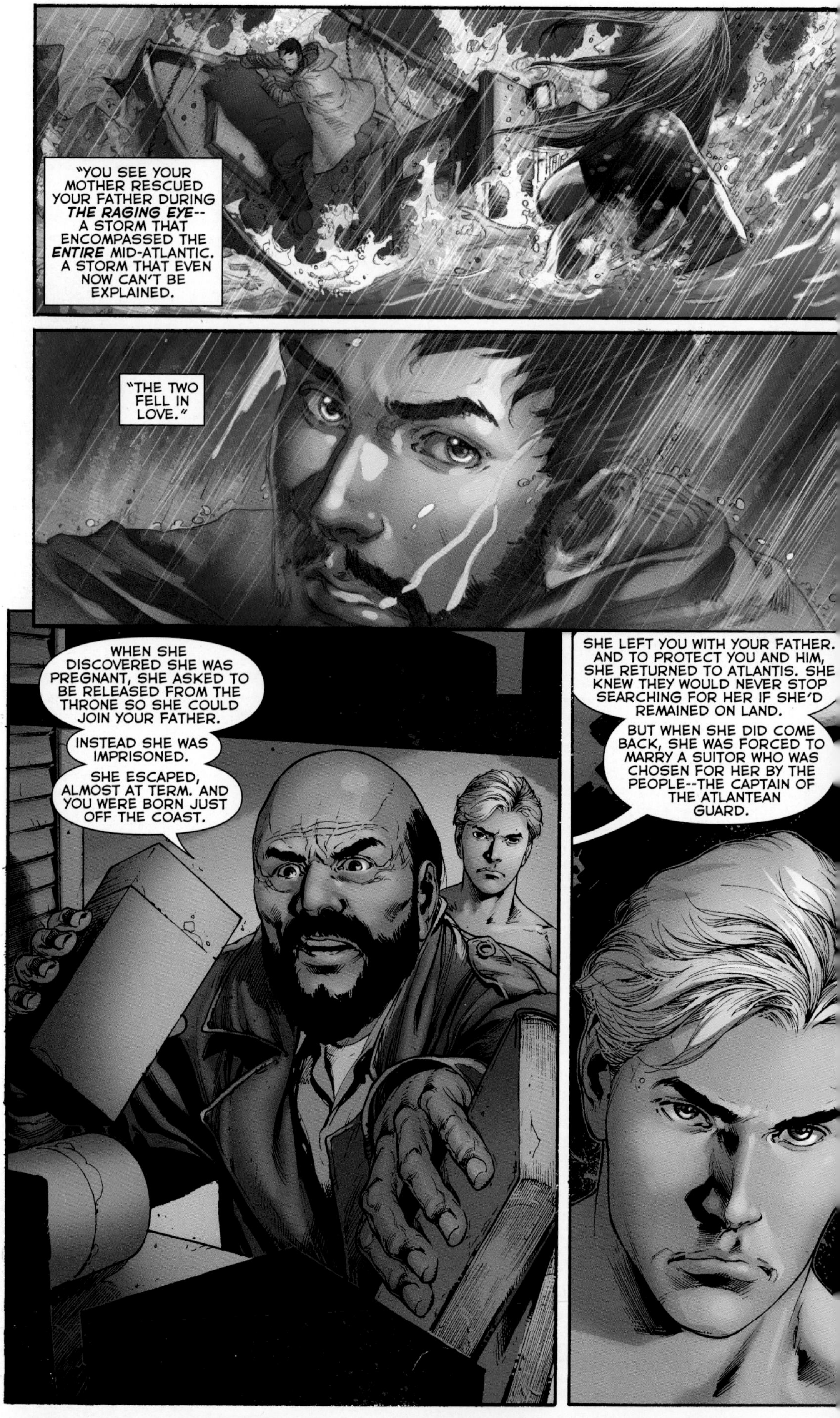
"YOU SEE YOUR MOTHER RESCUED YOUR FATHER DURING *THE RAGING EYE*-- A STORM THAT ENCOMPASSED THE *ENTIRE* MID-ATLANTIC. A STORM THAT EVEN NOW CAN'T BE EXPLAINED.
"THE TWO FELL IN LOVE."
WHEN SHE DISCOVERED SHE WAS PREGNANT, SHE ASKED TO BE RELEASED FROM THE THRONE SO SHE COULD JOIN YOUR FATHER.
INSTEAD SHE WAS IMPRISONED.
SHE ESCAPED, ALMOST AT TERM. AND YOU WERE BORN JUST OFF THE COAST.
SHE LEFT YOU WITH YOUR FATHER. AND TO PROTECT YOU AND HIM, SHE RETURNED TO ATLANTIS. SHE KNEW THEY WOULD NEVER STOP SEARCHING FOR HER IF SHE'D REMAINED ON LAND.
BUT WHEN SHE DID COME BACK, SHE WAS FORCED TO MARRY A SUITOR WHO WAS CHOSEN FOR HER BY THE PEOPLE--THE CAPTAIN OF THE ATLANTEAN GUARD.

"SHE SIRED A *SECOND* SON.

"YOUR YOUNGER BROTHER--ORM.

ON ORM'S TWELFTH BIRTHDAY, HIS FATHER WAS KILLED.

YOUR [MOTH]ER SAW THIS [AS HER] SECOND [CHAN]CE TO LEAVE [ATLAN]TIS. I HELPED [ARRAN]GE A ROUTE [BACK] TO YOU AND [YOUR] FATHER. SHE [IN]SISTED ON [BRIN]GING ORM.

[BUT SHE WAS] [M]URDERED THE [NI]GHT BEFORE HER ESCAPE.

WHO KILLED HER?

[I B]ELIEVE IT WAS [YO]UR BROTHER. [H]ER OWN SON.

[AFTER] HER DEATH HE BECAME THE *KING* OF *ATLANTIS.*

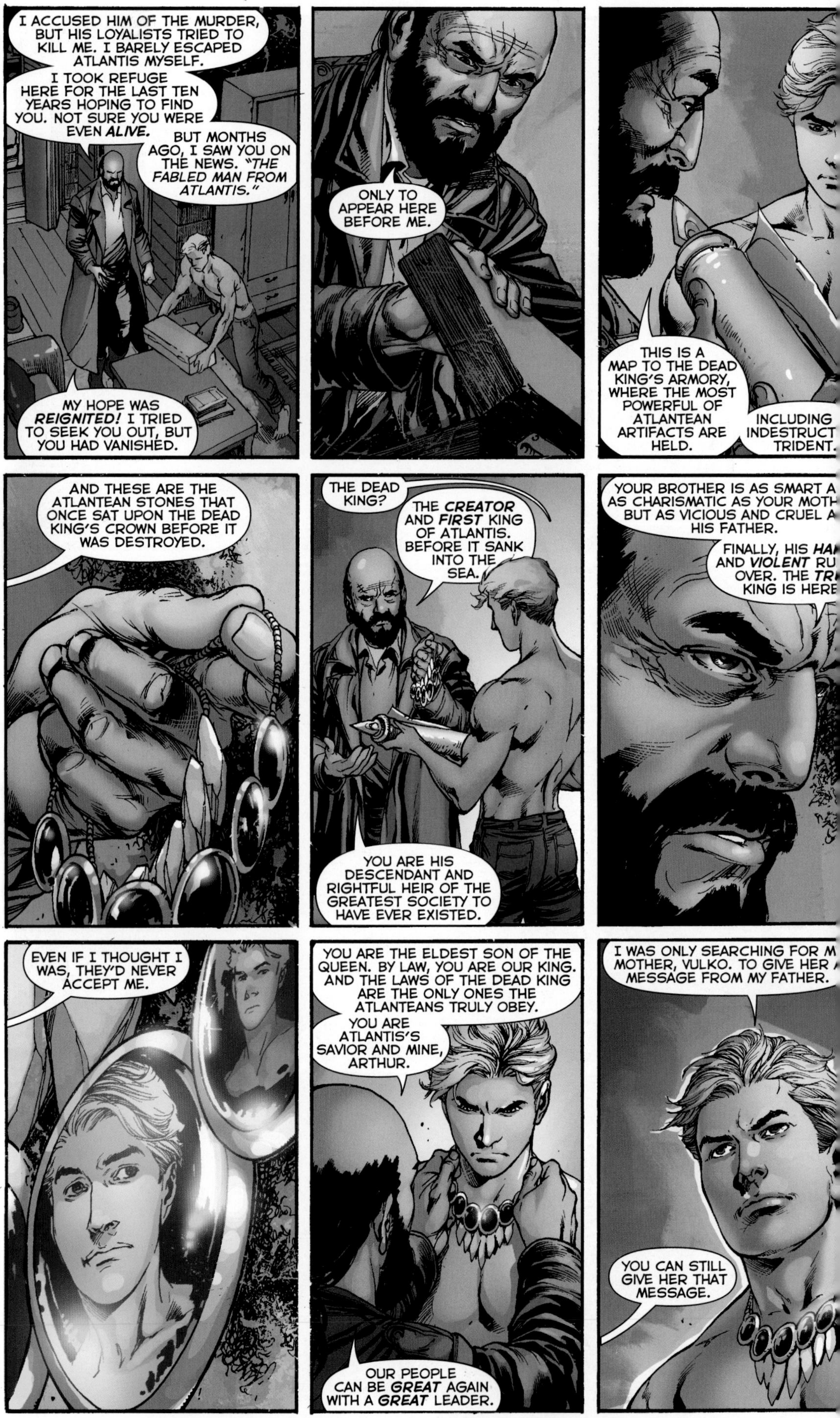
I ACCUSED HIM OF THE MURDER, BUT HIS LOYALISTS TRIED TO KILL ME. I BARELY ESCAPED ATLANTIS MYSELF.
I TOOK REFUGE HERE FOR THE LAST TEN YEARS HOPING TO FIND YOU. NOT SURE YOU WERE EVEN *ALIVE.*
BUT MONTHS AGO, I SAW YOU ON THE NEWS. *"THE FABLED MAN FROM ATLANTIS."*
MY HOPE WAS ***REIGNITED!*** I TRIED TO SEEK YOU OUT, BUT YOU HAD VANISHED.
ONLY TO APPEAR HERE BEFORE ME.
THIS IS A MAP TO THE DEAD KING'S ARMORY, WHERE THE MOST POWERFUL OF ATLANTEAN ARTIFACTS ARE HELD.
INCLUDING INDESTRUCT TRIDENT.
AND THESE ARE THE ATLANTEAN STONES THAT ONCE SAT UPON THE DEAD KING'S CROWN BEFORE IT WAS DESTROYED.
THE DEAD KING?
THE ***CREATOR*** AND ***FIRST*** KING OF ATLANTIS. BEFORE IT SANK INTO THE SEA.
YOU ARE HIS DESCENDANT AND RIGHTFUL HEIR OF THE GREATEST SOCIETY TO HAVE EVER EXISTED.
YOUR BROTHER IS AS SMART A AS CHARISMATIC AS YOUR MOTH BUT AS VICIOUS AND CRUEL A HIS FATHER.
FINALLY, HIS ***HA*** AND ***VIOLENT*** RU OVER. THE ***TR*** KING IS HERE
EVEN IF I THOUGHT I WAS, THEY'D NEVER ACCEPT ME.
YOU ARE THE ELDEST SON OF THE QUEEN. BY LAW, YOU ARE OUR KING. AND THE LAWS OF THE DEAD KING ARE THE ONLY ONES THE ATLANTEANS TRULY OBEY.
YOU ARE ATLANTIS'S SAVIOR AND MINE, ARTHUR.
OUR PEOPLE CAN BE ***GREAT*** AGAIN WITH A ***GREAT*** LEADER.
I WAS ONLY SEARCHING FOR M MOTHER, VULKO. TO GIVE HER MESSAGE FROM MY FATHER.
YOU CAN STILL GIVE HER THAT MESSAGE.

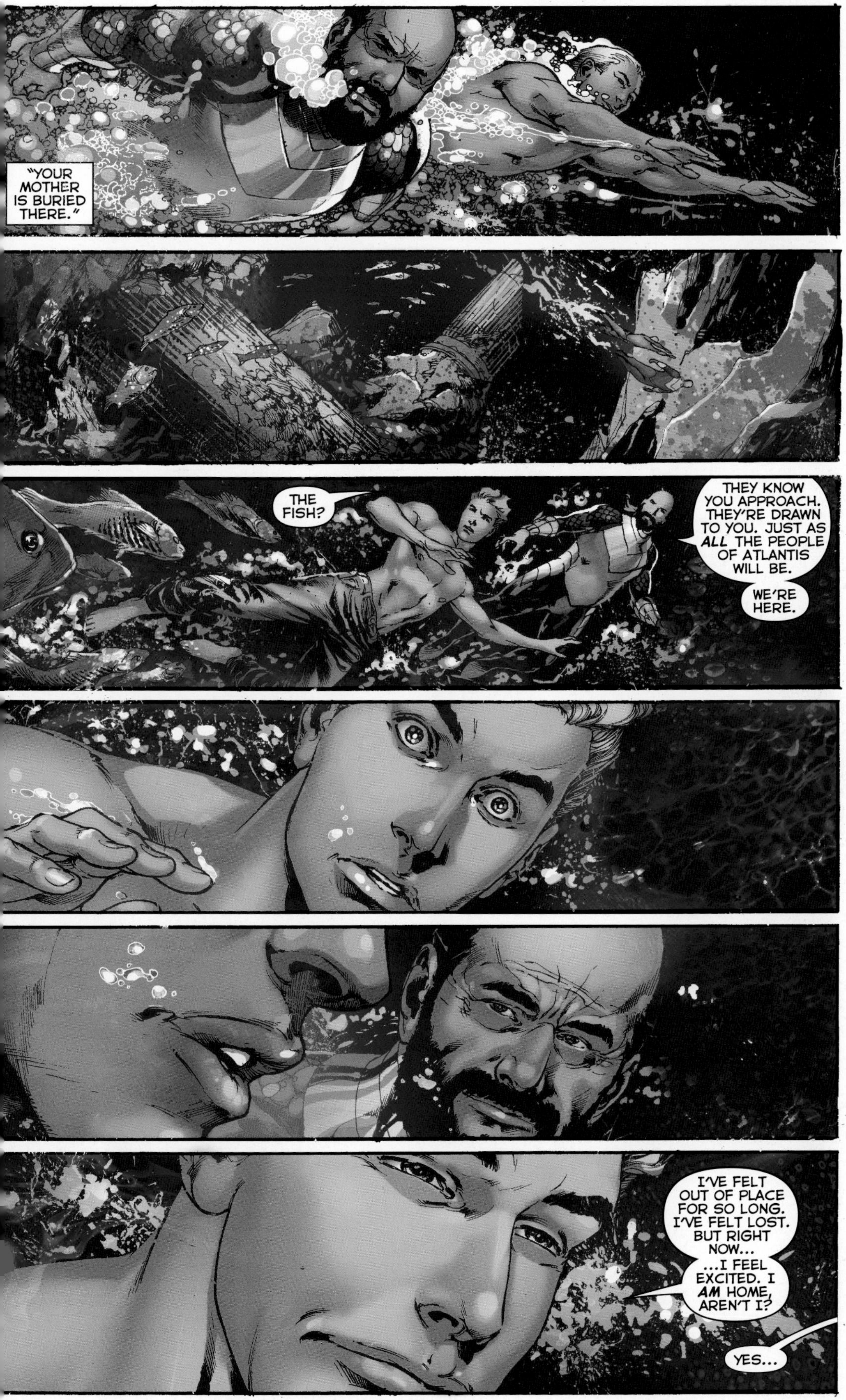
"YOUR MOTHER IS BURIED THERE."
THE FISH?
THEY KNOW YOU APPROACH. THEY'RE DRAWN TO YOU. JUST AS *ALL* THE PEOPLE OF ATLANTIS WILL BE.
WE'RE HERE.
I'VE FELT OUT OF PLACE FOR SO LONG. I'VE FELT LOST. BUT RIGHT NOW...
...I FEEL EXCITED. I *AM* HOME, AREN'T I?
YES...

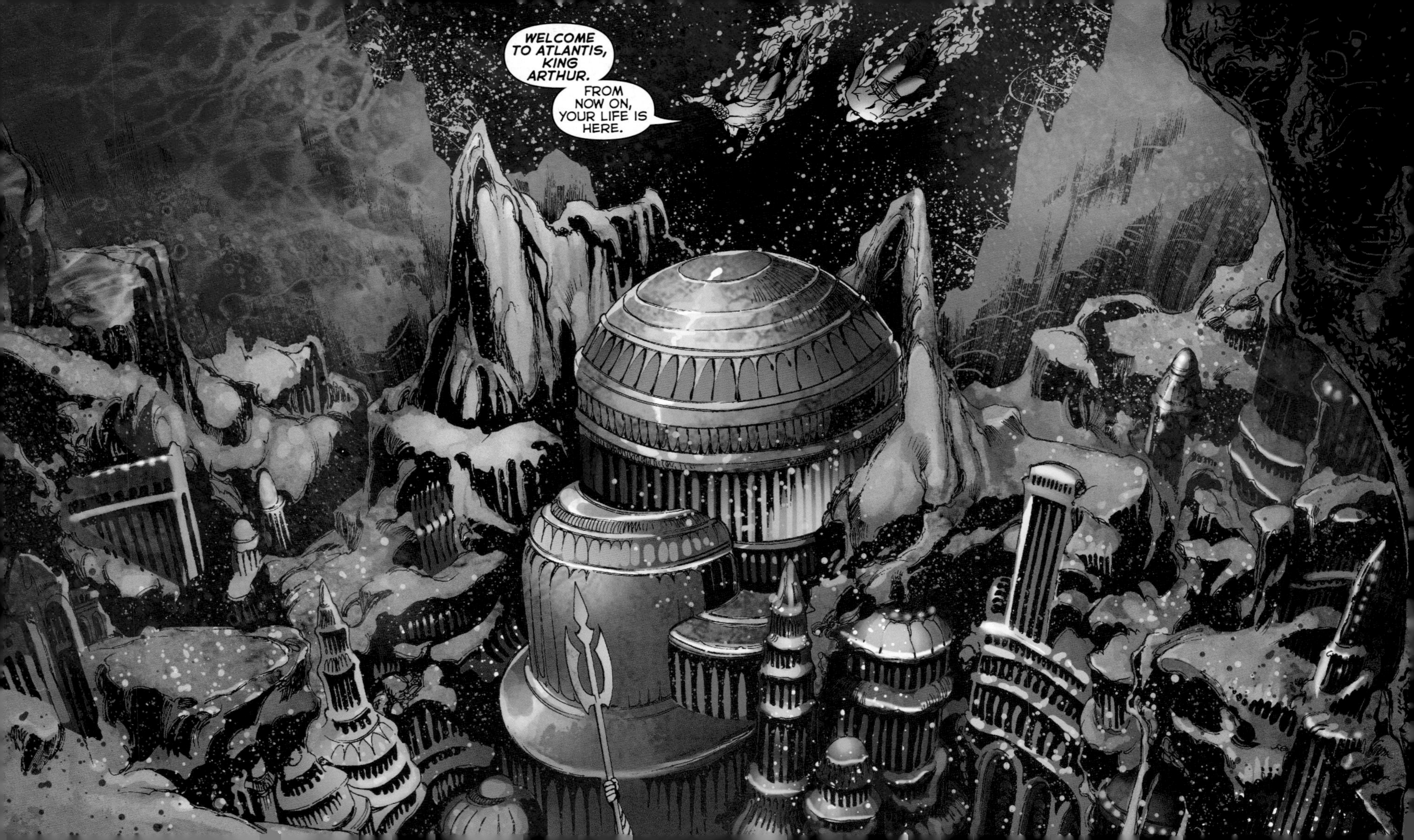
WELCOME TO ATLANTIS, KING ARTHUR.
FROM NOW ON, YOUR LIFE IS HERE.

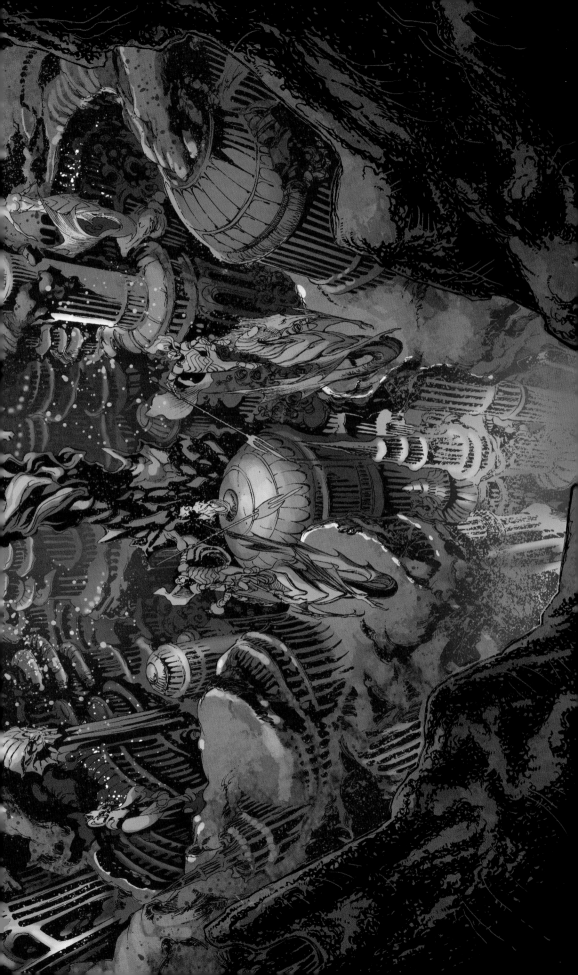

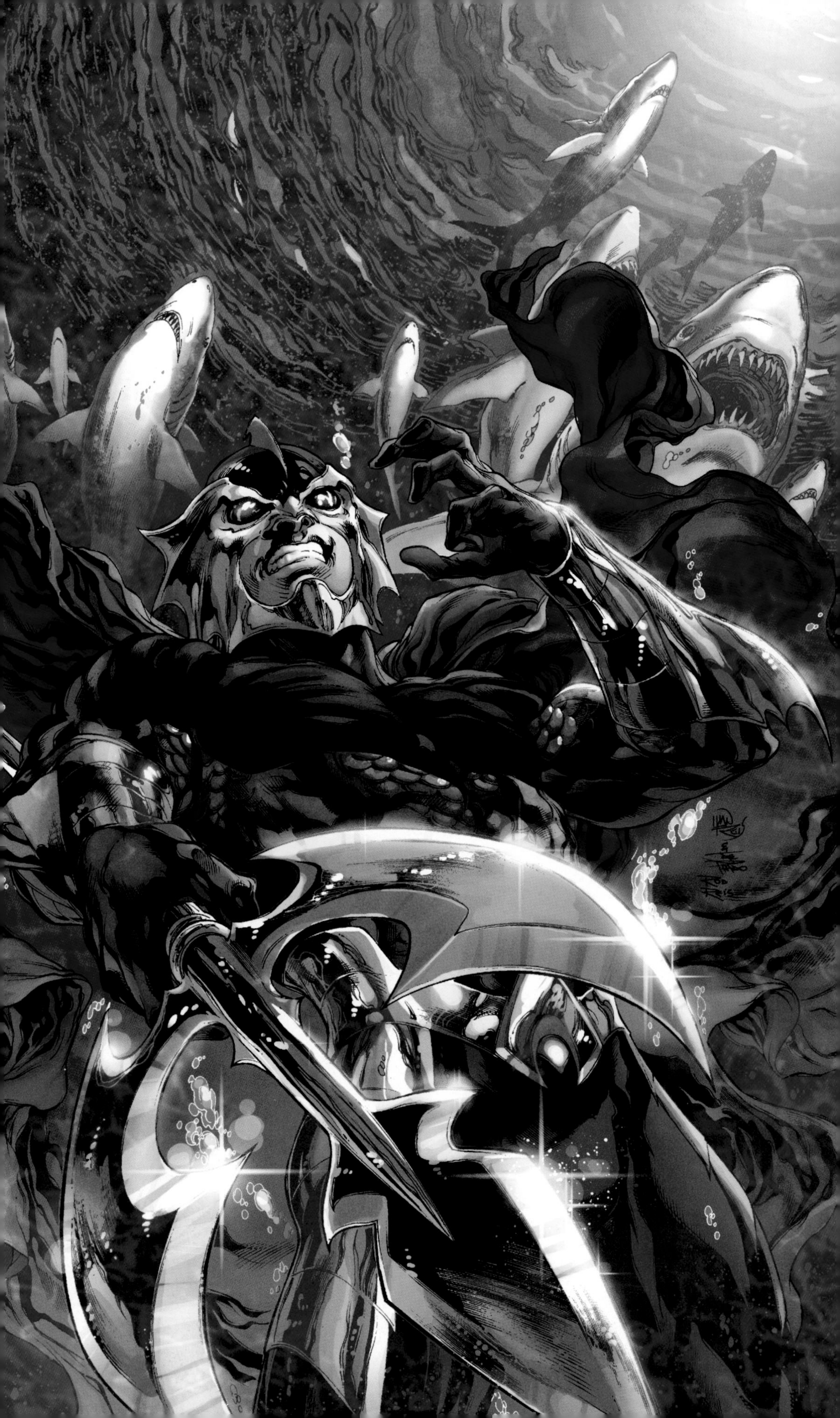

GEOFF JOHNS writer PETE WOODS PERE PÉREZ pencillers MARLO ALQUIZA RUY JOSE SEAN PARSONS PERE PÉREZ CAM SMITH
cover by IVAN REIS, JOE PRADO & ROD REIS

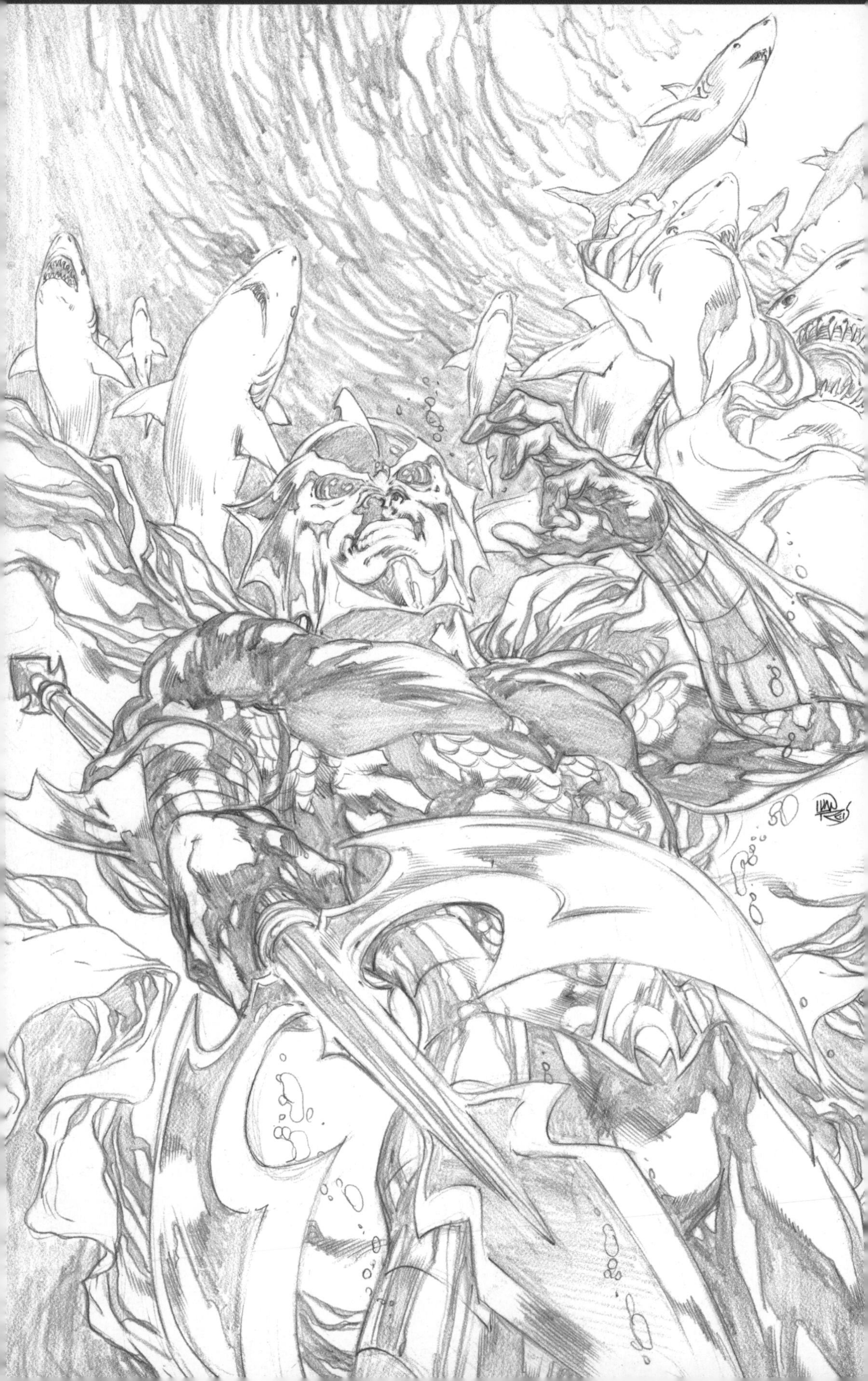

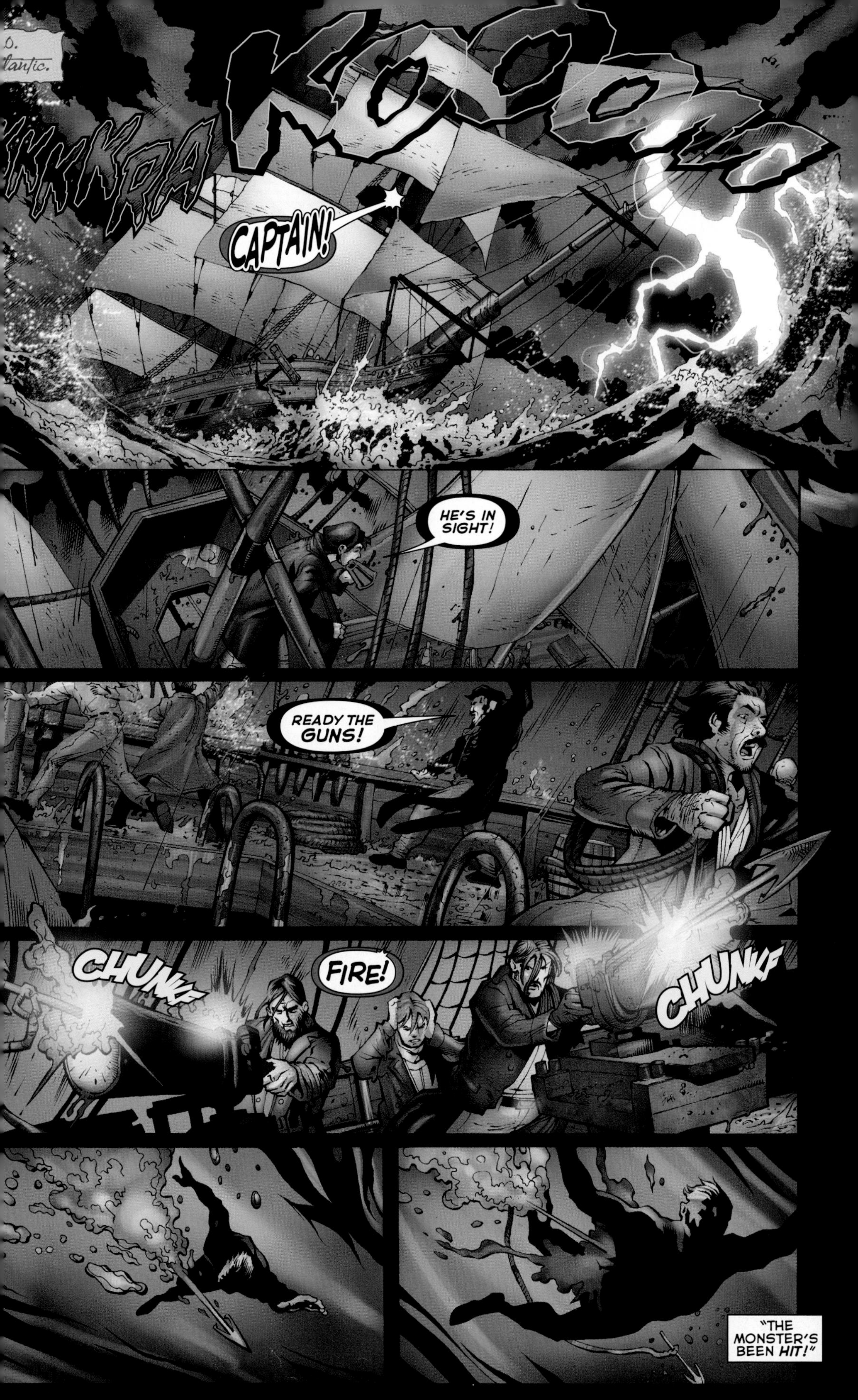
CAPTAIN!
HE'S IN SIGHT!
READY THE GUNS!
CHUNKF
FIRE!
CHUNKF
"THE MONSTER'S BEEN HIT!"

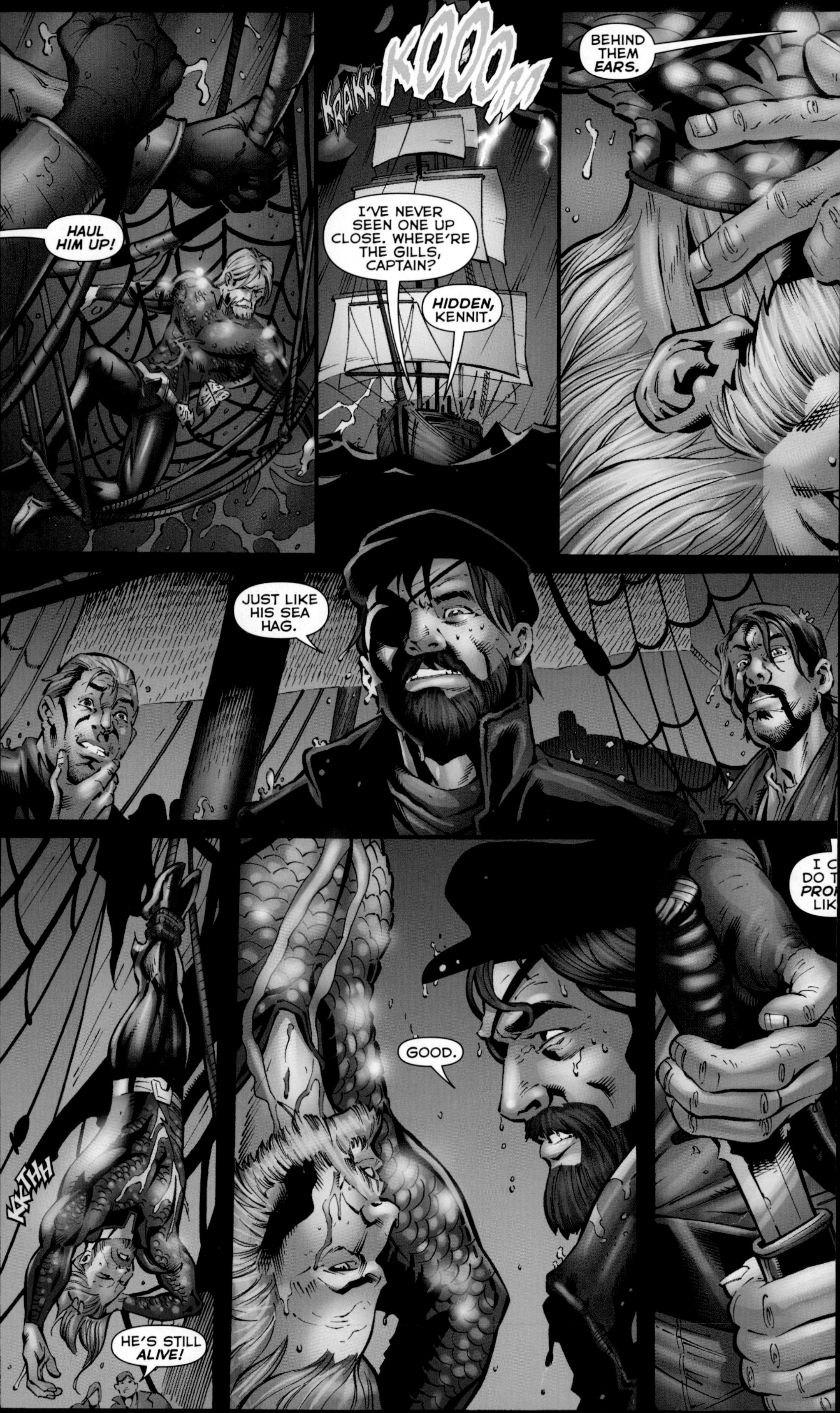
HAUL HIM UP!
KRAKK
KOOOM
I'VE NEVER SEEN ONE UP CLOSE. WHERE'RE THE GILLS, CAPTAIN?
HIDDEN, KENNIT.
BEHIND THEM *EARS.*
JUST LIKE HIS SEA HAG.
KRKTHH
HE'S STILL *ALIVE!*
GOOD.
I C
DO T
PROM
LIK

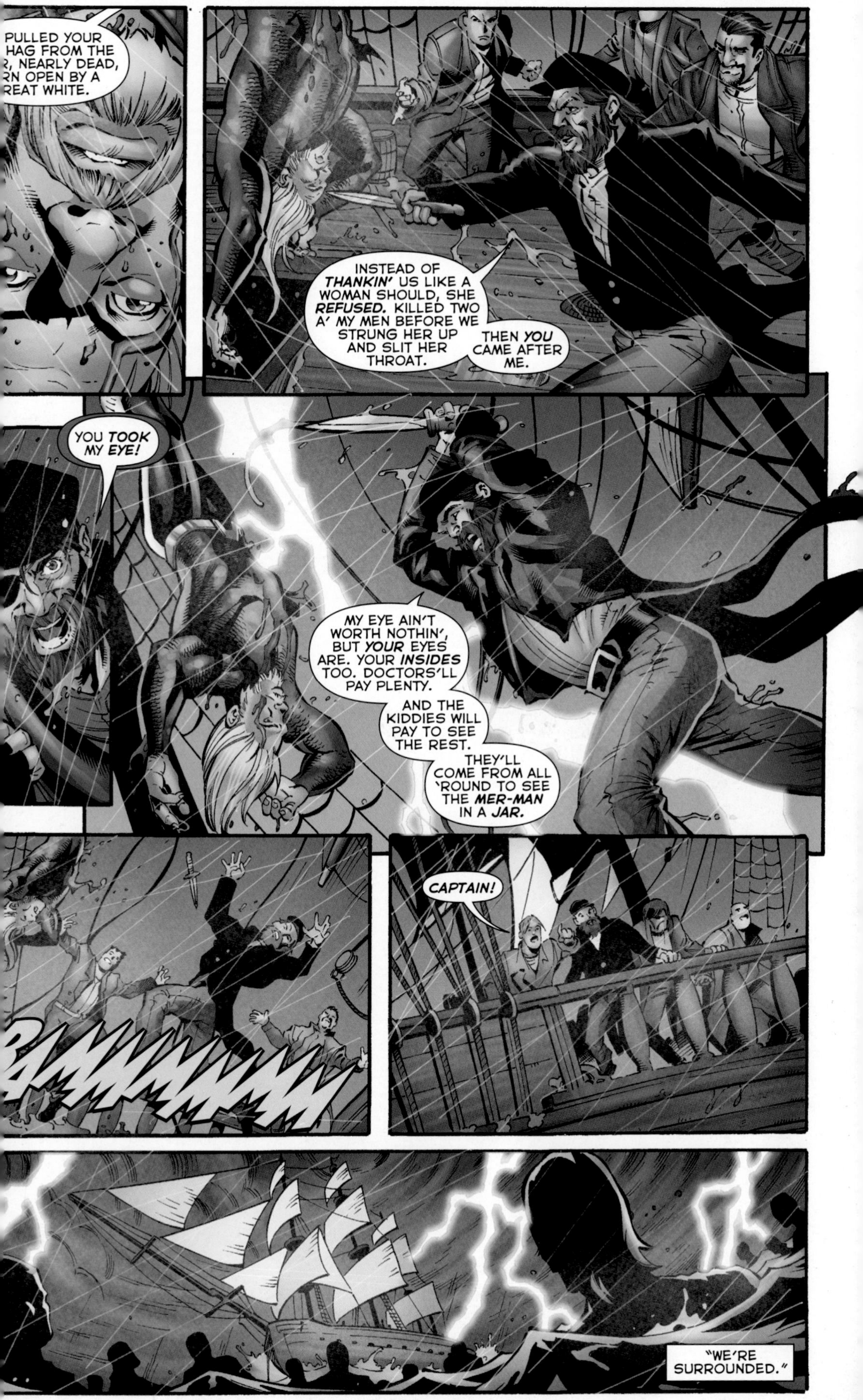
PULLED YOUR
HAG FROM THE
R, NEARLY DEAD,
RN OPEN BY A
REAT WHITE.
INSTEAD OF *THANKIN'* US LIKE A WOMAN SHOULD, SHE *REFUSED.* KILLED TWO A' MY MEN BEFORE WE STRUNG HER UP AND SLIT HER THROAT.
THEN *YOU* CAME AFTER ME.
YOU *TOOK* MY *EYE!*
MY EYE AIN'T WORTH NOTHIN', BUT *YOUR* EYES ARE. YOUR *INSIDES* TOO. DOCTORS'LL PAY PLENTY.
AND THE KIDDIES WILL PAY TO SEE THE REST.
THEY'LL COME FROM ALL 'ROUND TO SEE THE *MER-MAN* IN A *JAR.*
CAPTAIN!
"WE'RE SURROUNDED."

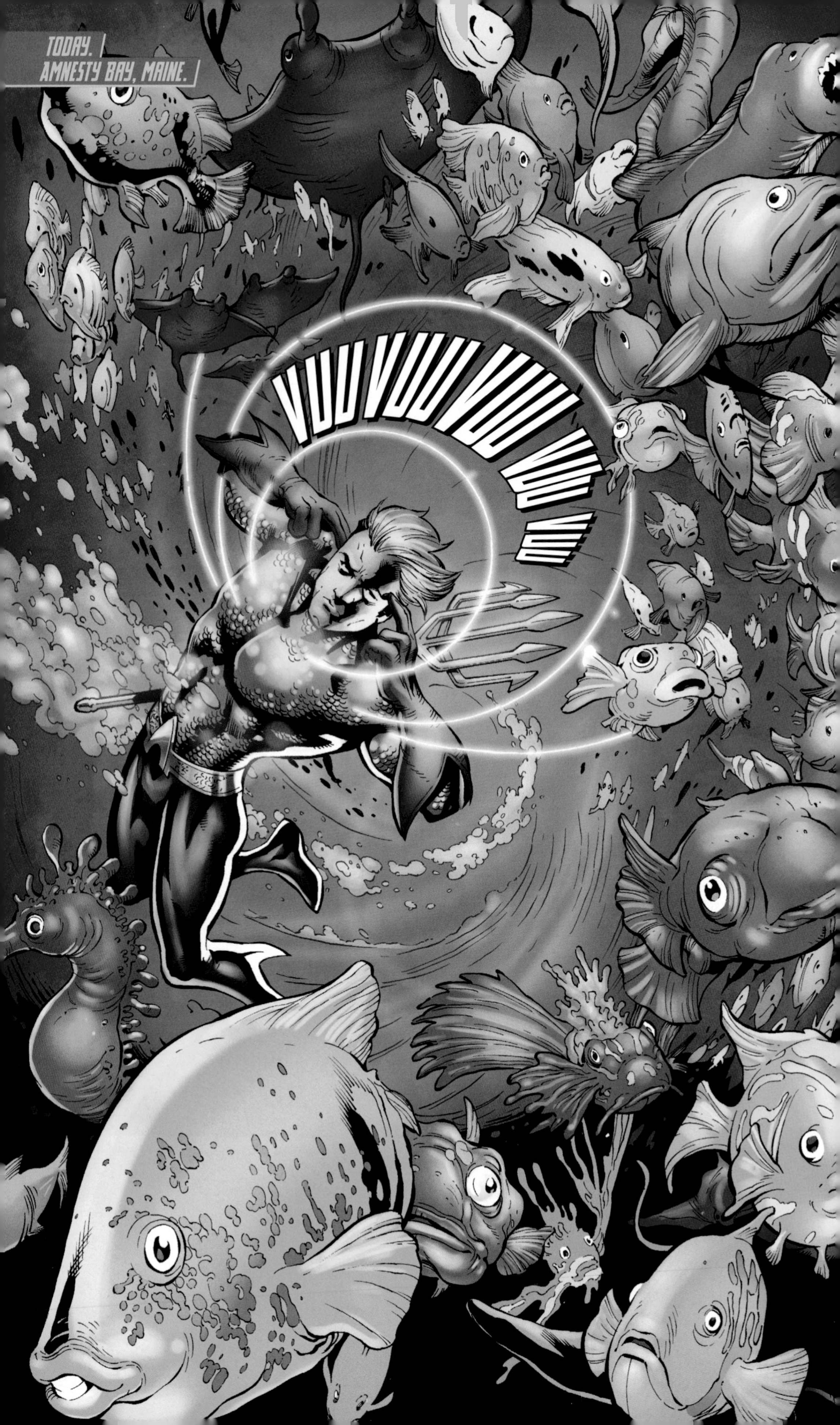
TODAY.
AMNESTY BAY, MAINE.
VUUVUUVUUVUUVUU

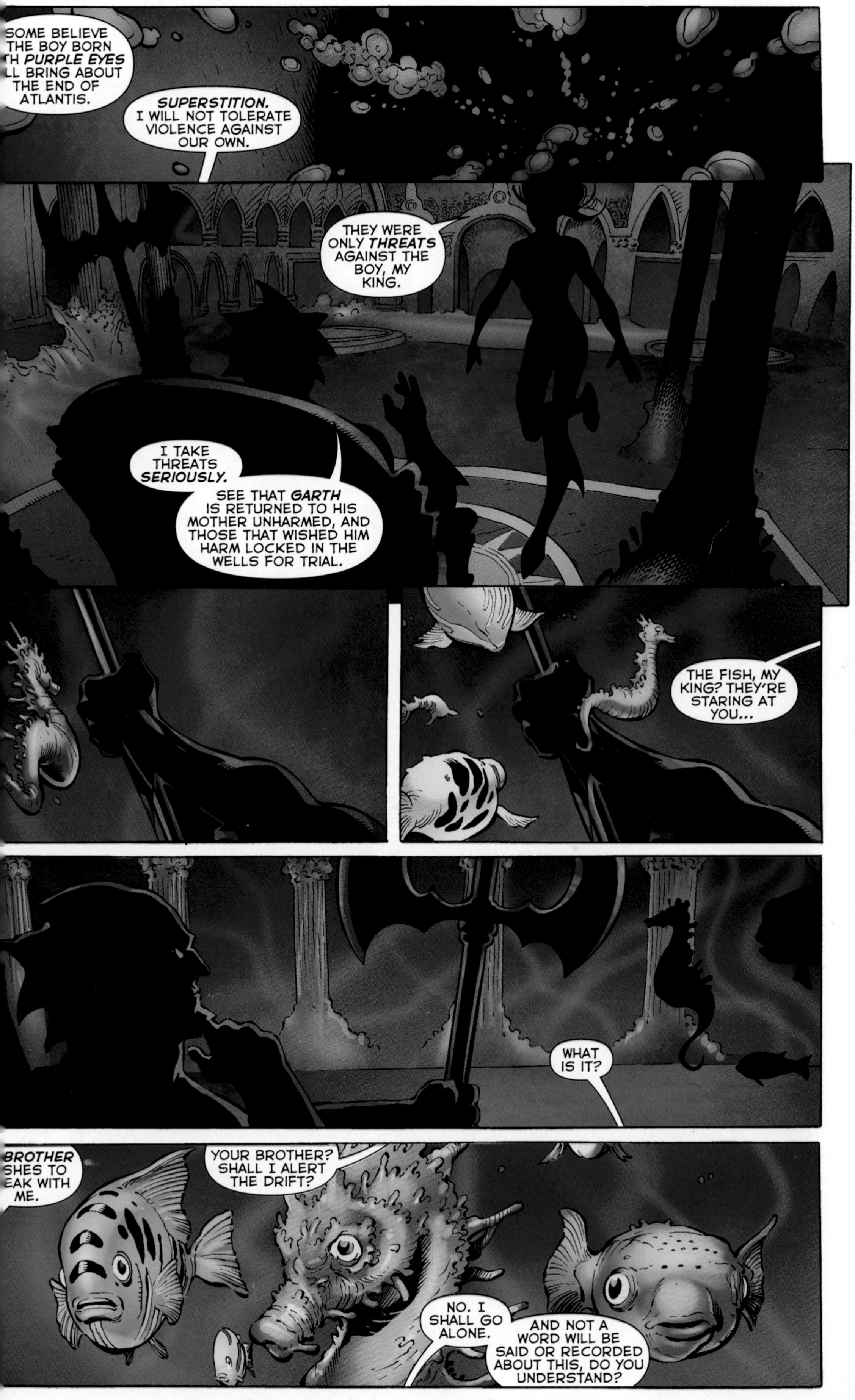
SOME BELIEVE THE BOY BORN TH *PURPLE EYES* LL BRING ABOUT THE END OF ATLANTIS.
SUPERSTITION. I WILL NOT TOLERATE VIOLENCE AGAINST OUR OWN.
THEY WERE ONLY *THREATS* AGAINST THE BOY, MY KING.
I TAKE THREATS *SERIOUSLY.*
SEE THAT *GARTH* IS RETURNED TO HIS MOTHER UNHARMED, AND THOSE THAT WISHED HIM HARM LOCKED IN THE WELLS FOR TRIAL.
THE FISH, MY KING? THEY'RE STARING AT YOU...
WHAT IS IT?
BROTHER SHES TO EAK WITH ME.
YOUR BROTHER? SHALL I ALERT THE DRIFT?
NO. I SHALL GO ALONE.
AND NOT A WORD WILL BE SAID OR RECORDED ABOUT THIS, DO YOU UNDERSTAND?

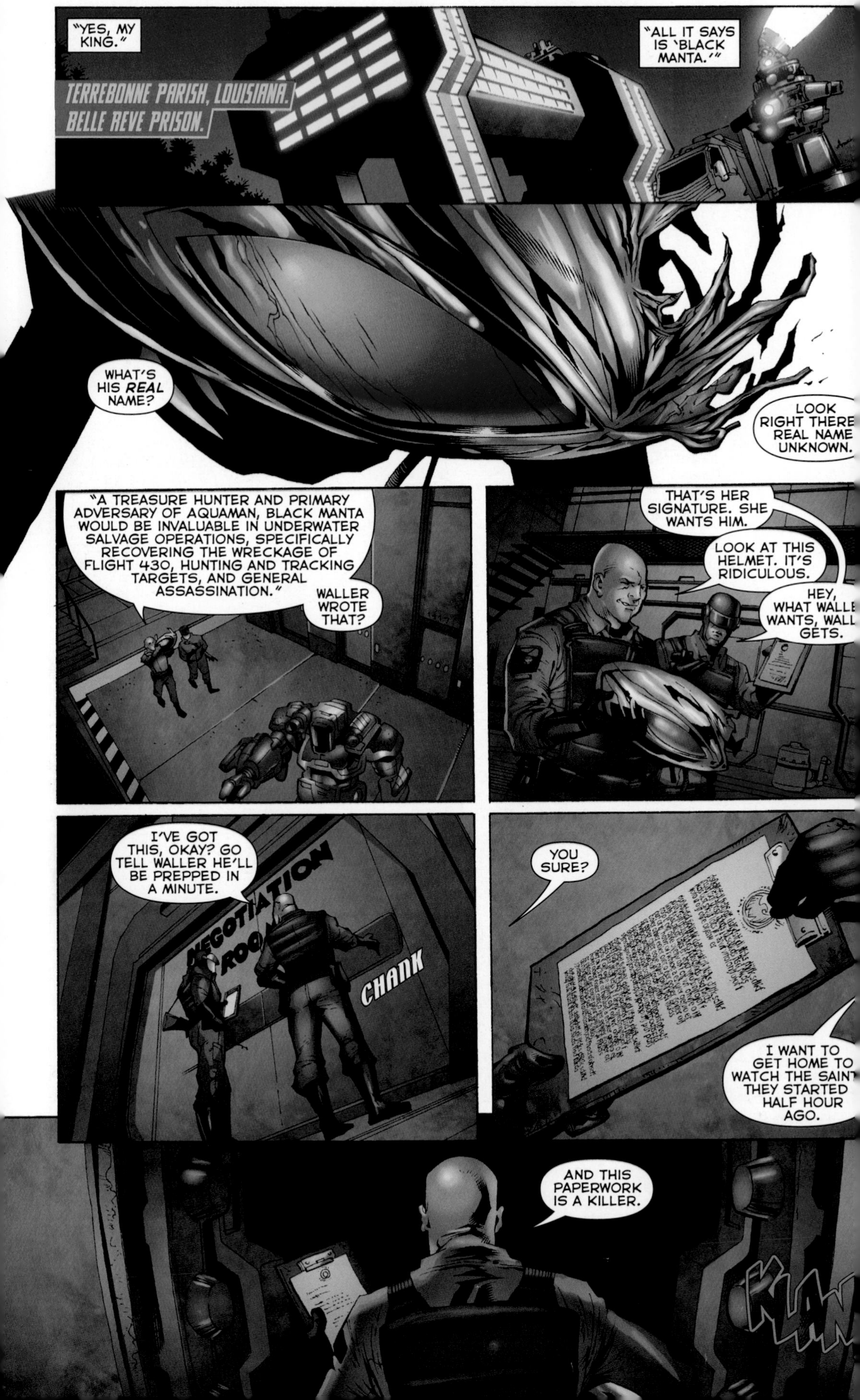

"YES, MY KING."
TERREBONNE PARISH, LOUISIANA.
BELLE REVE PRISON.
"ALL IT SAYS IS 'BLACK MANTA.'"
WHAT'S HIS *REAL* NAME?
LOOK RIGHT THERE REAL NAME UNKNOWN.
"A TREASURE HUNTER AND PRIMARY ADVERSARY OF AQUAMAN, BLACK MANTA WOULD BE INVALUABLE IN UNDERWATER SALVAGE OPERATIONS, SPECIFICALLY RECOVERING THE WRECKAGE OF FLIGHT 430, HUNTING AND TRACKING TARGETS, AND GENERAL ASSASSINATION."
WALLER WROTE THAT?
THAT'S HER SIGNATURE. SHE WANTS HIM.
LOOK AT THIS HELMET. IT'S RIDICULOUS.
HEY, WHAT WALLE WANTS, WALL GETS.
I'VE GOT THIS, OKAY? GO TELL WALLER HE'LL BE PREPPED IN A MINUTE.
NEGOTIATION ROO
CHANK
YOU SURE?
I WANT TO GET HOME TO WATCH THE SAIN THEY STARTED HALF HOUR AGO.
AND THIS PAPERWORK IS A KILLER.
KLAN

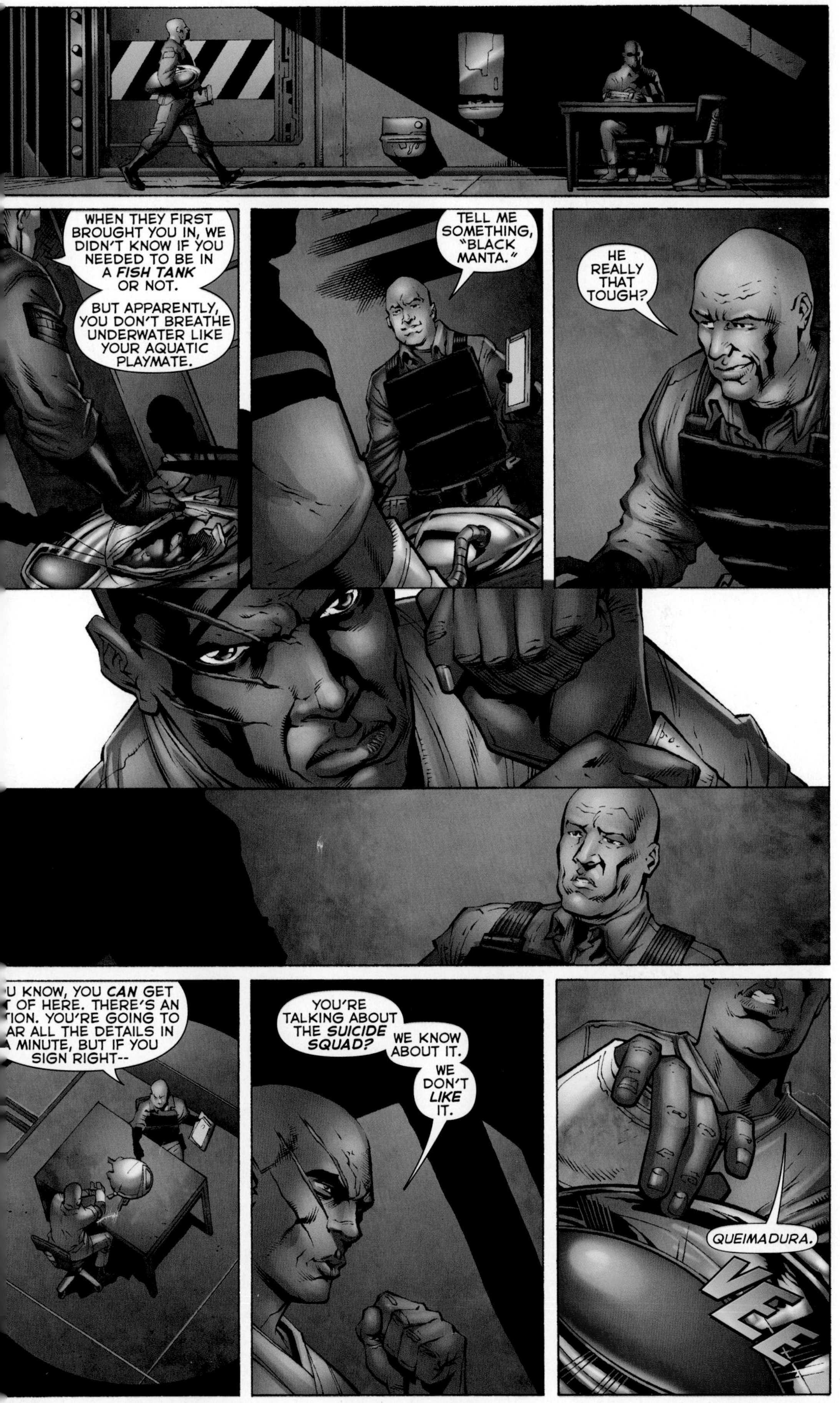
WHEN THEY FIRST BROUGHT YOU IN, WE DIDN'T KNOW IF YOU NEEDED TO BE IN A *FISH TANK* OR NOT.
BUT APPARENTLY, YOU DON'T BREATHE UNDERWATER LIKE YOUR AQUATIC PLAYMATE.
TELL ME SOMETHING, "BLACK MANTA."
HE REALLY THAT TOUGH?
U KNOW, YOU *CAN* GET T OF HERE. THERE'S AN TION. YOU'RE GOING TO AR ALL THE DETAILS IN A MINUTE, BUT IF YOU SIGN RIGHT--
YOU'RE TALKING ABOUT THE *SUICIDE SQUAD?*
WE KNOW ABOUT IT.
WE DON'T *LIKE* IT.
QUEIMADURA.
VEE

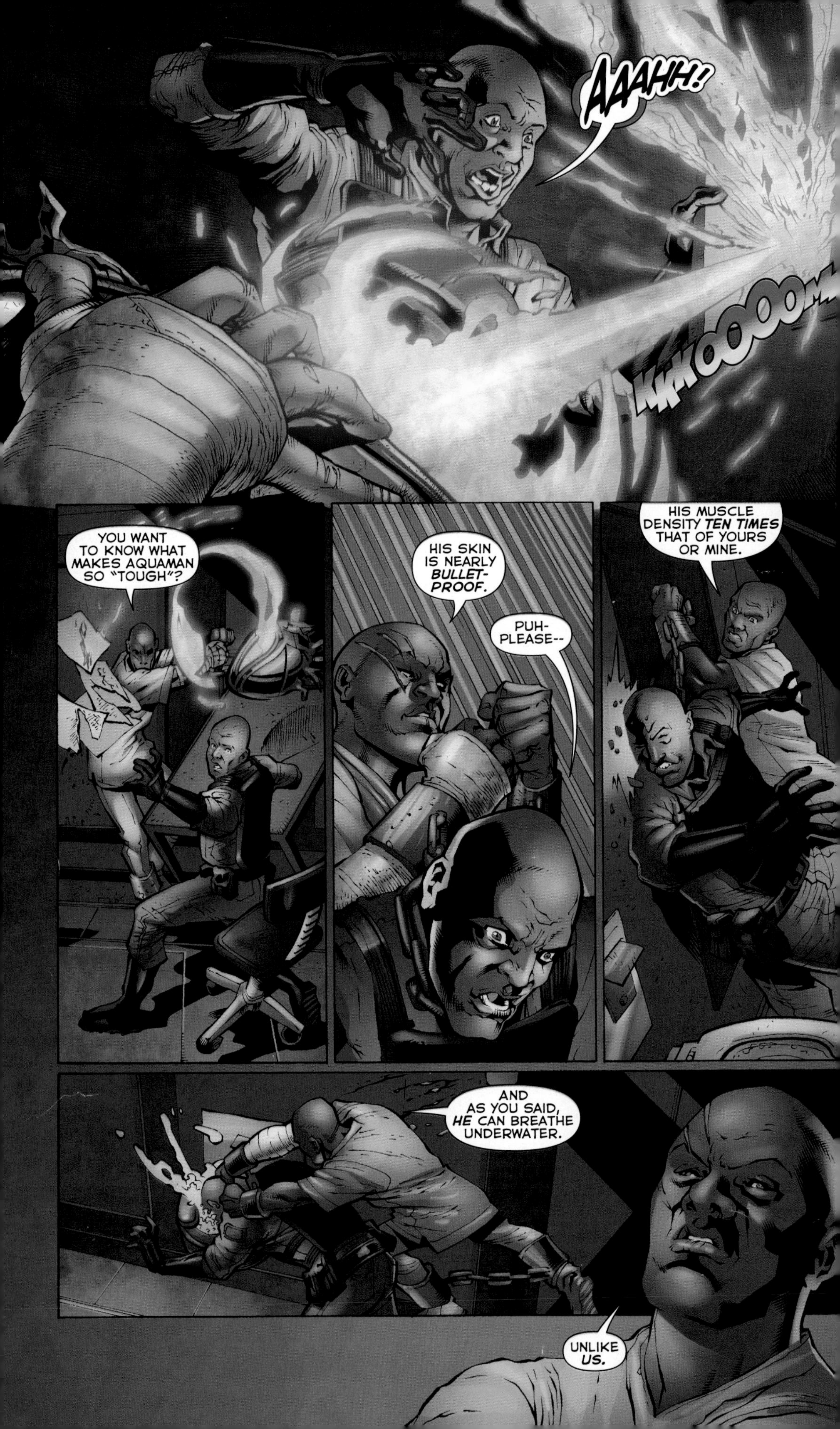
AAAHH!
KKKOOOOM
YOU WANT TO KNOW WHAT MAKES AQUAMAN SO "TOUGH"?
HIS SKIN IS NEARLY *BULLET-PROOF*.
PUH-PLEASE--
HIS MUSCLE DENSITY *TEN TIMES* THAT OF YOURS OR MINE.
AND AS YOU SAID, *HE* CAN BREATHE UNDERWATER.
UNLIKE *US*.

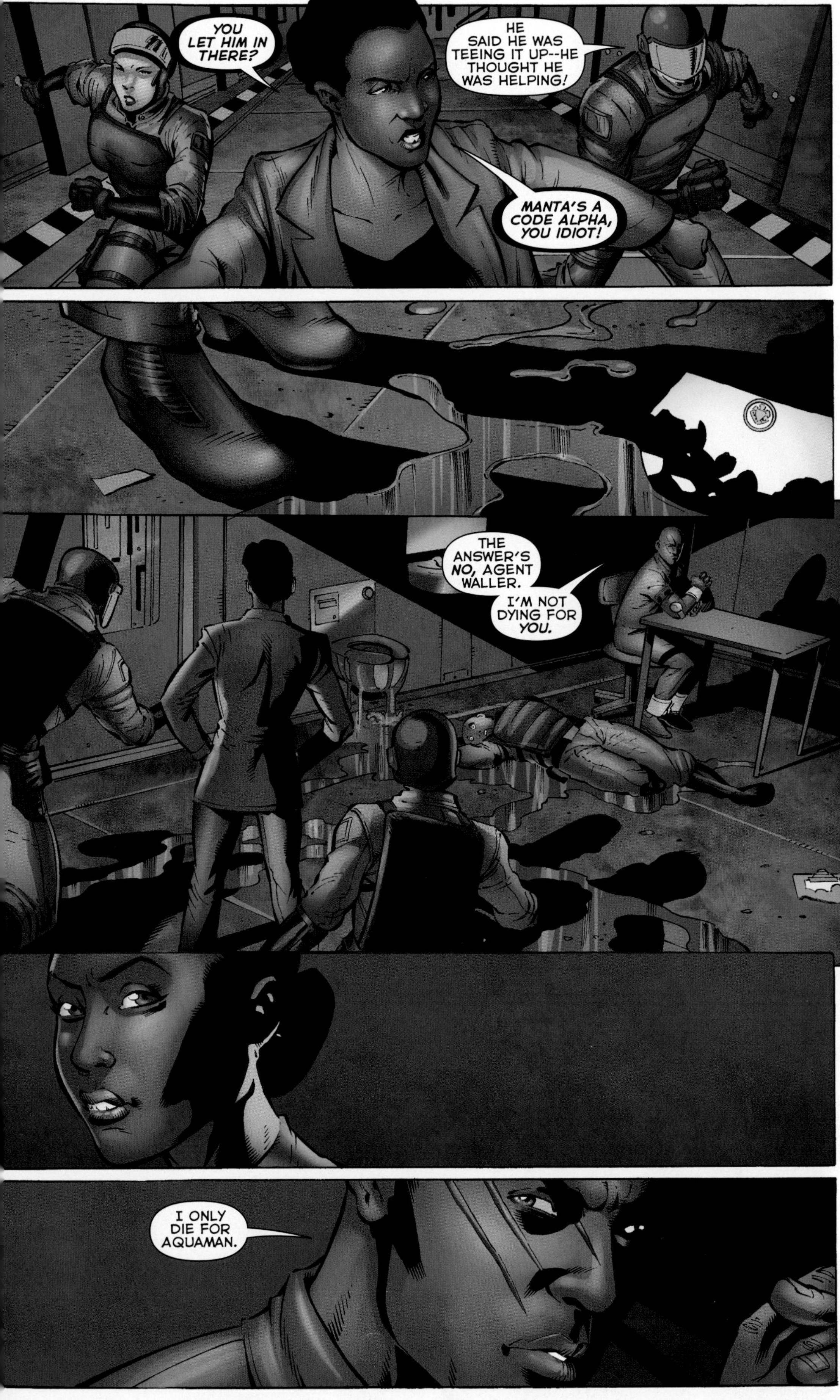
YOU LET HIM IN THERE?
HE SAID HE WAS TEEING IT UP--HE THOUGHT HE WAS HELPING!
MANTA'S A CODE ALPHA, YOU IDIOT!
THE ANSWER'S NO, AGENT WALLER.
I'M NOT DYING FOR YOU.
I ONLY DIE FOR AQUAMAN.

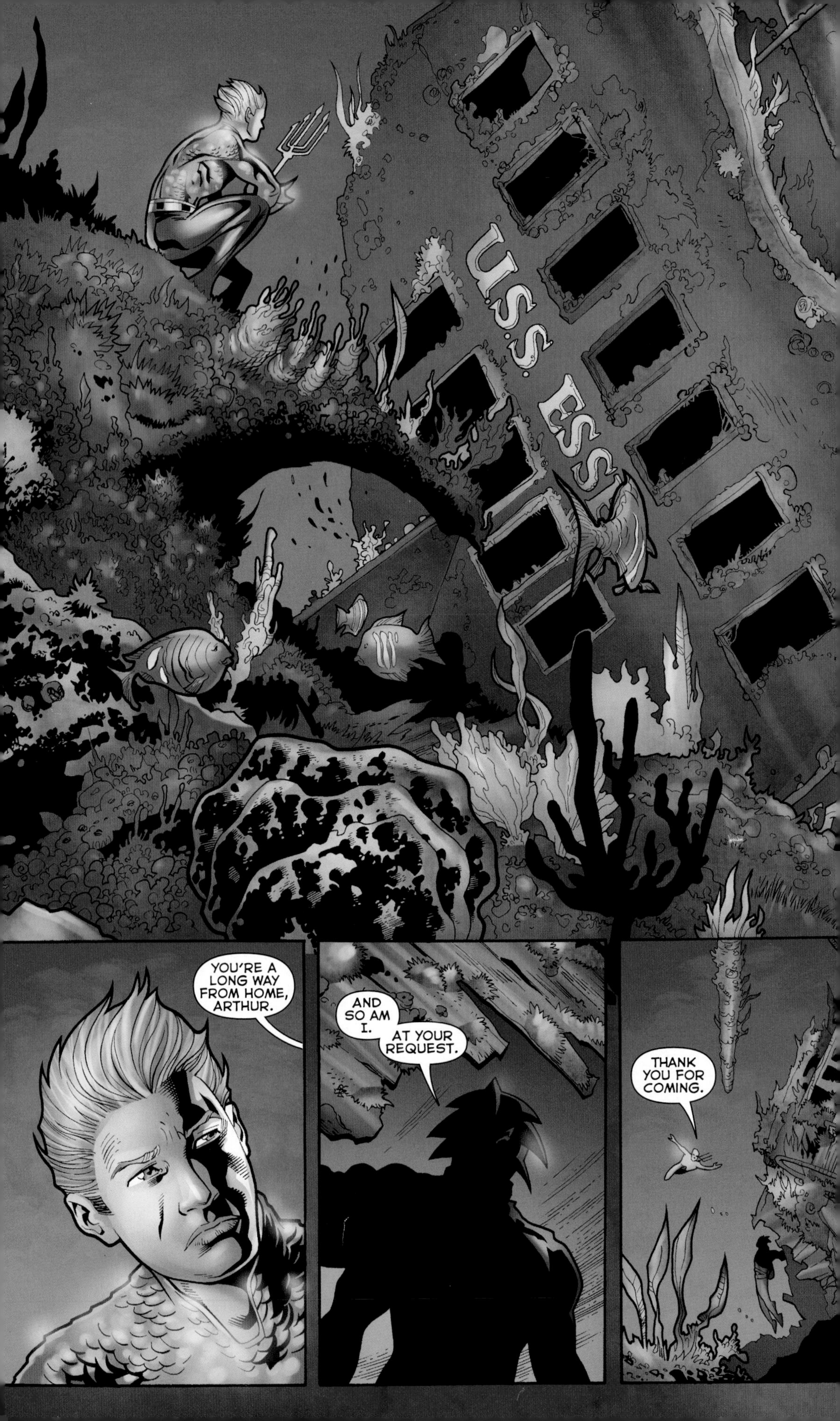
YOU'RE A LONG WAY FROM HOME, ARTHUR.
AND SO AM I.
AT YOUR REQUEST.
THANK YOU FOR COMING.

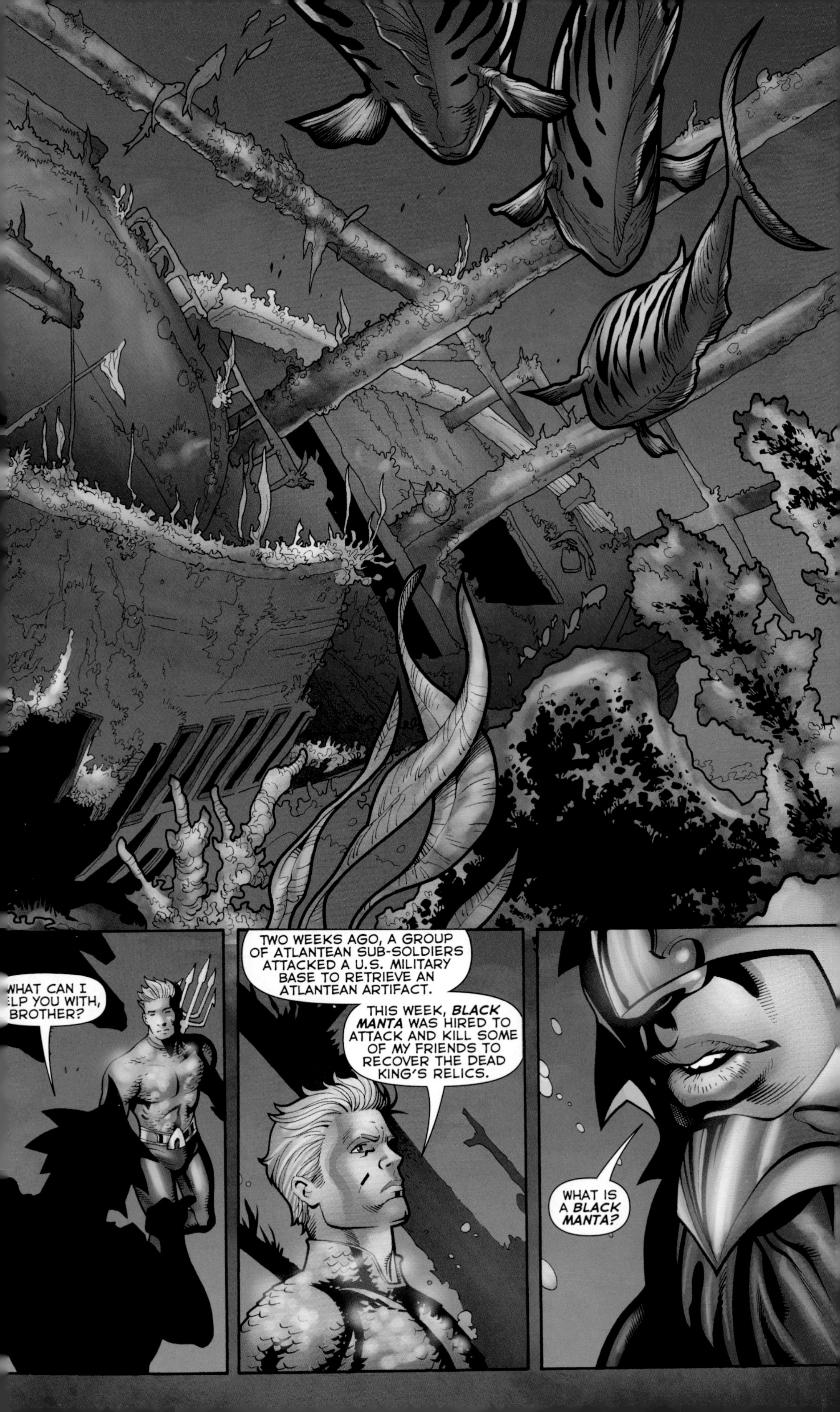
WHAT CAN I
ELP YOU WITH,
BROTHER?
TWO WEEKS AGO, A GROUP OF ATLANTEAN SUB-SOLDIERS ATTACKED A U.S. MILITARY BASE TO RETRIEVE AN ATLANTEAN ARTIFACT.
THIS WEEK, *BLACK MANTA* WAS HIRED TO ATTACK AND KILL SOME OF MY FRIENDS TO RECOVER THE DEAD KING'S RELICS.
WHAT IS A *BLACK MANTA?*

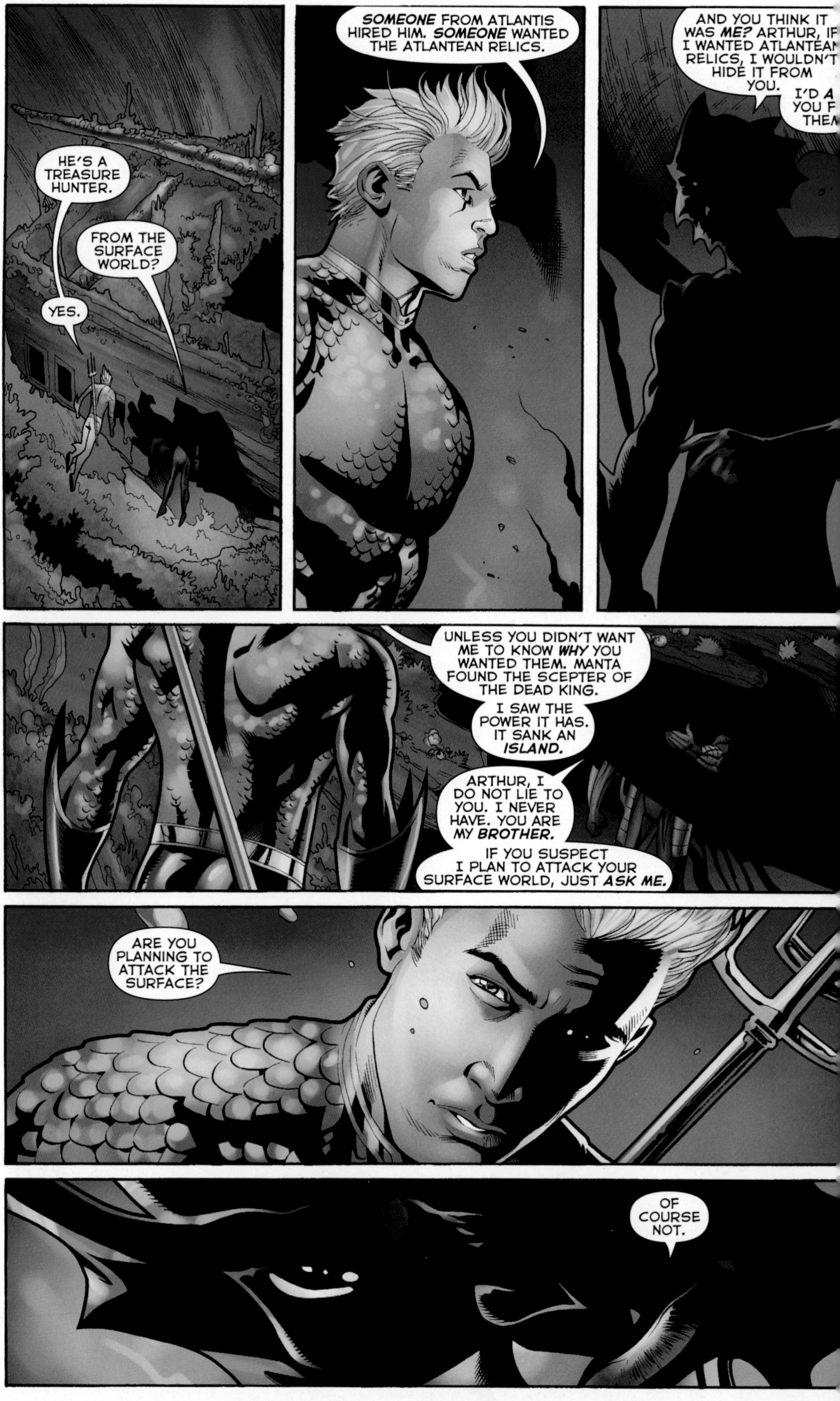
HE'S A TREASURE HUNTER.
FROM THE SURFACE WORLD?
YES.
SOMEONE FROM ATLANTIS HIRED HIM. ***SOMEONE*** WANTED THE ATLANTEAN RELICS.
AND YOU THINK IT WAS ***ME?*** ARTHUR, IF I WANTED ATLANTEAN RELICS, I WOULDN'T HIDE IT FROM YOU.
I'D A
YOU F
THEM
UNLESS YOU DIDN'T WANT ME TO KNOW ***WHY*** YOU WANTED THEM. MANTA FOUND THE SCEPTER OF THE DEAD KING.
I SAW THE POWER IT HAS. IT SANK AN ***ISLAND.***
ARTHUR, I DO NOT LIE TO YOU. I NEVER HAVE. YOU ARE MY ***BROTHER.***
IF YOU SUSPECT I PLAN TO ATTACK YOUR SURFACE WORLD, JUST ***ASK ME.***
ARE YOU PLANNING TO ATTACK THE SURFACE?
OF COURSE NOT.

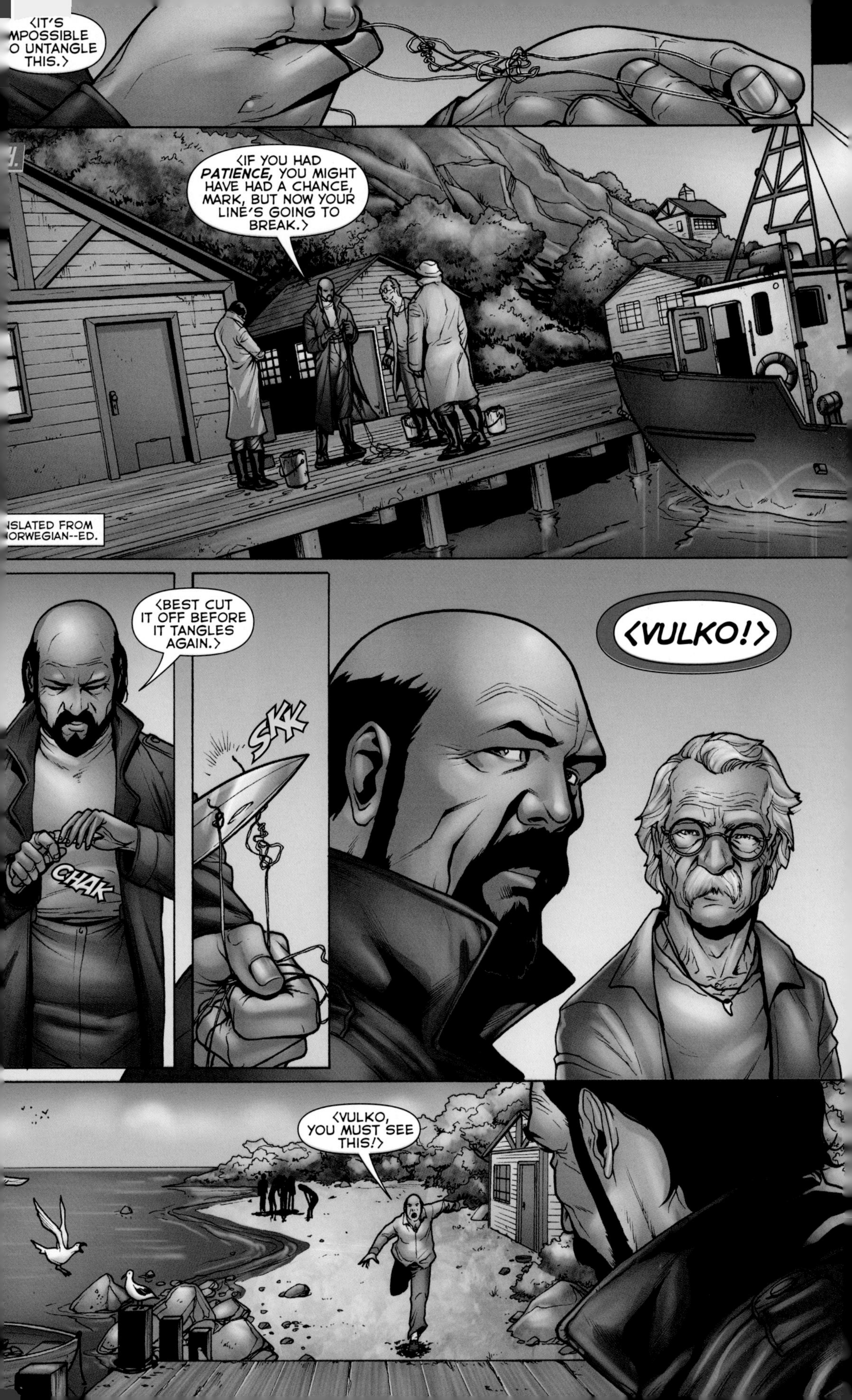
<IT'S
MPOSSIBLE
O UNTANGLE
THIS.>
<IF YOU HAD PATIENCE, YOU MIGHT HAVE HAD A CHANCE, MARK, BUT NOW YOUR LINE'S GOING TO BREAK.>
NSLATED FROM
NORWEGIAN--ED.
<BEST CUT IT OFF BEFORE IT TANGLES AGAIN.>
CHAK
SKK
<VULKO!>
<VULKO, YOU MUST SEE THIS!>

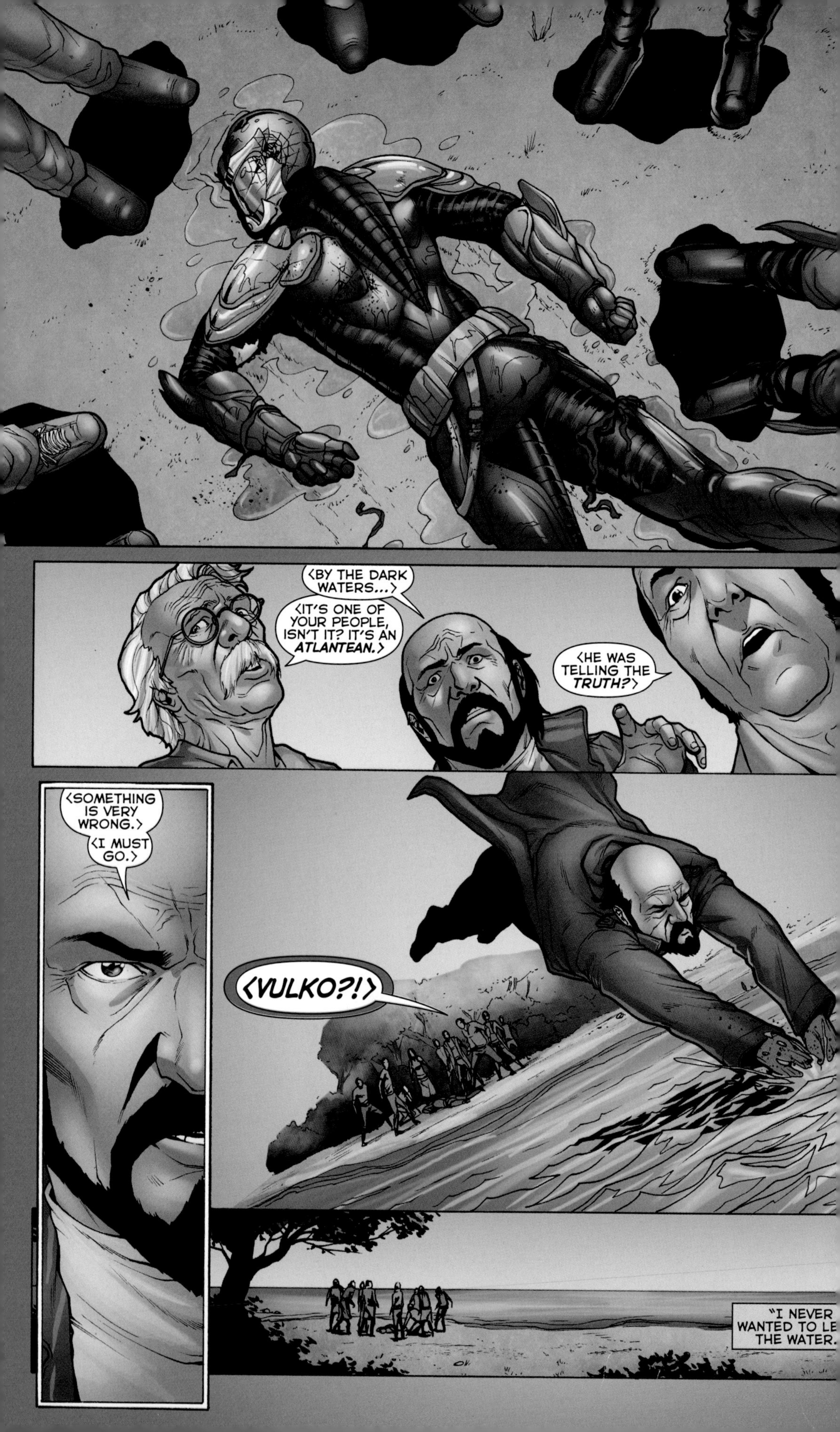

<BY THE DARK WATERS...>
<IT'S ONE OF YOUR PEOPLE, ISN'T IT? IT'S AN ATLANTEAN.>
<HE WAS TELLING THE TRUTH?>
<SOMETHING IS VERY WRONG.>
<I MUST GO.>
<VULKO?!>
"I NEVER WANTED TO LE THE WATER.

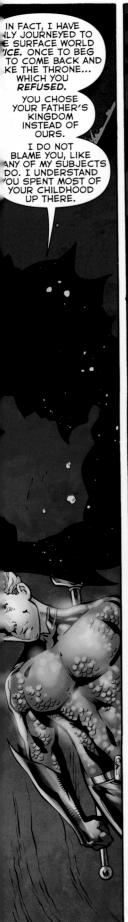

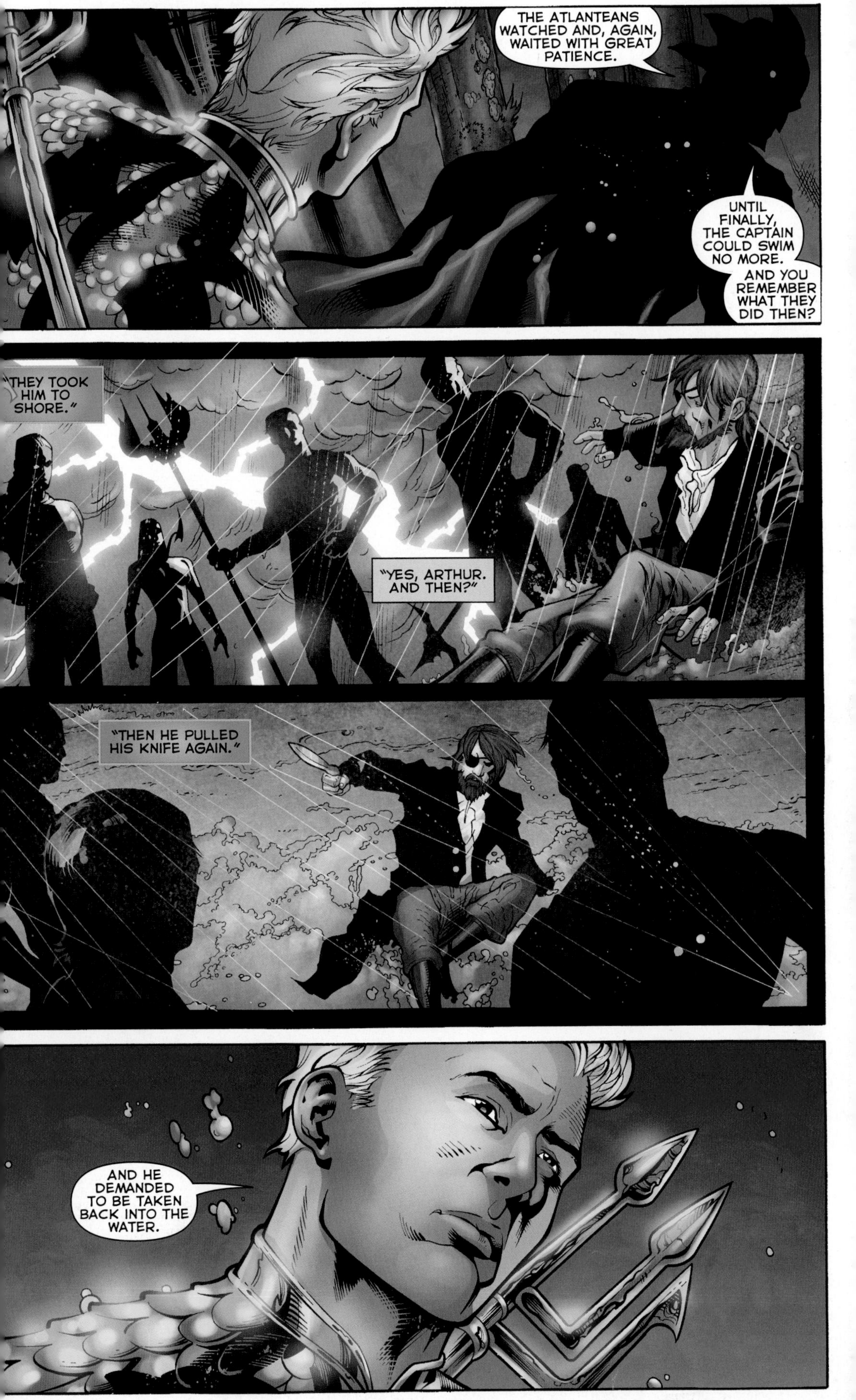
THE ATLANTEANS WATCHED AND, AGAIN, WAITED WITH GREAT PATIENCE.
UNTIL FINALLY, THE CAPTAIN COULD SWIM NO MORE.
AND YOU REMEMBER WHAT THEY DID THEN?
"THEY TOOK HIM TO SHORE."
"YES, ARTHUR. AND THEN?"
"THEN HE PULLED HIS KNIFE AGAIN."
AND HE DEMANDED TO BE TAKEN BACK INTO THE WATER.

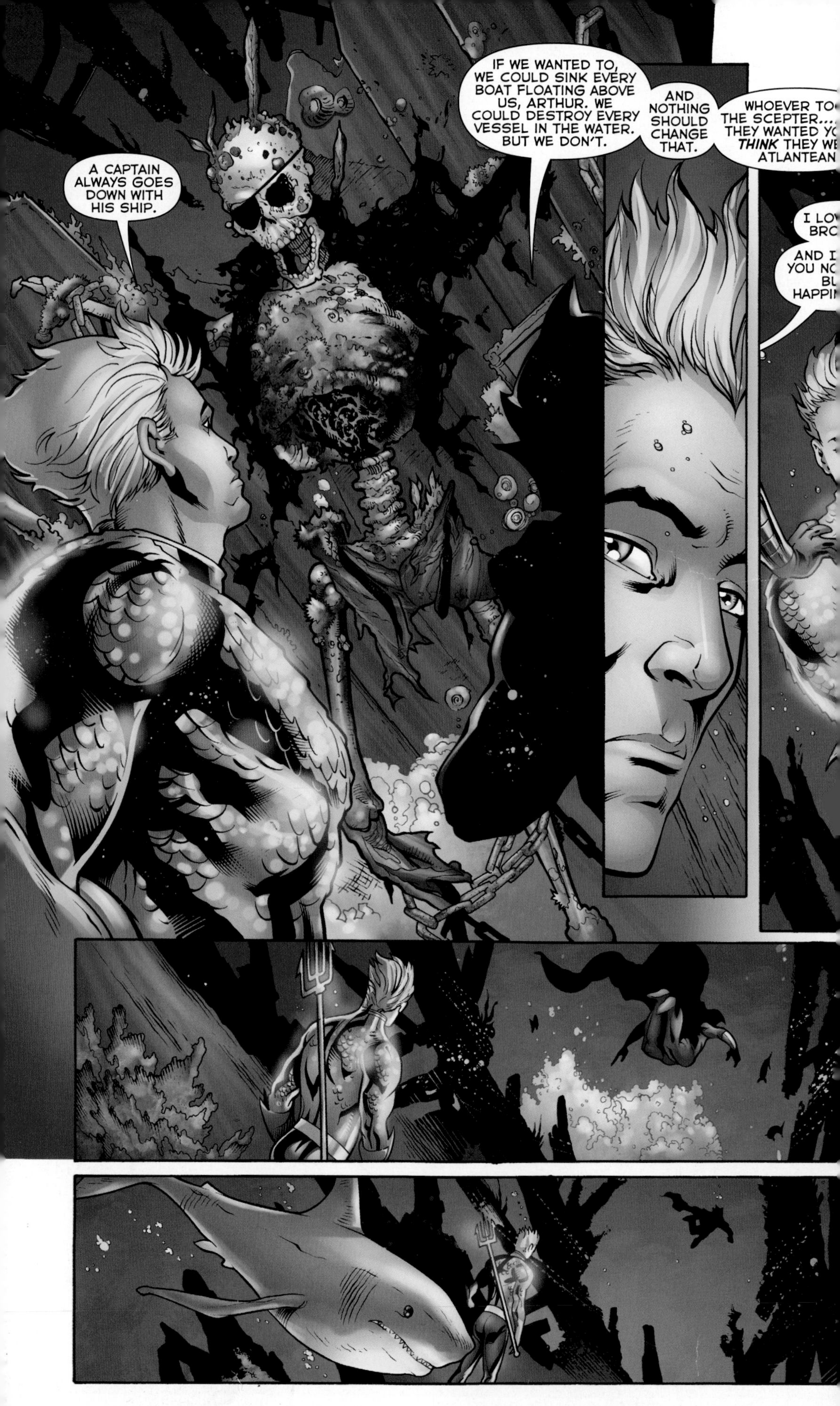
A CAPTAIN ALWAYS GOES DOWN WITH HIS SHIP.
IF WE WANTED TO, WE COULD SINK EVERY BOAT FLOATING ABOVE US, ARTHUR. WE COULD DESTROY EVERY VESSEL IN THE WATER. BUT WE DON'T.
AND NOTHING SHOULD CHANGE THAT.
WHOEVER TO THE SCEPTER... THEY WANTED YO THINK THEY WE ATLANTEAN
I LOV BRO
AND I YOU NO BU HAPPI

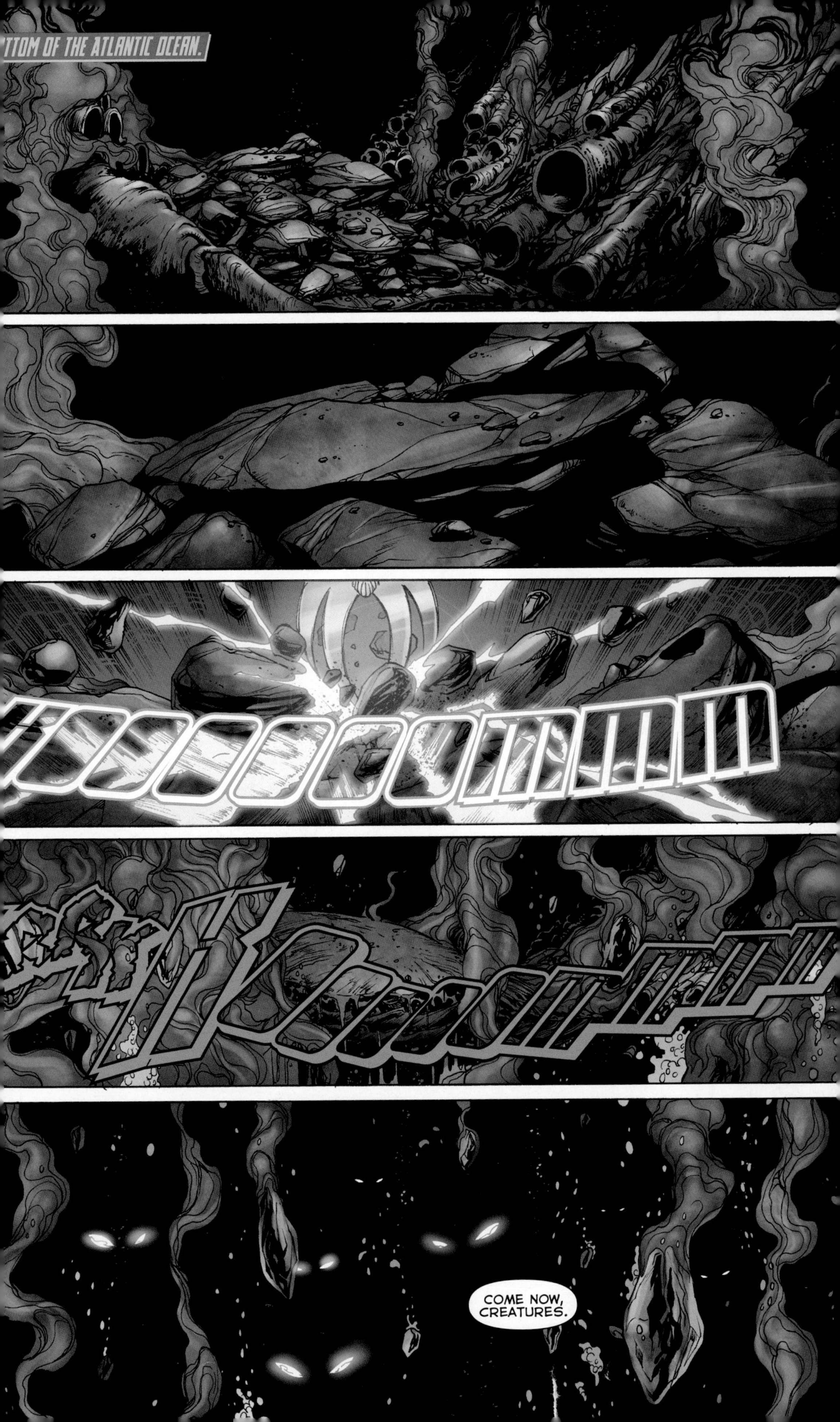
TTOM OF THE ATLANTIC OCEAN.
COME NOW, CREATURES.

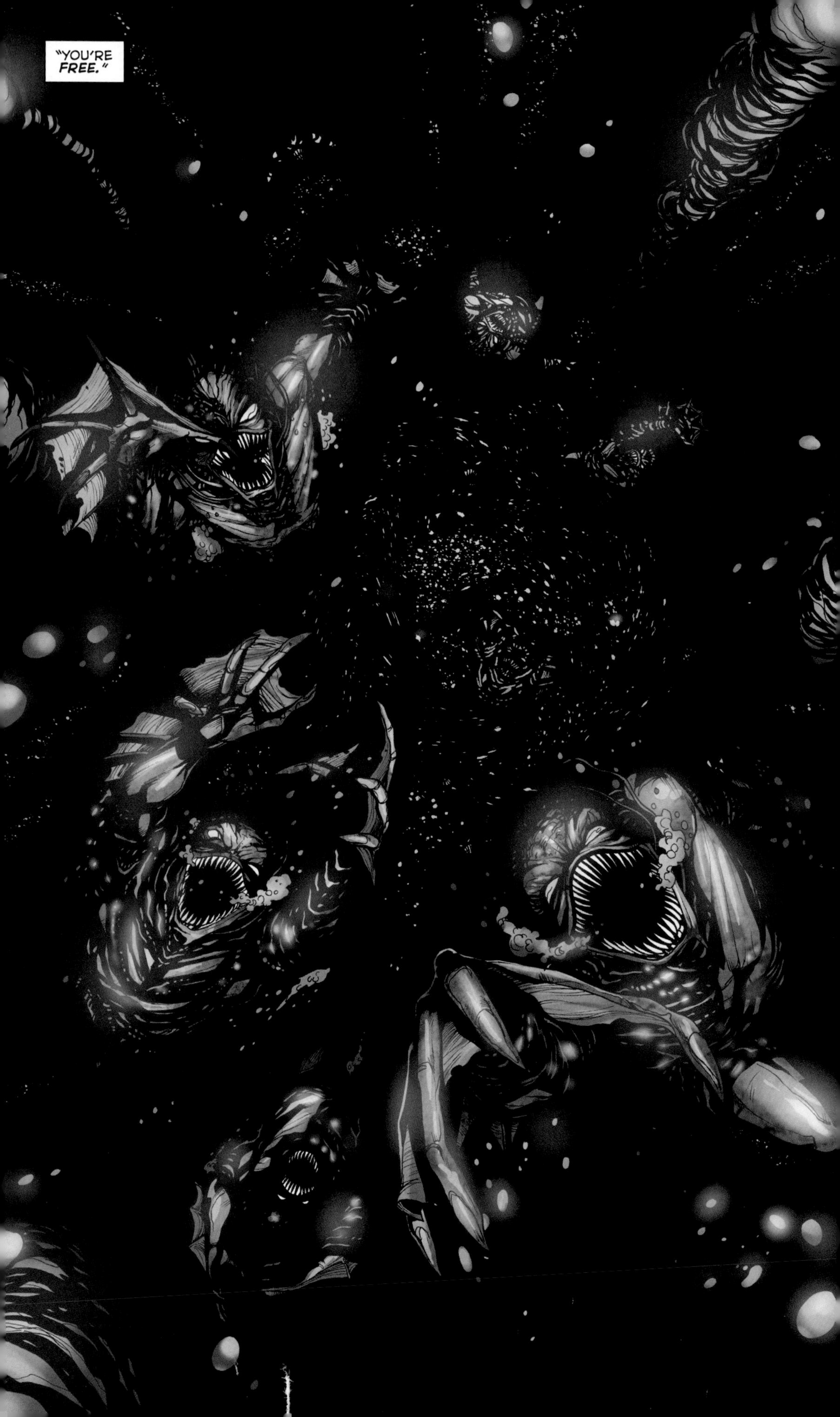
"YOU'RE FREE."

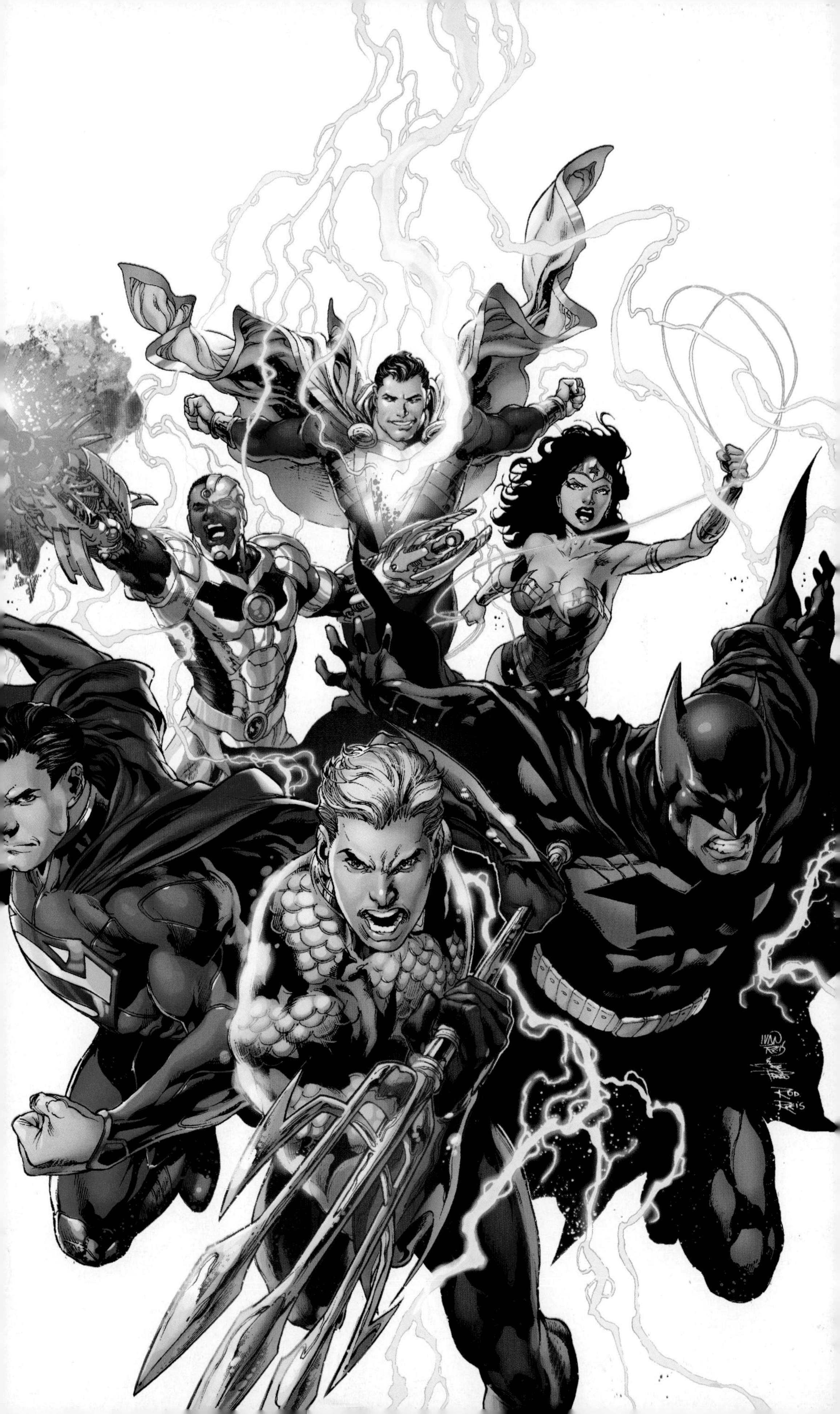

GEOFF JOHNS writer IVAN REIS penciller JOE PRADO inker cover by IVAN REIS, JOE PRADO & ROD REIS

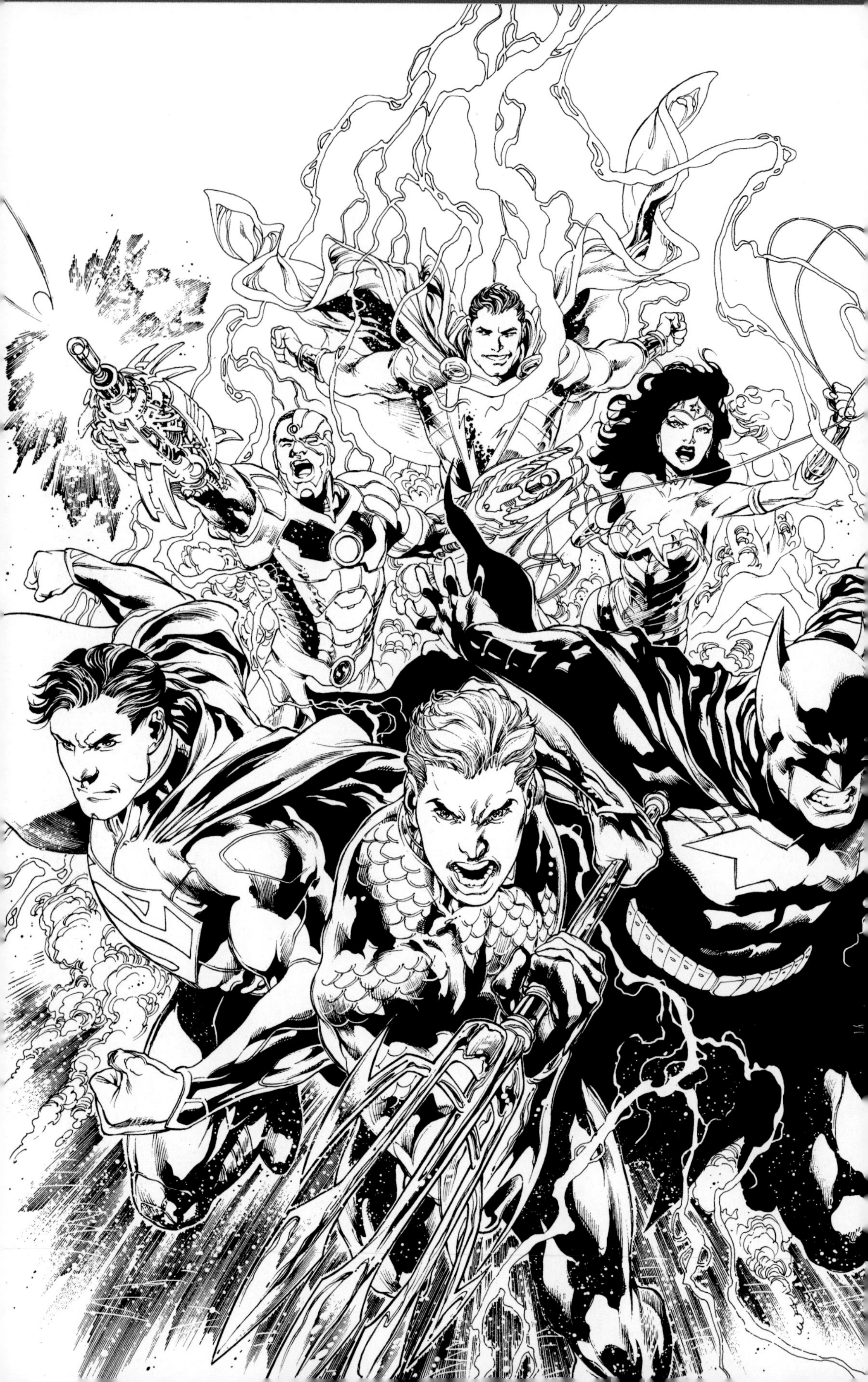

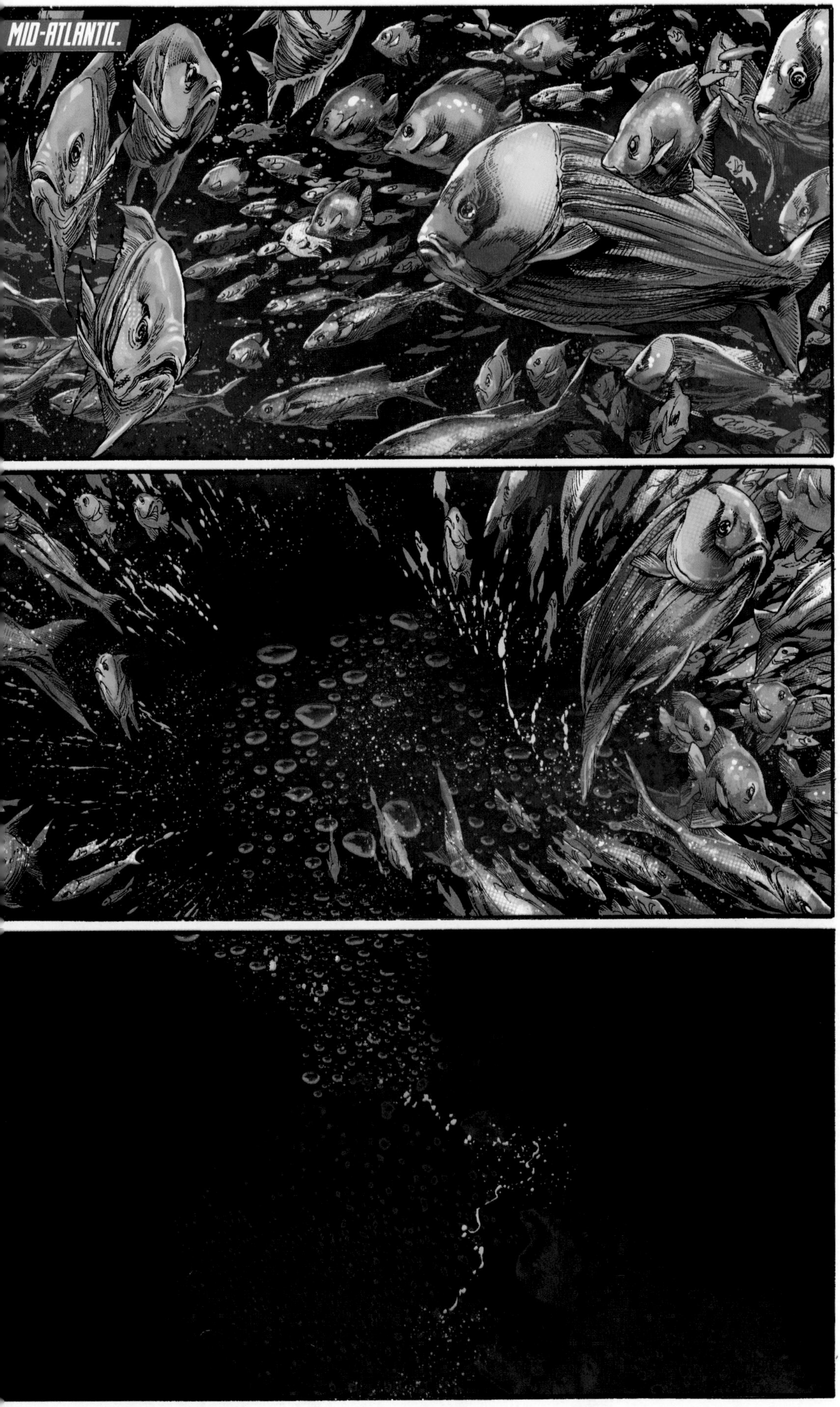
MID-ATLANTIC.

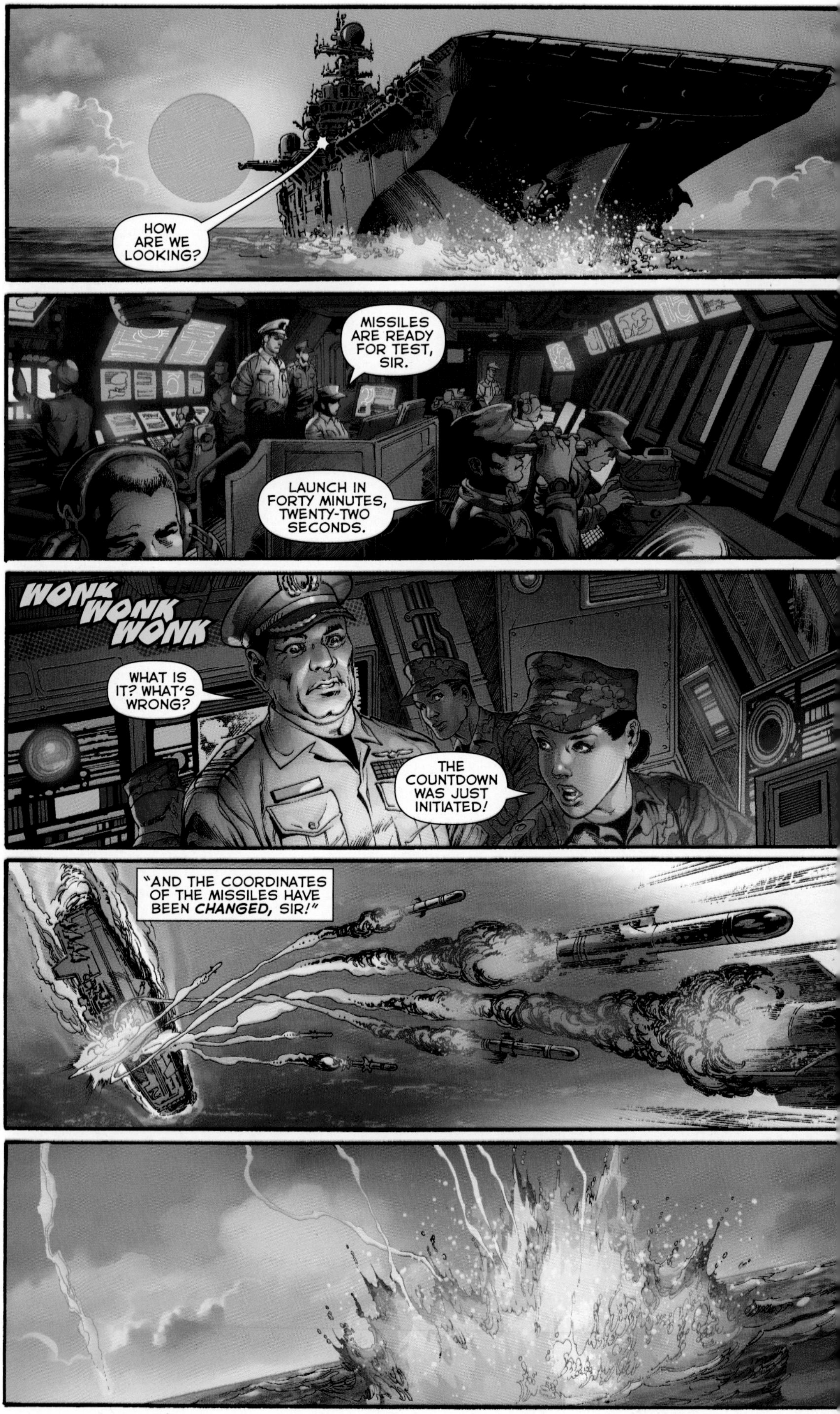
HOW ARE WE LOOKING?
MISSILES ARE READY FOR TEST, SIR.
LAUNCH IN FORTY MINUTES, TWENTY-TWO SECONDS.
WONK WONK WONK
WHAT IS IT? WHAT'S WRONG?
THE COUNTDOWN WAS JUST INITIATED!
"AND THE COORDINATES OF THE MISSILES HAVE BEEN CHANGED, SIR!"

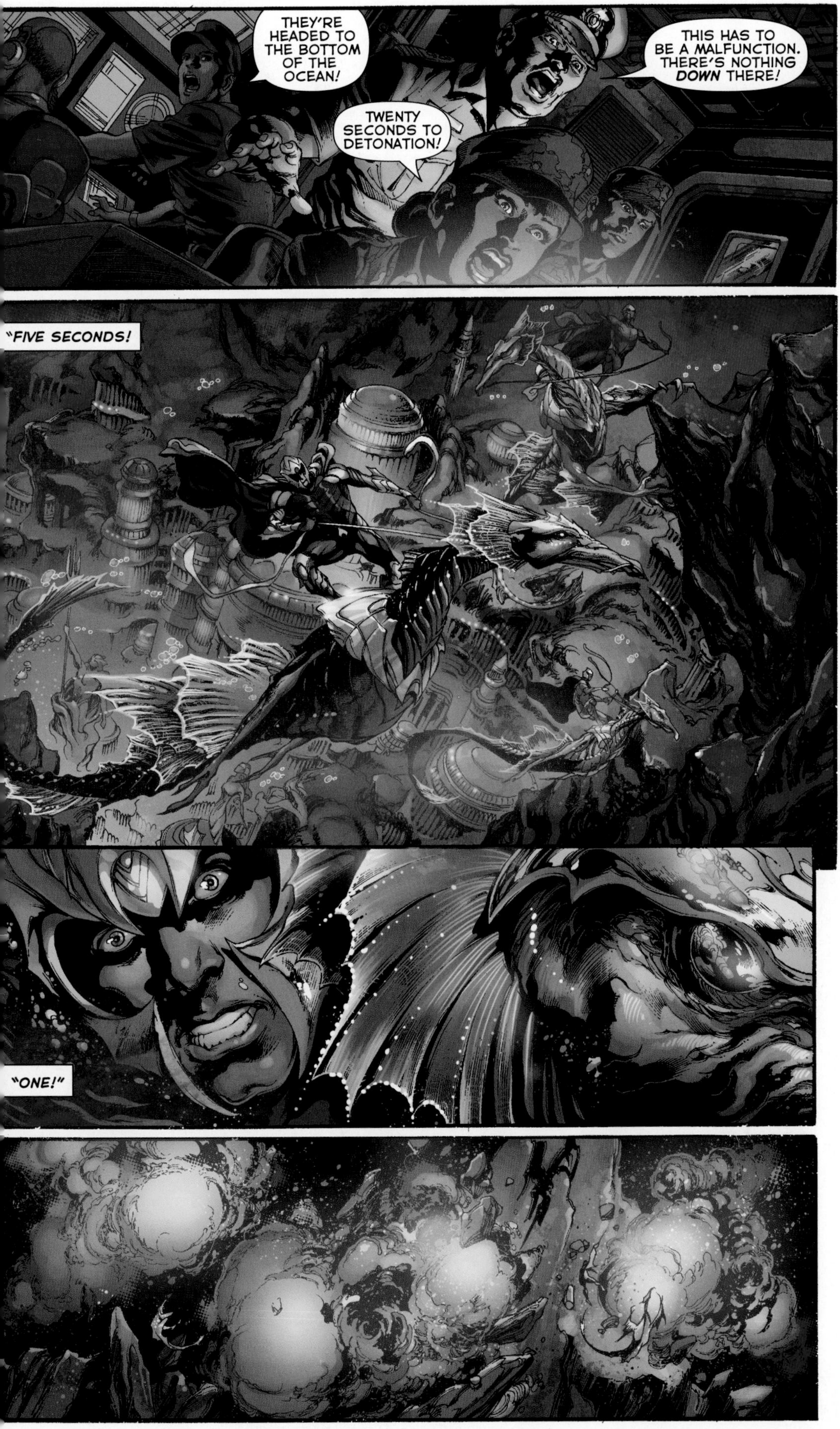
THEY'RE HEADED TO THE BOTTOM OF THE OCEAN!
THIS HAS TO BE A MALFUNCTION. THERE'S NOTHING DOWN THERE!
TWENTY SECONDS TO DETONATION!
"FIVE SECONDS!
"ONE!"

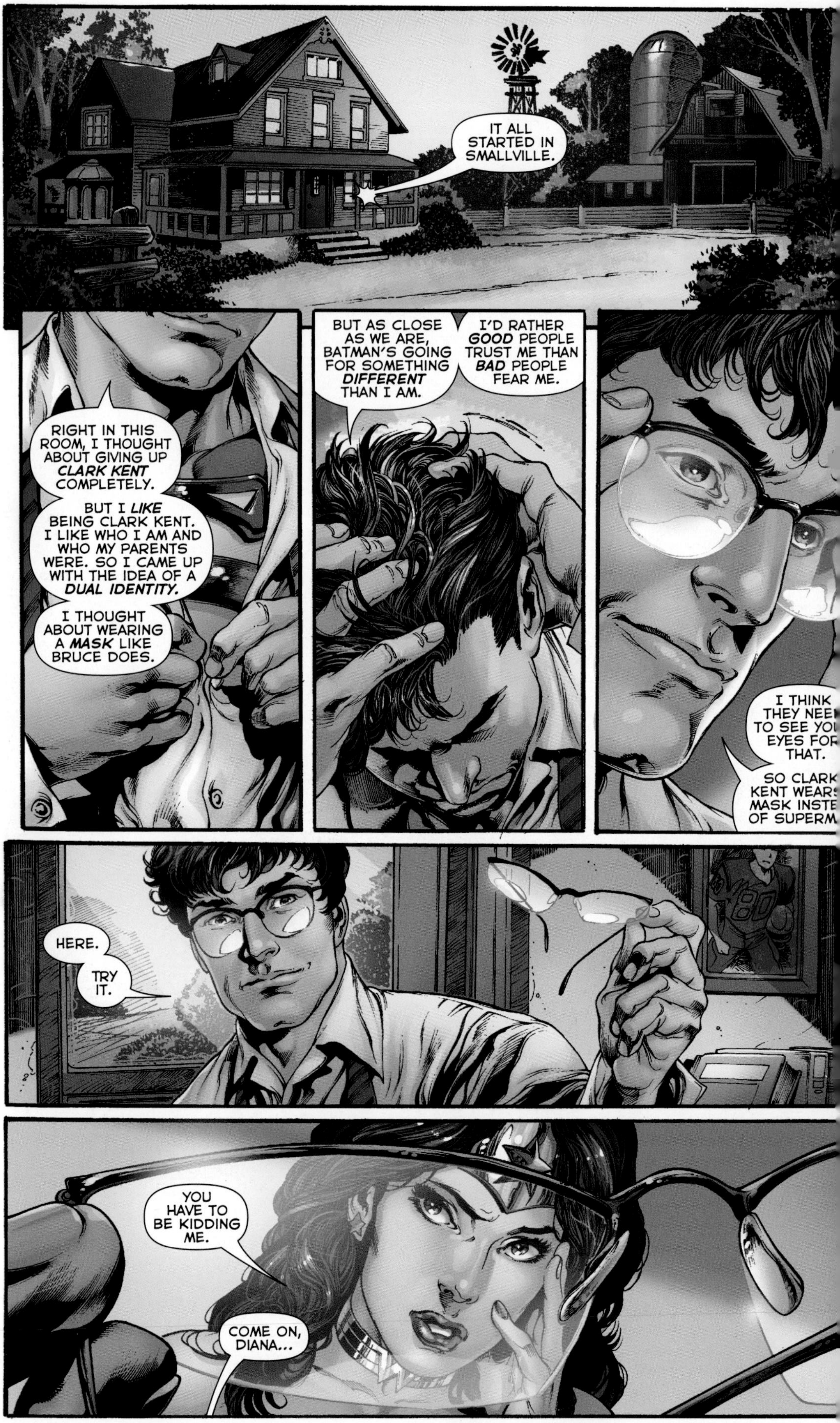
IT ALL STARTED IN SMALLVILLE.
RIGHT IN THIS ROOM, I THOUGHT ABOUT GIVING UP CLARK KENT COMPLETELY.
BUT I LIKE BEING CLARK KENT. I LIKE WHO I AM AND WHO MY PARENTS WERE. SO I CAME UP WITH THE IDEA OF A DUAL IDENTITY.
I THOUGHT ABOUT WEARING A MASK LIKE BRUCE DOES.
BUT AS CLOSE AS WE ARE, BATMAN'S GOING FOR SOMETHING DIFFERENT THAN I AM.
I'D RATHER GOOD PEOPLE TRUST ME THAN BAD PEOPLE FEAR ME.
I THINK THEY NEE TO SEE YO EYES FOR THAT.
SO CLARK KENT WEARS MASK INSTE OF SUPERM
HERE.
TRY IT.
YOU HAVE TO BE KIDDING ME.
COME ON, DIANA...

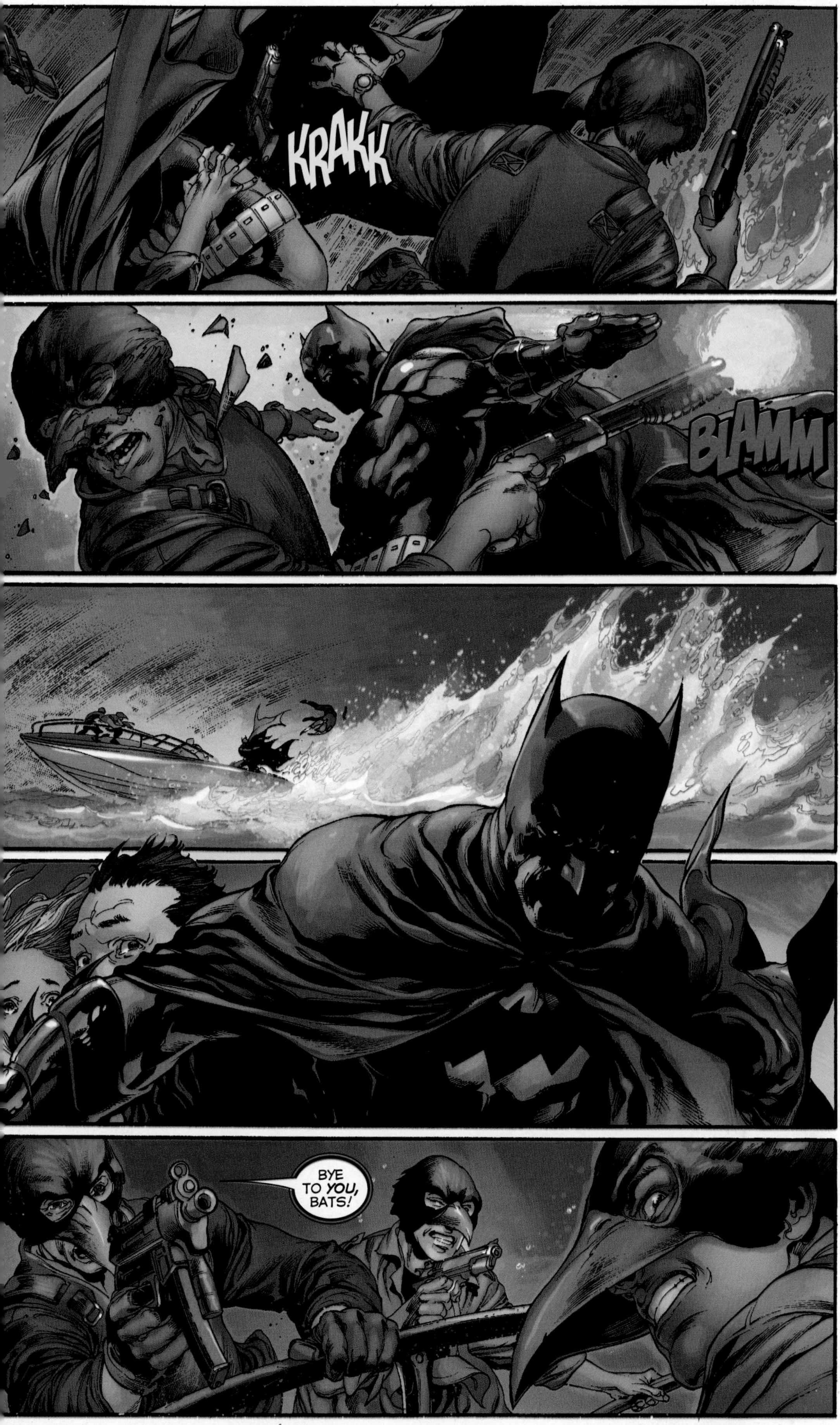
KRAKK
BLAMM
BYE TO YOU, BATS!

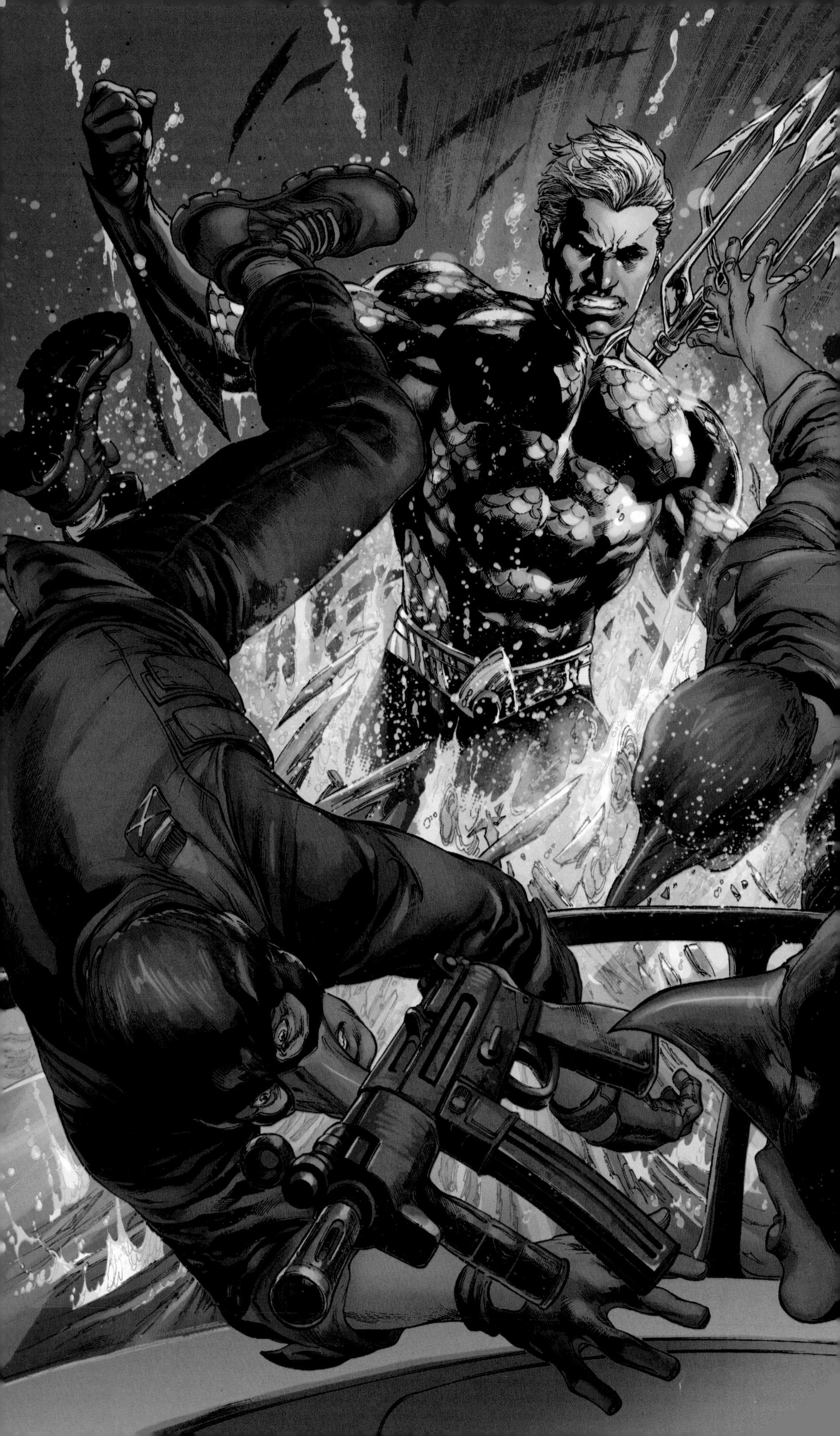

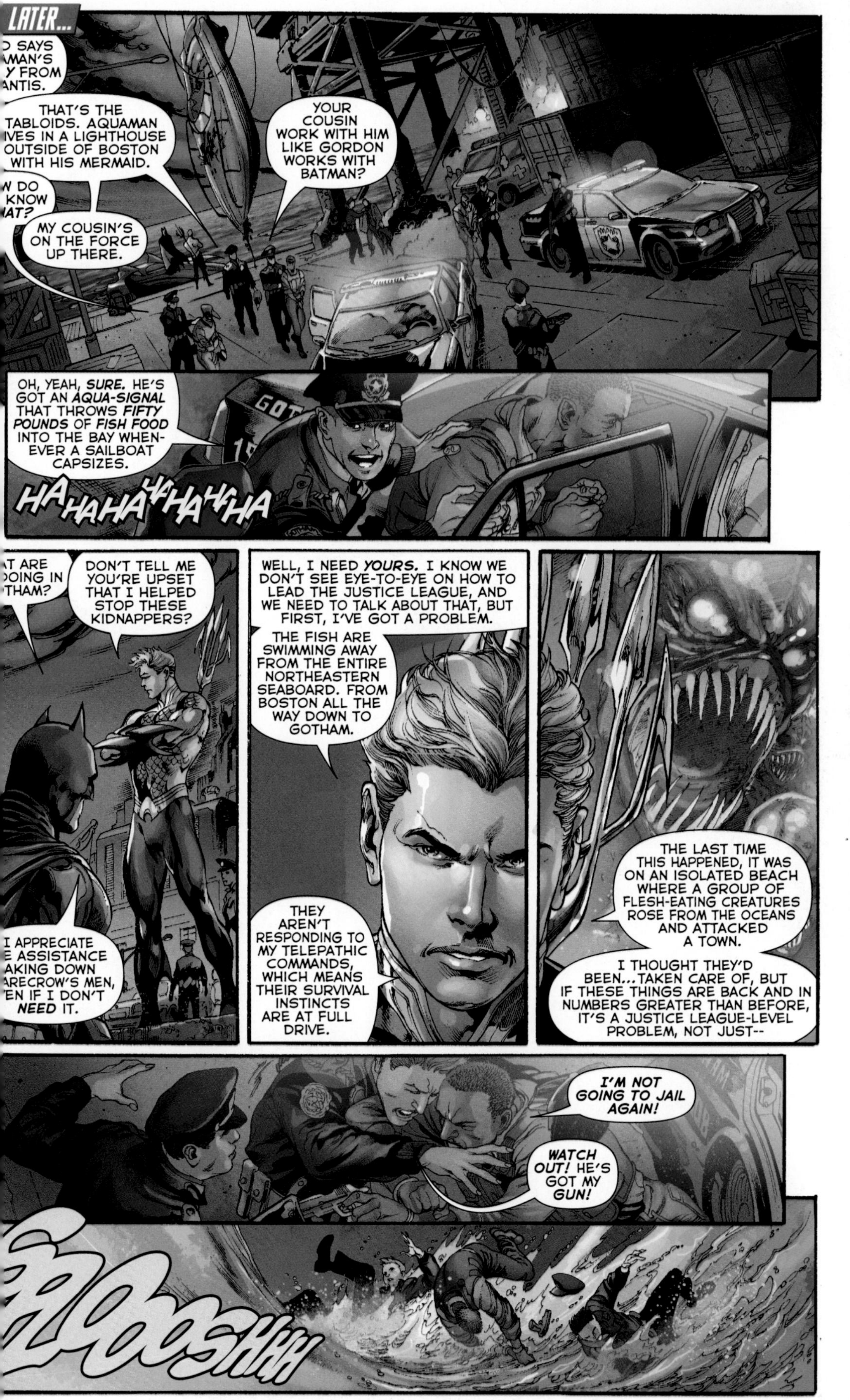
LATER...
O SAYS
AMAN'S
Y FROM
ANTIS.
THAT'S THE TABLOIDS. AQUAMAN IVES IN A LIGHTHOUSE OUTSIDE OF BOSTON WITH HIS MERMAID.
YOUR COUSIN WORK WITH HIM LIKE GORDON WORKS WITH BATMAN?
W DO
KNOW
HAT?
MY COUSIN'S ON THE FORCE UP THERE.
OH, YEAH, SURE. HE'S GOT AN AQUA-SIGNAL THAT THROWS FIFTY POUNDS OF FISH FOOD INTO THE BAY WHEN-EVER A SAILBOAT CAPSIZES.
HAHAHAHAHAHAHA
AT ARE
DOING IN
THAM?
DON'T TELL ME YOU'RE UPSET THAT I HELPED STOP THESE KIDNAPPERS?
I APPRECIATE
E ASSISTANCE
AKING DOWN
ARECROW'S MEN,
EN IF I DON'T
NEED IT.
WELL, I NEED YOURS. I KNOW WE DON'T SEE EYE-TO-EYE ON HOW TO LEAD THE JUSTICE LEAGUE, AND WE NEED TO TALK ABOUT THAT, BUT FIRST, I'VE GOT A PROBLEM.
THE FISH ARE SWIMMING AWAY FROM THE ENTIRE NORTHEASTERN SEABOARD. FROM BOSTON ALL THE WAY DOWN TO GOTHAM.
THEY AREN'T RESPONDING TO MY TELEPATHIC COMMANDS, WHICH MEANS THEIR SURVIVAL INSTINCTS ARE AT FULL DRIVE.
THE LAST TIME THIS HAPPENED, IT WAS ON AN ISOLATED BEACH WHERE A GROUP OF FLESH-EATING CREATURES ROSE FROM THE OCEANS AND ATTACKED A TOWN.
I THOUGHT THEY'D BEEN...TAKEN CARE OF, BUT IF THESE THINGS ARE BACK AND IN NUMBERS GREATER THAN BEFORE, IT'S A JUSTICE LEAGUE-LEVEL PROBLEM, NOT JUST--
I'M NOT GOING TO JAIL AGAIN!
WATCH OUT! HE'S GOT MY GUN!
SPLOOSHHH

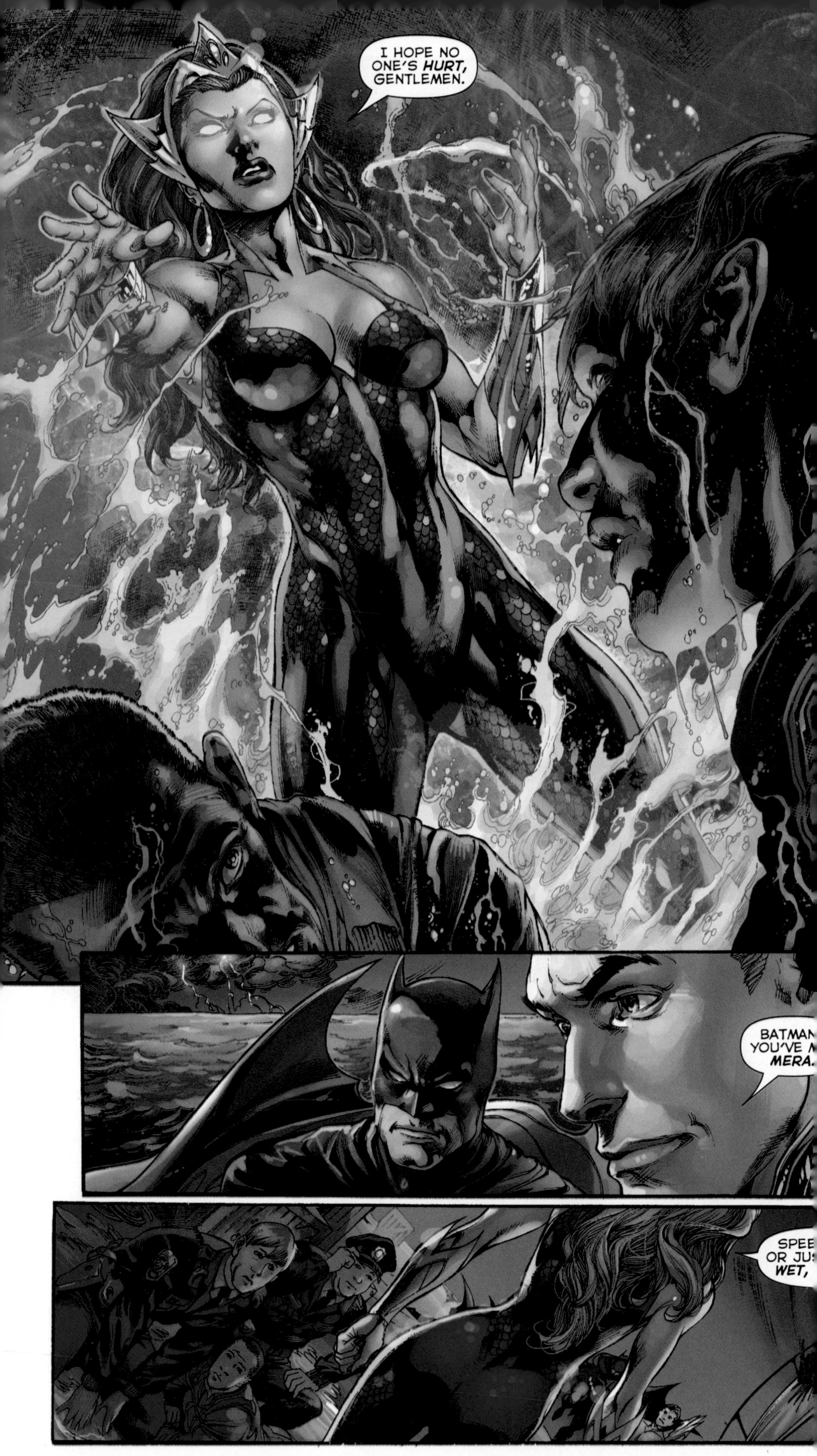
I HOPE NO ONE'S *HURT,* GENTLEMEN.
BATMAN YOU'VE M *MERA.*
SPEE OR JUS *WET,*

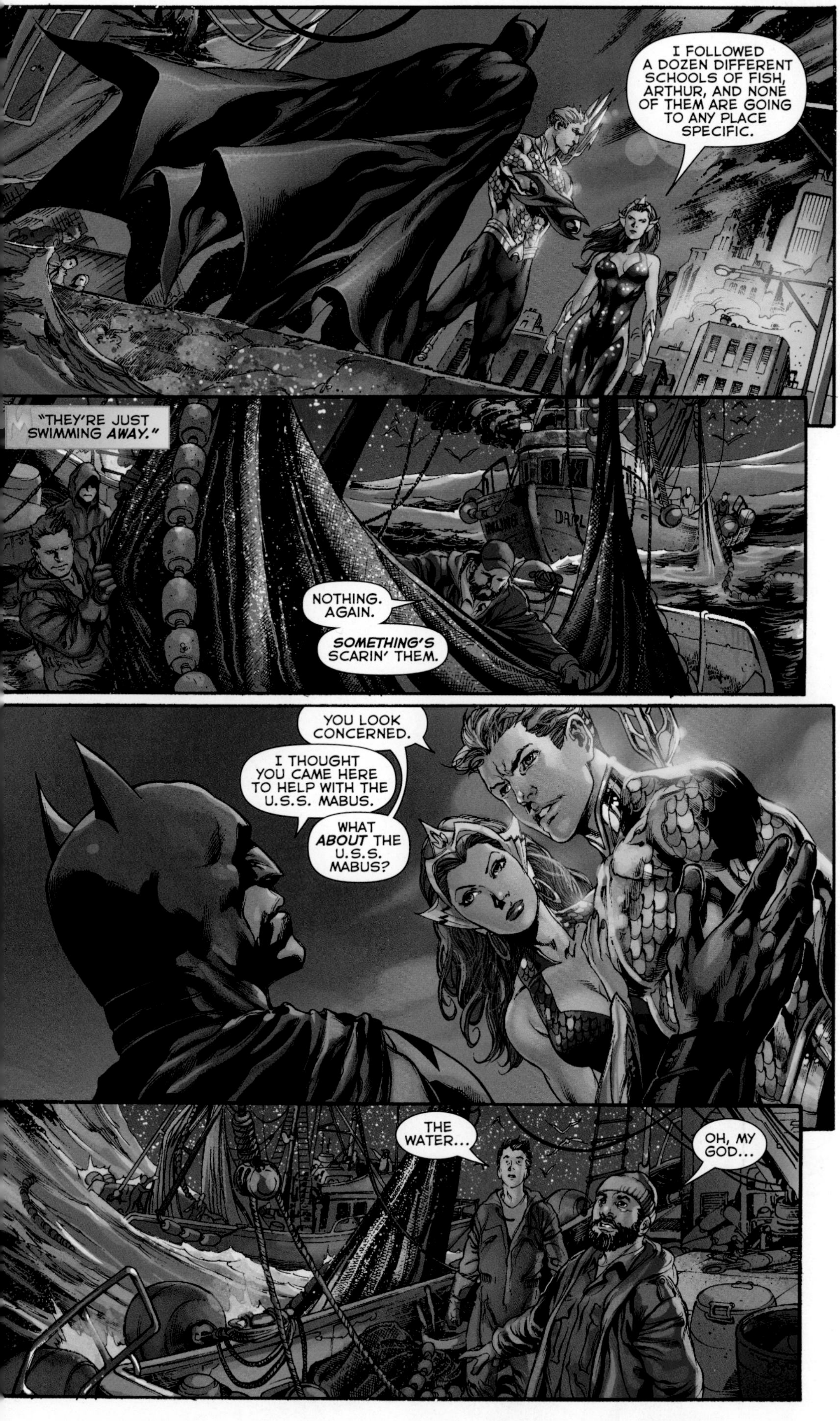
I FOLLOWED A DOZEN DIFFERENT SCHOOLS OF FISH, ARTHUR, AND NONE OF THEM ARE GOING TO ANY PLACE SPECIFIC.
"THEY'RE JUST SWIMMING AWAY."
NOTHING. AGAIN.
SOMETHING'S SCARIN' THEM.
YOU LOOK CONCERNED.
I THOUGHT YOU CAME HERE TO HELP WITH THE U.S.S. MABUS.
WHAT ABOUT THE U.S.S. MABUS?
THE WATER...
OH, MY GOD...

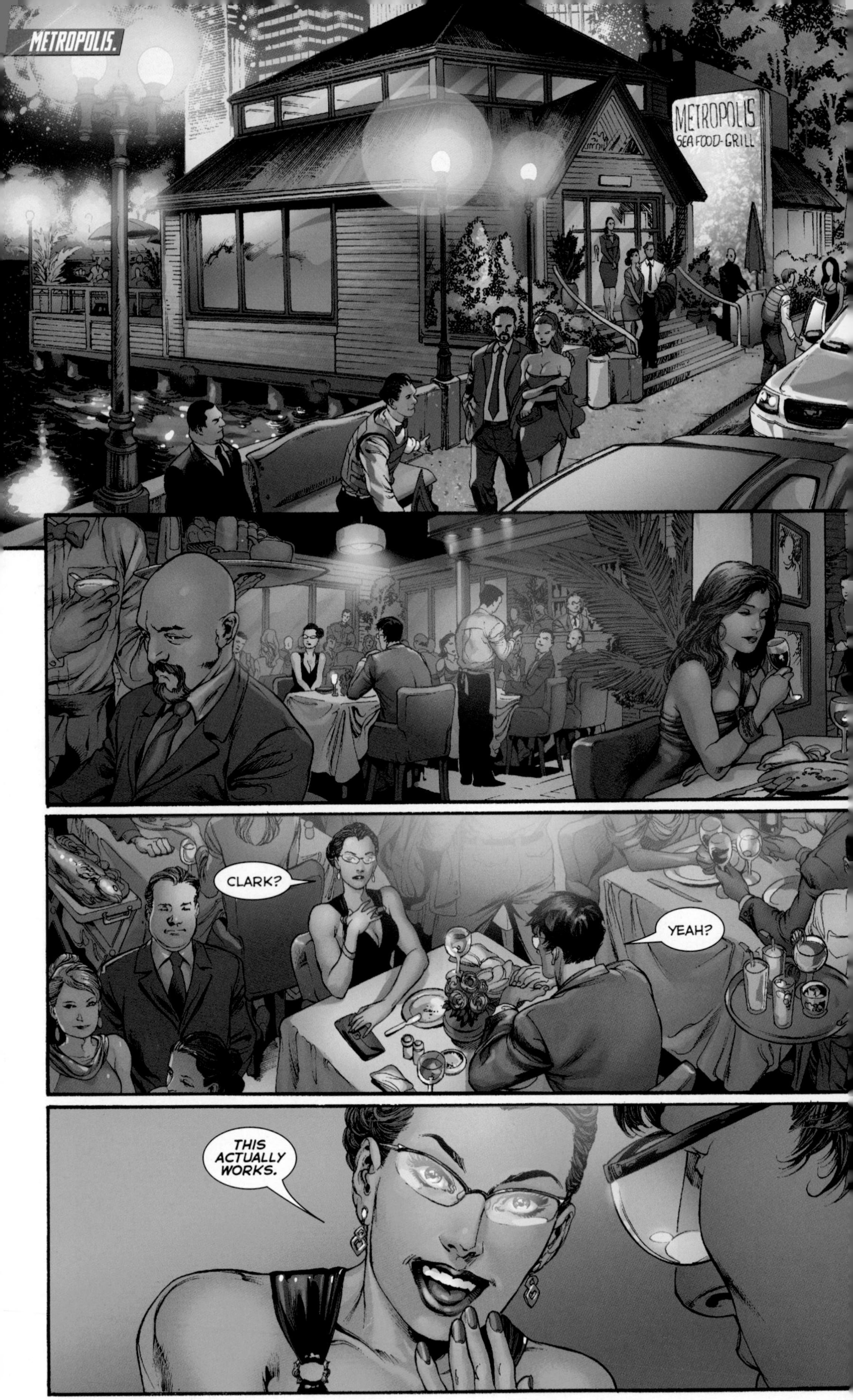
METROPOLIS.
METROPOLIS
SEA FOOD-GRILL
CLARK?
YEAH?
THIS ACTUALLY WORKS.

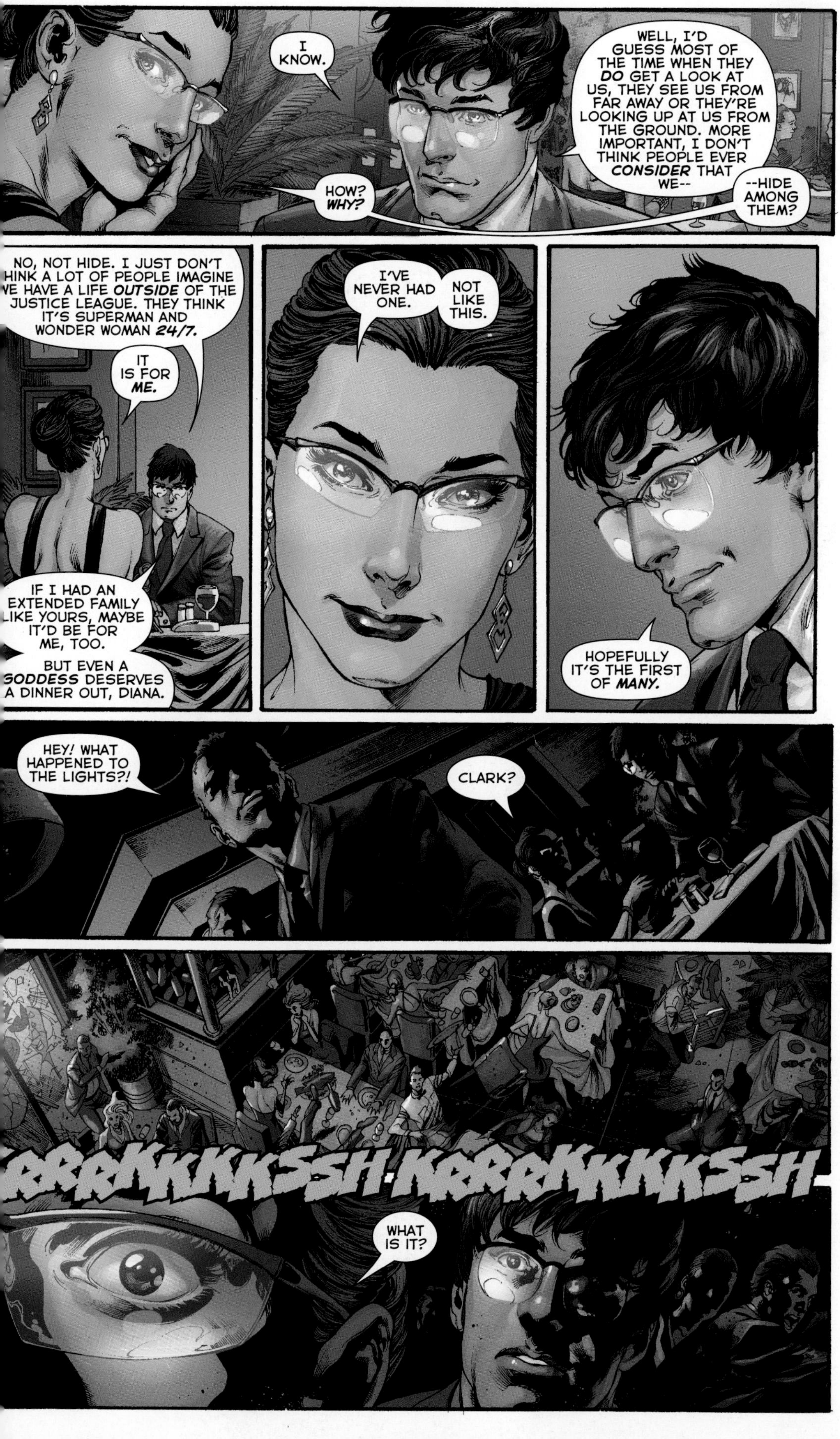
I KNOW.
WELL, I'D GUESS MOST OF THE TIME WHEN THEY DO GET A LOOK AT US, THEY SEE US FROM FAR AWAY OR THEY'RE LOOKING UP AT US FROM THE GROUND. MORE IMPORTANT, I DON'T THINK PEOPLE EVER CONSIDER THAT WE--
HOW? WHY?
--HIDE AMONG THEM?
NO, NOT HIDE. I JUST DON'T THINK A LOT OF PEOPLE IMAGINE WE HAVE A LIFE OUTSIDE OF THE JUSTICE LEAGUE. THEY THINK IT'S SUPERMAN AND WONDER WOMAN 24/7.
IT IS FOR ME.
IF I HAD AN EXTENDED FAMILY LIKE YOURS, MAYBE IT'D BE FOR ME, TOO.
BUT EVEN A GODDESS DESERVES A DINNER OUT, DIANA.
I'VE NEVER HAD ONE.
NOT LIKE THIS.
HOPEFULLY IT'S THE FIRST OF MANY.
HEY! WHAT HAPPENED TO THE LIGHTS?!
CLARK?
KRRRKKKKSSH KRRRKKKKKSSH
WHAT IS IT?

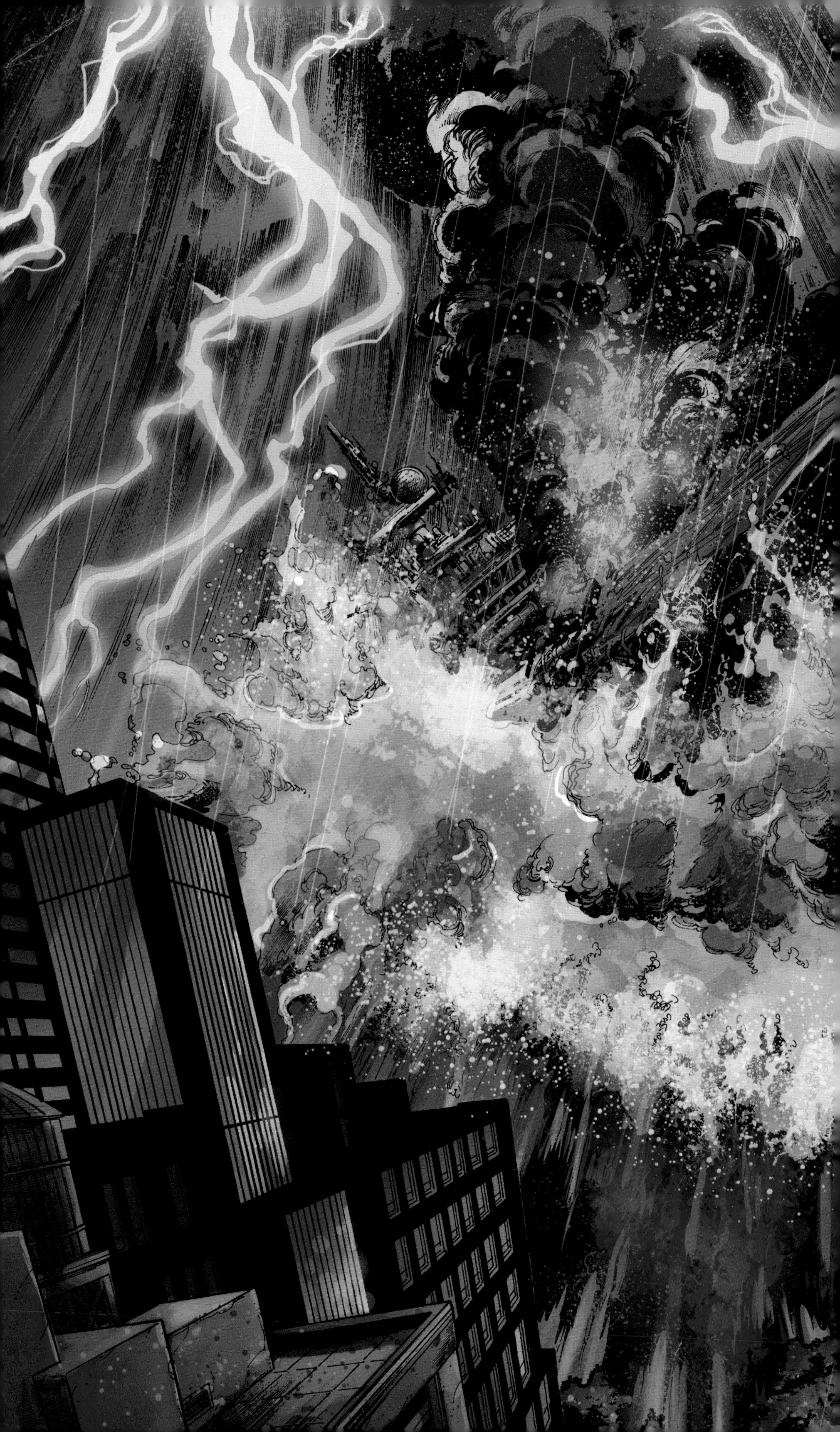

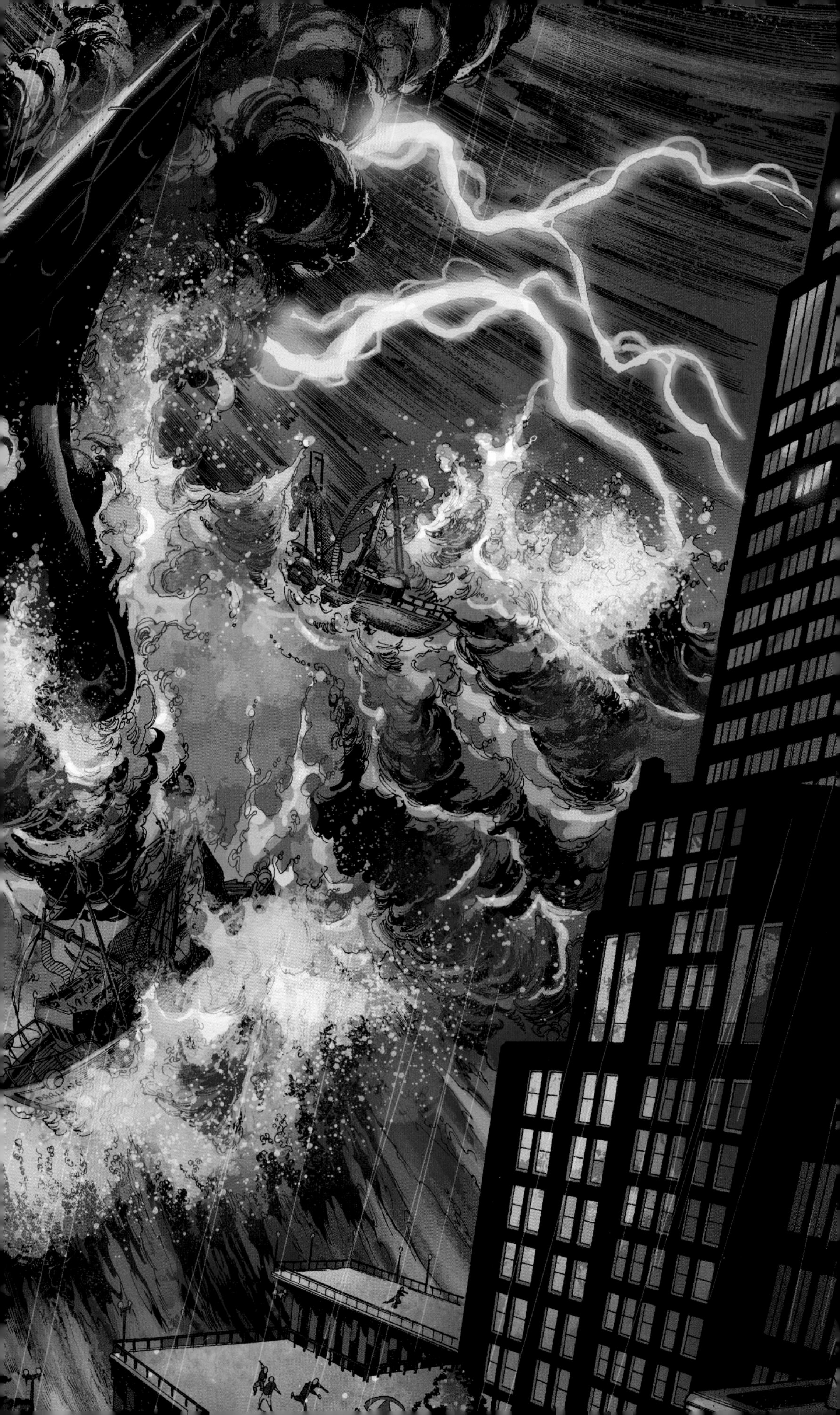
DARLING

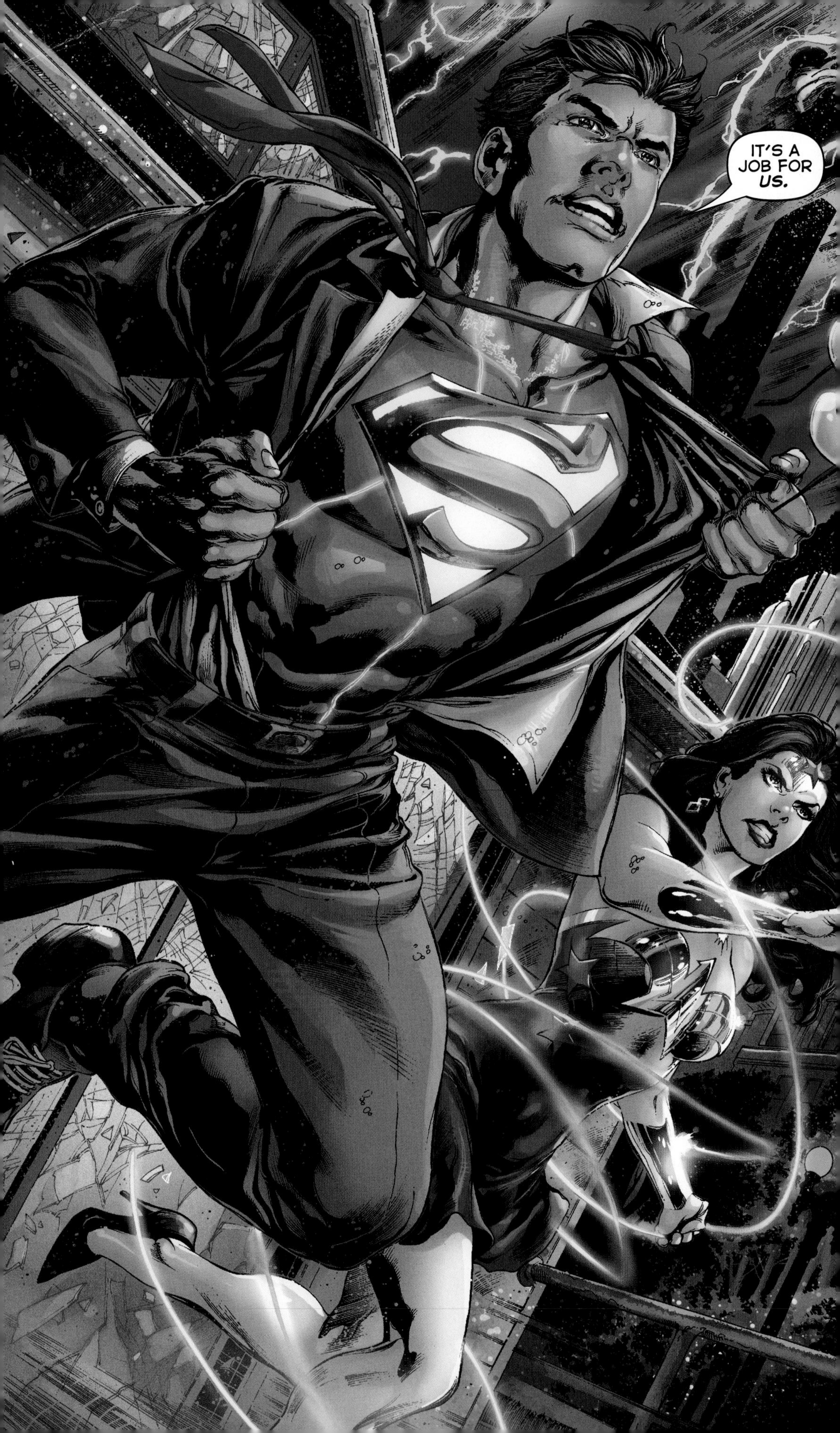
IT'S A JOB FOR US.

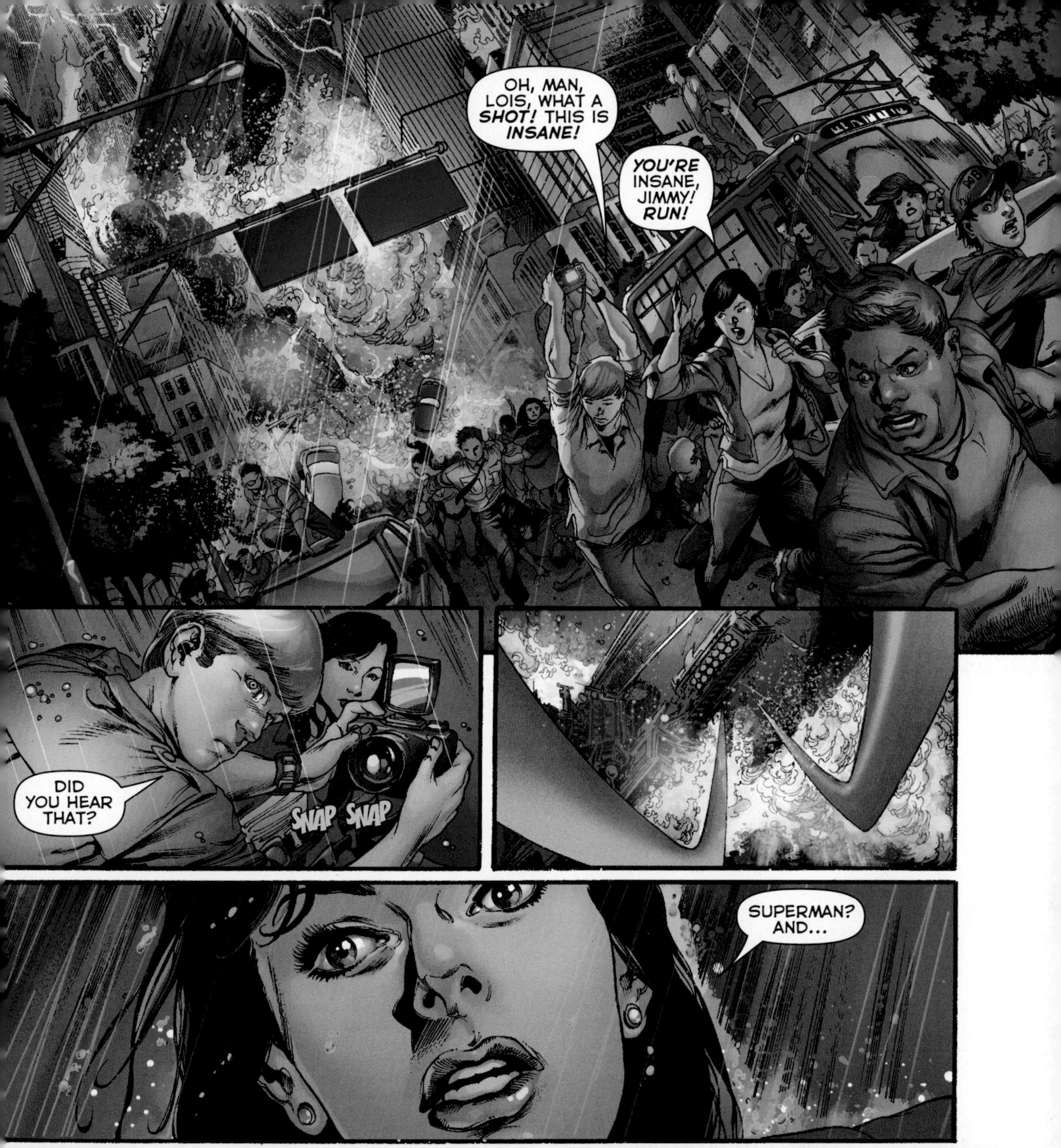
OH, MAN, LOIS, WHAT A SHOT! THIS IS INSANE!
YOU'RE INSANE, JIMMY! RUN!
DID YOU HEAR THAT?
SNAP SNAP
SUPERMAN? AND...
NNGG
DDT

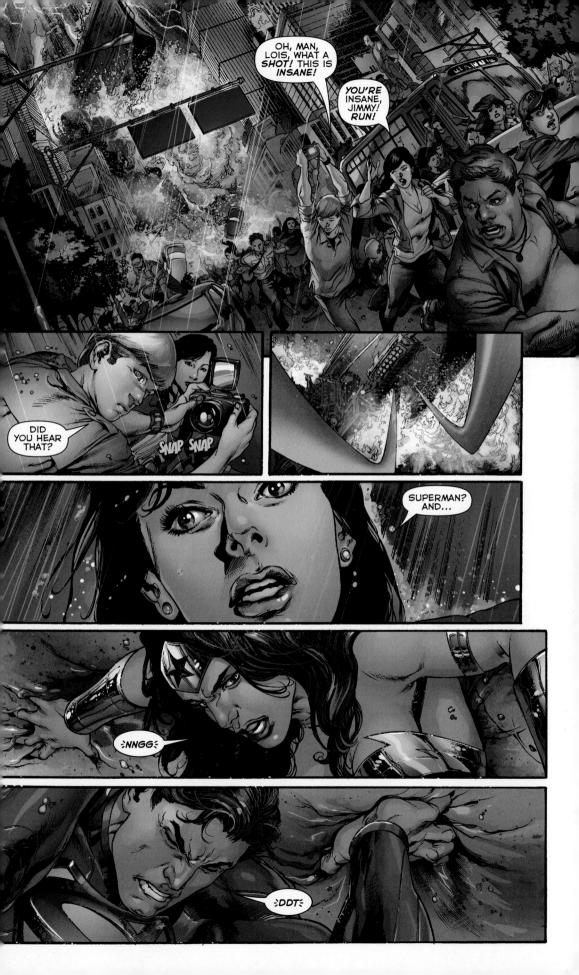

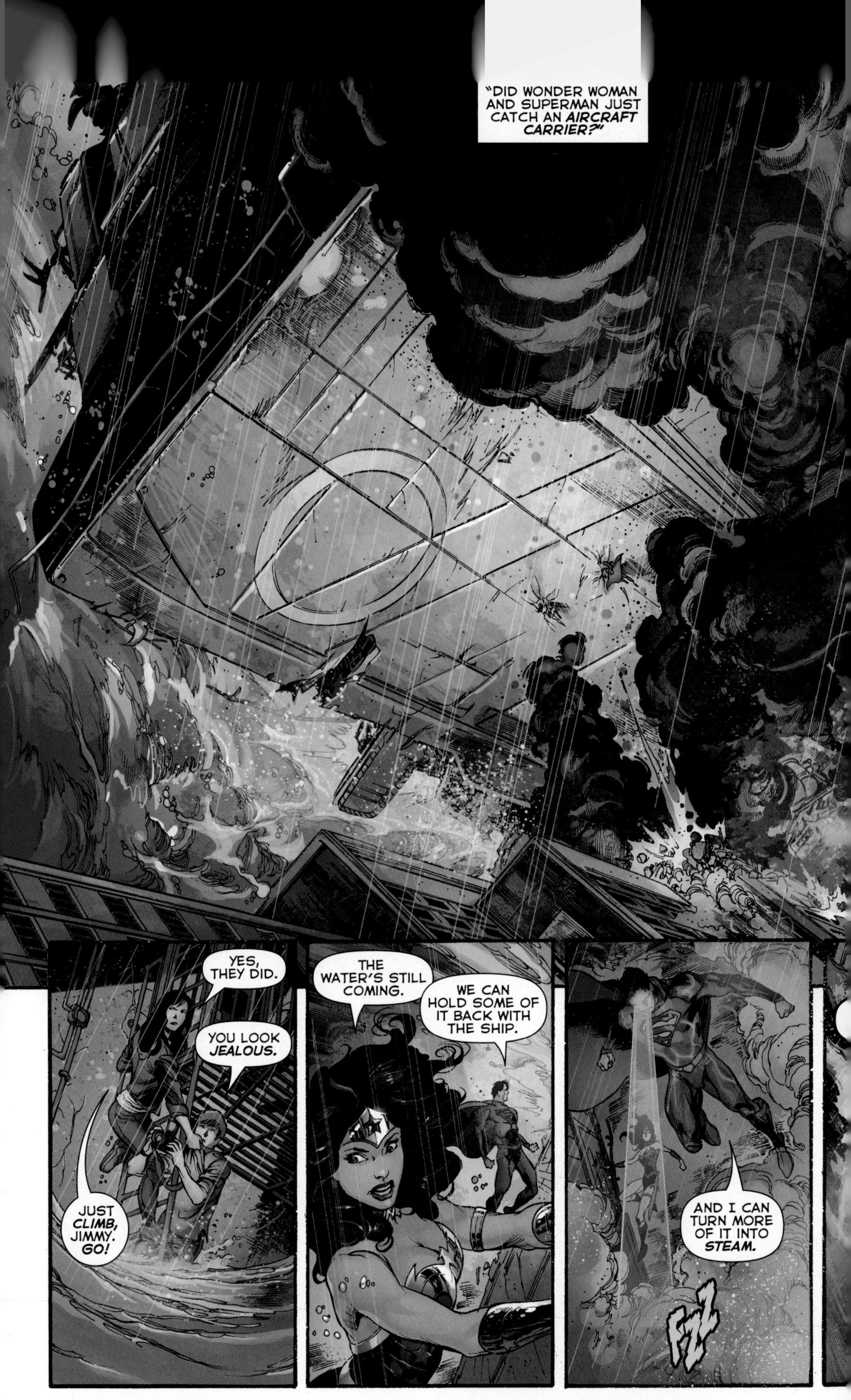
"DID WONDER WOMAN AND SUPERMAN JUST CATCH AN *AIRCRAFT CARRIER?*"
YES, THEY DID.
YOU LOOK *JEALOUS.*
JUST *CLIMB,* JIMMY. *GO!*
THE WATER'S STILL COMING.
WE CAN HOLD SOME OF IT BACK WITH THE SHIP.
AND I CAN TURN MORE OF IT INTO *STEAM.*
FZZ

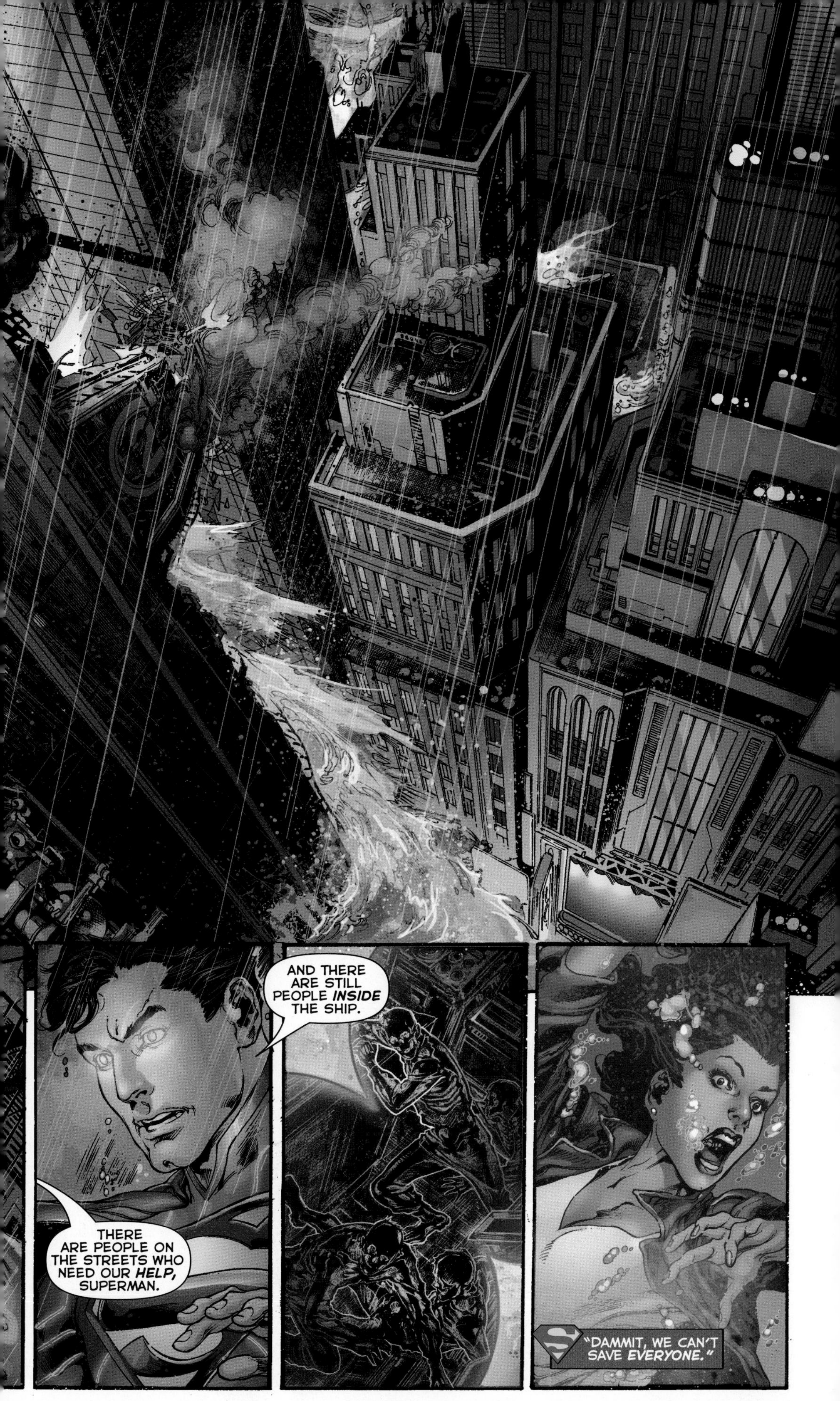
THERE ARE PEOPLE ON THE STREETS WHO NEED OUR HELP, SUPERMAN.
AND THERE ARE STILL PEOPLE INSIDE THE SHIP.
"DAMMIT, WE CAN'T SAVE EVERYONE."

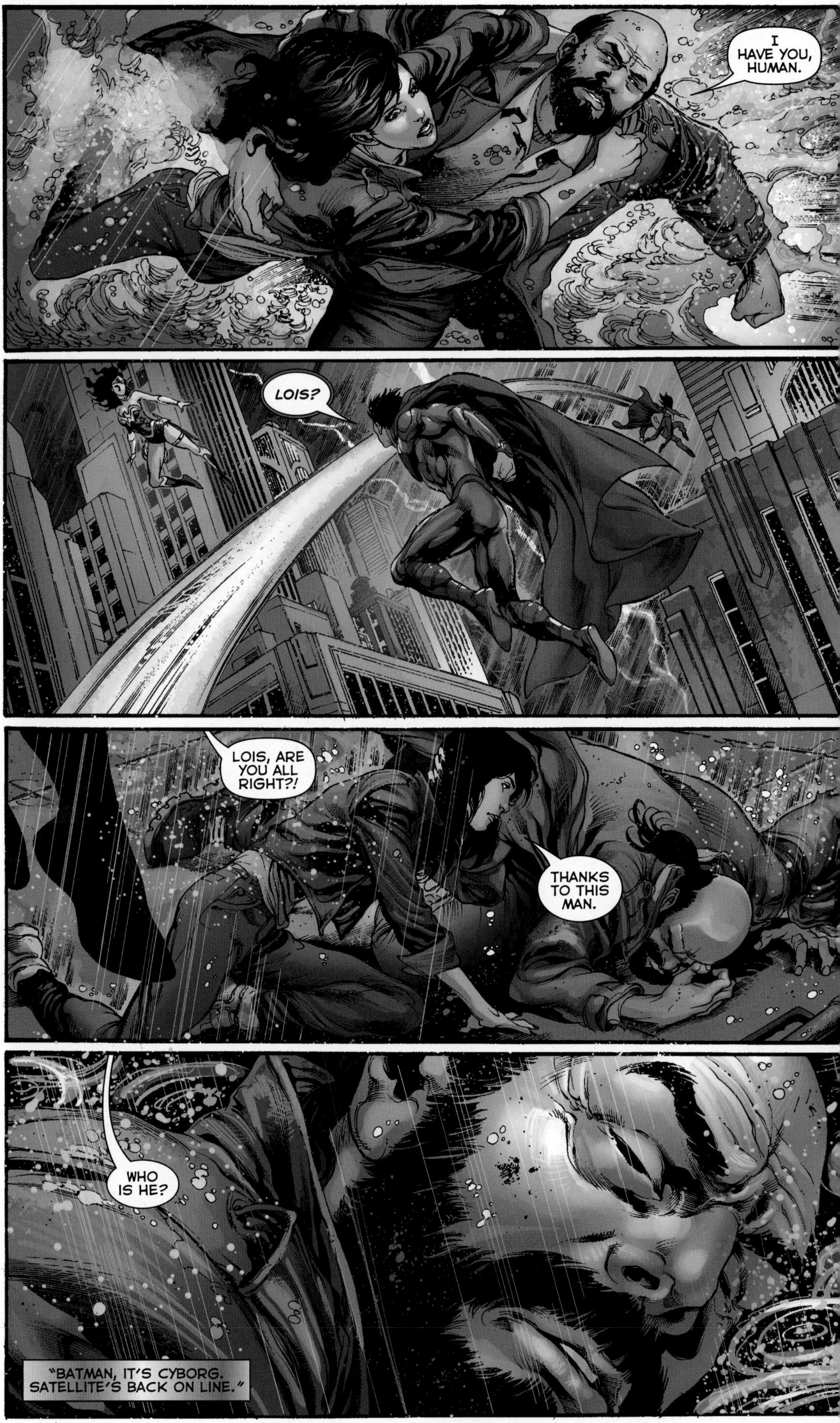
I HAVE YOU, HUMAN.
LOIS?
LOIS, ARE YOU ALL RIGHT?!
THANKS TO THIS MAN.
WHO IS HE?
"BATMAN, IT'S CYBORG. SATELLITE'S BACK ON LINE."

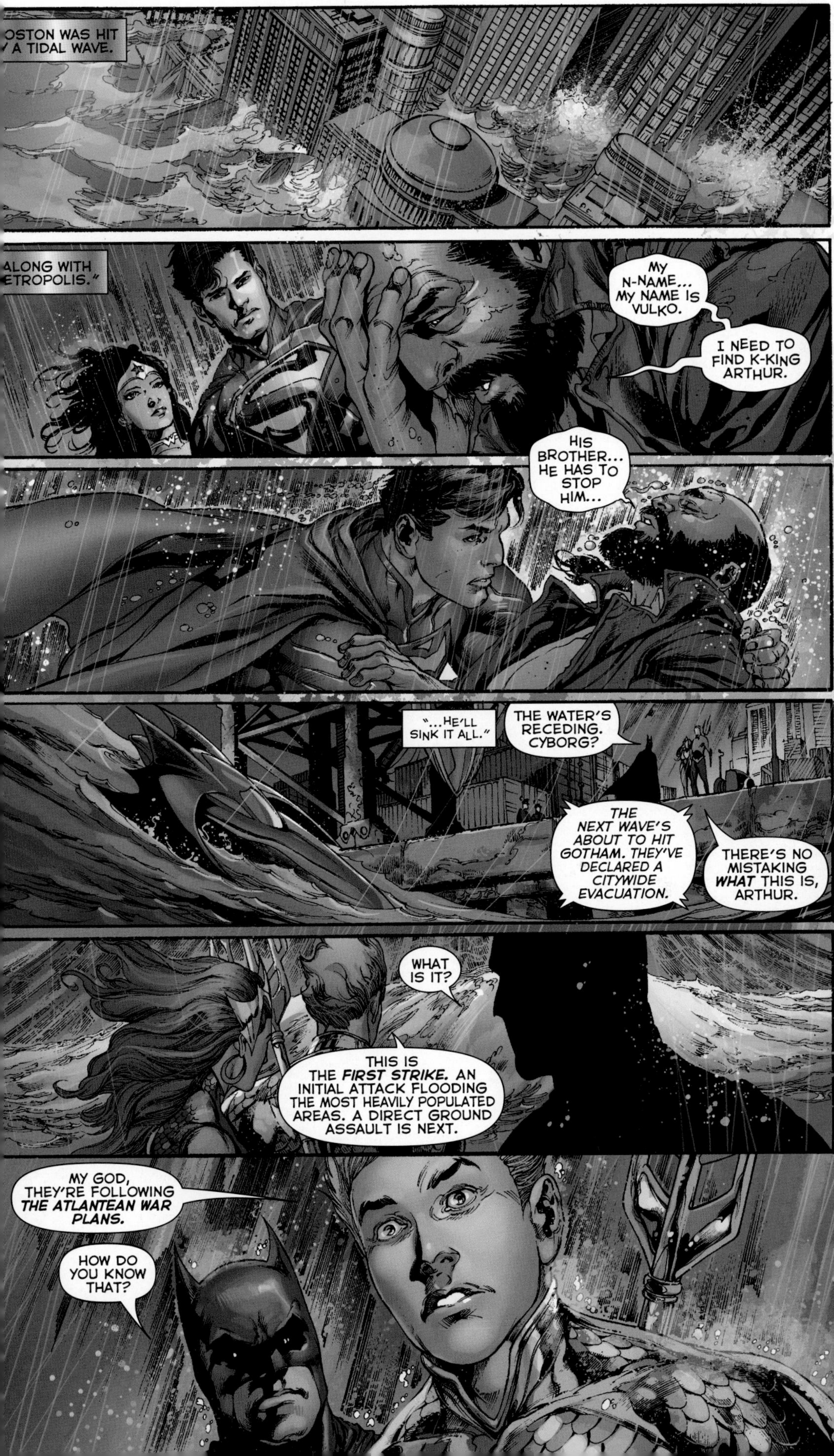
OSTON WAS HIT
A TIDAL WAVE.
ALONG WITH
ETROPOLIS."
MY N-NAME... MY NAME IS VULKO.
I NEED TO FIND K-KING ARTHUR.
HIS BROTHER... HE HAS TO STOP HIM...
"...HE'LL SINK IT ALL."
THE WATER'S RECEDING. CYBORG?
THE NEXT WAVE'S ABOUT TO HIT GOTHAM. THEY'VE DECLARED A CITYWIDE EVACUATION.
THERE'S NO MISTAKING WHAT THIS IS, ARTHUR.
WHAT IS IT?
THIS IS THE FIRST STRIKE. AN INITIAL ATTACK FLOODING THE MOST HEAVILY POPULATED AREAS. A DIRECT GROUND ASSAULT IS NEXT.
MY GOD, THEY'RE FOLLOWING THE ATLANTEAN WAR PLANS.
HOW DO YOU KNOW THAT?

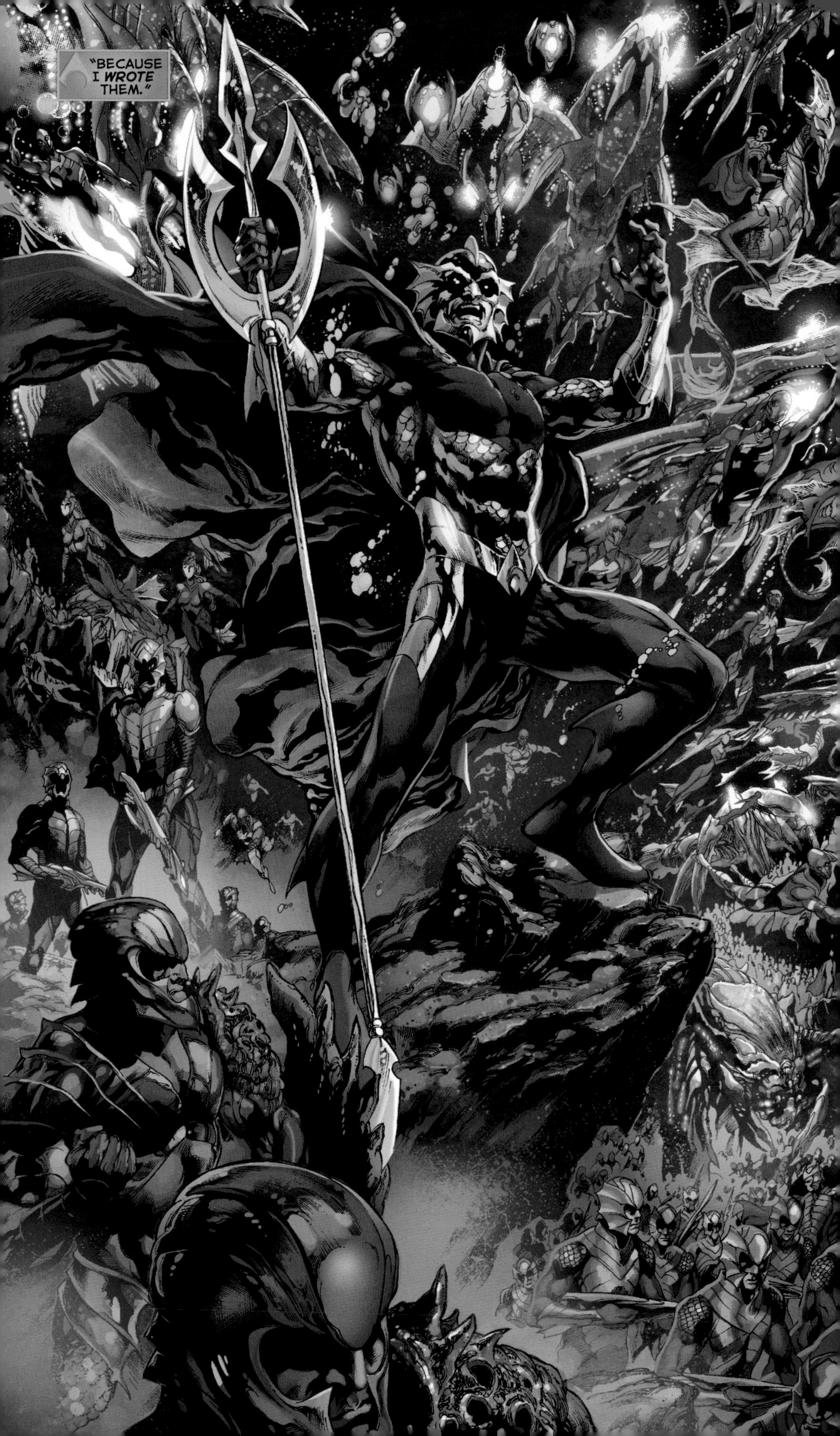
"BECAUSE I *WROTE* THEM."

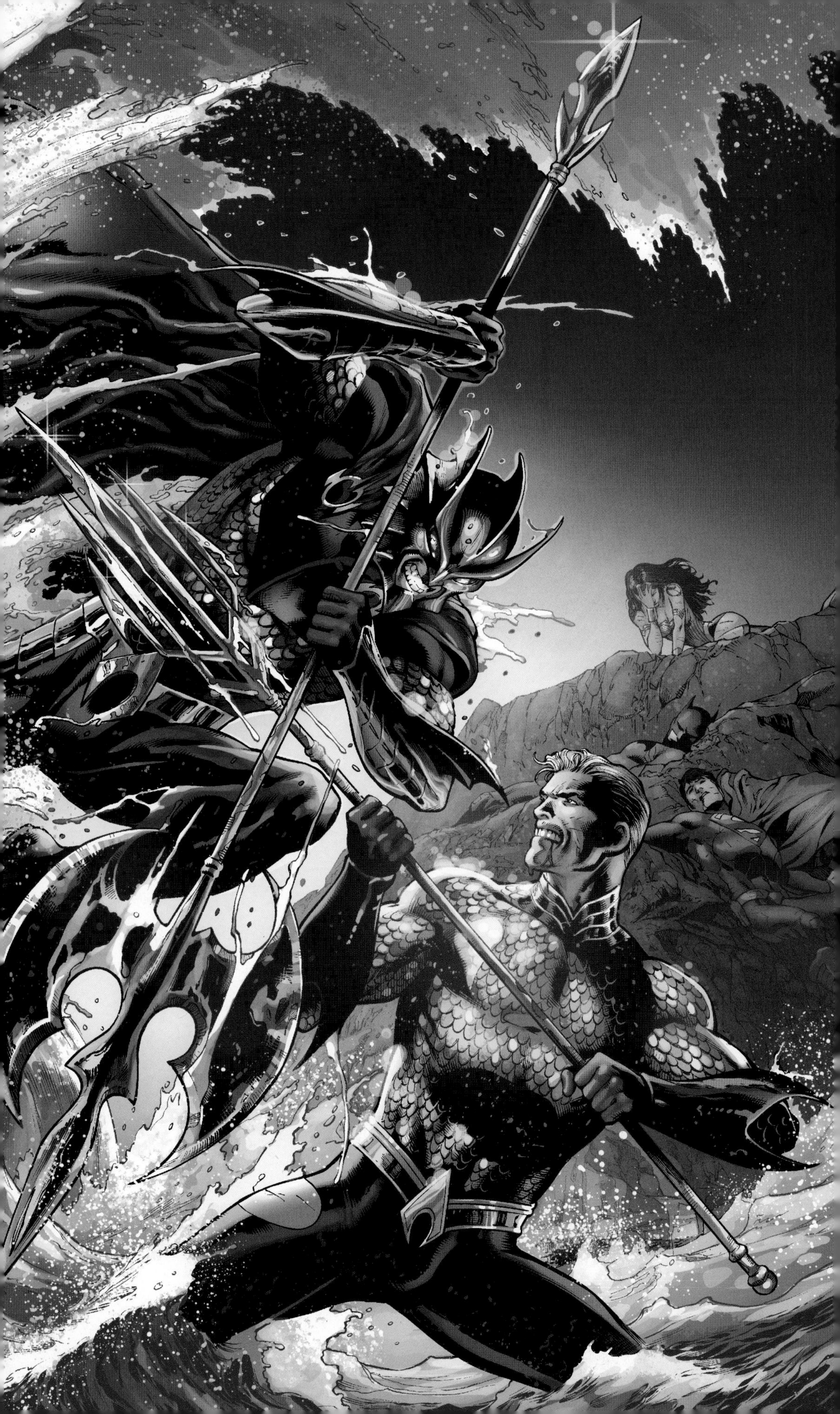

GEOFF JOHNS writer **PAUL PELLETIER** penciller **ART THIBERT** with **KARL KESEL** inkers cover by **EDDY BARROWS, EBER FERREIRA & R**

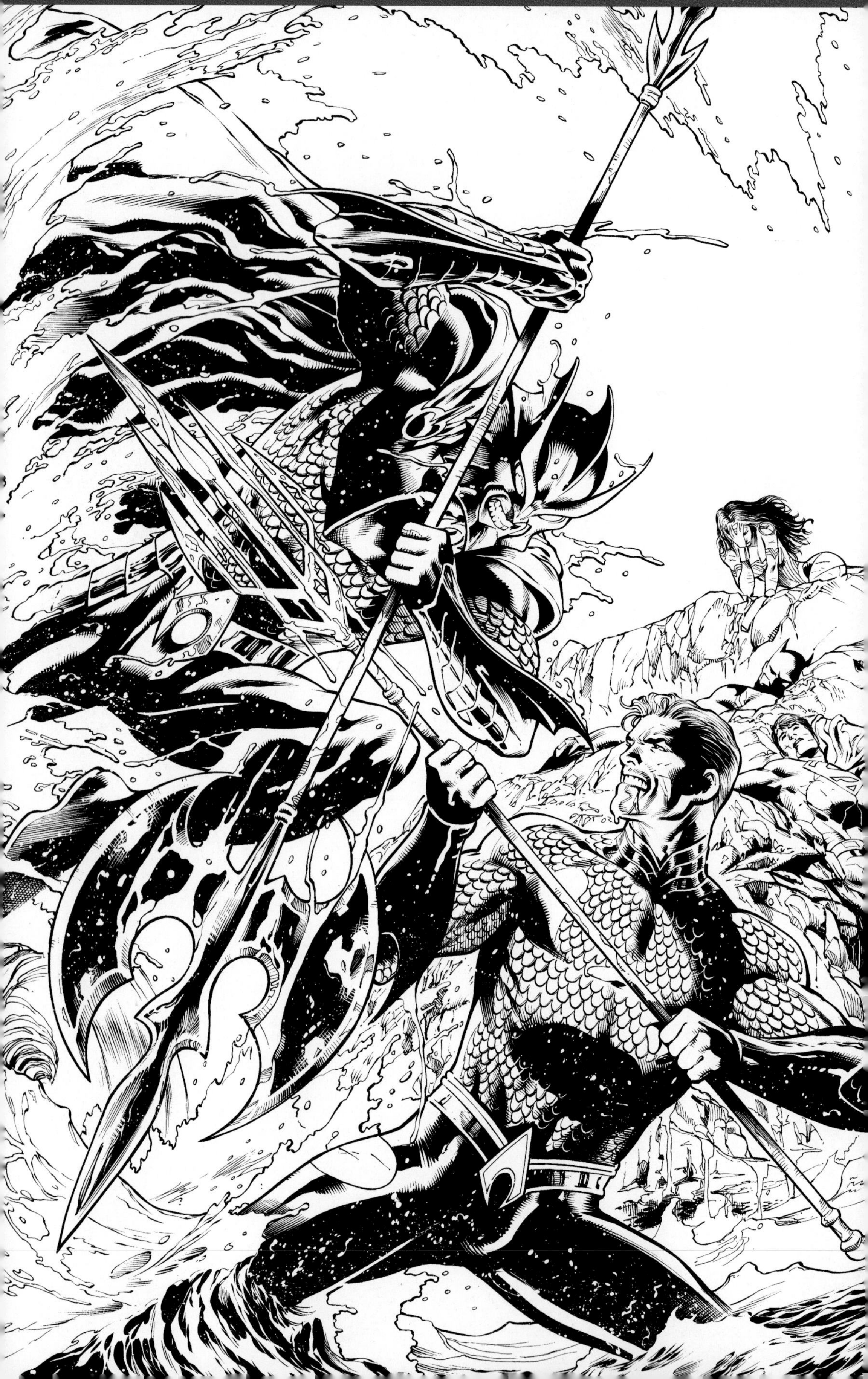

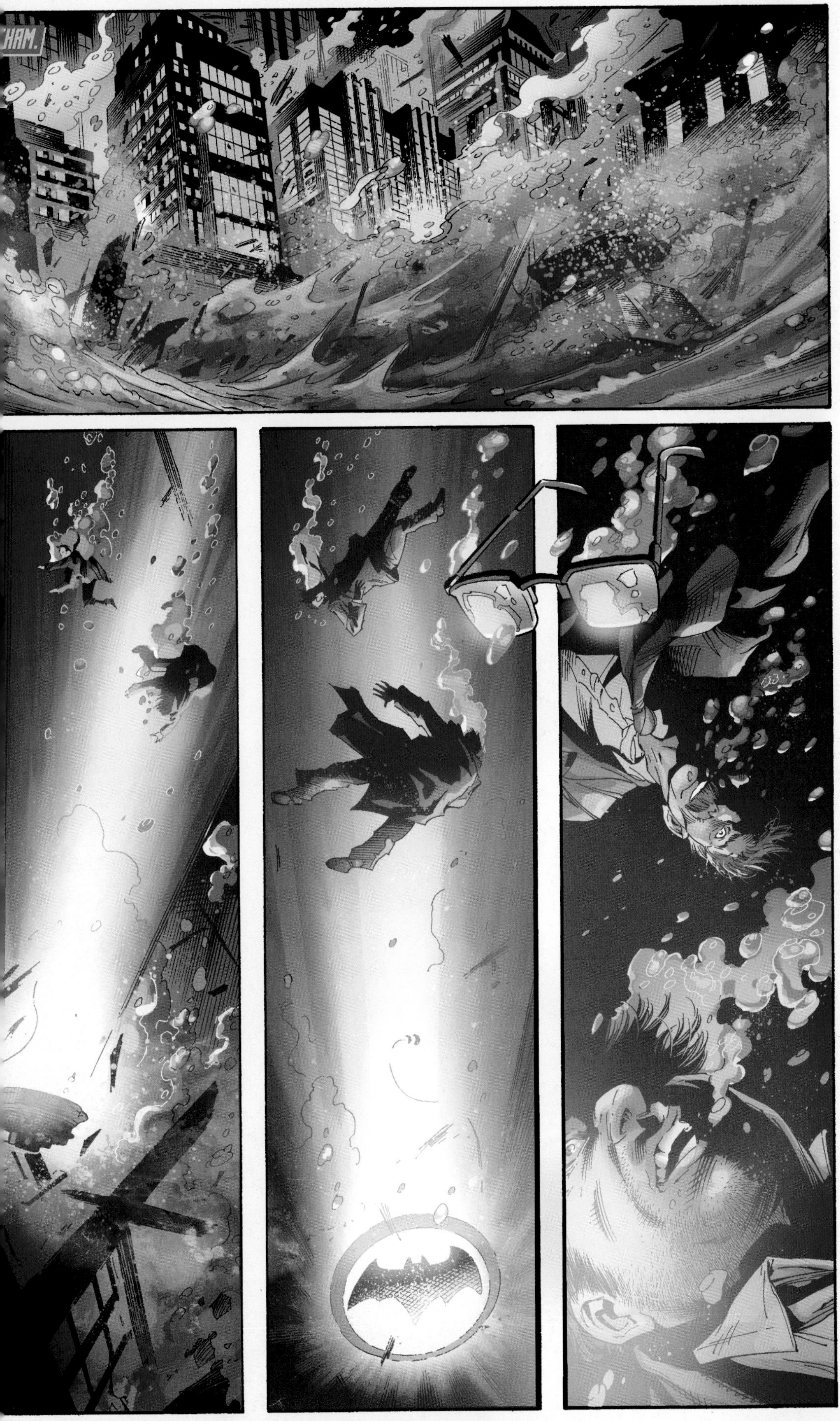
HAM.

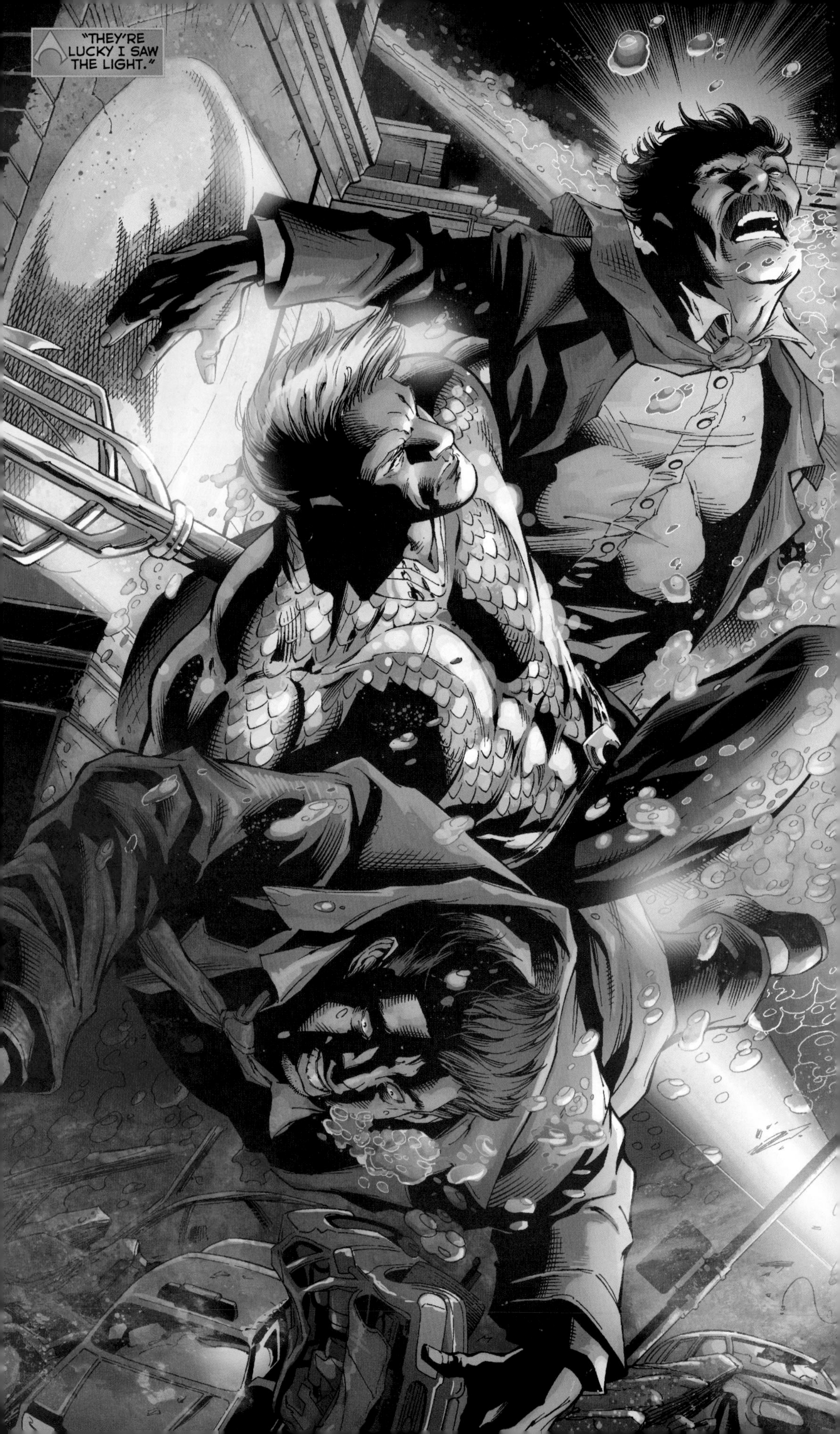
"THEY'RE LUCKY I SAW THE LIGHT."

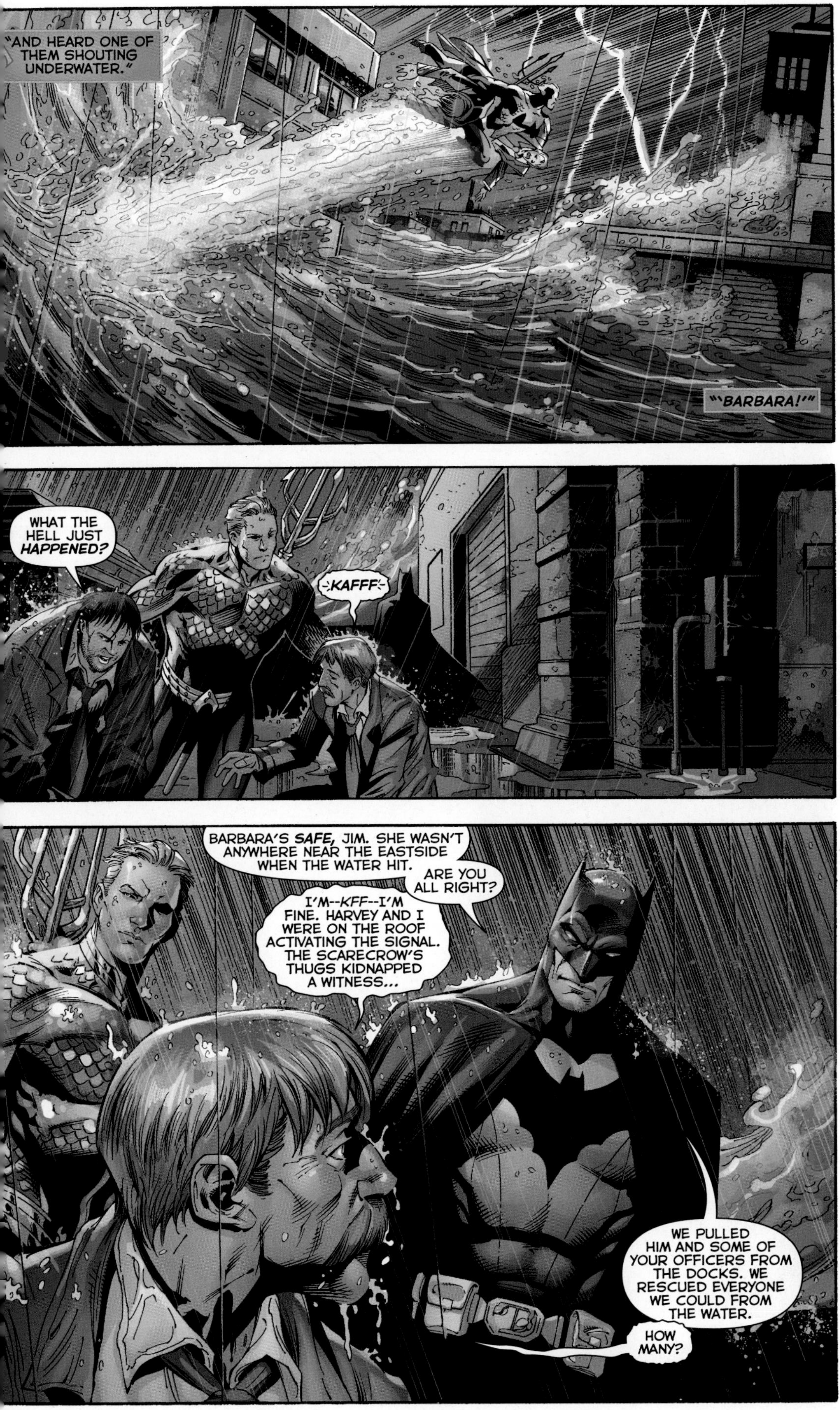
"AND HEARD ONE OF THEM SHOUTING UNDERWATER."
"'BARBARA!'"
WHAT THE HELL JUST *HAPPENED?*
-KAFFF-
BARBARA'S *SAFE,* JIM. SHE WASN'T ANYWHERE NEAR THE EASTSIDE WHEN THE WATER HIT.
ARE YOU ALL RIGHT?
I'M--*KFF*--I'M FINE. HARVEY AND I WERE ON THE ROOF ACTIVATING THE SIGNAL. THE SCARECROW'S THUGS KIDNAPPED A WITNESS...
WE PULLED HIM AND SOME OF YOUR OFFICERS FROM THE DOCKS. WE RESCUED EVERYONE WE COULD FROM THE WATER.
HOW MANY?

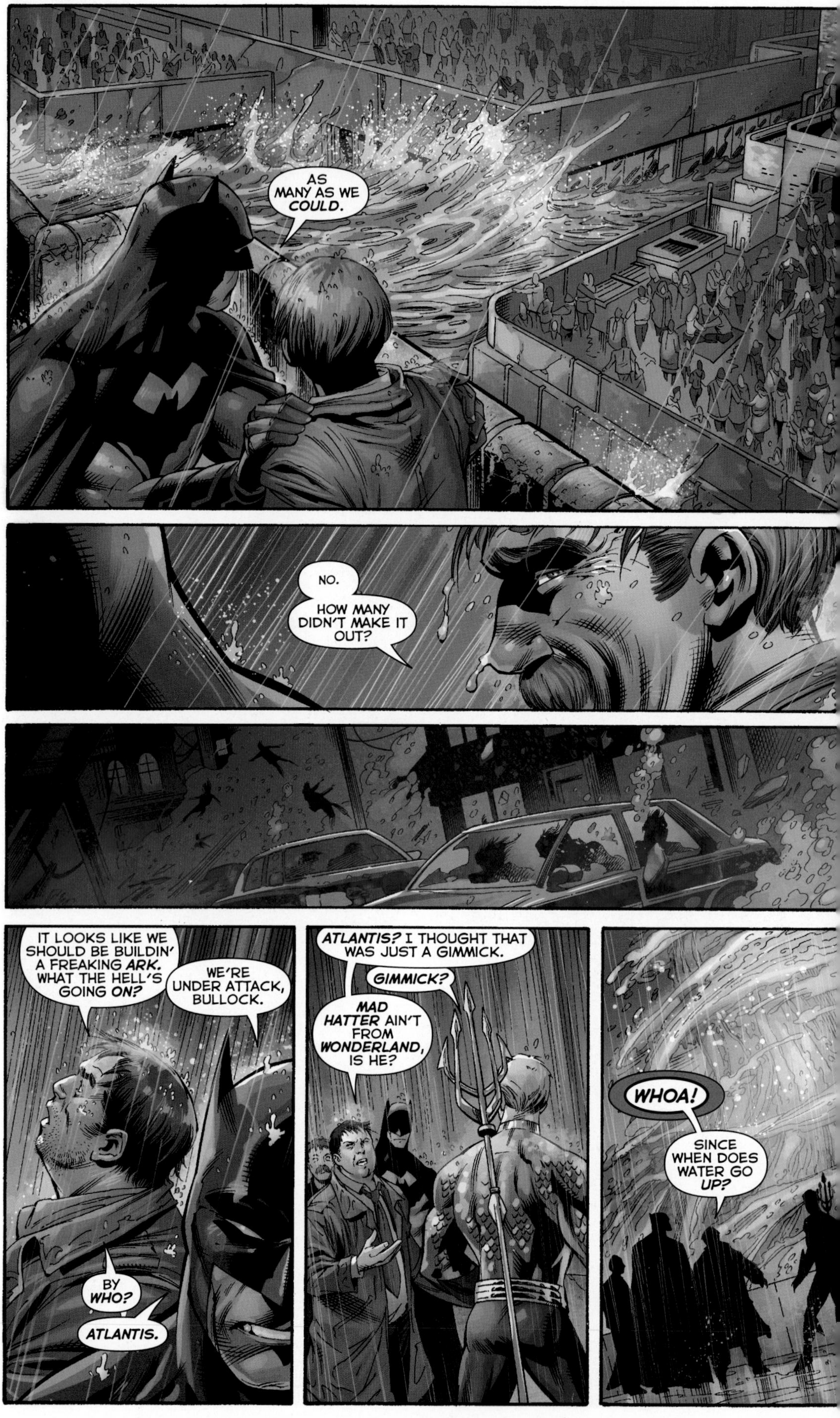
AS MANY AS WE COULD.
NO.
HOW MANY DIDN'T MAKE IT OUT?
IT LOOKS LIKE WE SHOULD BE BUILDIN' A FREAKING ARK. WHAT THE HELL'S GOING ON?
WE'RE UNDER ATTACK, BULLOCK.
BY WHO?
ATLANTIS.
ATLANTIS? I THOUGHT THAT WAS JUST A GIMMICK.
GIMMICK?
MAD HATTER AIN'T FROM WONDERLAND, IS HE?
WHOA!
SINCE WHEN DOES WATER GO UP?

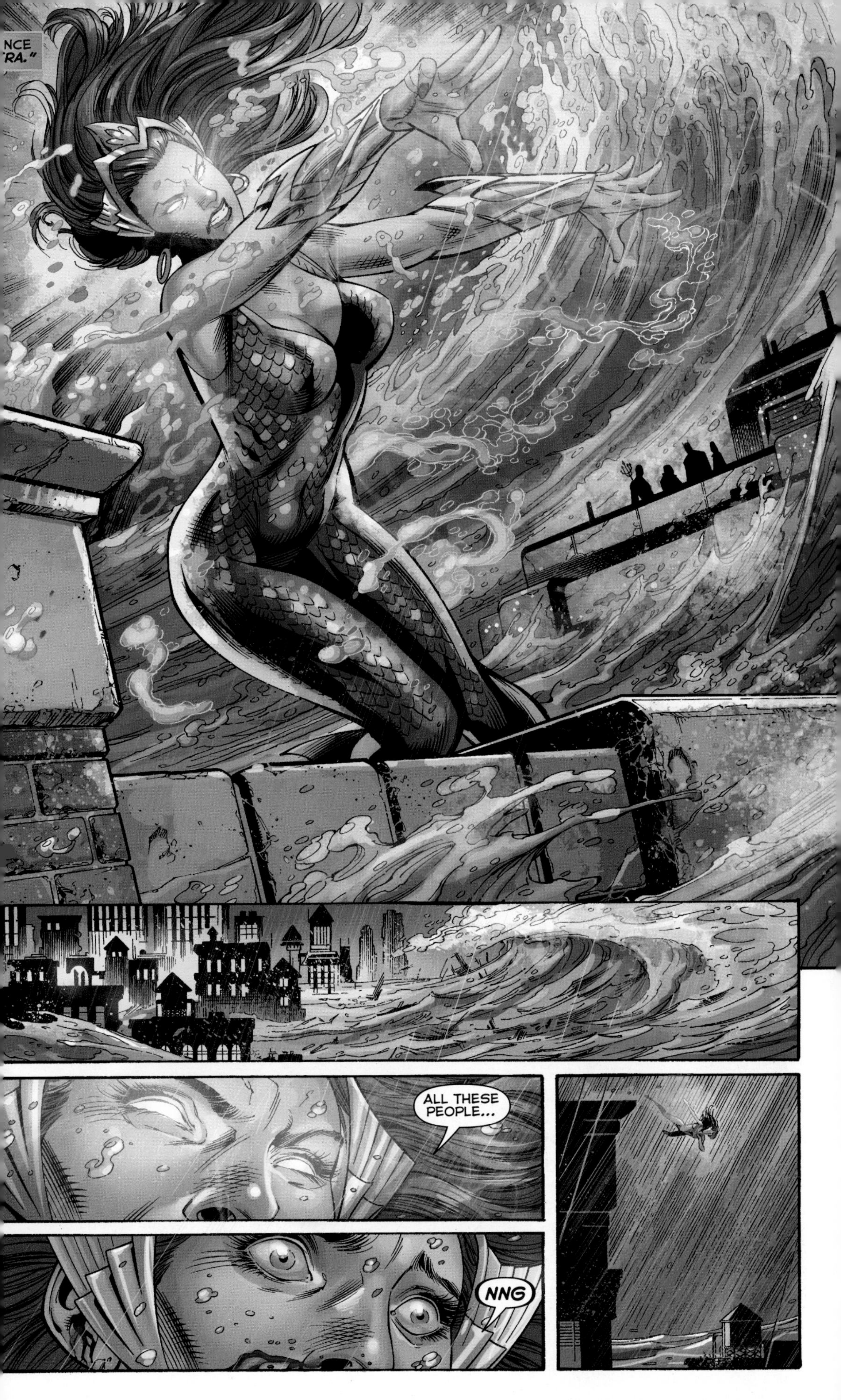
NCE
RA."
ALL THESE PEOPLE...
NNG

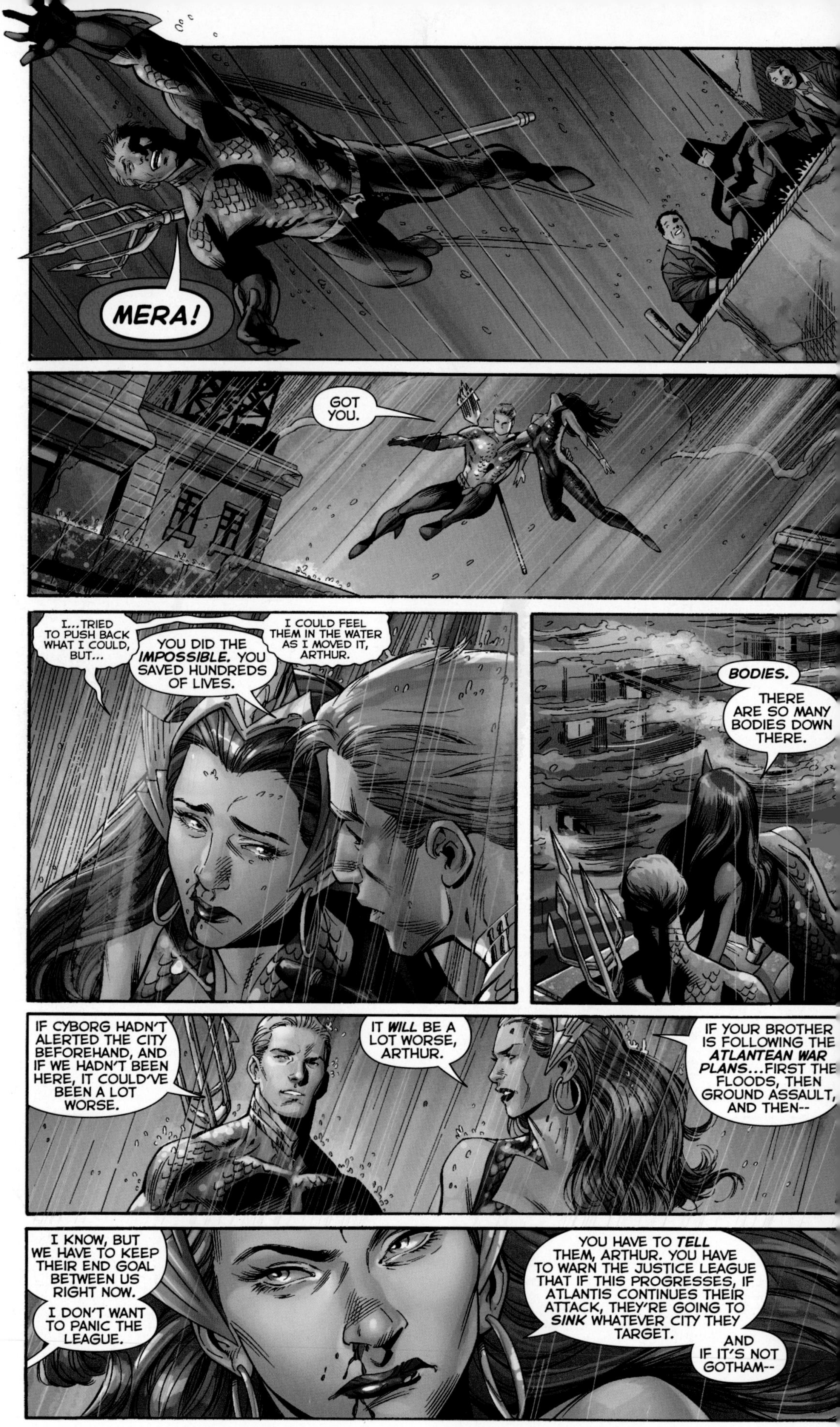
MERA!
GOT YOU.
I...TRIED TO PUSH BACK WHAT I COULD, BUT...
YOU DID THE IMPOSSIBLE. YOU SAVED HUNDREDS OF LIVES.
I COULD FEEL THEM IN THE WATER AS I MOVED IT, ARTHUR.
BODIES.
THERE ARE SO MANY BODIES DOWN THERE.
IF CYBORG HADN'T ALERTED THE CITY BEFOREHAND, AND IF WE HADN'T BEEN HERE, IT COULD'VE BEEN A LOT WORSE.
IT WILL BE A LOT WORSE, ARTHUR.
IF YOUR BROTHER IS FOLLOWING THE ATLANTEAN WAR PLANS...FIRST THE FLOODS, THEN GROUND ASSAULT, AND THEN--
YOU HAVE TO TELL THEM, ARTHUR. YOU HAVE TO WARN THE JUSTICE LEAGUE THAT IF THIS PROGRESSES, IF ATLANTIS CONTINUES THEIR ATTACK, THEY'RE GOING TO SINK WHATEVER CITY THEY TARGET.
AND IF IT'S NOT GOTHAM--
I KNOW, BUT WE HAVE TO KEEP THEIR END GOAL BETWEEN US RIGHT NOW.
I DON'T WANT TO PANIC THE LEAGUE.

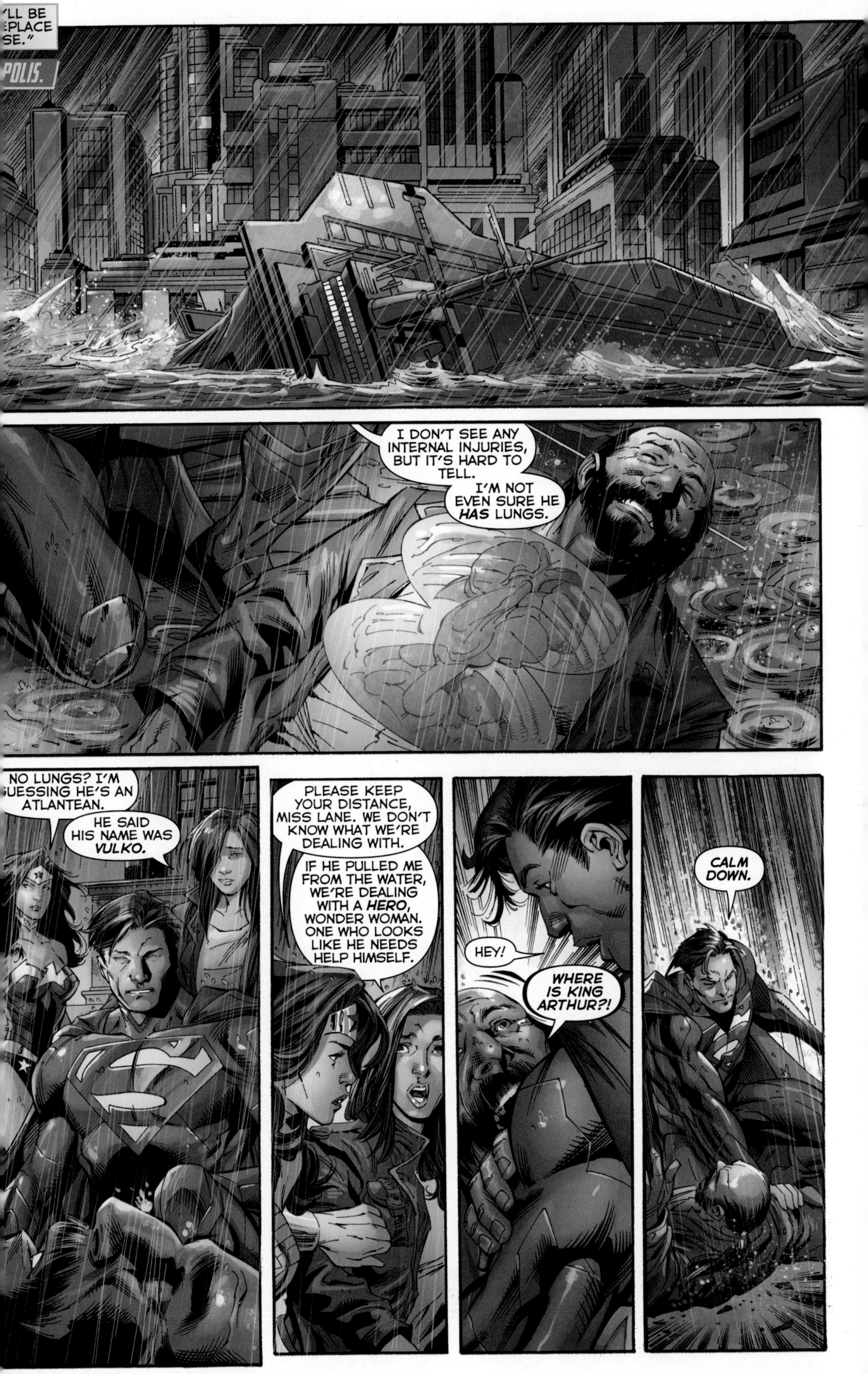

'LL BE
EPLACE
SE."
POLIS.
I DON'T SEE ANY INTERNAL INJURIES, BUT IT'S HARD TO TELL.
I'M NOT EVEN SURE HE HAS LUNGS.
NO LUNGS? I'M GUESSING HE'S AN ATLANTEAN.
HE SAID HIS NAME WAS VULKO.
PLEASE KEEP YOUR DISTANCE, MISS LANE. WE DON'T KNOW WHAT WE'RE DEALING WITH.
IF HE PULLED ME FROM THE WATER, WE'RE DEALING WITH A HERO, WONDER WOMAN. ONE WHO LOOKS LIKE HE NEEDS HELP HIMSELF.
HEY!
WHERE IS KING ARTHUR?!
CALM DOWN.

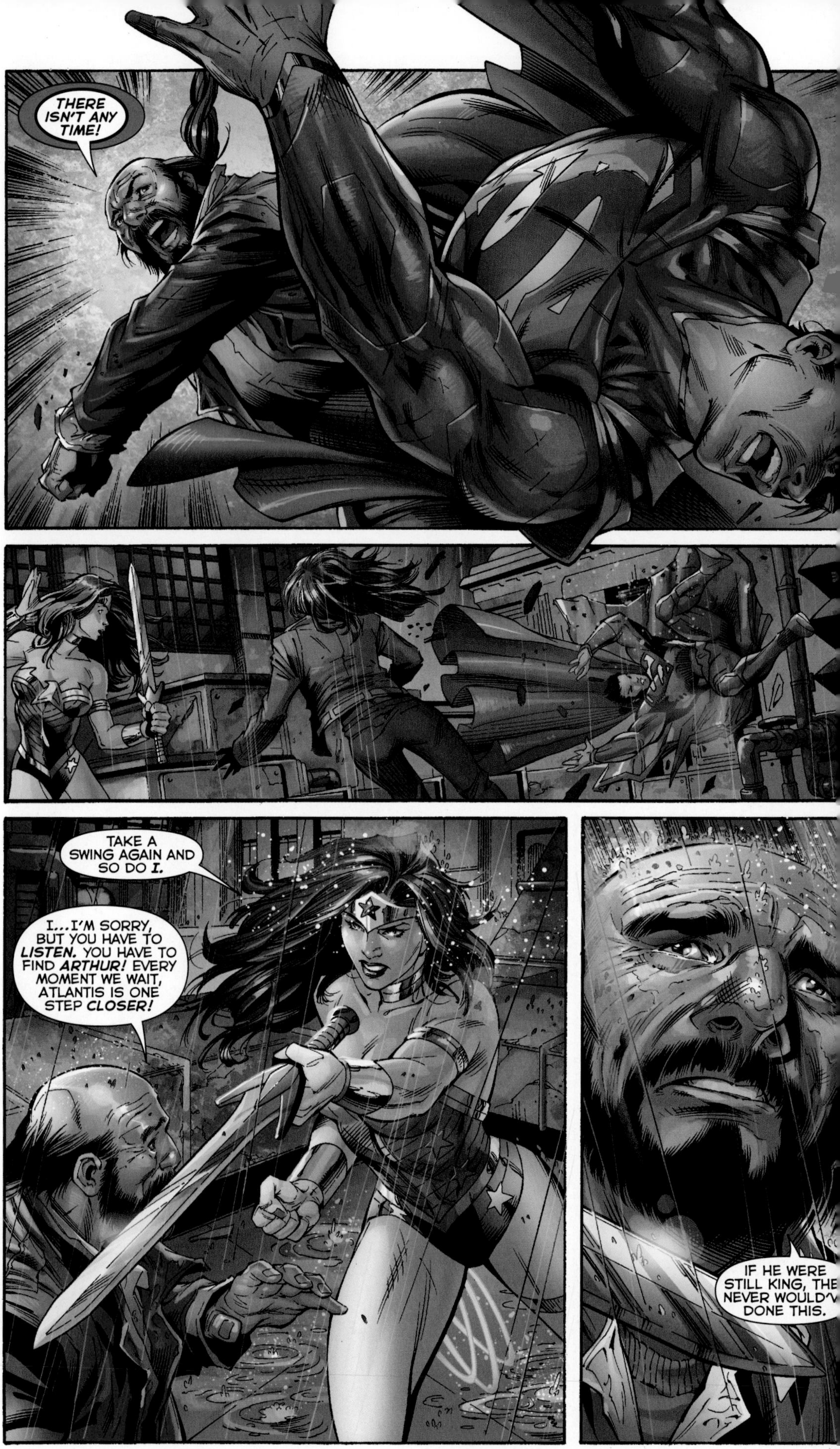
THERE ISN'T ANY TIME!
TAKE A SWING AGAIN AND SO DO I.
I...I'M SORRY, BUT YOU HAVE TO LISTEN. YOU HAVE TO FIND ARTHUR! EVERY MOMENT WE WAIT, ATLANTIS IS ONE STEP CLOSER!
IF HE WERE STILL KING, THE NEVER WOULD'V DONE THIS.

"MERA'S CLEARING OUT THE REST OF THE STREETS. COMMISSIONER GORDON AND HIS MEN ARE GOING TO HELP RECOVER THE BODIES."

ONCE MERA'S DONE IN GOTHAM, SHE'LL HEAD TO METROPOLIS TO DO THE SAME.

THE WAVES HIT AND IT ALL GOES *QUIET?*

WHERE'S ATLANTIS?

THEY'RE WAITING.

FOR WHAT?

TO SEE WHAT CITY WAS HIT THE *HARDEST.* THAT'S WHERE THEY'LL RISE OUT OF THE OCEAN.

ACCORDING TO THESE *ATLANTEAN WAR PLANS* YOU MENTIONED?

YES... THEY PLAN TO SINK A CITY.

AND YOU KNOW THIS BECAUSE YOU *WROTE* THOSE WAR PLANS?

WITH MY BROTHER, YEARS AGO.

I WAS IN A DIFFERENT FRAME OF MIND.

SO I GATHERED.

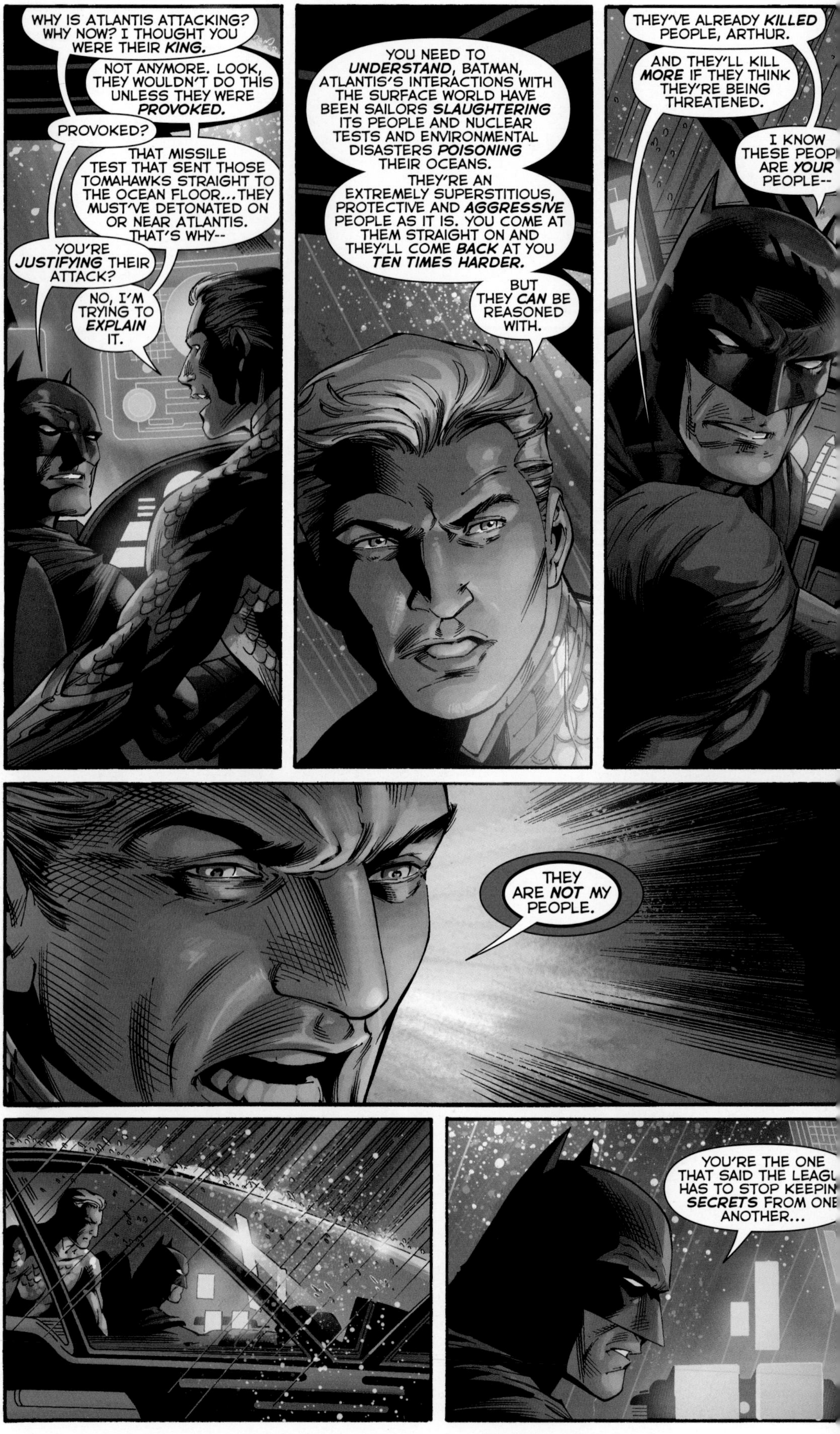
WHY IS ATLANTIS ATTACKING? WHY NOW? I THOUGHT YOU WERE THEIR KING.
NOT ANYMORE. LOOK, THEY WOULDN'T DO THIS UNLESS THEY WERE PROVOKED.
PROVOKED?
THAT MISSILE TEST THAT SENT THOSE TOMAHAWKS STRAIGHT TO THE OCEAN FLOOR... THEY MUST'VE DETONATED ON OR NEAR ATLANTIS. THAT'S WHY--
YOU'RE JUSTIFYING THEIR ATTACK?
NO, I'M TRYING TO EXPLAIN IT.
YOU NEED TO UNDERSTAND, BATMAN, ATLANTIS'S INTERACTIONS WITH THE SURFACE WORLD HAVE BEEN SAILORS SLAUGHTERING ITS PEOPLE AND NUCLEAR TESTS AND ENVIRONMENTAL DISASTERS POISONING THEIR OCEANS.
THEY'RE AN EXTREMELY SUPERSTITIOUS, PROTECTIVE AND AGGRESSIVE PEOPLE AS IT IS. YOU COME AT THEM STRAIGHT ON AND THEY'LL COME BACK AT YOU TEN TIMES HARDER.
BUT THEY CAN BE REASONED WITH.
THEY'VE ALREADY KILLED PEOPLE, ARTHUR.
AND THEY'LL KILL MORE IF THEY THINK THEY'RE BEING THREATENED.
I KNOW THESE PEOP ARE YOUR PEOPLE--
THEY ARE NOT MY PEOPLE.
YOU'RE THE ONE THAT SAID THE LEAGU HAS TO STOP KEEPIN SECRETS FROM ONE ANOTHER...

...WHAT AREN'T YOU TELLING ME?

I...

I NEARLY *DIED* TRYING TO FIND ATLANTIS. WHEN I FINALLY DID, YES, THEY WELCOMED ME WITH OPEN ARMS.

EVEN MY BROTHER, WHO CHERISHES ATLANTEAN LAW, STEPPED DOWN FROM THE THRONE.

BUT WITHIN WEEKS, THERE WAS *DISSENSION.* SOME CALLED ME THE *IMPURE* KING. A HALF-HUMAN SURFACE DWELLER. THERE WAS A MOVEMENT TO *CHANGE* THE LAWS AND REINSTATE MY YOUNGER BROTHER...A *FULL* ATLANTEAN.

DURING THAT TIME, I TRIED TO BE WHAT THEY *WANTED* ME TO BE.

I TURNED MY BACK ON THE SURFACE WORLD. I SAW IT THE UGLY WAY *THEY* DO.

"UNTIL *DARKSEID* CAME AND THE JUSTICE LEAGUE WAS FOUNDED.

"IT GAVE ME A PLACE TO GO."

I'M BEGINNING TO UNDERSTAND HOW HARD THIS IS GOING TO BE FOR YOU, ARTHUR. BUT YOU'RE STILL TRYING TO RATIONALIZE THEIR ACTIONS.

AND THERE *IS* NO RATIONALIZING AN ATTACK LIKE THIS. *WHATEVER* THE CATALYST.

PROVOKED OR NOT, IF YOUR BROTHER IS BEHIND THIS, THE JUSTICE LEAGUE IS BRINGING HIM IN. THAT'S THE WAY IT HAS TO BE.

VEETVEETVEETVEET

WHAT'S THAT?

INCOMING. WE NEED TO MOVE.

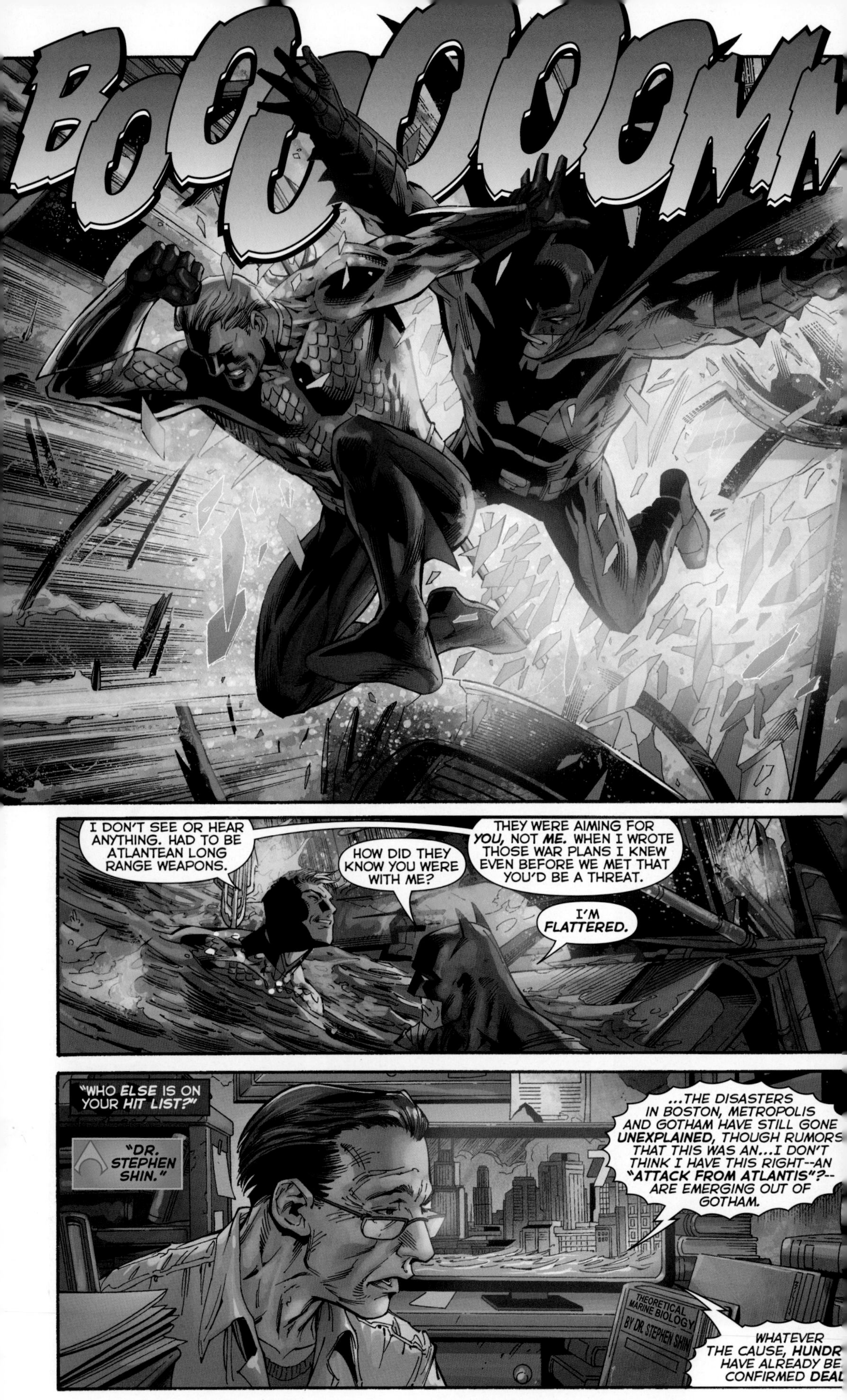
BOOOOOOM
I DON'T SEE OR HEAR ANYTHING. HAD TO BE ATLANTEAN LONG RANGE WEAPONS.
HOW DID THEY KNOW YOU WERE WITH ME?
THEY WERE AIMING FOR YOU, NOT ME. WHEN I WROTE THOSE WAR PLANS I KNEW EVEN BEFORE WE MET THAT YOU'D BE A THREAT.
I'M FLATTERED.
"WHO ELSE IS ON YOUR HIT LIST?"
"DR. STEPHEN SHIN."
...THE DISASTERS IN BOSTON, METROPOLIS AND GOTHAM HAVE STILL GONE UNEXPLAINED, THOUGH RUMORS THAT THIS WAS AN...I DON'T THINK I HAVE THIS RIGHT--AN "ATTACK FROM ATLANTIS"?--ARE EMERGING OUT OF GOTHAM.
THEORETICAL MARINE BIOLOGY BY DR. STEPHEN SHIN
WHATEVER THE CAUSE, HUNDR HAVE ALREADY BE CONFIRMED DEAL

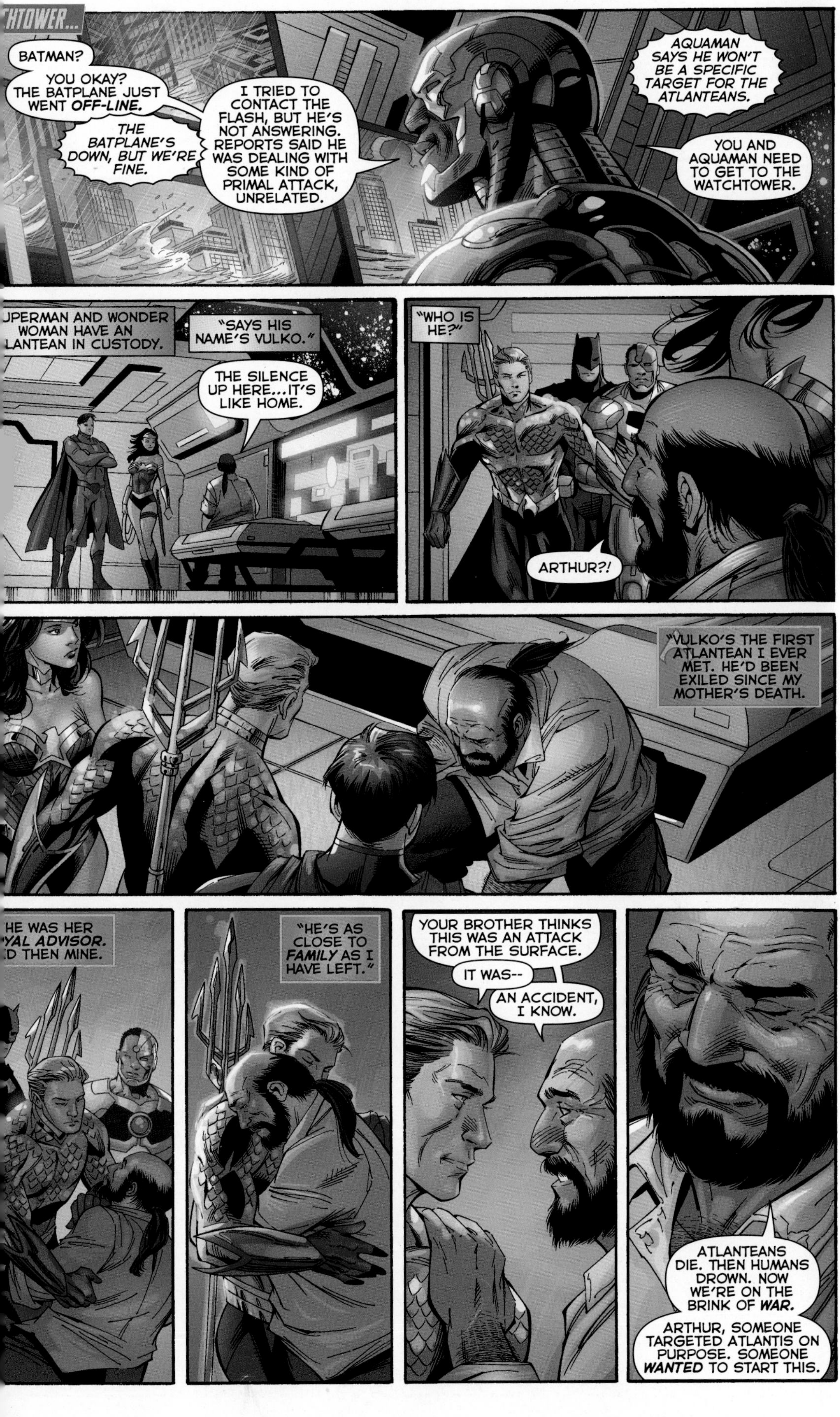
HTOWER...
BATMAN?
YOU OKAY? THE BATPLANE JUST WENT *OFF-LINE.*
THE BATPLANE'S DOWN, BUT WE'RE FINE.
I TRIED TO CONTACT THE FLASH, BUT HE'S NOT ANSWERING. REPORTS SAID HE WAS DEALING WITH SOME KIND OF PRIMAL ATTACK, UNRELATED.
AQUAMAN SAYS HE WON'T BE A SPECIFIC TARGET FOR THE ATLANTEANS.
YOU AND AQUAMAN NEED TO GET TO THE WATCHTOWER.
UPERMAN AND WONDER WOMAN HAVE AN LANTEAN IN CUSTODY.
"SAYS HIS NAME'S VULKO."
THE SILENCE UP HERE...IT'S LIKE HOME.
"WHO IS HE?"
ARTHUR?!
"VULKO'S THE FIRST ATLANTEAN I EVER MET. HE'D BEEN EXILED SINCE MY MOTHER'S DEATH.
HE WAS HER YAL ADVISOR. D THEN MINE.
"HE'S AS CLOSE TO *FAMILY* AS I HAVE LEFT."
YOUR BROTHER THINKS THIS WAS AN ATTACK FROM THE SURFACE.
IT WAS--
AN ACCIDENT, I KNOW.
ATLANTEANS DIE. THEN HUMANS DROWN. NOW WE'RE ON THE BRINK OF *WAR.*
ARTHUR, SOMEONE TARGETED ATLANTIS ON PURPOSE. SOMEONE *WANTED* TO START THIS.

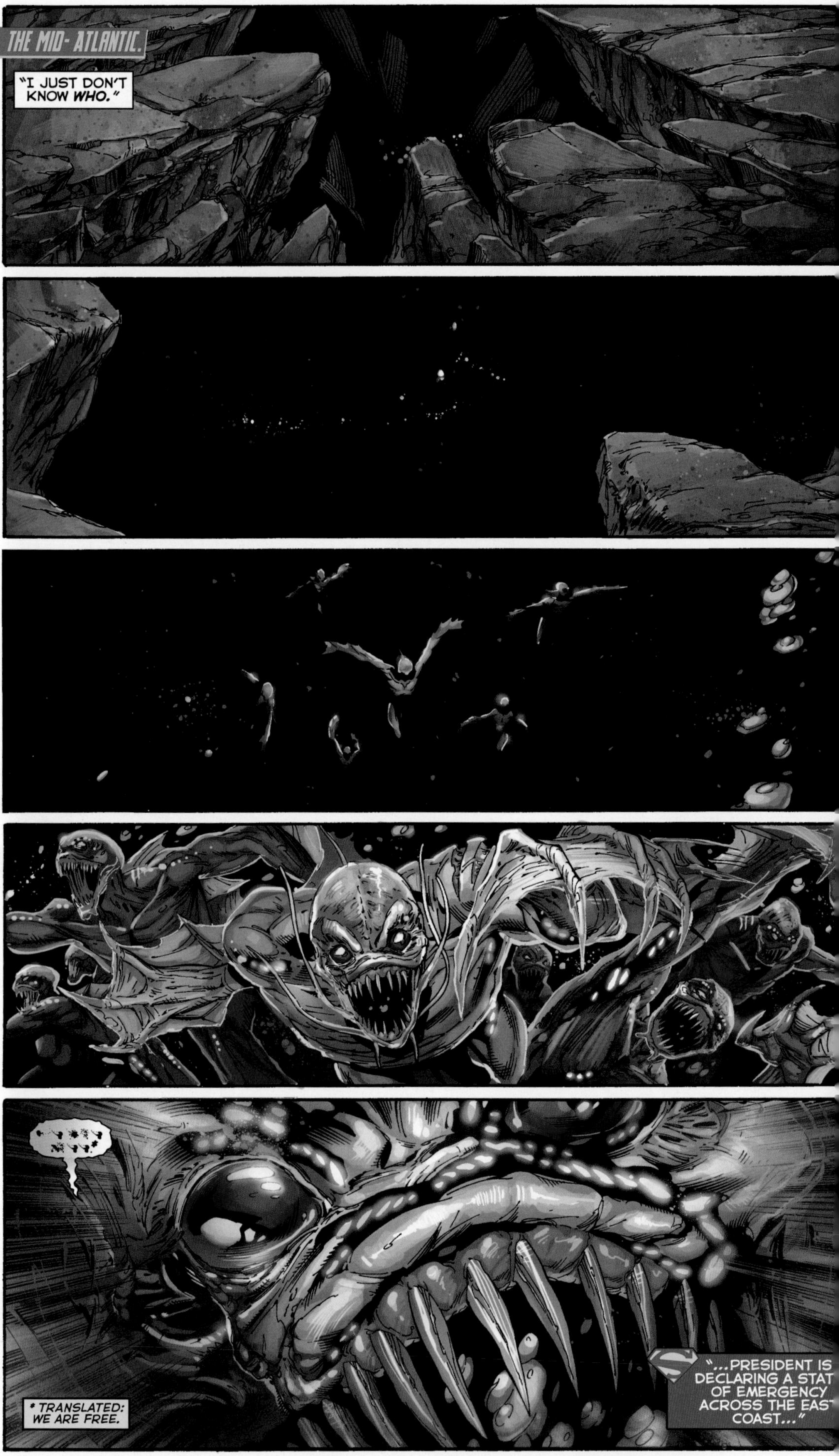
THE MID- ATLANTIC.
"I JUST DON'T KNOW WHO."
*TRANSLATED: WE ARE FREE.
"...PRESIDENT IS DECLARING A STAT OF EMERGENCY ACROSS THE EAS COAST..."

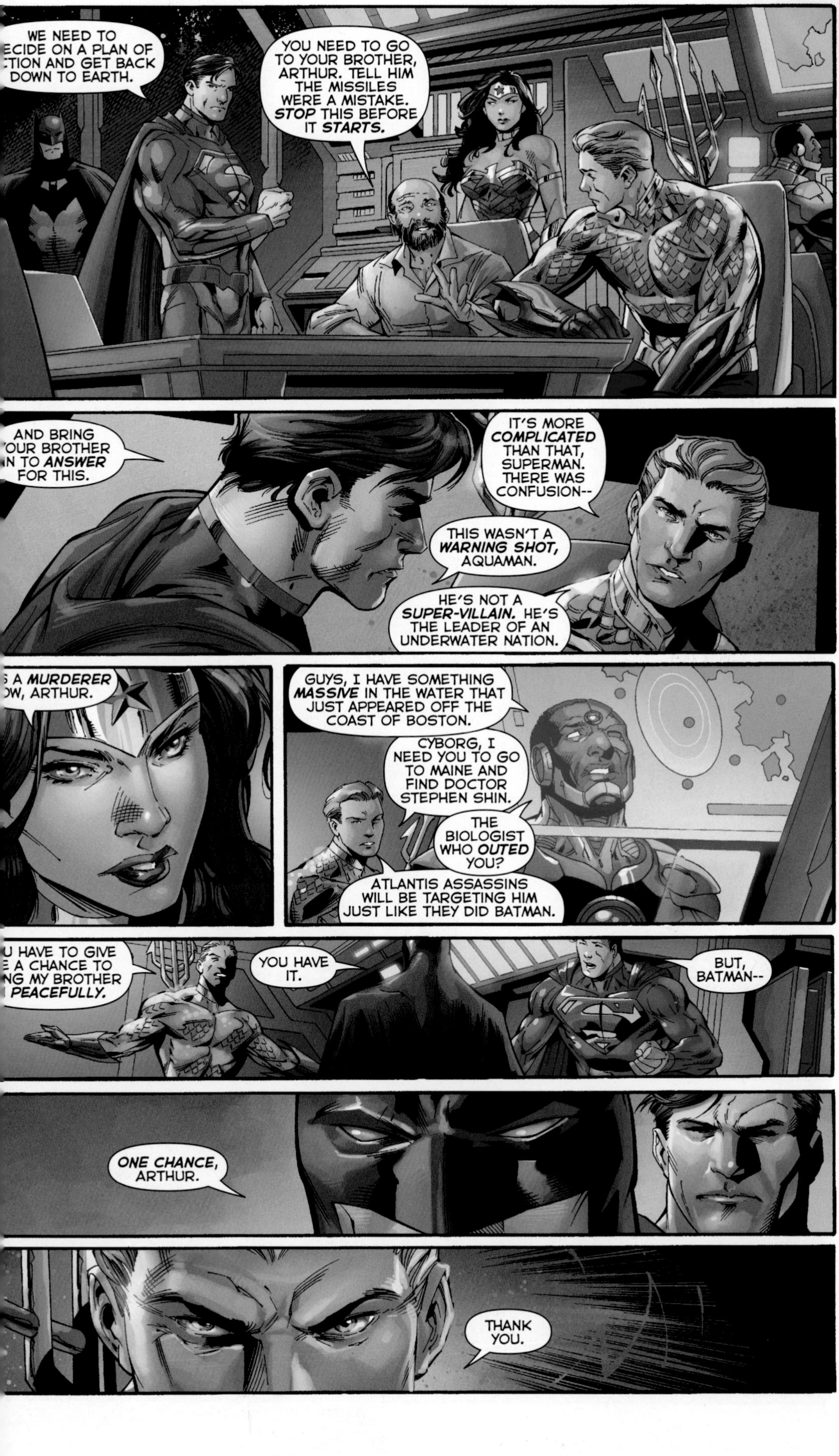

WE NEED TO ECIDE ON A PLAN OF CTION AND GET BACK DOWN TO EARTH.
YOU NEED TO GO TO YOUR BROTHER, ARTHUR. TELL HIM THE MISSILES WERE A MISTAKE. *STOP* THIS BEFORE IT *STARTS.*
AND BRING OUR BROTHER N TO *ANSWER* FOR THIS.
IT'S MORE *COMPLICATED* THAN THAT, SUPERMAN. THERE WAS CONFUSION--
THIS WASN'T A *WARNING SHOT,* AQUAMAN.
HE'S NOT A *SUPER-VILLAIN.* HE'S THE LEADER OF AN UNDERWATER NATION.
S A *MURDERER* OW, ARTHUR.
GUYS, I HAVE SOMETHING *MASSIVE* IN THE WATER THAT JUST APPEARED OFF THE COAST OF BOSTON.
CYBORG, I NEED YOU TO GO TO MAINE AND FIND DOCTOR STEPHEN SHIN.
THE BIOLOGIST WHO *OUTED* YOU?
ATLANTIS ASSASSINS WILL BE TARGETING HIM JUST LIKE THEY DID BATMAN.
U HAVE TO GIVE E A CHANCE TO NG MY BROTHER *PEACEFULLY.*
YOU HAVE IT.
BUT, BATMAN--
ONE CHANCE, ARTHUR.
THANK YOU.

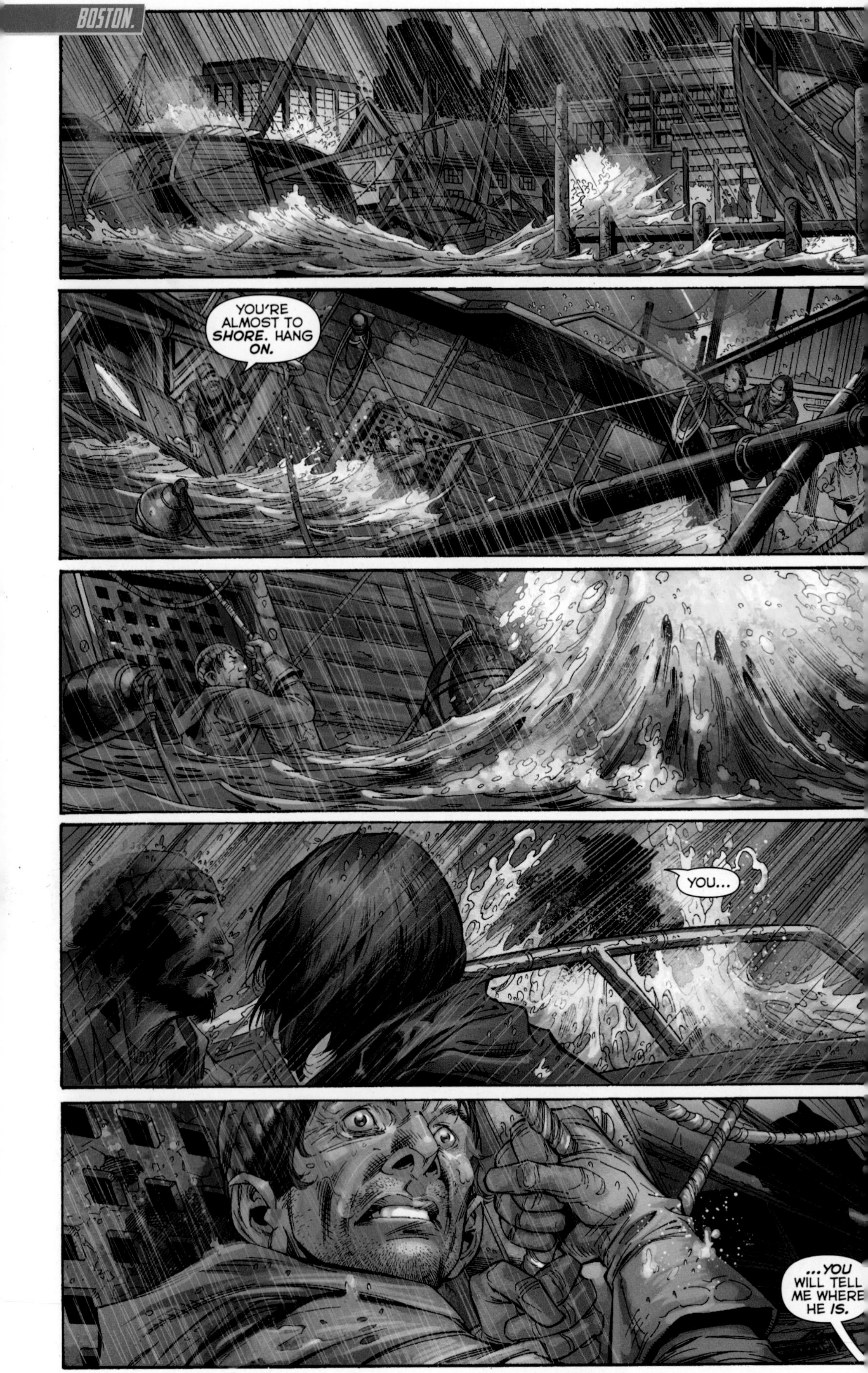
BOSTON.
YOU'RE ALMOST TO SHORE. HANG ON.
YOU...
...YOU WILL TELL ME WHERE HE IS.

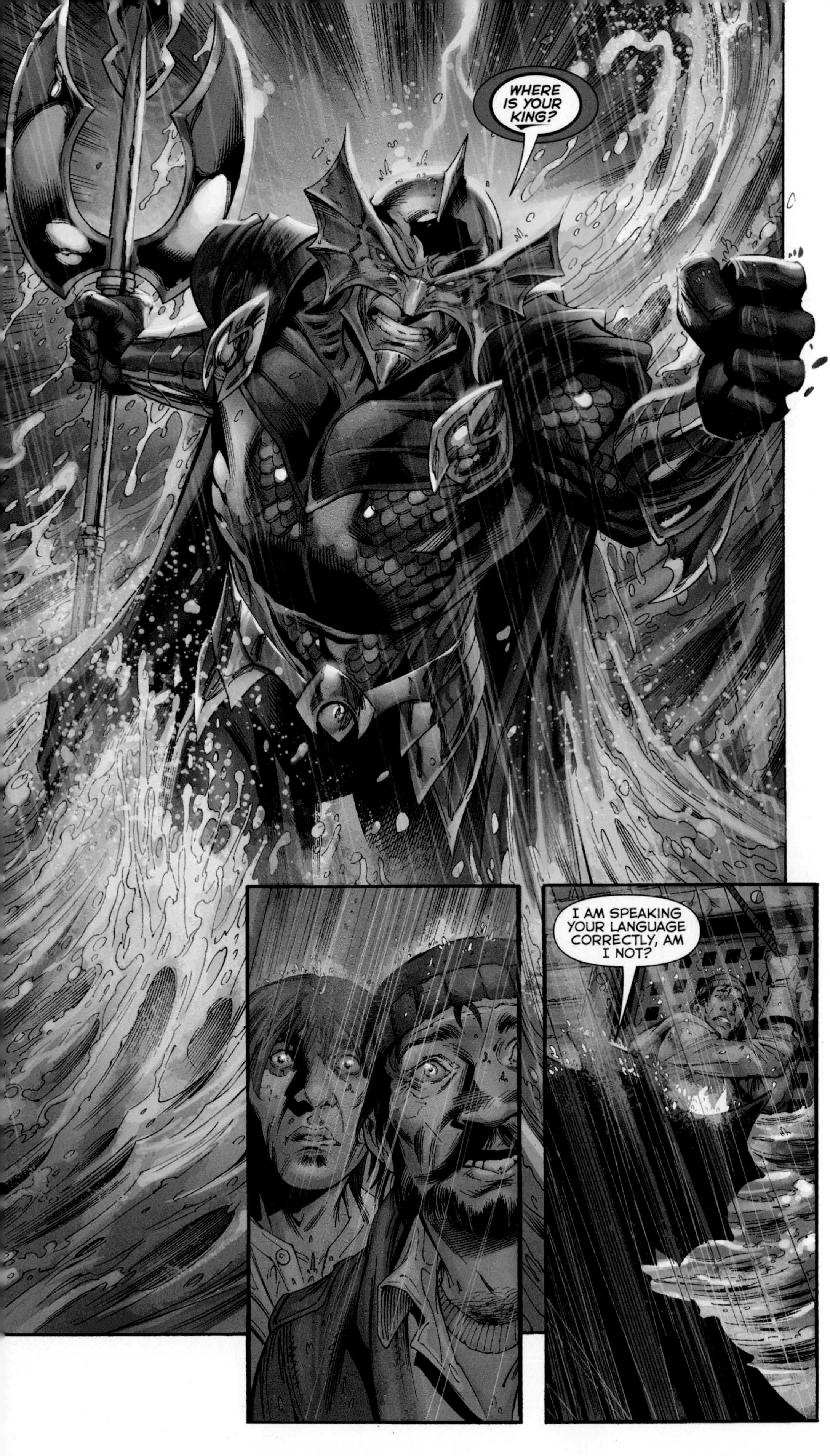
WHERE IS YOUR KING?
I AM SPEAKING YOUR LANGUAGE CORRECTLY, AM I NOT?

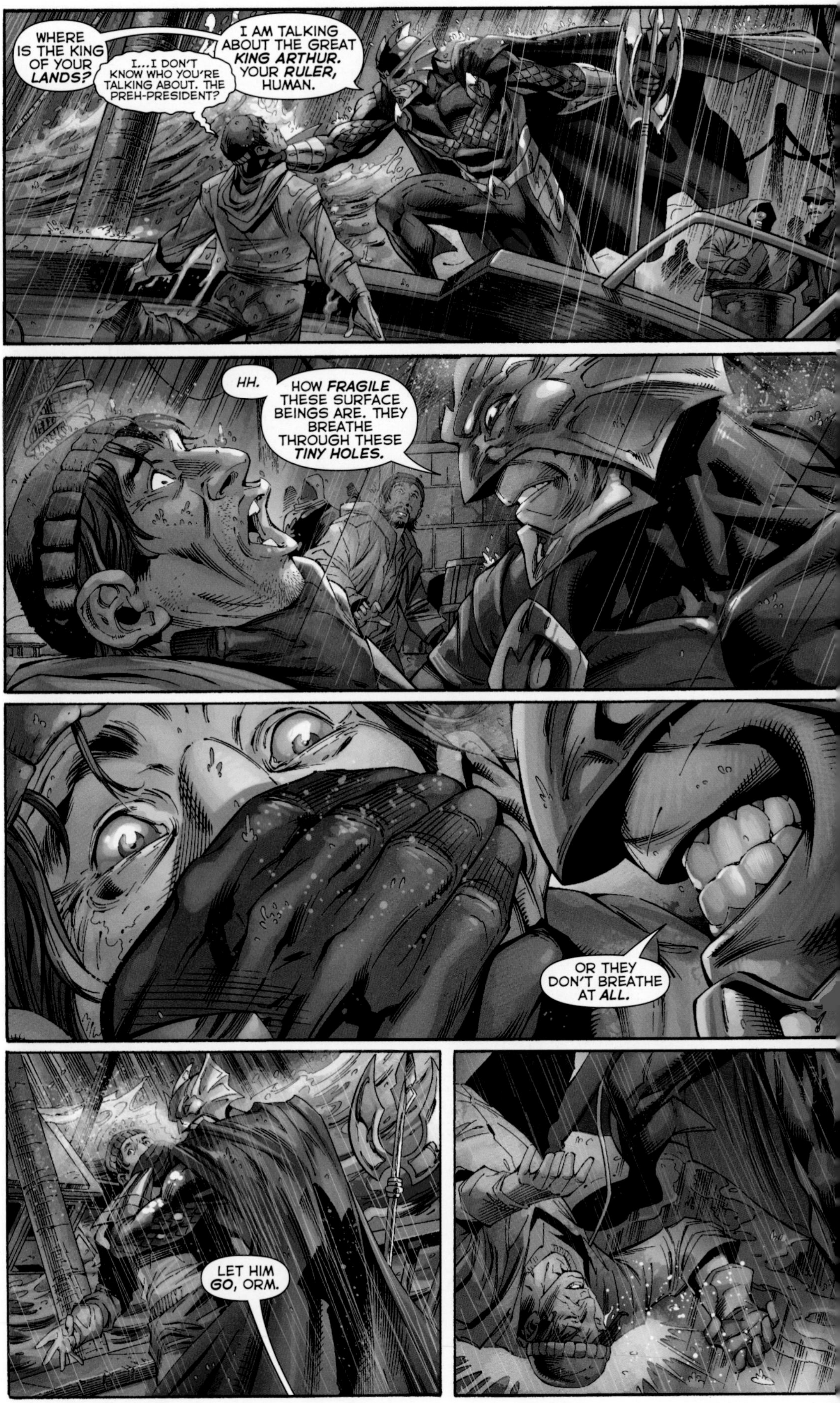
WHERE IS THE KING OF YOUR LANDS?
I AM TALKING ABOUT THE GREAT KING ARTHUR. YOUR RULER, HUMAN.
I...I DON'T KNOW WHO YOU'RE TALKING ABOUT. THE PREH-PRESIDENT?
HH.
HOW FRAGILE THESE SURFACE BEINGS ARE. THEY BREATHE THROUGH THESE TINY HOLES.
OR THEY DON'T BREATHE AT ALL.
LET HIM GO, ORM.

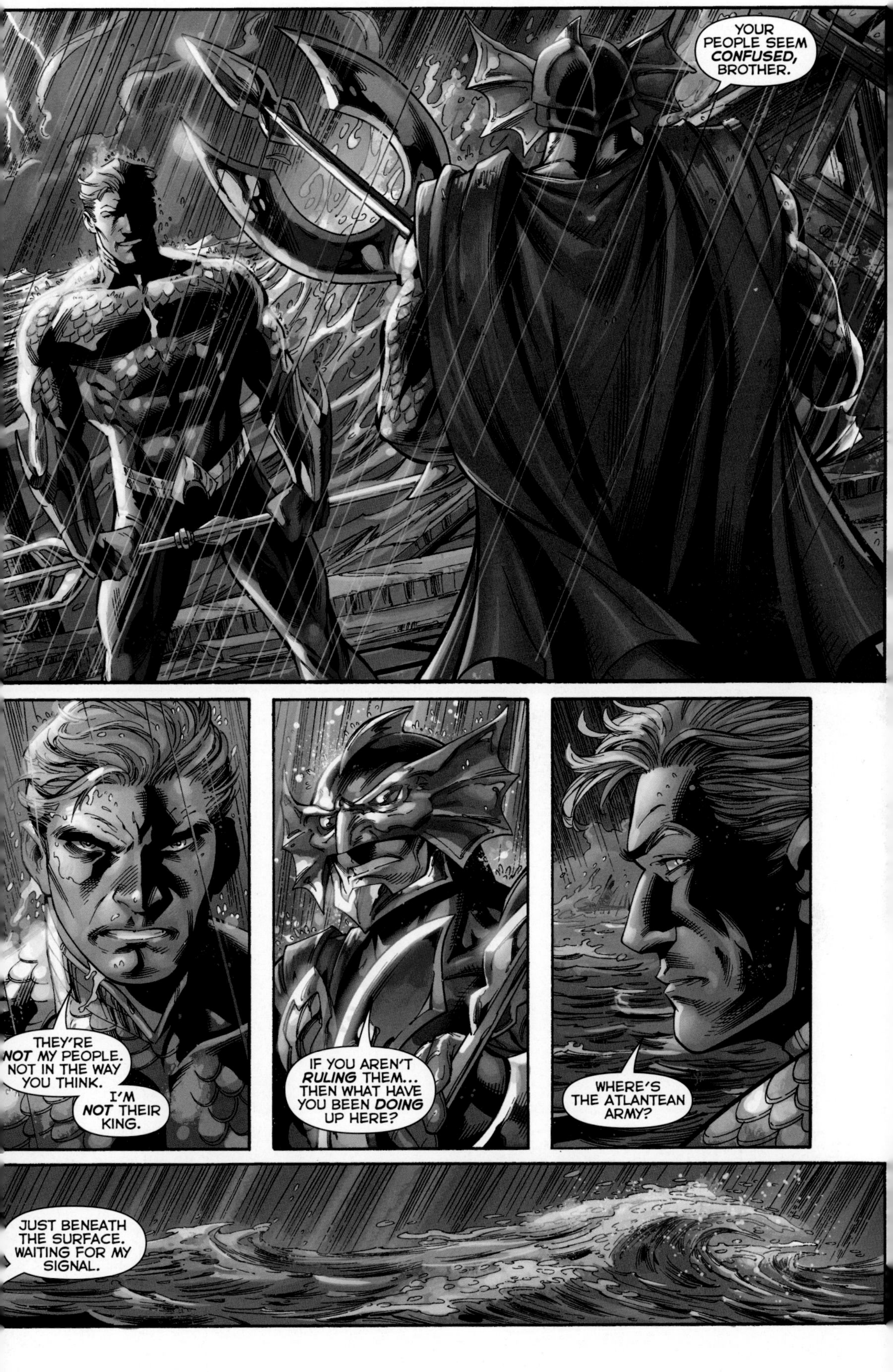
YOUR PEOPLE SEEM *CONFUSED,* BROTHER.
THEY'RE *NOT* MY PEOPLE. NOT IN THE WAY YOU THINK.
I'M *NOT* THEIR KING.
IF YOU AREN'T *RULING* THEM... THEN WHAT HAVE YOU BEEN *DOING* UP HERE?
WHERE'S THE ATLANTEAN ARMY?
JUST BENEATH THE SURFACE. WAITING FOR MY SIGNAL.

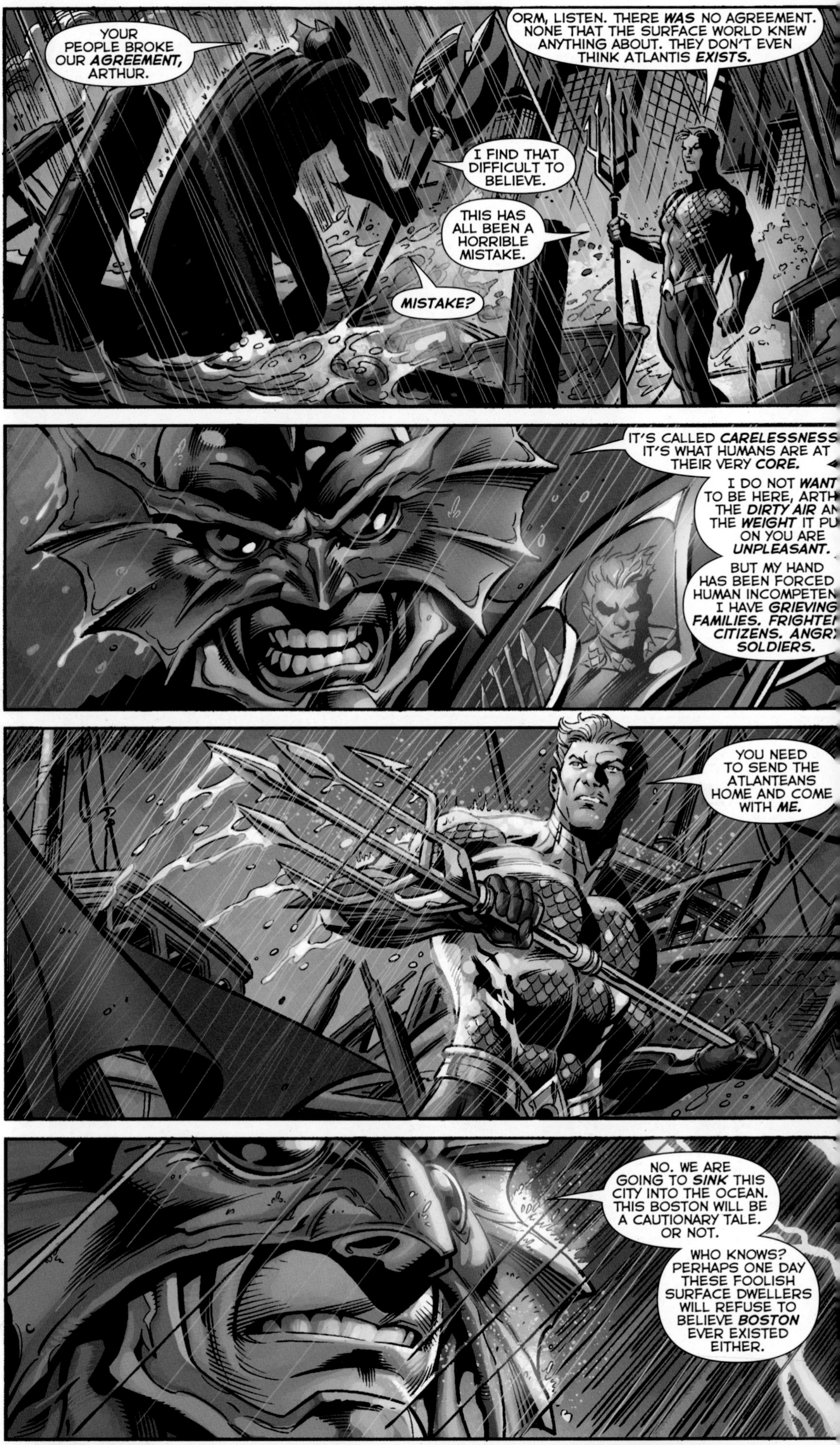
YOUR PEOPLE BROKE OUR *AGREEMENT,* ARTHUR.
ORM, LISTEN. THERE *WAS* NO AGREEMENT. NONE THAT THE SURFACE WORLD KNEW ANYTHING ABOUT. THEY DON'T EVEN THINK ATLANTIS *EXISTS.*
I FIND THAT DIFFICULT TO BELIEVE.
THIS HAS ALL BEEN A HORRIBLE MISTAKE.
MISTAKE?
IT'S CALLED *CARELESSNESS* IT'S WHAT HUMANS ARE AT THEIR VERY *CORE.*
I DO NOT *WANT* TO BE HERE, ARTH THE *DIRTY AIR* AN THE *WEIGHT* IT PU ON YOU ARE *UNPLEASANT.*
BUT MY HAND HAS BEEN FORCED HUMAN INCOMPETEN I HAVE *GRIEVING FAMILIES. FRIGHTE CITIZENS. ANGR SOLDIERS.*
YOU NEED TO SEND THE ATLANTEANS HOME AND COME WITH *ME.*
NO. WE ARE GOING TO *SINK* THIS CITY INTO THE OCEAN. THIS BOSTON WILL BE A CAUTIONARY TALE. OR NOT.
WHO KNOWS? PERHAPS ONE DAY THESE FOOLISH SURFACE DWELLERS WILL REFUSE TO BELIEVE *BOSTON* EVER EXISTED EITHER.

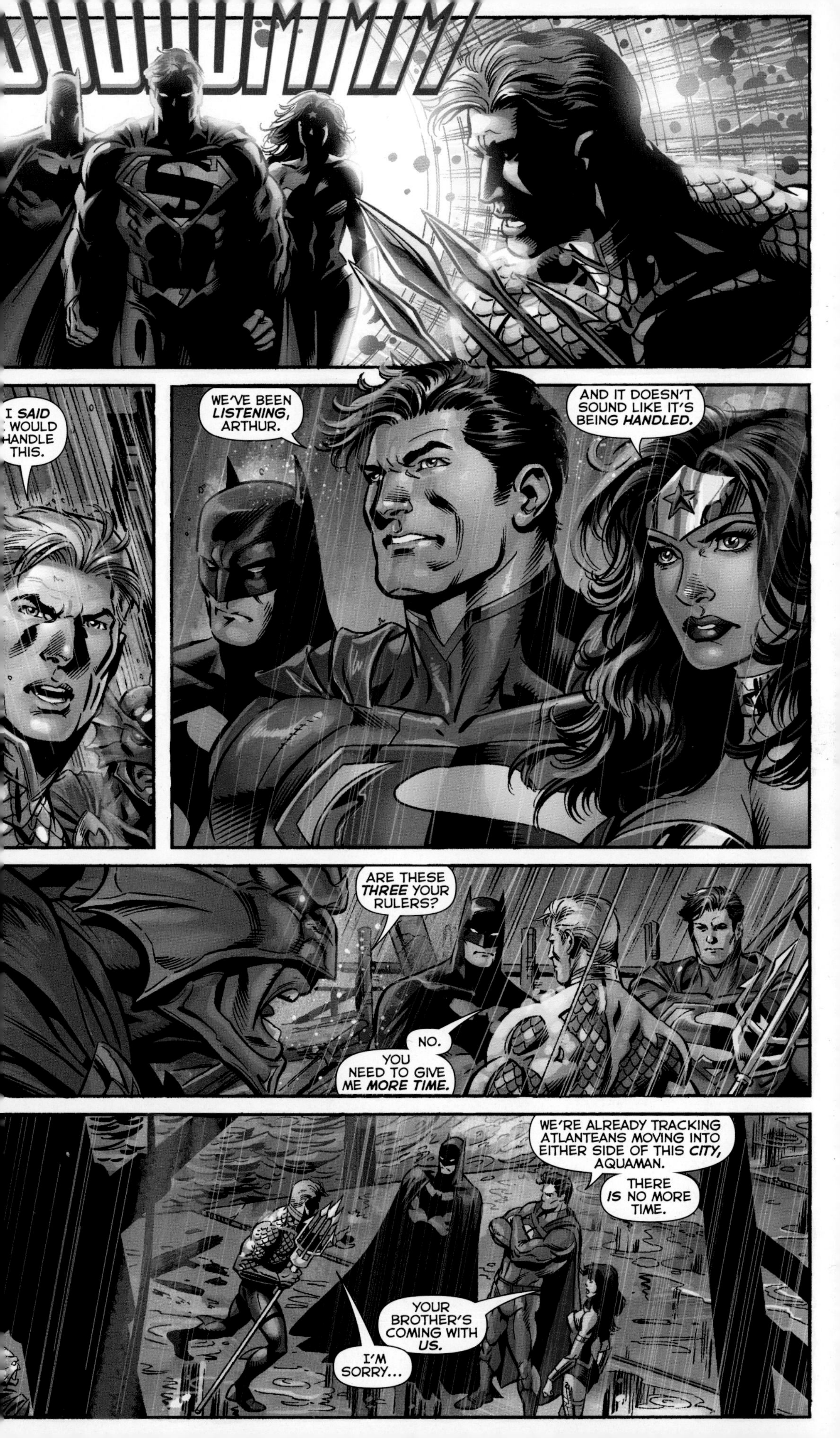
I SAID
I WOULD
HANDLE
THIS.
WE'VE BEEN LISTENING, ARTHUR.
AND IT DOESN'T SOUND LIKE IT'S BEING HANDLED.
ARE THESE THREE YOUR RULERS?
NO.
YOU NEED TO GIVE ME MORE TIME.
WE'RE ALREADY TRACKING ATLANTEANS MOVING INTO EITHER SIDE OF THIS CITY, AQUAMAN.
THERE IS NO MORE TIME.
YOUR BROTHER'S COMING WITH US.
I'M SORRY...

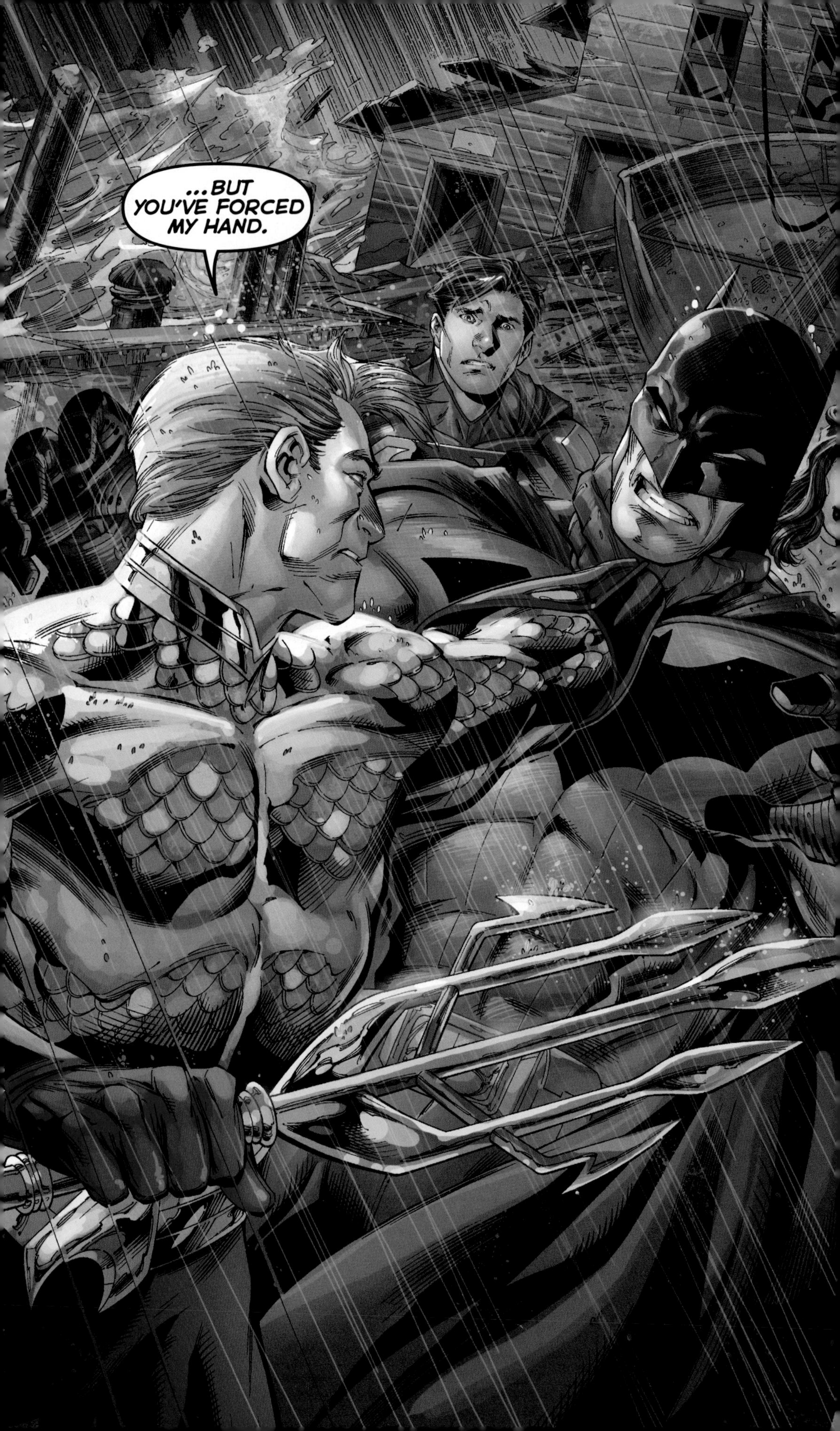
...BUT YOU'VE FORCED MY HAND.

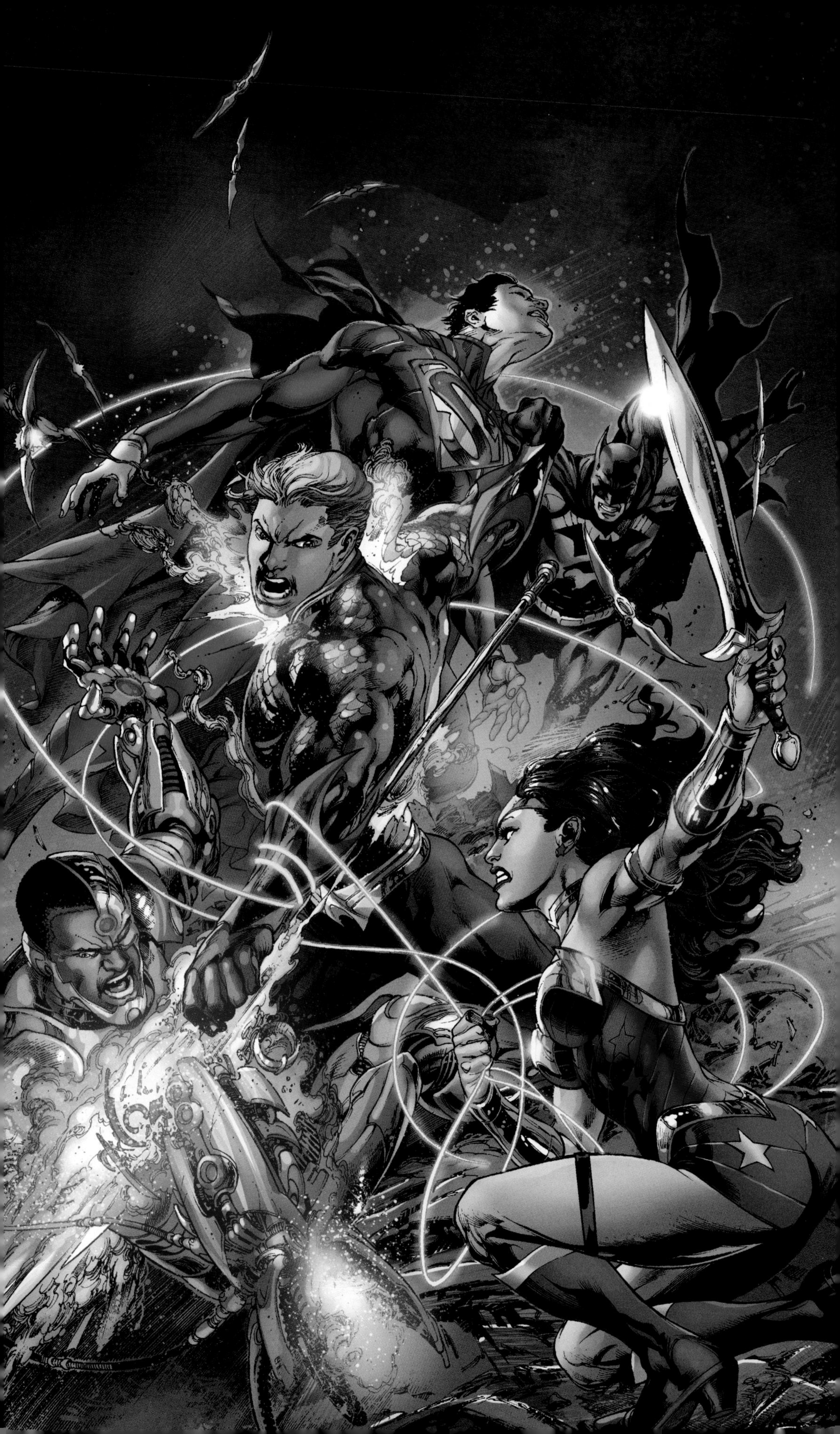

GEOFF JOHNS writer **IVAN REIS** penciller **JOE PRADO & IVAN REIS** inkers cover by **IVAN REIS, JOE PRADO & ROD REIS**

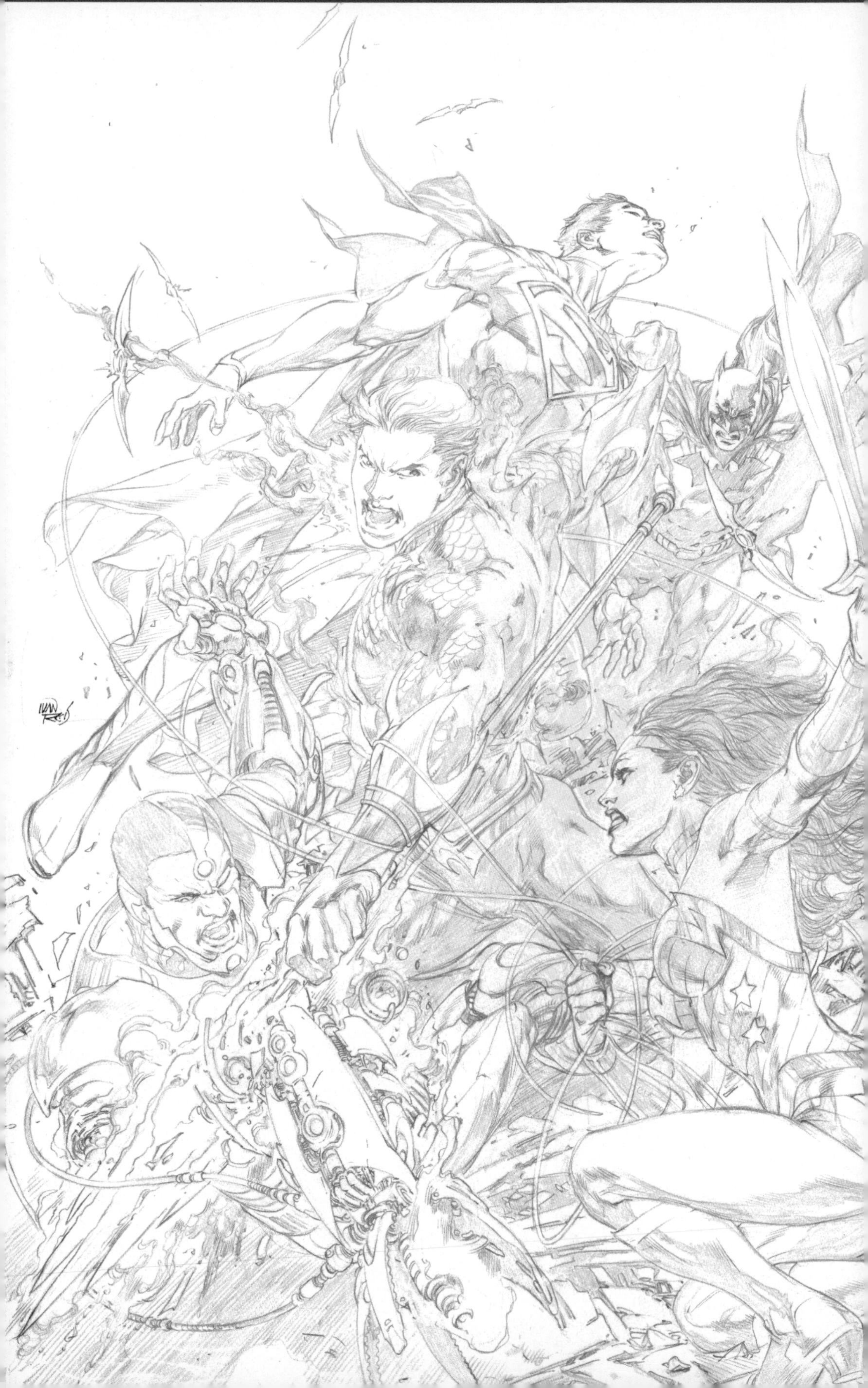

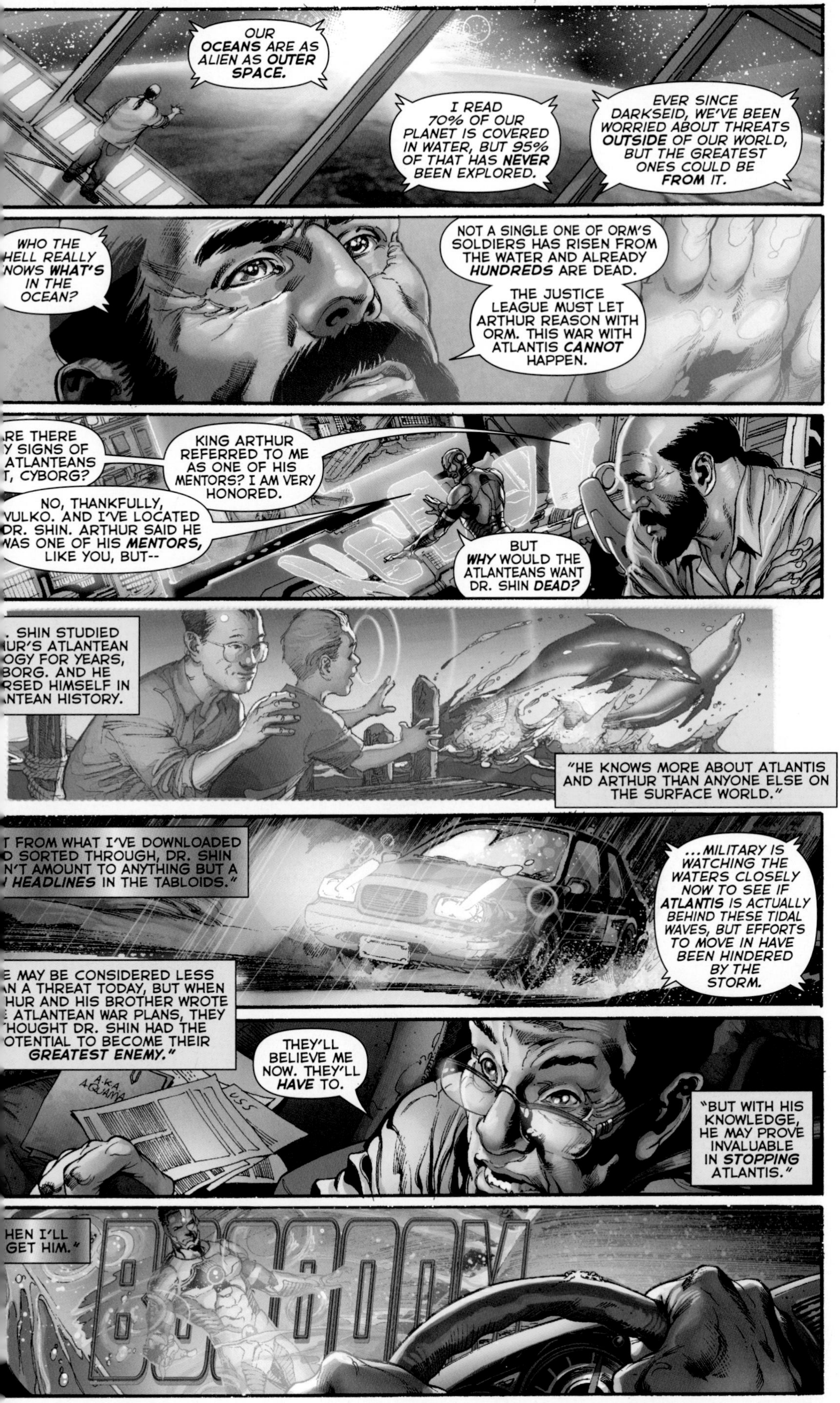

OUR OCEANS ARE AS ALIEN AS OUTER SPACE.
I READ 70% OF OUR PLANET IS COVERED IN WATER, BUT 95% OF THAT HAS NEVER BEEN EXPLORED.
EVER SINCE DARKSEID, WE'VE BEEN WORRIED ABOUT THREATS OUTSIDE OF OUR WORLD, BUT THE GREATEST ONES COULD BE FROM IT.
WHO THE HELL REALLY NOWS WHAT'S IN THE OCEAN?
NOT A SINGLE ONE OF ORM'S SOLDIERS HAS RISEN FROM THE WATER AND ALREADY HUNDREDS ARE DEAD.
THE JUSTICE LEAGUE MUST LET ARTHUR REASON WITH ORM. THIS WAR WITH ATLANTIS CANNOT HAPPEN.
RE THERE SIGNS OF ATLANTEANS , CYBORG?
KING ARTHUR REFERRED TO ME AS ONE OF HIS MENTORS? I AM VERY HONORED.
NO, THANKFULLY, VULKO. AND I'VE LOCATED DR. SHIN. ARTHUR SAID HE WAS ONE OF HIS MENTORS, LIKE YOU, BUT--
BUT WHY WOULD THE ATLANTEANS WANT DR. SHIN DEAD?
. SHIN STUDIED UR'S ATLANTEAN OGY FOR YEARS, BORG. AND HE RSED HIMSELF IN NTEAN HISTORY.
"HE KNOWS MORE ABOUT ATLANTIS AND ARTHUR THAN ANYONE ELSE ON THE SURFACE WORLD."
T FROM WHAT I'VE DOWNLOADED SORTED THROUGH, DR. SHIN N'T AMOUNT TO ANYTHING BUT A HEADLINES IN THE TABLOIDS."
...MILITARY IS WATCHING THE WATERS CLOSELY NOW TO SEE IF ATLANTIS IS ACTUALLY BEHIND THESE TIDAL WAVES, BUT EFFORTS TO MOVE IN HAVE BEEN HINDERED BY THE STORM.
E MAY BE CONSIDERED LESS N A THREAT TODAY, BUT WHEN HUR AND HIS BROTHER WROTE ATLANTEAN WAR PLANS, THEY THOUGHT DR. SHIN HAD THE OTENTIAL TO BECOME THEIR GREATEST ENEMY."
THEY'LL BELIEVE ME NOW. THEY'LL HAVE TO.
A-K-A AQUAMA
"BUT WITH HIS KNOWLEDGE, HE MAY PROVE INVALUABLE IN STOPPING ATLANTIS."
HEN I'LL GET HIM."

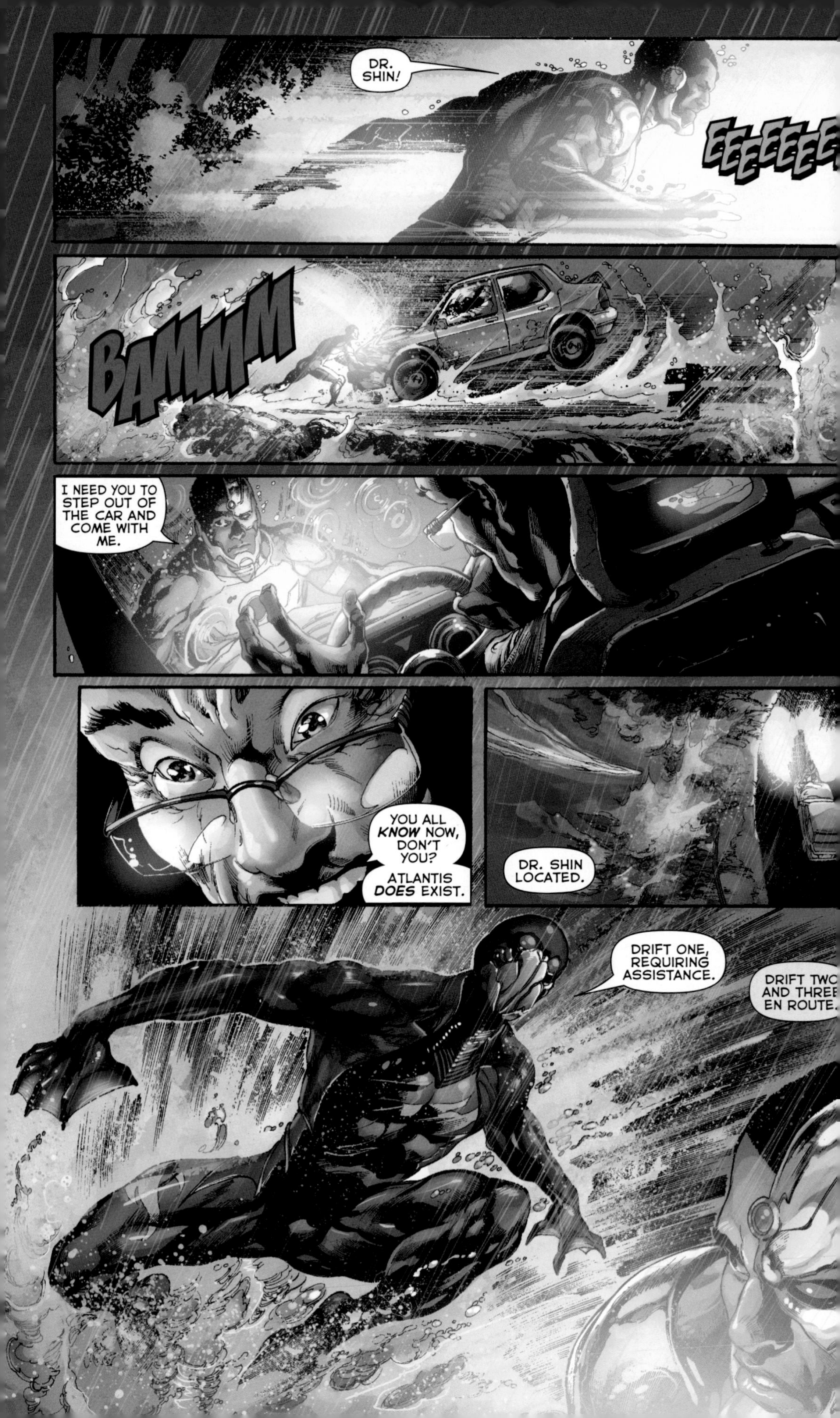

DR. SHIN!
EEEEEEEE
BAMMMM
I NEED YOU TO STEP OUT OF THE CAR AND COME WITH ME.
YOU ALL KNOW NOW, DON'T YOU?
ATLANTIS DOES EXIST.
DR. SHIN LOCATED.
DRIFT ONE, REQUIRING ASSISTANCE.
DRIFT TWO AND THREE EN ROUTE.

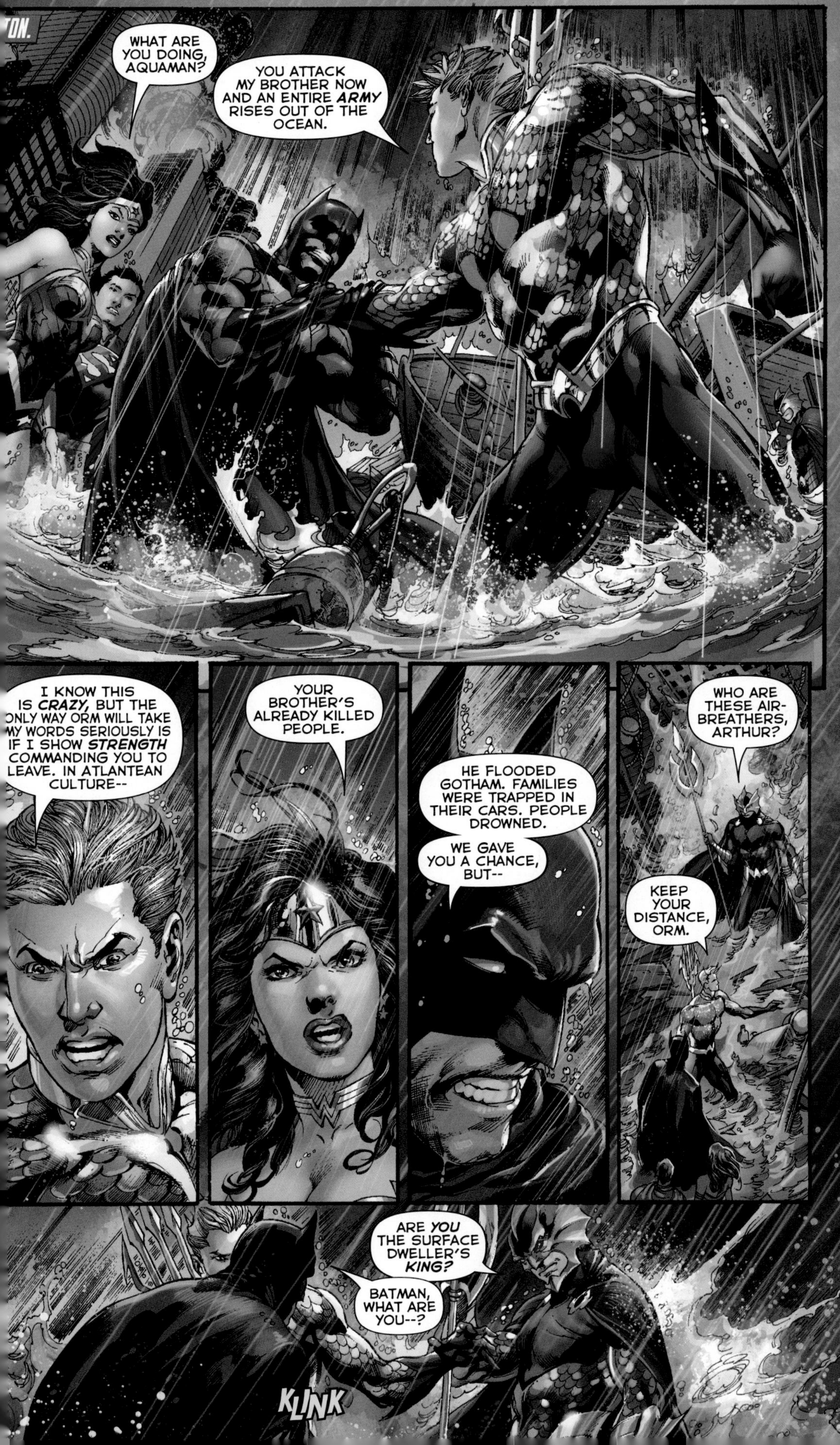
TON.
WHAT ARE YOU DOING, AQUAMAN?
YOU ATTACK MY BROTHER NOW AND AN ENTIRE ARMY RISES OUT OF THE OCEAN.
I KNOW THIS IS CRAZY, BUT THE ONLY WAY ORM WILL TAKE MY WORDS SERIOUSLY IS IF I SHOW STRENGTH COMMANDING YOU TO LEAVE. IN ATLANTEAN CULTURE--
YOUR BROTHER'S ALREADY KILLED PEOPLE.
HE FLOODED GOTHAM. FAMILIES WERE TRAPPED IN THEIR CARS. PEOPLE DROWNED.
WE GAVE YOU A CHANCE, BUT--
WHO ARE THESE AIR-BREATHERS, ARTHUR?
KEEP YOUR DISTANCE, ORM.
ARE YOU THE SURFACE DWELLER'S KING?
BATMAN, WHAT ARE YOU--?
KLINK

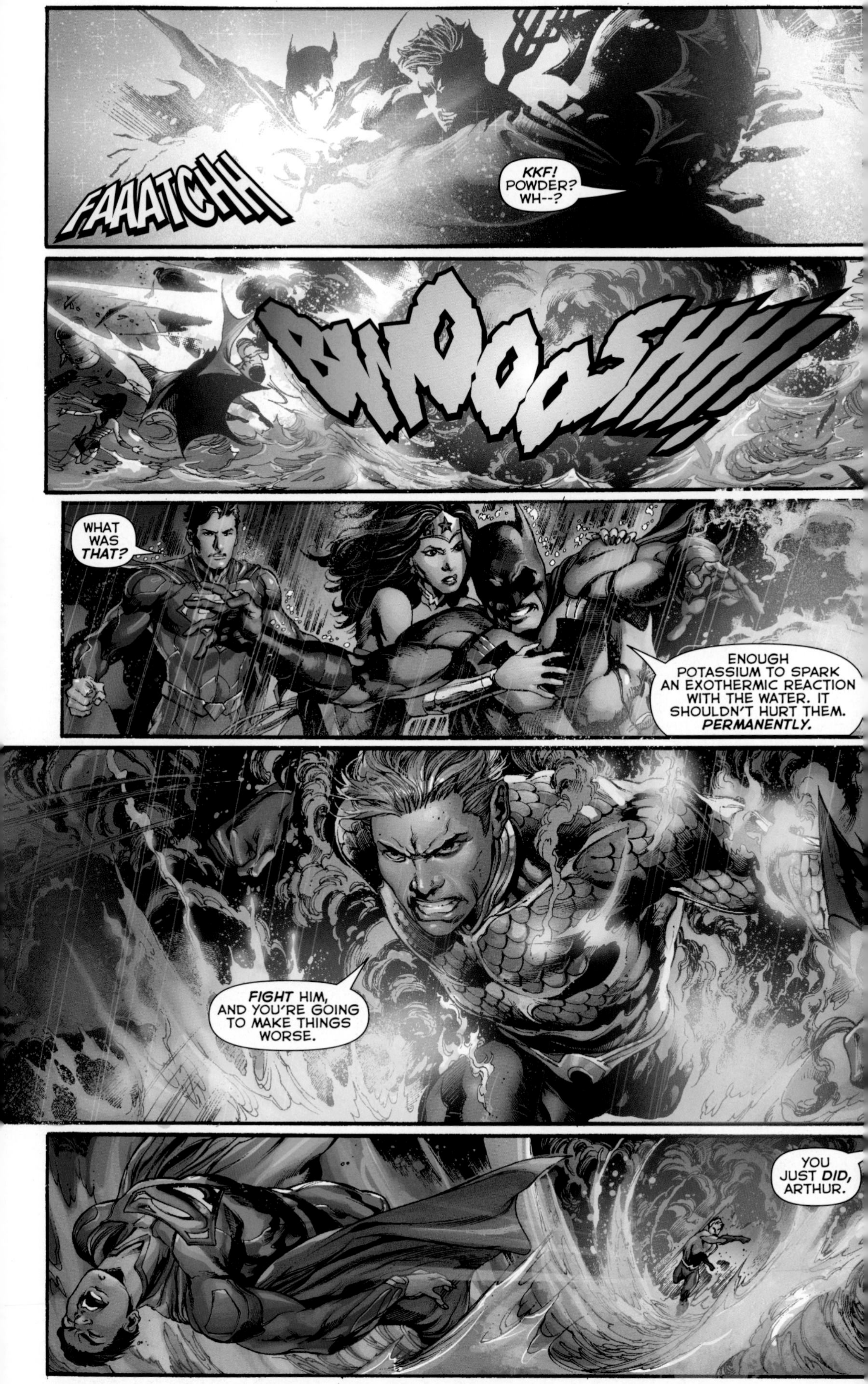
FAAATCHH
KKF! POWDER? WH--?
BWOOSHH
WHAT WAS THAT?
ENOUGH POTASSIUM TO SPARK AN EXOTHERMIC REACTION WITH THE WATER. IT SHOULDN'T HURT THEM. PERMANENTLY.
FIGHT HIM, AND YOU'RE GOING TO MAKE THINGS WORSE.
YOU JUST DID, ARTHUR.

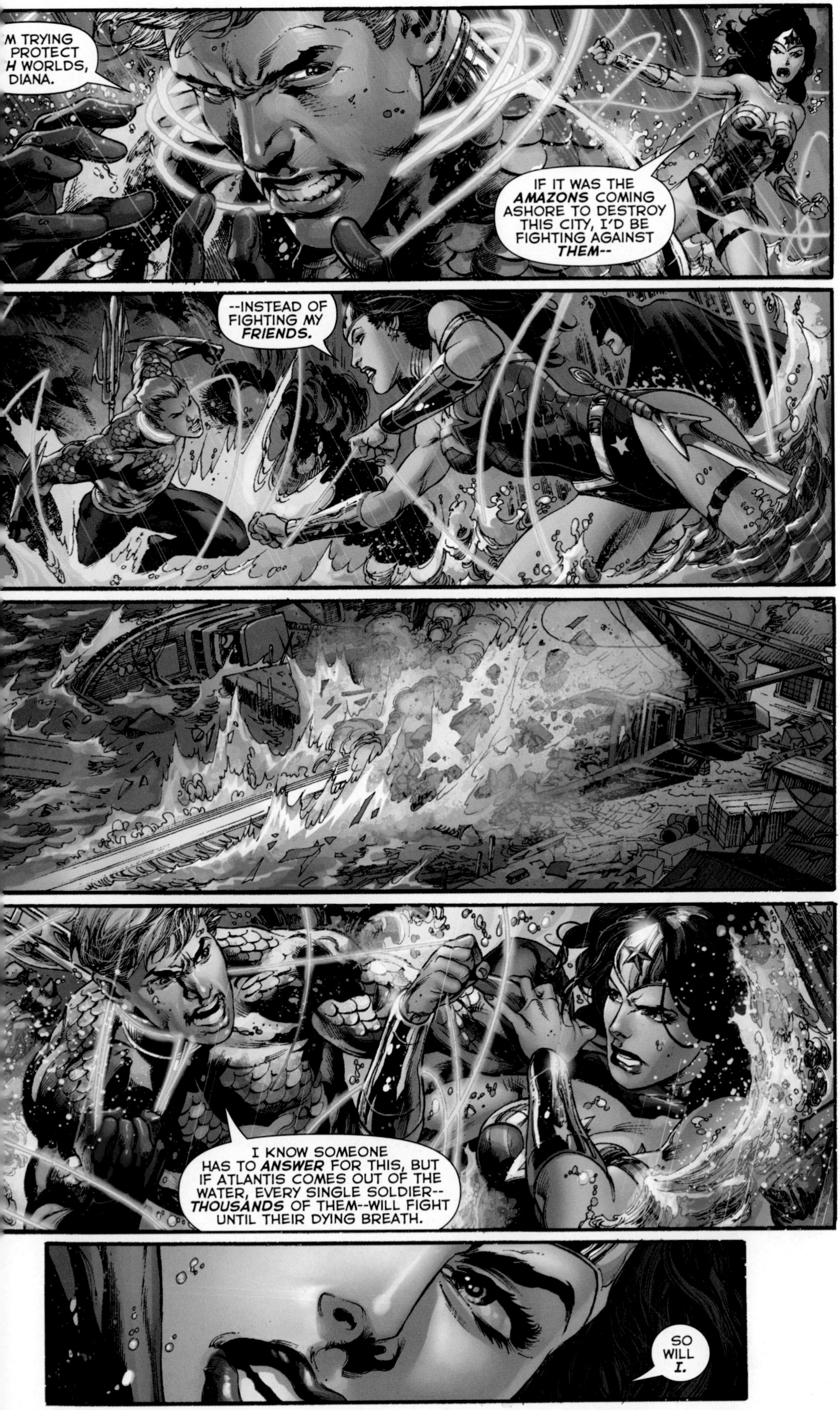
M TRYING PROTECT H WORLDS, DIANA.
IF IT WAS THE AMAZONS COMING ASHORE TO DESTROY THIS CITY, I'D BE FIGHTING AGAINST THEM--
--INSTEAD OF FIGHTING MY FRIENDS.
I KNOW SOMEONE HAS TO ANSWER FOR THIS, BUT IF ATLANTIS COMES OUT OF THE WATER, EVERY SINGLE SOLDIER-- THOUSANDS OF THEM--WILL FIGHT UNTIL THEIR DYING BREATH.
SO WILL I.

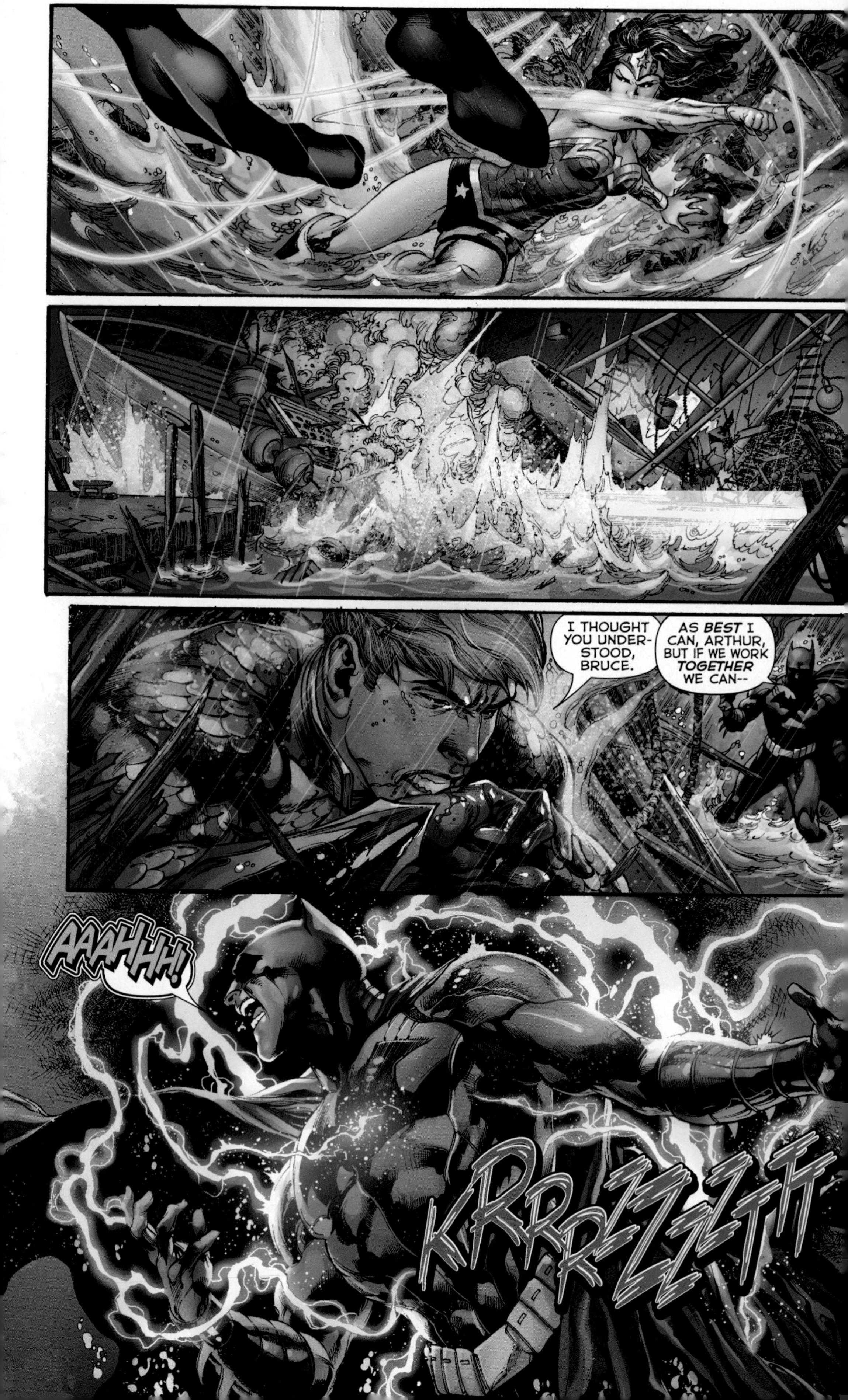
I THOUGHT YOU UNDER-STOOD, BRUCE.
AS BEST I CAN, ARTHUR, BUT IF WE WORK TOGETHER WE CAN--
AAAHHH!
KRRRZZZZTH

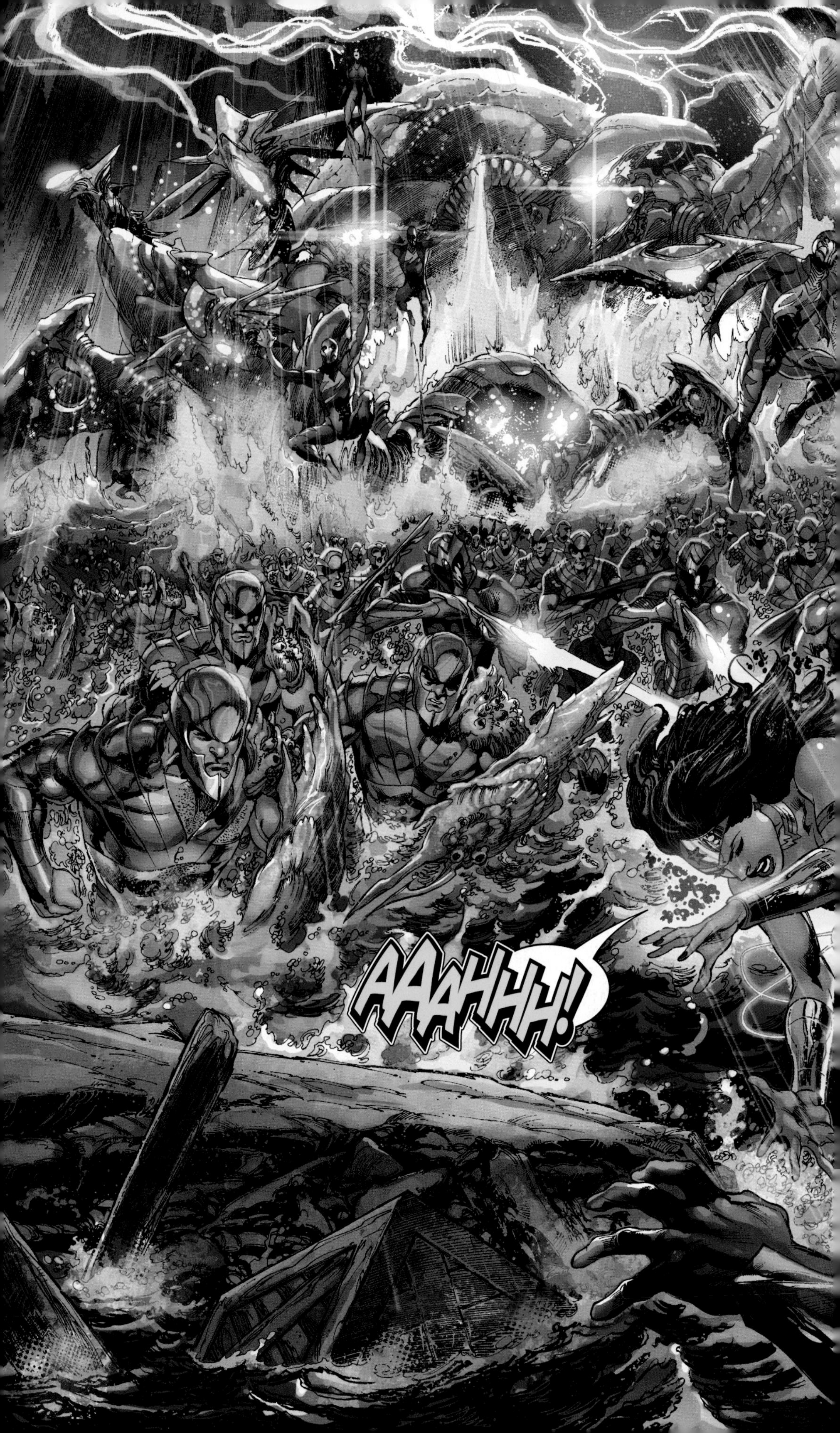
AAAHHH!

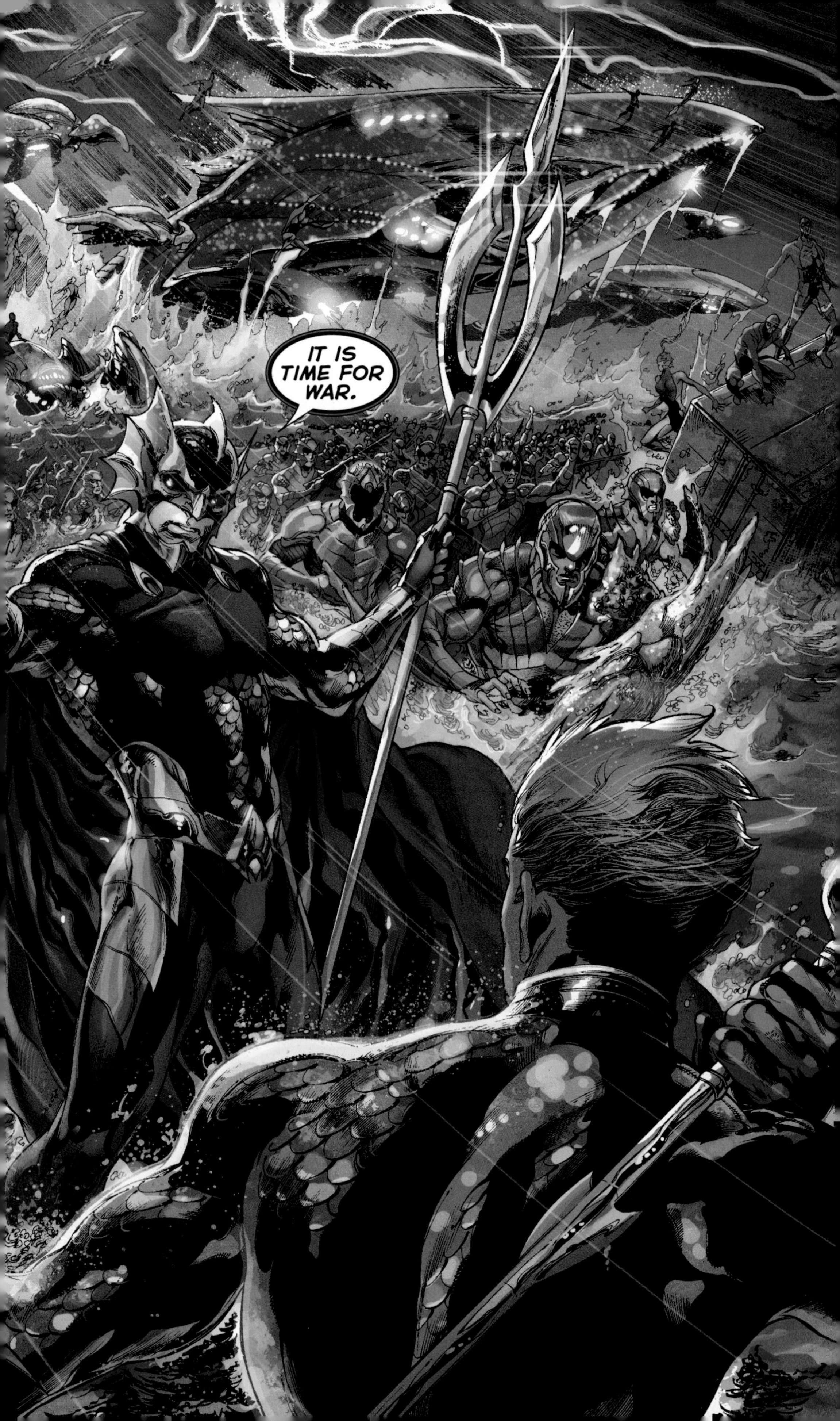
IT IS TIME FOR WAR.

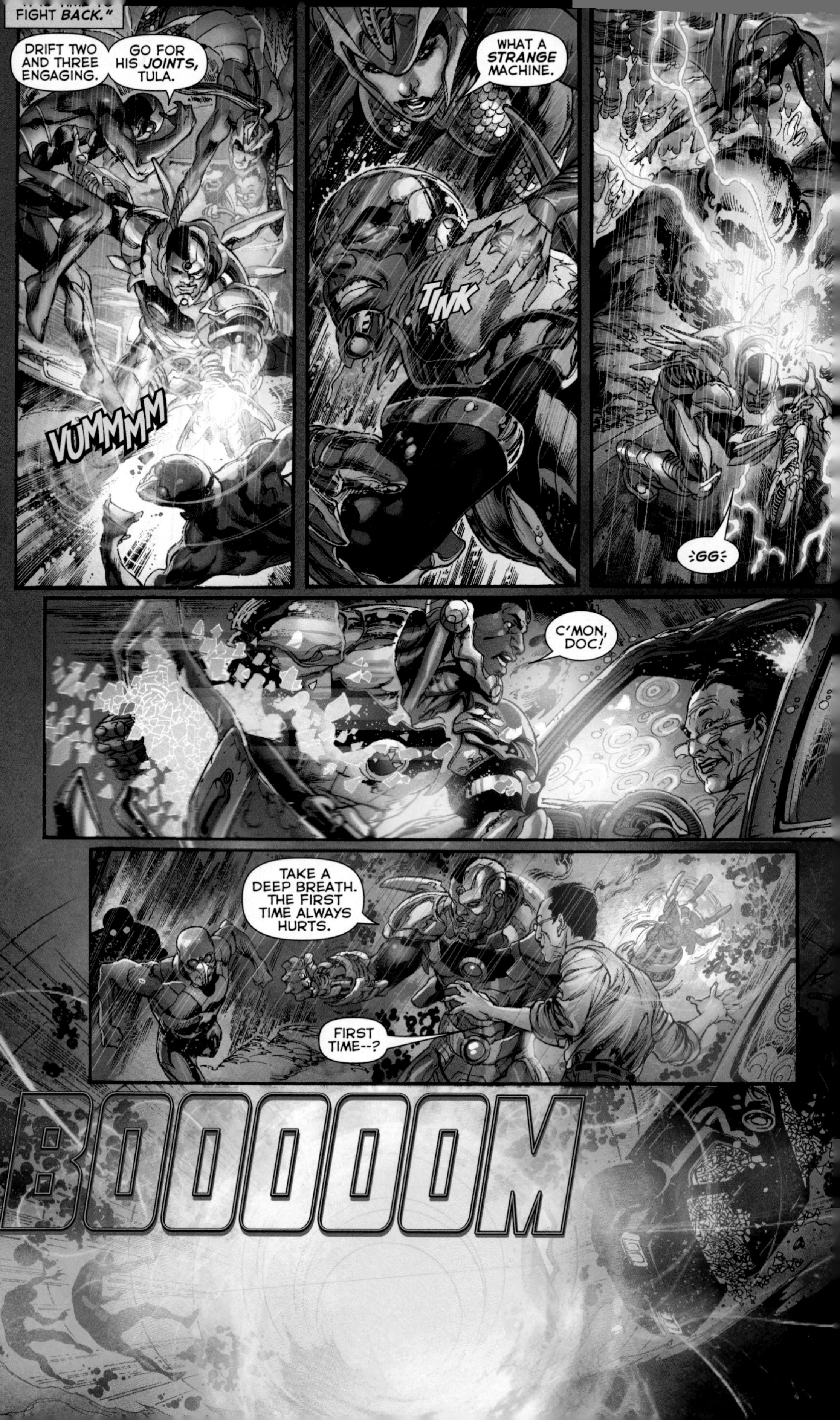
FIGHT BACK."
DRIFT TWO AND THREE ENGAGING.
GO FOR HIS JOINTS, TULA.
VUMMMM
WHAT A STRANGE MACHINE.
TINK
GG
C'MON, DOC!
TAKE A DEEP BREATH. THE FIRST TIME ALWAYS HURTS.
FIRST TIME--?
BOOOOOM

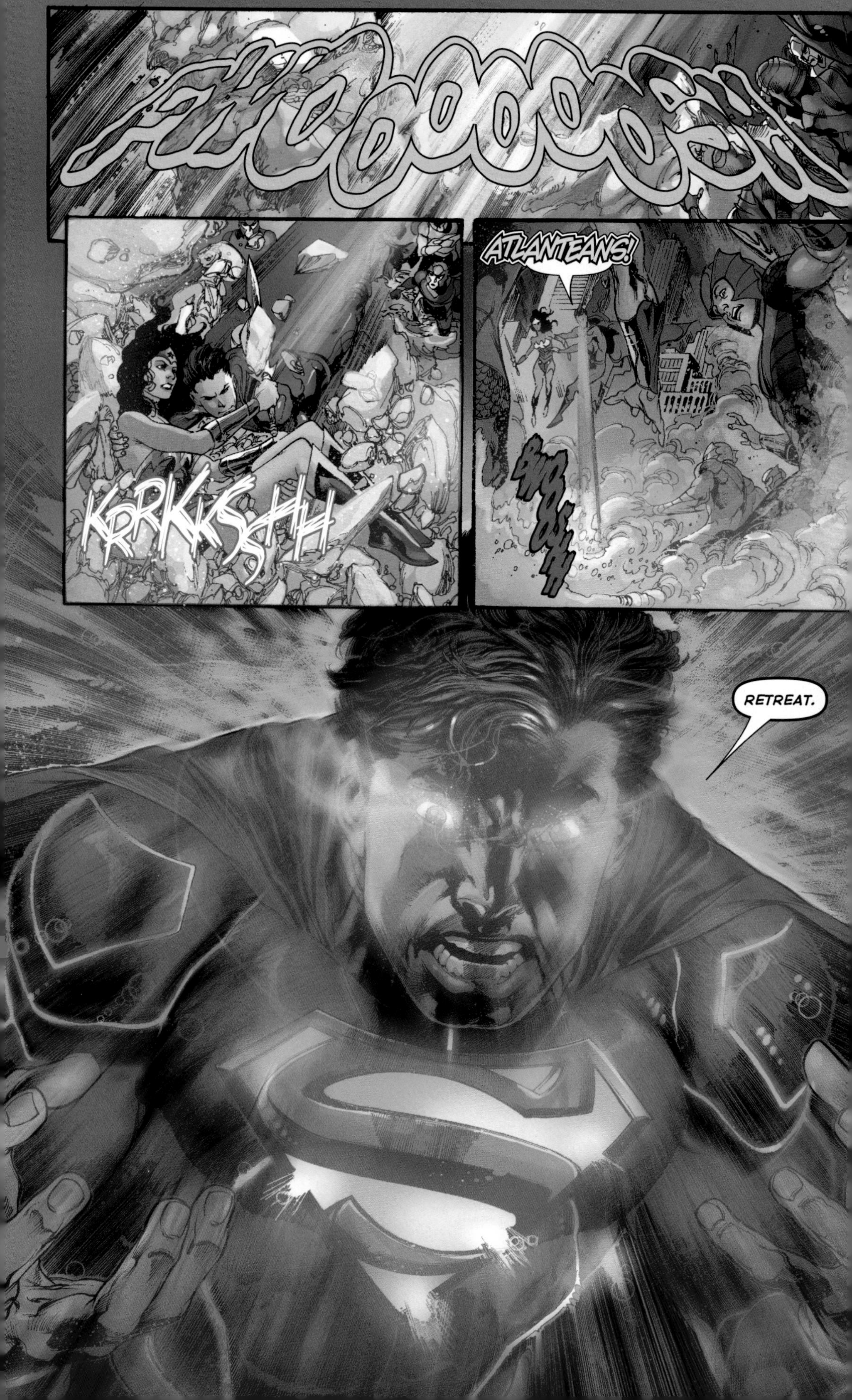
FZHOOOOOOSH
KRRKKSHHH
ATLANTEANS!
BWOOOSHH
RETREAT.

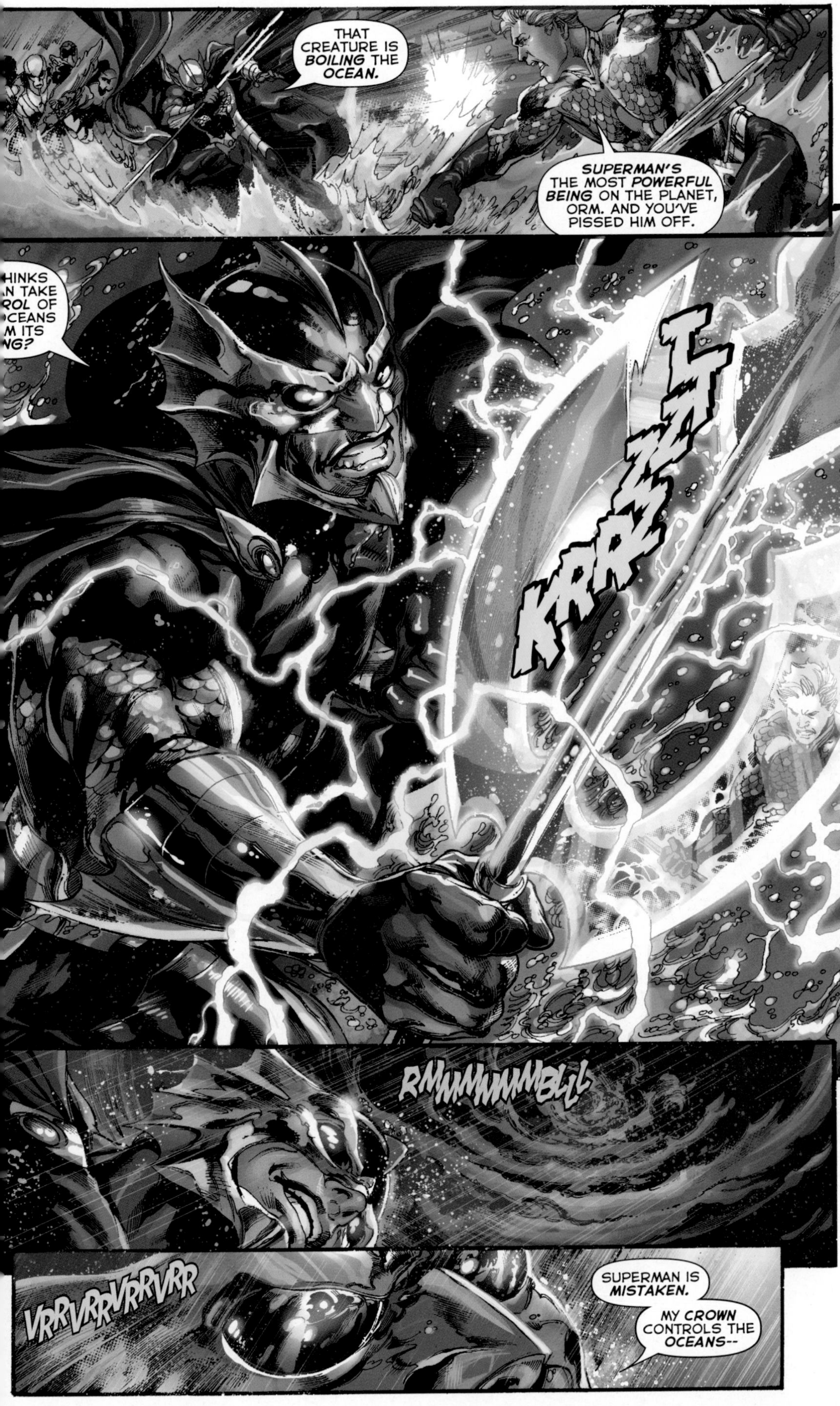
THAT CREATURE IS BOILING THE OCEAN.
SUPERMAN'S THE MOST POWERFUL BEING ON THE PLANET, ORM. AND YOU'VE PISSED HIM OFF.
KRRZZZT
RMMMMMMBLL
VRRVRRVRRVRR
SUPERMAN IS MISTAKEN.
MY CROWN CONTROLS THE OCEANS--

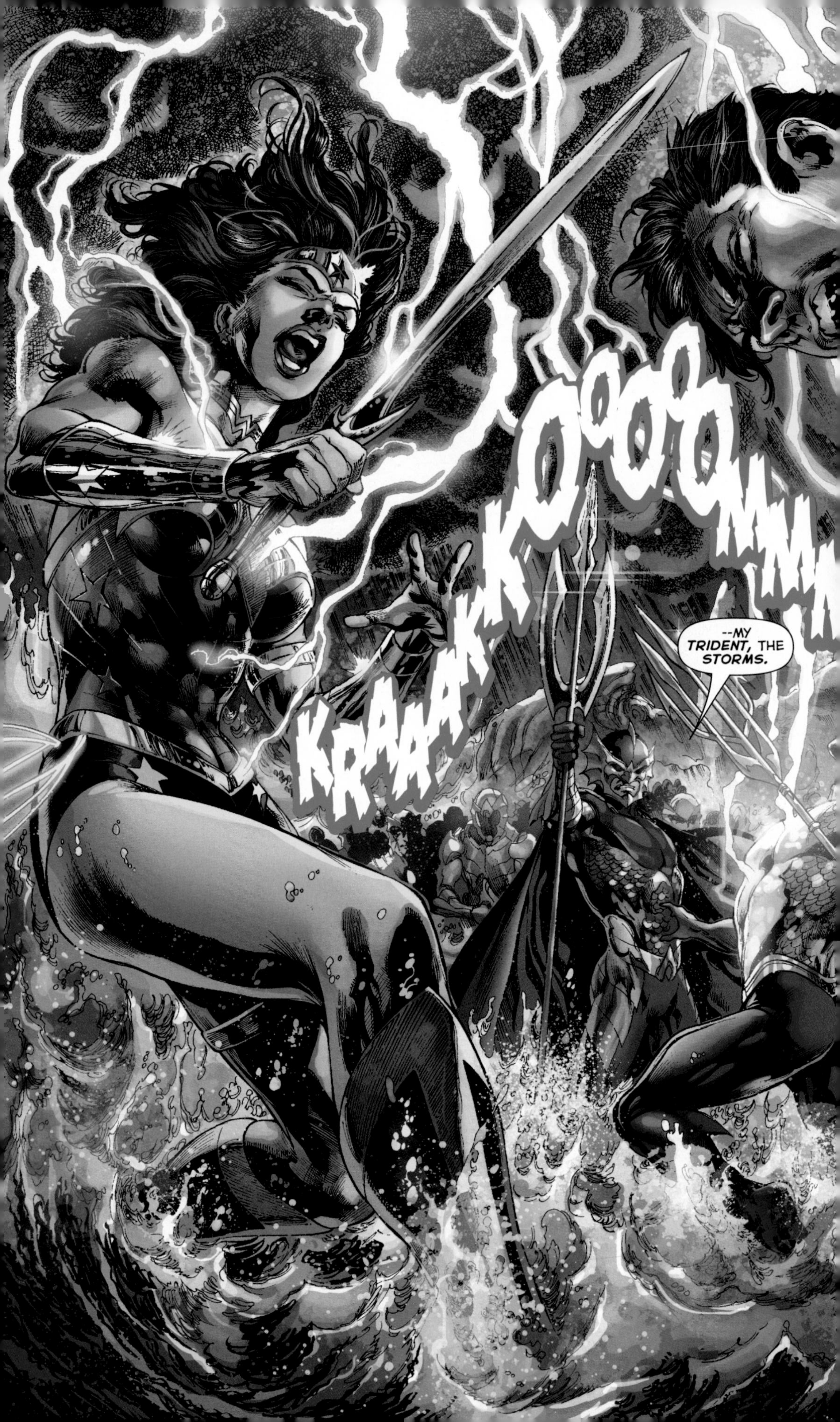
KRAAAKKOOOOOMM
--MY TRIDENT, THE STORMS.

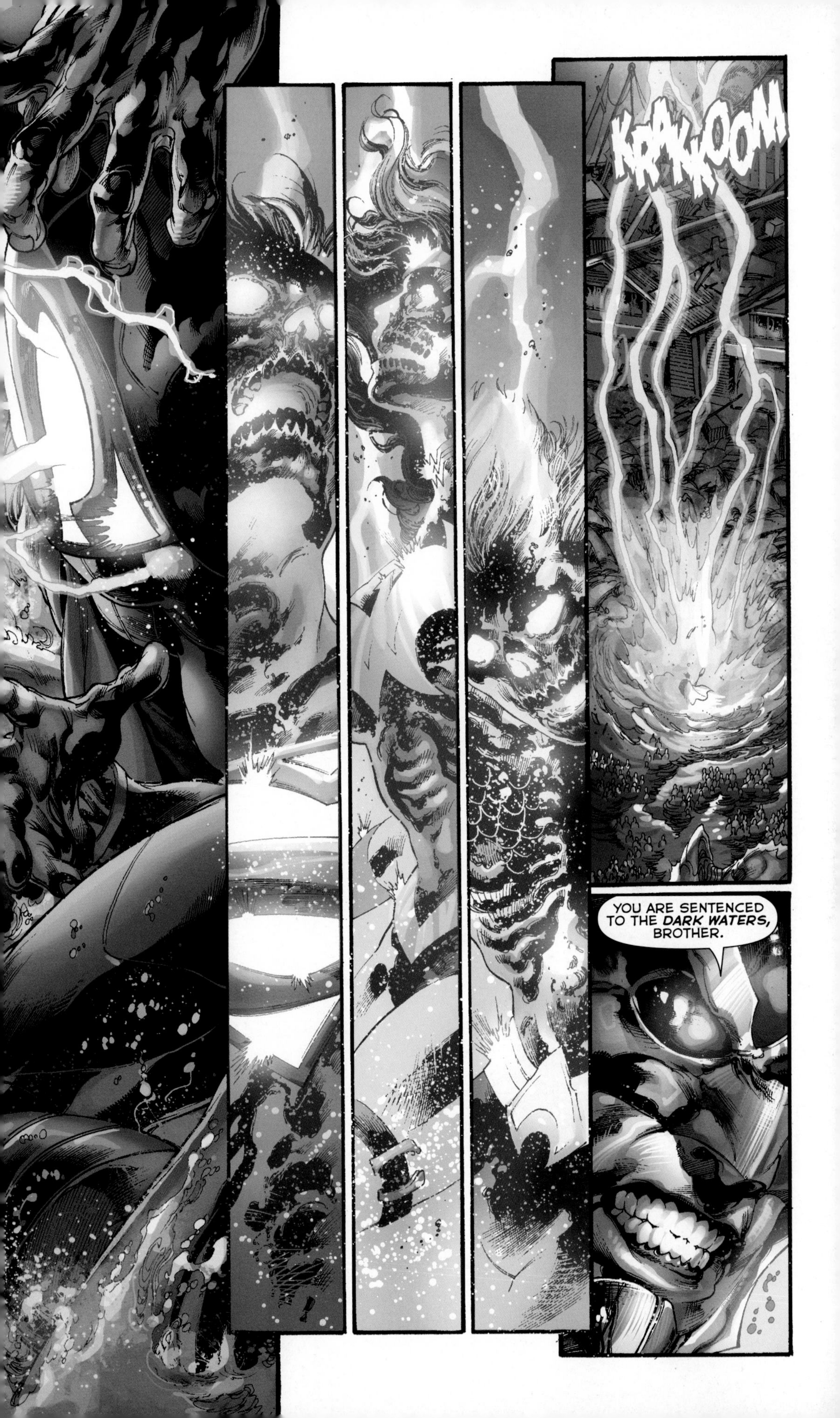
KRAKOOM
YOU ARE SENTENCED TO THE *DARK WATERS*, BROTHER.

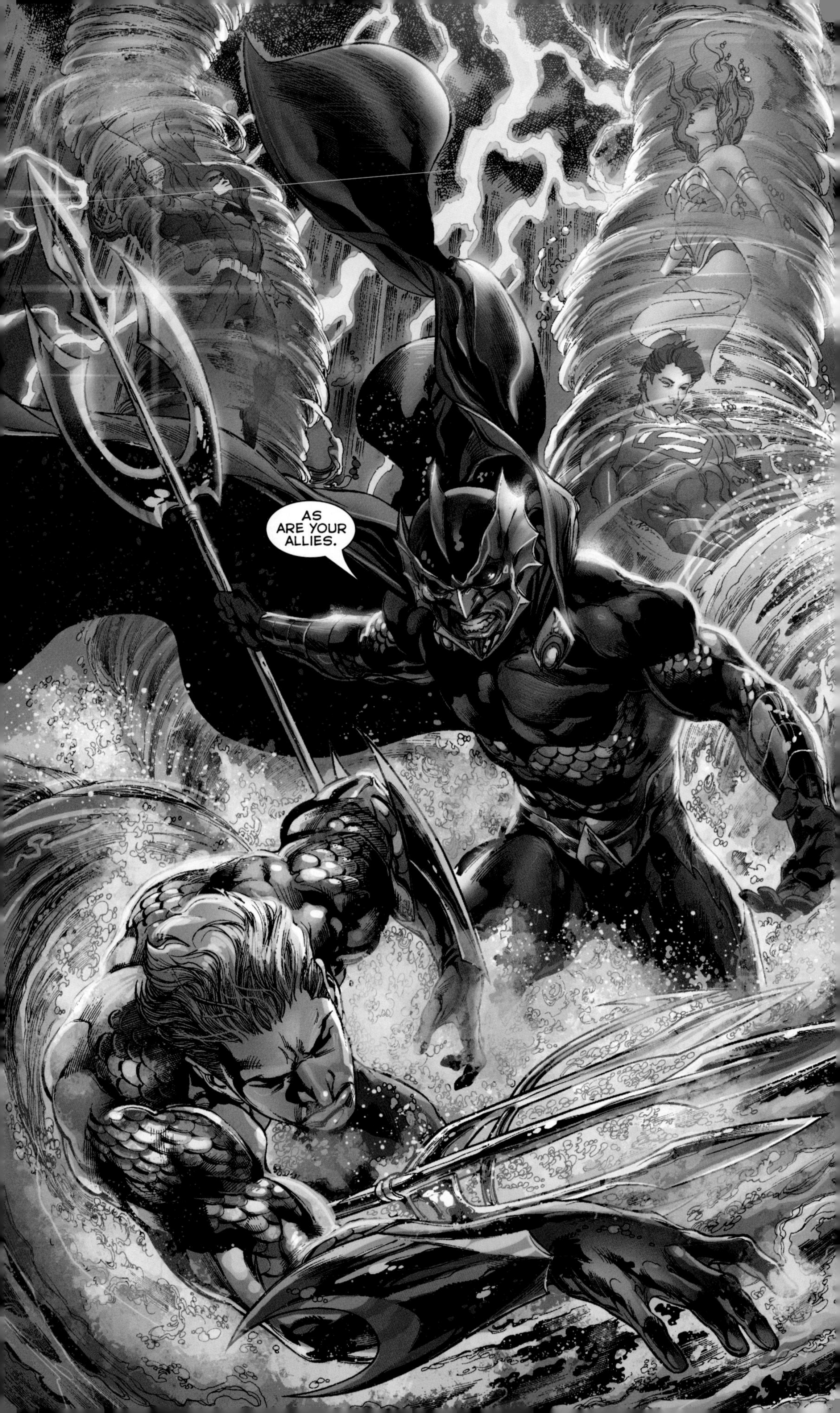
AS ARE YOUR ALLIES.

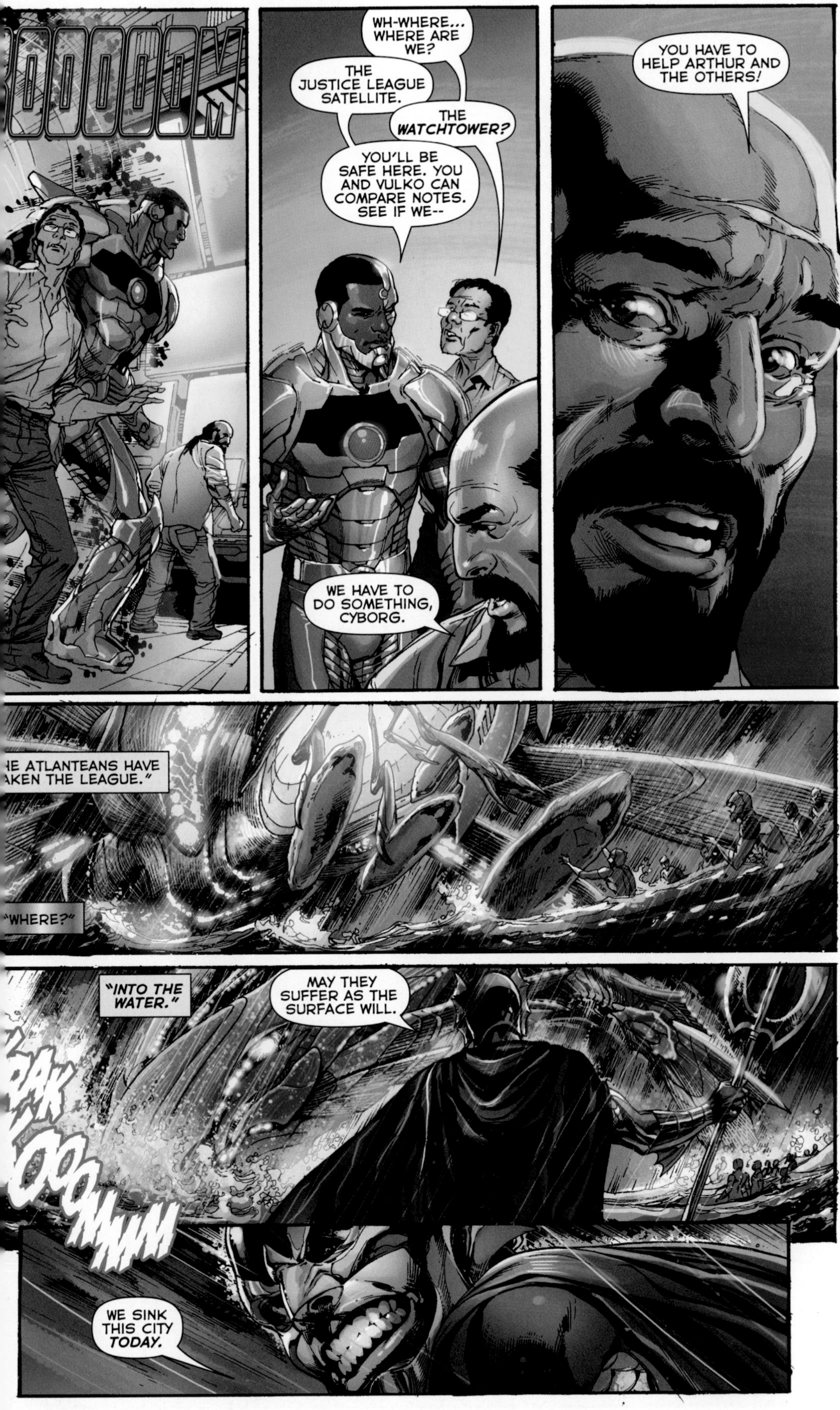
BOOOOOOM
WH-WHERE... WHERE ARE WE?
THE JUSTICE LEAGUE SATELLITE.
THE WATCHTOWER?
YOU'LL BE SAFE HERE. YOU AND VULKO CAN COMPARE NOTES. SEE IF WE--
WE HAVE TO DO SOMETHING, CYBORG.
YOU HAVE TO HELP ARTHUR AND THE OTHERS!
HE ATLANTEANS HAVE AKEN THE LEAGUE."
"WHERE?"
"INTO THE WATER."
MAY THEY SUFFER AS THE SURFACE WILL.
WE SINK THIS CITY TODAY.

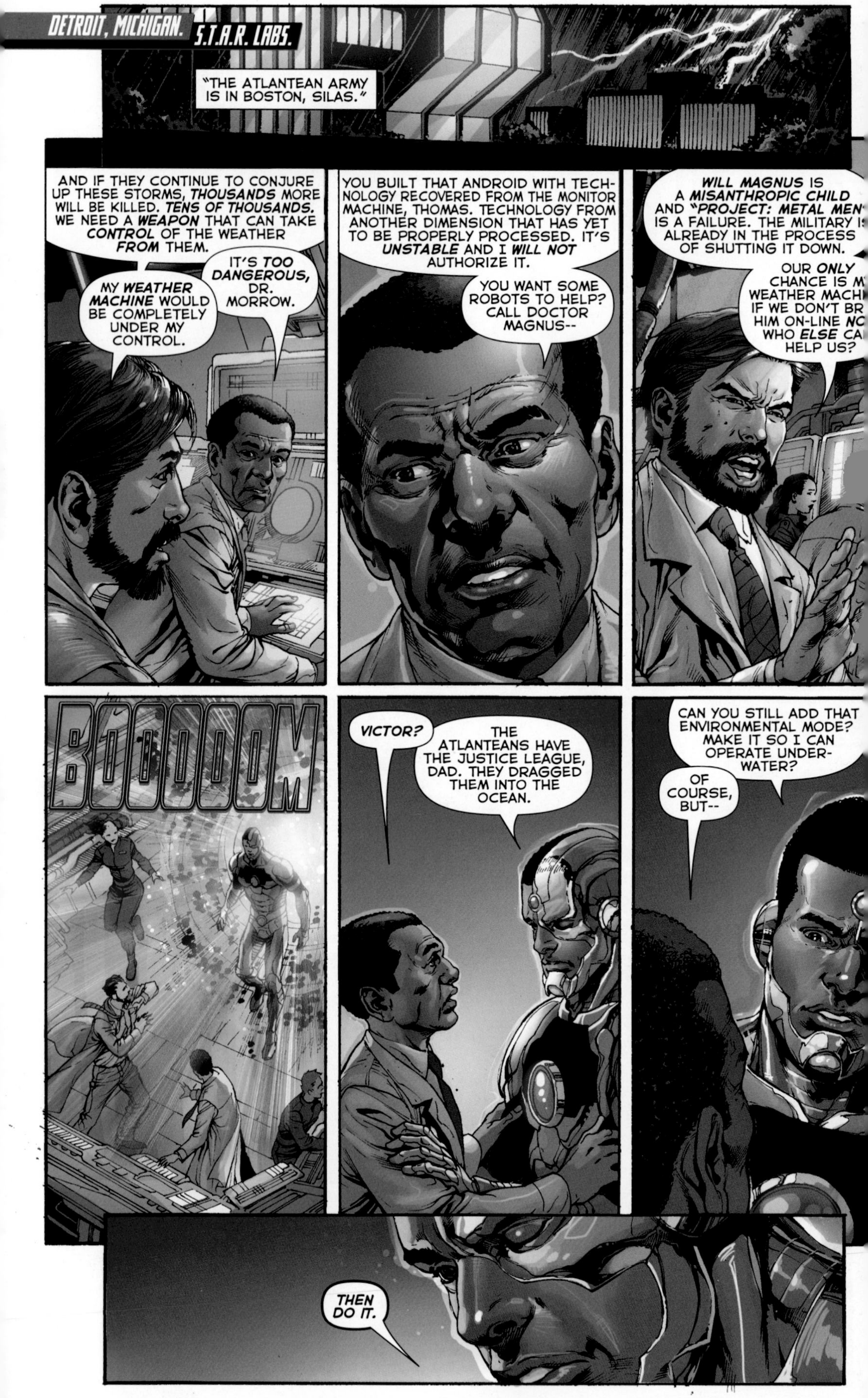

"THE ATLANTEAN ARMY IS IN BOSTON, SILAS."

AND IF THEY CONTINUE TO CONJURE UP THESE STORMS, *THOUSANDS* MORE WILL BE KILLED. *TENS OF THOUSANDS.* WE NEED A *WEAPON* THAT CAN TAKE *CONTROL* OF THE WEATHER FROM THEM.

MY *WEATHER MACHINE* WOULD BE COMPLETELY UNDER MY CONTROL.

IT'S *TOO DANGEROUS,* DR. MORROW.

YOU BUILT THAT ANDROID WITH TECHNOLOGY RECOVERED FROM THE MONITOR MACHINE, THOMAS. TECHNOLOGY FROM ANOTHER DIMENSION THAT HAS YET TO BE PROPERLY PROCESSED. IT'S *UNSTABLE* AND I *WILL NOT* AUTHORIZE IT.

YOU WANT SOME ROBOTS TO HELP? CALL DOCTOR MAGNUS--

WILL MAGNUS IS A *MISANTHROPIC CHILD* AND *"PROJECT: METAL MEN"* IS A FAILURE. THE MILITARY I[S] ALREADY IN THE PROCESS OF SHUTTING IT DOWN.

OUR *ONLY* CHANCE IS M[Y] WEATHER MACH[INE] IF WE DON'T BR[ING] HIM ON-LINE NO[W] WHO *ELSE* CA[N] HELP US?

BOOOOOM

VICTOR?

THE ATLANTEANS HAVE THE JUSTICE LEAGUE, DAD. THEY DRAGGED THEM INTO THE OCEAN.

CAN YOU STILL ADD THAT ENVIRONMENTAL MODE? MAKE IT SO I CAN OPERATE UNDER-WATER?

OF COURSE, BUT--

THEN DO IT.

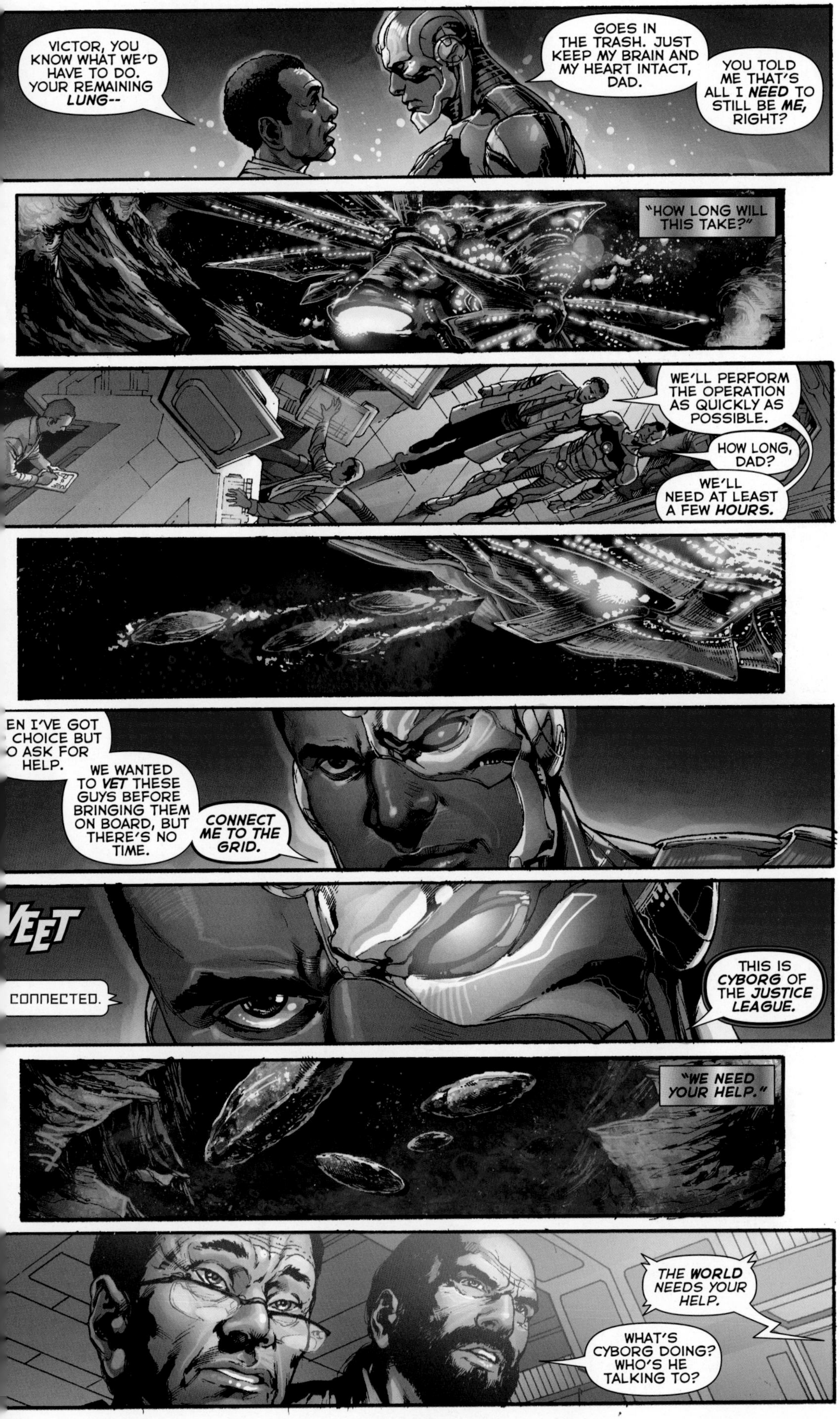
VICTOR, YOU KNOW WHAT WE'D HAVE TO DO. YOUR REMAINING *LUNG*--
GOES IN THE TRASH. JUST KEEP MY BRAIN AND MY HEART INTACT, DAD.
YOU TOLD ME THAT'S ALL I ***NEED*** TO STILL BE ***ME,*** RIGHT?
"HOW LONG WILL THIS TAKE?"
WE'LL PERFORM THE OPERATION AS QUICKLY AS POSSIBLE.
HOW LONG, DAD?
WE'LL NEED AT LEAST A FEW ***HOURS.***
EN I'VE GOT CHOICE BUT O ASK FOR HELP.
WE WANTED TO ***VET*** THESE GUYS BEFORE BRINGING THEM ON BOARD, BUT THERE'S NO TIME.
CONNECT ME TO THE GRID.
VEET
CONNECTED.
THIS IS ***CYBORG*** OF THE ***JUSTICE LEAGUE.***
"WE NEED YOUR HELP."
*THE **WORLD** NEEDS YOUR HELP.*
WHAT'S CYBORG DOING? WHO'S HE TALKING TO?

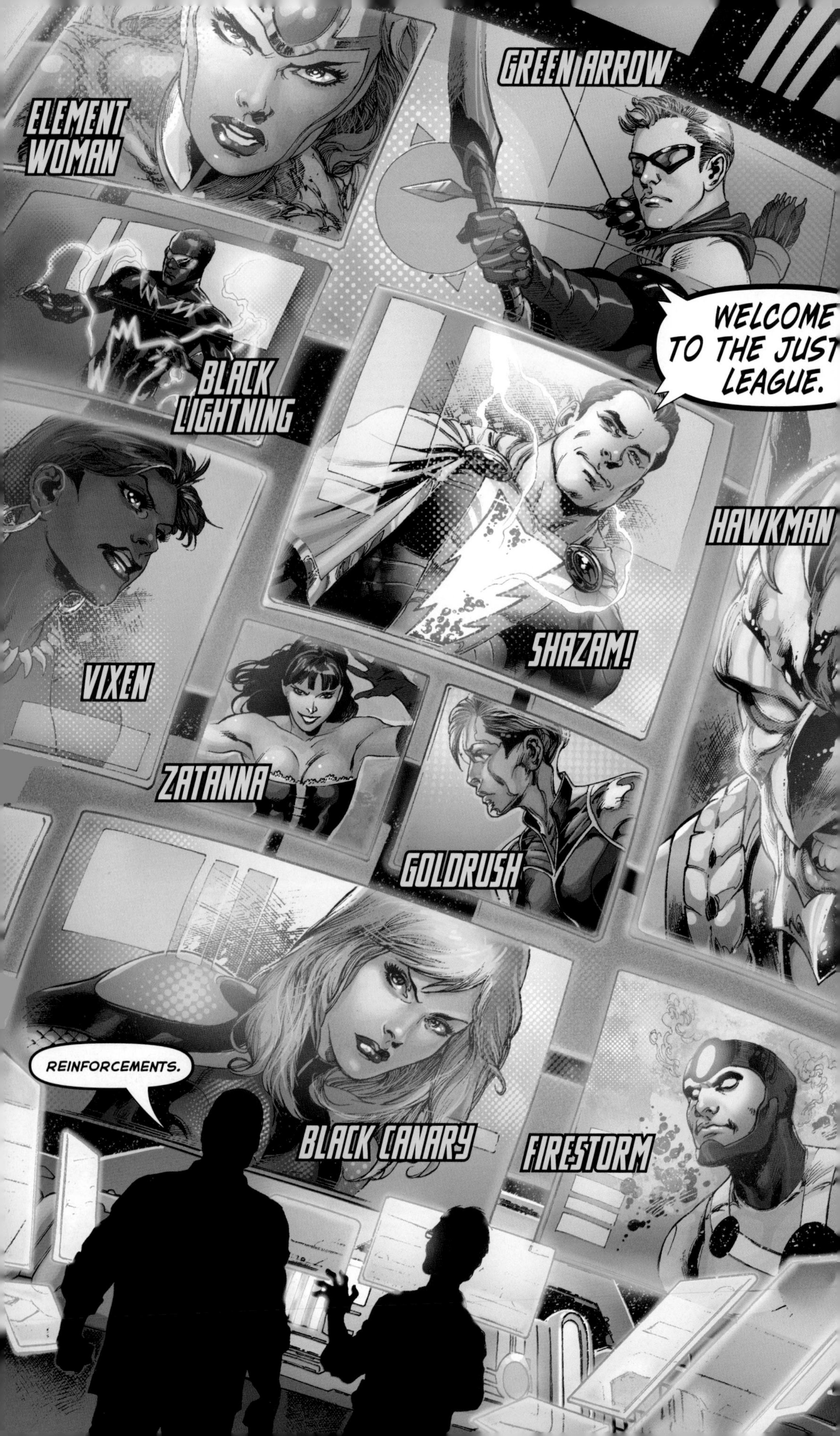
GREEN ARROW
ELEMENT WOMAN
WELCOME TO THE JUST LEAGUE.
BLACK LIGHTNING
HAWKMAN
SHAZAM!
VIXEN
ZATANNA
GOLDRUSH
REINFORCEMENTS.
BLACK CANARY
FIRESTORM

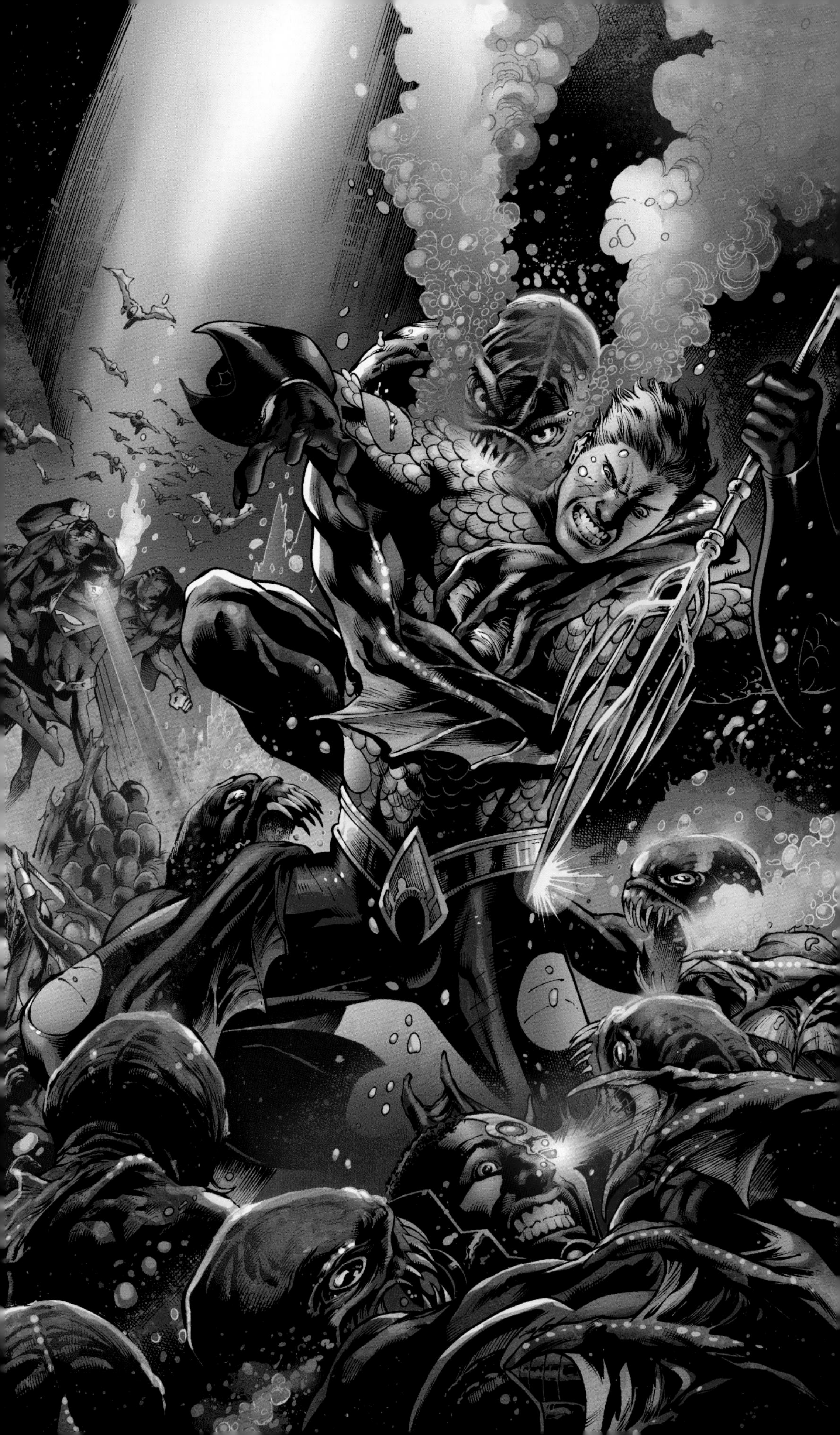

GEOFF JOHNS writer PAUL PELLETIER penciller SEAN PARSONS inker cover by EDDY BARROWS, EBER FERREIRA & ROD REIS

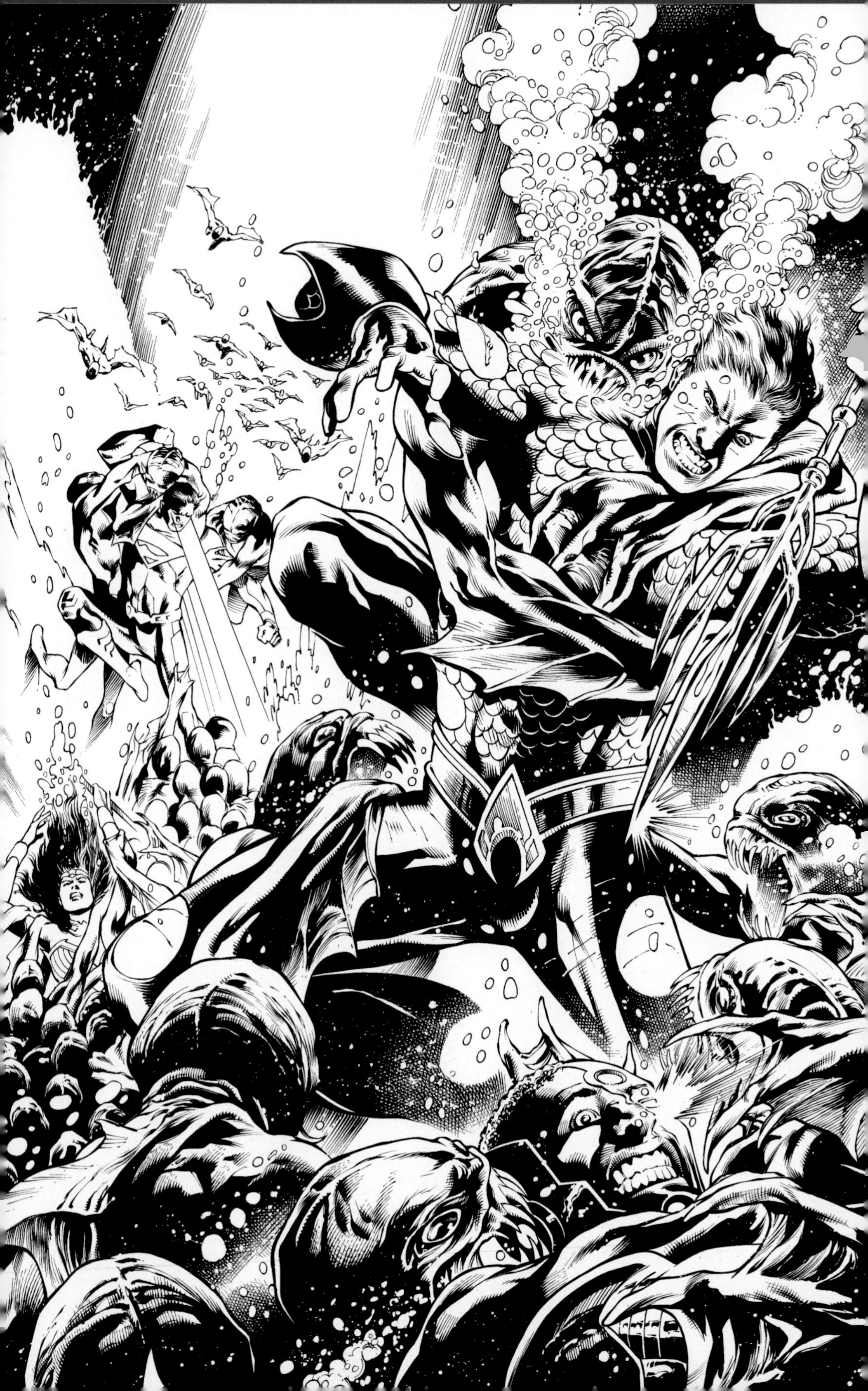

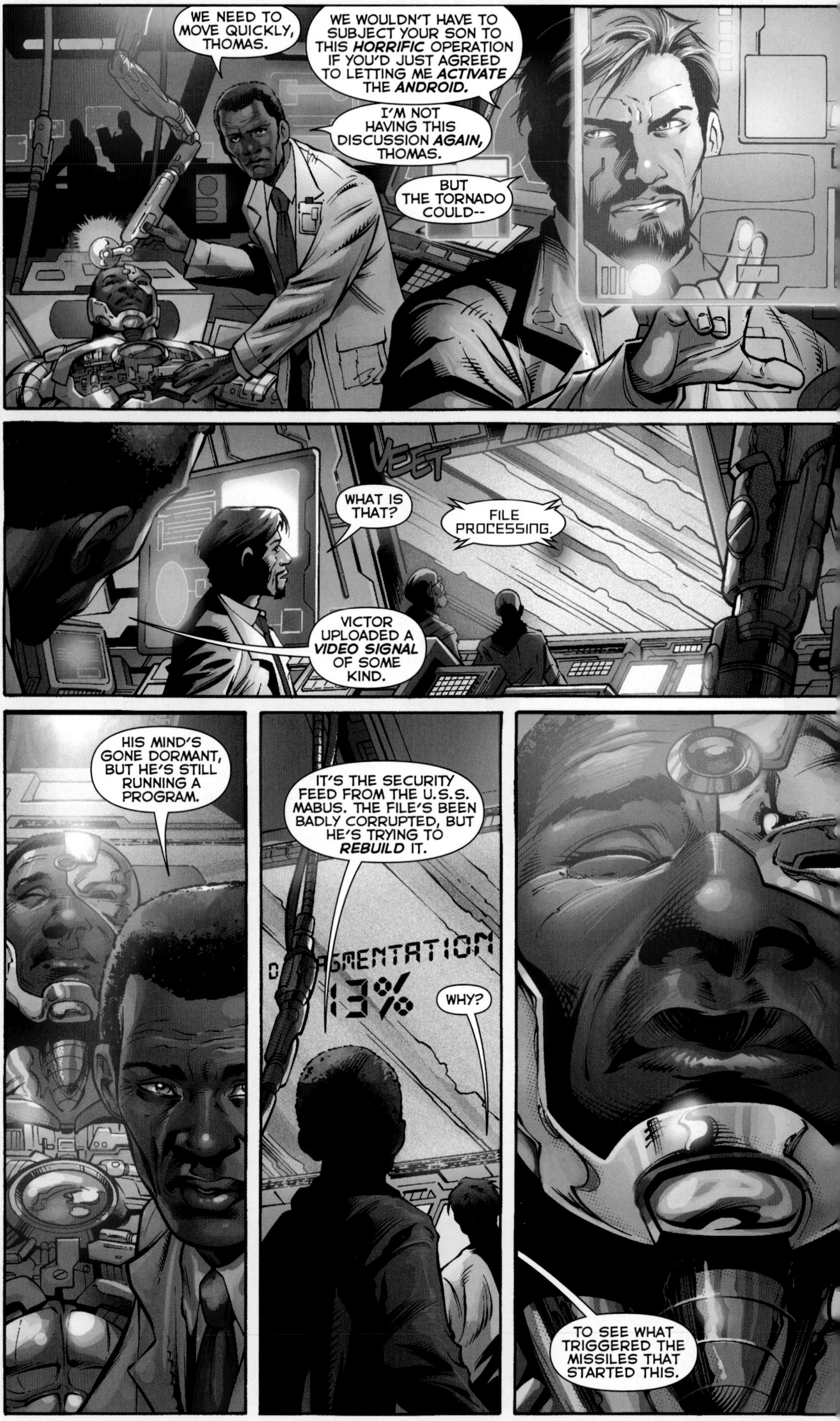
WE NEED TO MOVE QUICKLY, THOMAS.
WE WOULDN'T HAVE TO SUBJECT YOUR SON TO THIS *HORRIFIC* OPERATION IF YOU'D JUST AGREED TO LETTING ME *ACTIVATE* THE *ANDROID.*
I'M NOT HAVING THIS DISCUSSION *AGAIN,* THOMAS.
BUT THE TORNADO COULD--
VEET
WHAT IS THAT?
FILE PROCESSING.
VICTOR UPLOADED A *VIDEO SIGNAL* OF SOME KIND.
HIS MIND'S GONE DORMANT, BUT HE'S STILL RUNNING A PROGRAM.
IT'S THE SECURITY FEED FROM THE U.S.S. MABUS. THE FILE'S BEEN BADLY CORRUPTED, BUT HE'S TRYING TO *REBUILD* IT.
13%
WHY?
TO SEE WHAT TRIGGERED THE MISSILES THAT STARTED THIS.

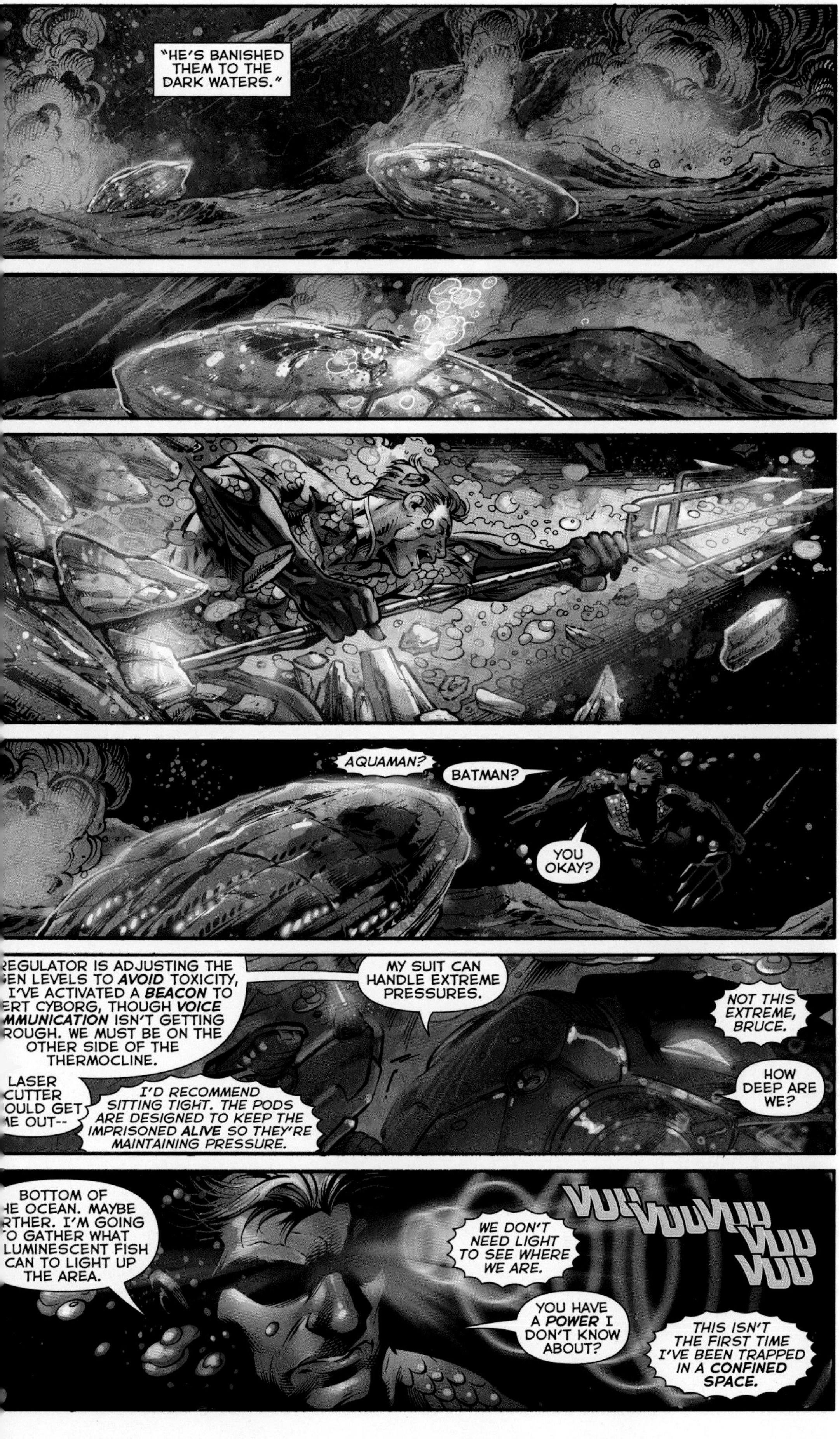
"HE'S BANISHED THEM TO THE DARK WATERS."
AQUAMAN?
BATMAN?
YOU OKAY?
REGULATOR IS ADJUSTING THE
GEN LEVELS TO AVOID TOXICITY,
I'VE ACTIVATED A BEACON TO
ERT CYBORG, THOUGH VOICE
MMUNICATION ISN'T GETTING
ROUGH. WE MUST BE ON THE
OTHER SIDE OF THE
THERMOCLINE.
MY SUIT CAN HANDLE EXTREME PRESSURES.
NOT THIS EXTREME, BRUCE.
LASER
CUTTER
OULD GET
E OUT--
I'D RECOMMEND SITTING TIGHT. THE PODS ARE DESIGNED TO KEEP THE IMPRISONED ALIVE SO THEY'RE MAINTAINING PRESSURE.
HOW DEEP ARE WE?
BOTTOM OF
HE OCEAN. MAYBE
RTHER. I'M GOING
O GATHER WHAT
LUMINESCENT FISH
CAN TO LIGHT UP
THE AREA.
WE DON'T NEED LIGHT TO SEE WHERE WE ARE.
VUU VUU VUU VUU VUU VUU
YOU HAVE A POWER I DON'T KNOW ABOUT?
THIS ISN'T THE FIRST TIME I'VE BEEN TRAPPED IN A CONFINED SPACE.

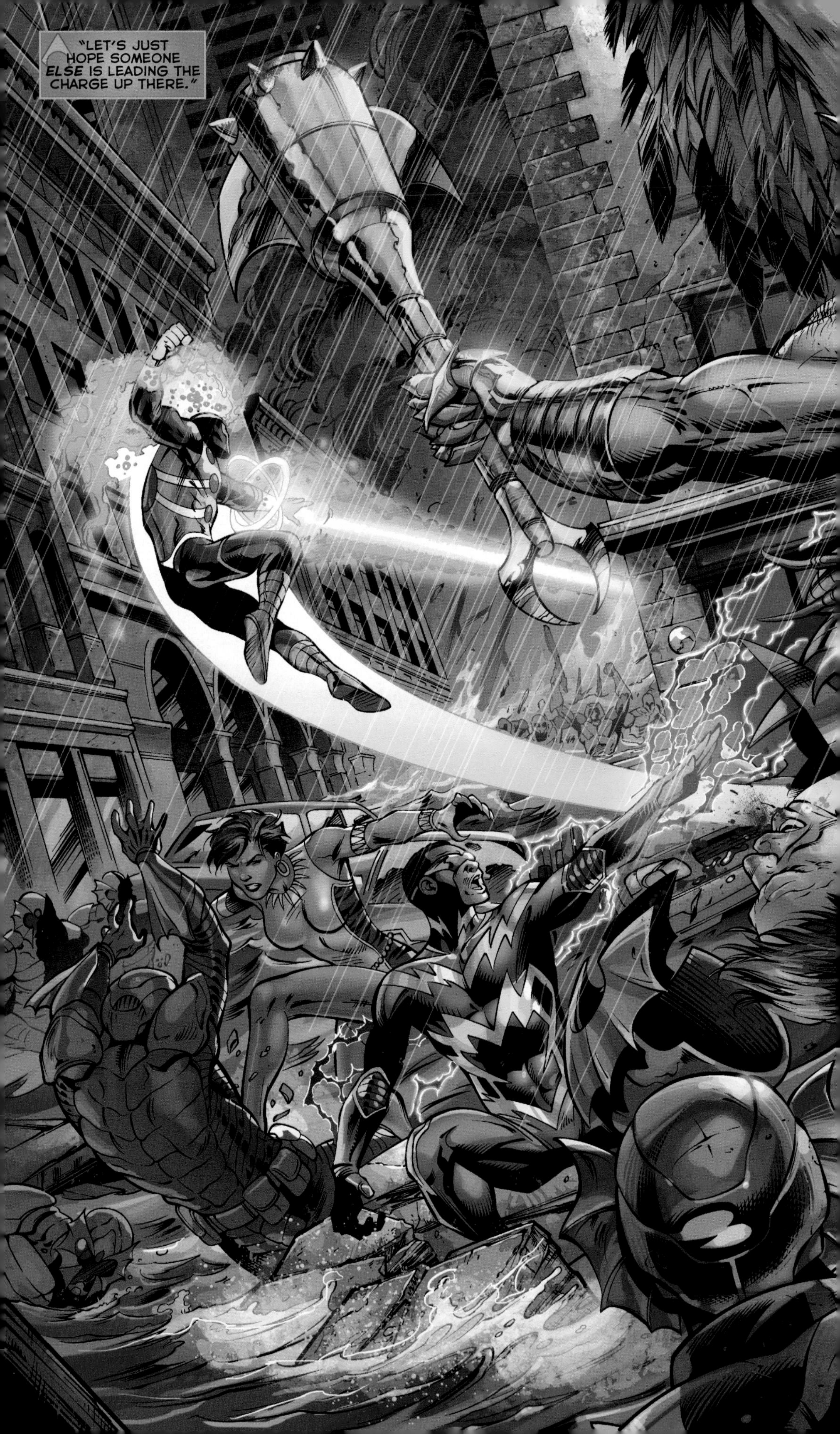
"LET'S JUST HOPE SOMEONE ELSE IS LEADING THE CHARGE UP THERE."

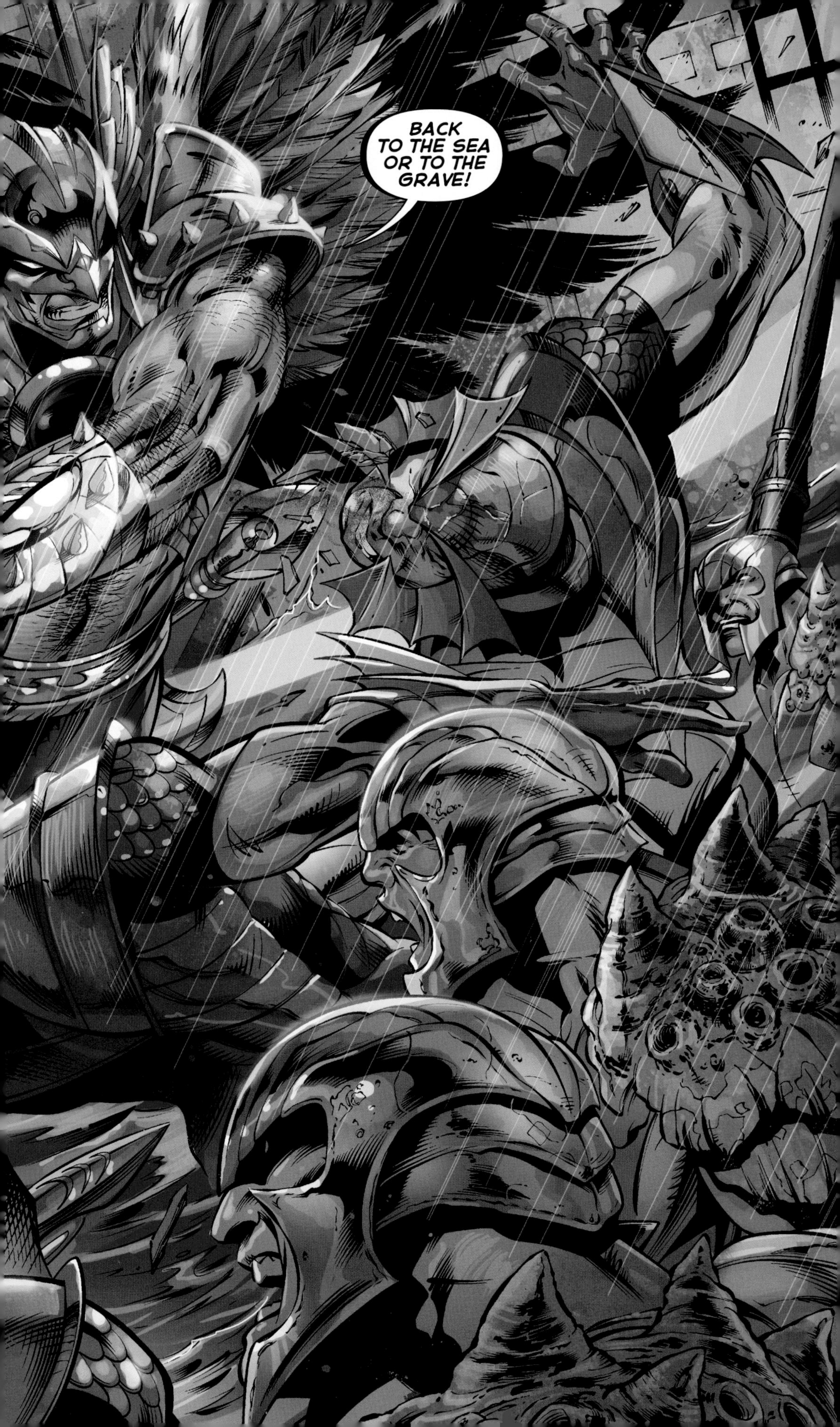
BACK TO THE SEA OR TO THE GRAVE!

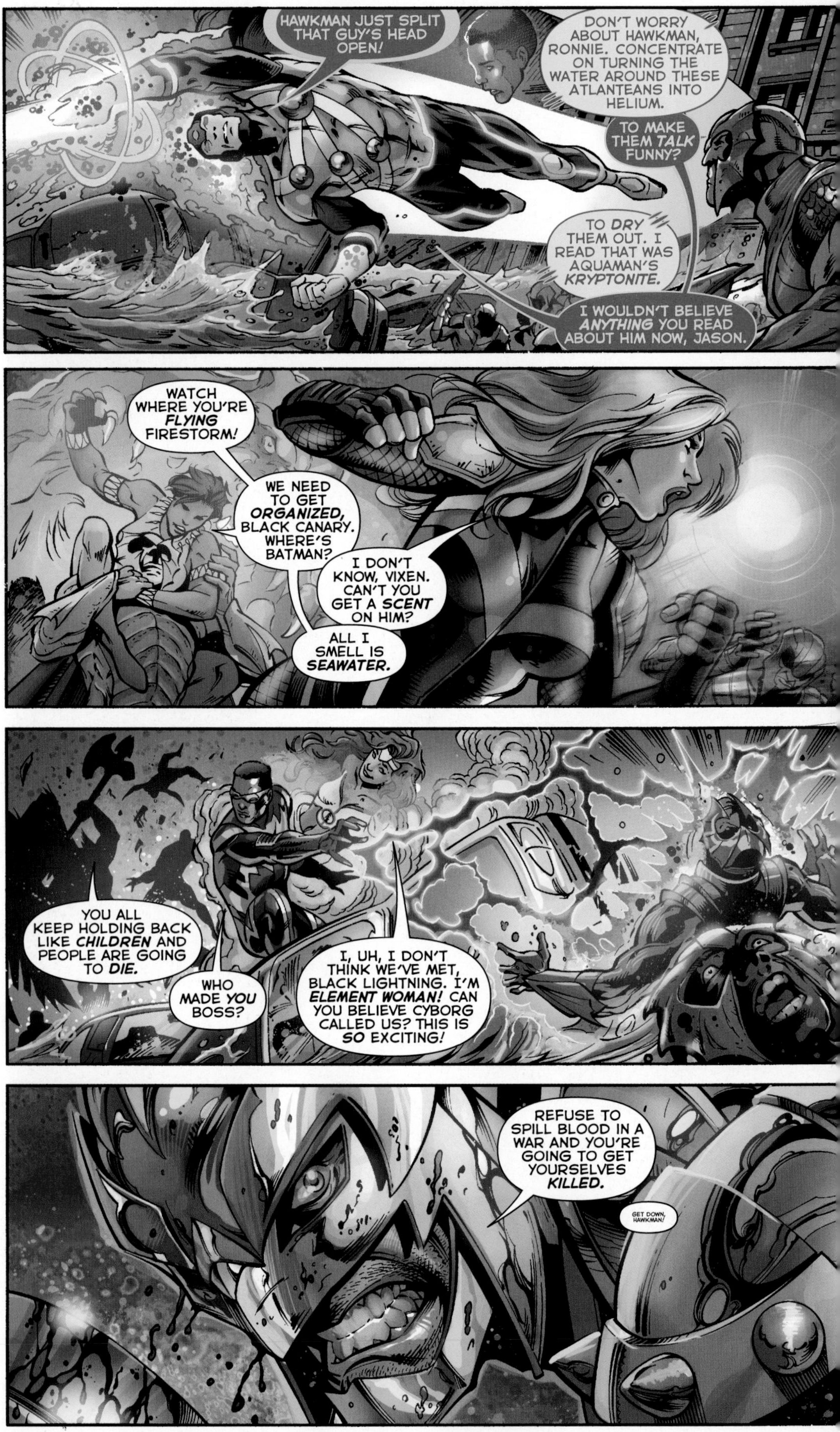
HAWKMAN JUST SPLIT THAT GUY'S HEAD OPEN!
DON'T WORRY ABOUT HAWKMAN, RONNIE. CONCENTRATE ON TURNING THE WATER AROUND THESE ATLANTEANS INTO HELIUM.
TO MAKE THEM *TALK* FUNNY?
TO *DRY* THEM OUT. I READ THAT WAS AQUAMAN'S *KRYPTONITE.*
I WOULDN'T BELIEVE *ANYTHING* YOU READ ABOUT HIM NOW, JASON.
WATCH WHERE YOU'RE *FLYING* FIRESTORM!
WE NEED TO GET *ORGANIZED,* BLACK CANARY. WHERE'S BATMAN?
I DON'T KNOW, VIXEN. CAN'T YOU GET A *SCENT* ON HIM?
ALL I SMELL IS *SEAWATER.*
YOU ALL KEEP HOLDING BACK LIKE *CHILDREN* AND PEOPLE ARE GOING TO *DIE.*
WHO MADE *YOU* BOSS?
I, UH, I DON'T THINK WE'VE MET, BLACK LIGHTNING. I'M *ELEMENT WOMAN!* CAN YOU BELIEVE CYBORG CALLED US? THIS IS *SO* EXCITING!
REFUSE TO SPILL BLOOD IN A WAR AND YOU'RE GOING TO GET YOURSELVES *KILLED.*
GET DOWN, HAWKMAN!

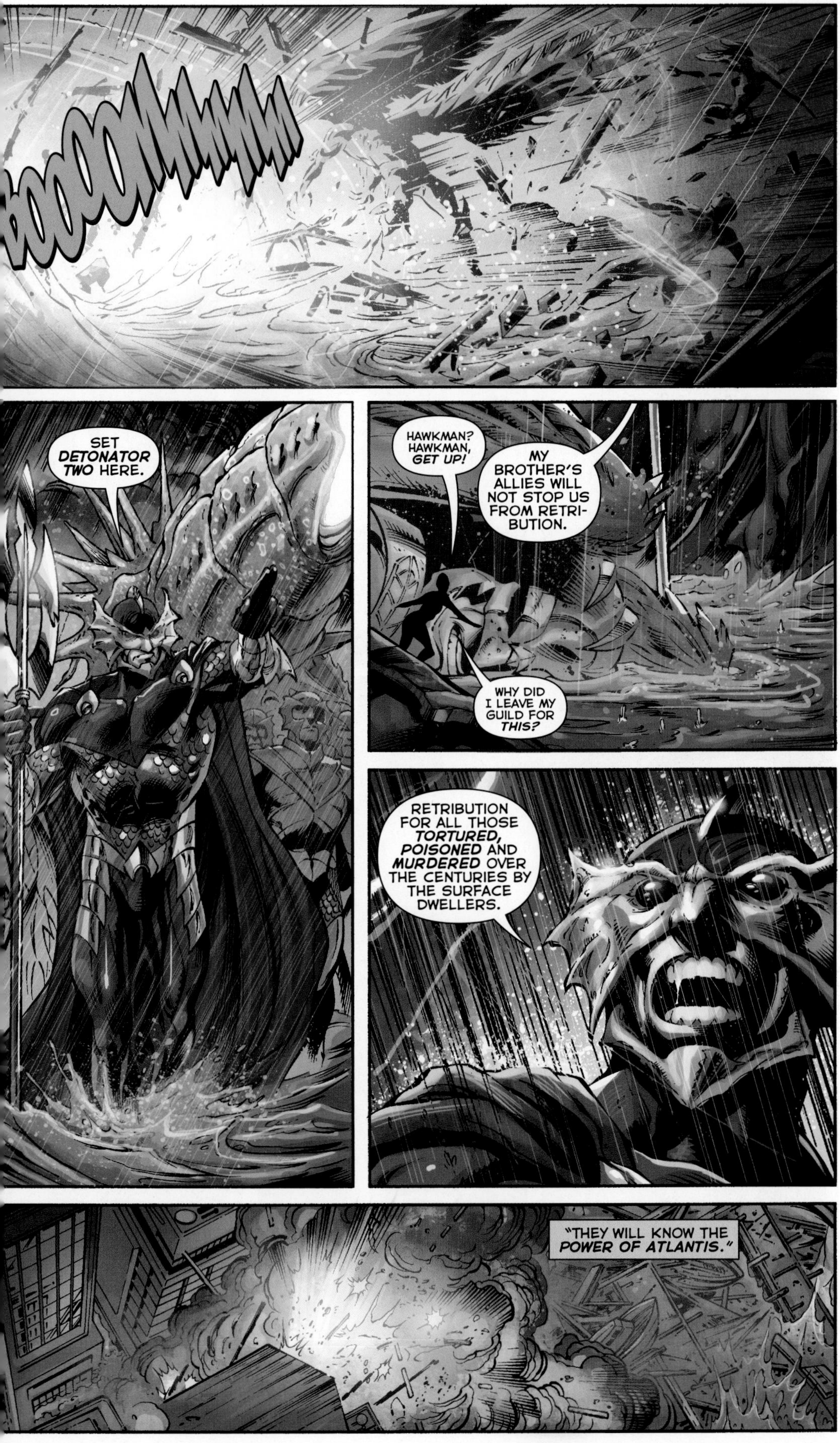
BOOOMMMMM
SET DETONATOR TWO HERE.
HAWKMAN? HAWKMAN, GET UP!
MY BROTHER'S ALLIES WILL NOT STOP US FROM RETRIBUTION.
WHY DID I LEAVE MY GUILD FOR THIS?
RETRIBUTION FOR ALL THOSE TORTURED, POISONED AND MURDERED OVER THE CENTURIES BY THE SURFACE DWELLERS.
"THEY WILL KNOW THE POWER OF ATLANTIS."

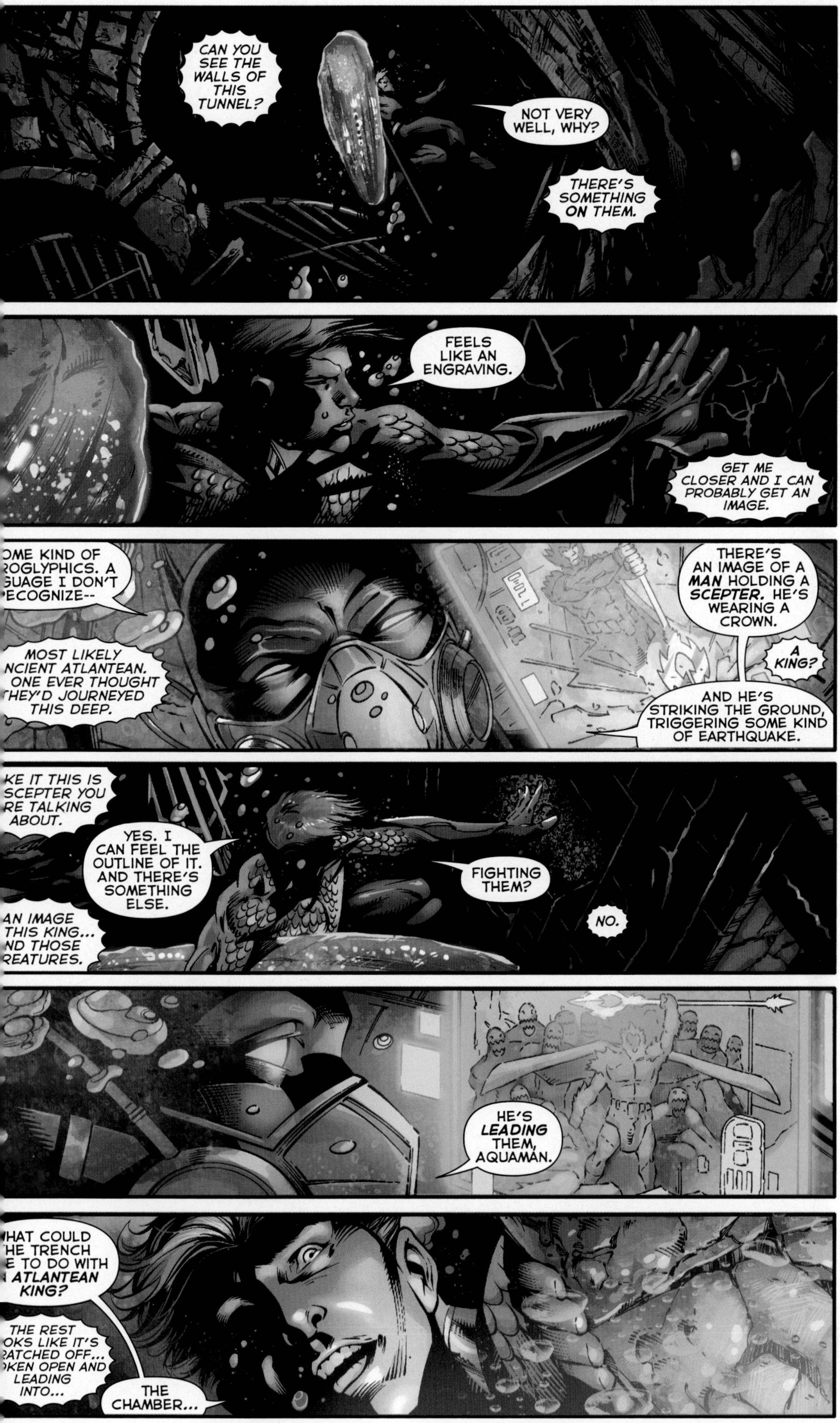
CAN YOU SEE THE WALLS OF THIS TUNNEL?
NOT VERY WELL, WHY?
THERE'S SOMETHING ON THEM.
FEELS LIKE AN ENGRAVING.
GET ME CLOSER AND I CAN PROBABLY GET AN IMAGE.
OME KIND OF ROGLYPHICS. A GUAGE I DON'T ECOGNIZE--
MOST LIKELY NCIENT ATLANTEAN. ONE EVER THOUGHT THEY'D JOURNEYED THIS DEEP.
THERE'S AN IMAGE OF A MAN HOLDING A SCEPTER. HE'S WEARING A CROWN.
A KING?
AND HE'S STRIKING THE GROUND, TRIGGERING SOME KIND OF EARTHQUAKE.
KE IT THIS IS SCEPTER YOU RE TALKING ABOUT.
YES. I CAN FEEL THE OUTLINE OF IT. AND THERE'S SOMETHING ELSE.
AN IMAGE THIS KING... ND THOSE REATURES.
FIGHTING THEM?
NO.
HE'S LEADING THEM, AQUAMAN.
HAT COULD HE TRENCH E TO DO WITH ATLANTEAN KING?
THE REST OKS LIKE IT'S ATCHED OFF... OKEN OPEN AND LEADING INTO...
THE CHAMBER...

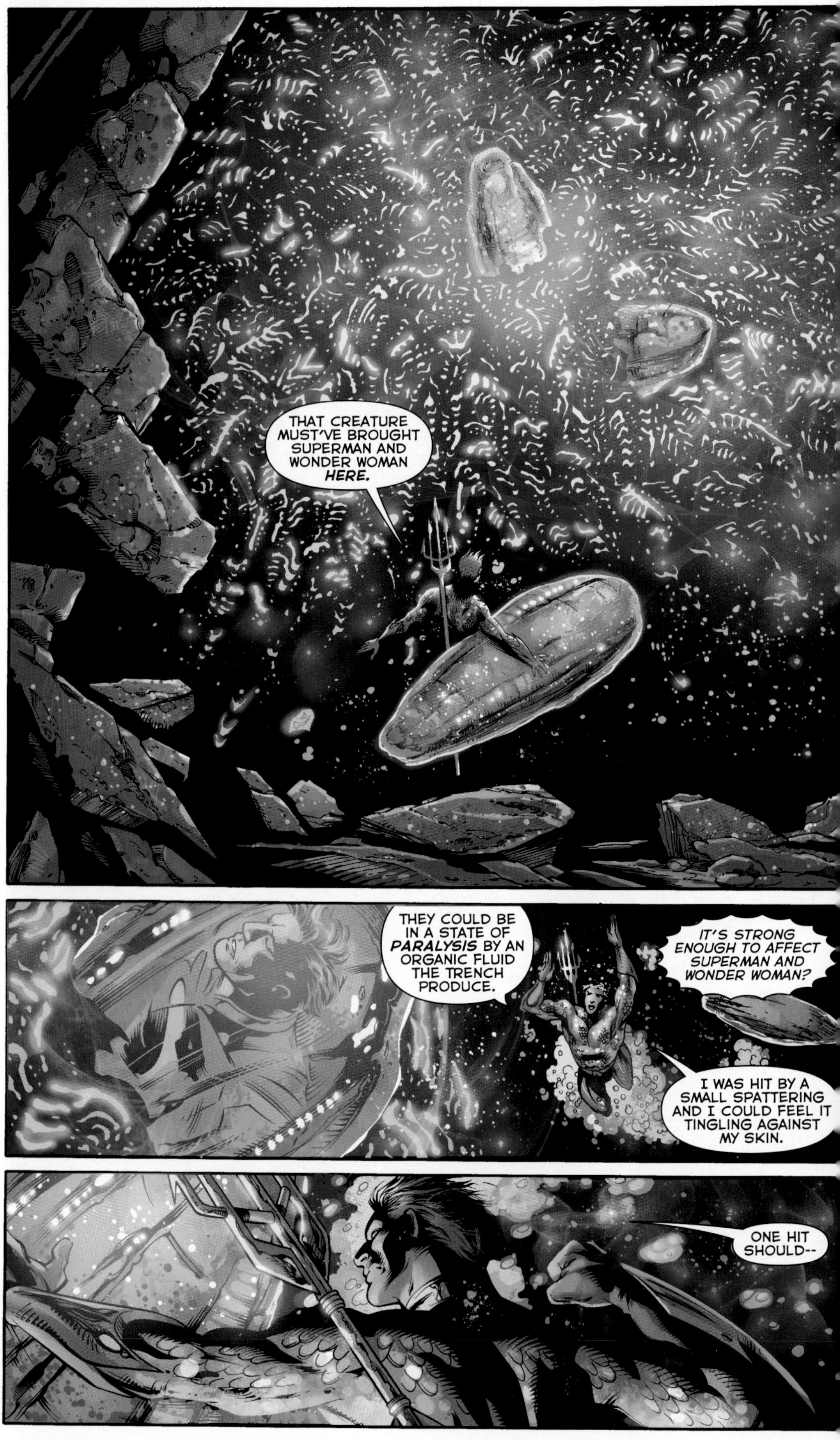
THAT CREATURE MUST'VE BROUGHT SUPERMAN AND WONDER WOMAN *HERE.*
THEY COULD BE IN A STATE OF *PARALYSIS* BY AN ORGANIC FLUID THE TRENCH PRODUCE.
IT'S STRONG ENOUGH TO AFFECT SUPERMAN AND WONDER WOMAN?
I WAS HIT BY A SMALL SPATTERING AND I COULD FEEL IT TINGLING AGAINST MY SKIN.
ONE HIT SHOULD--

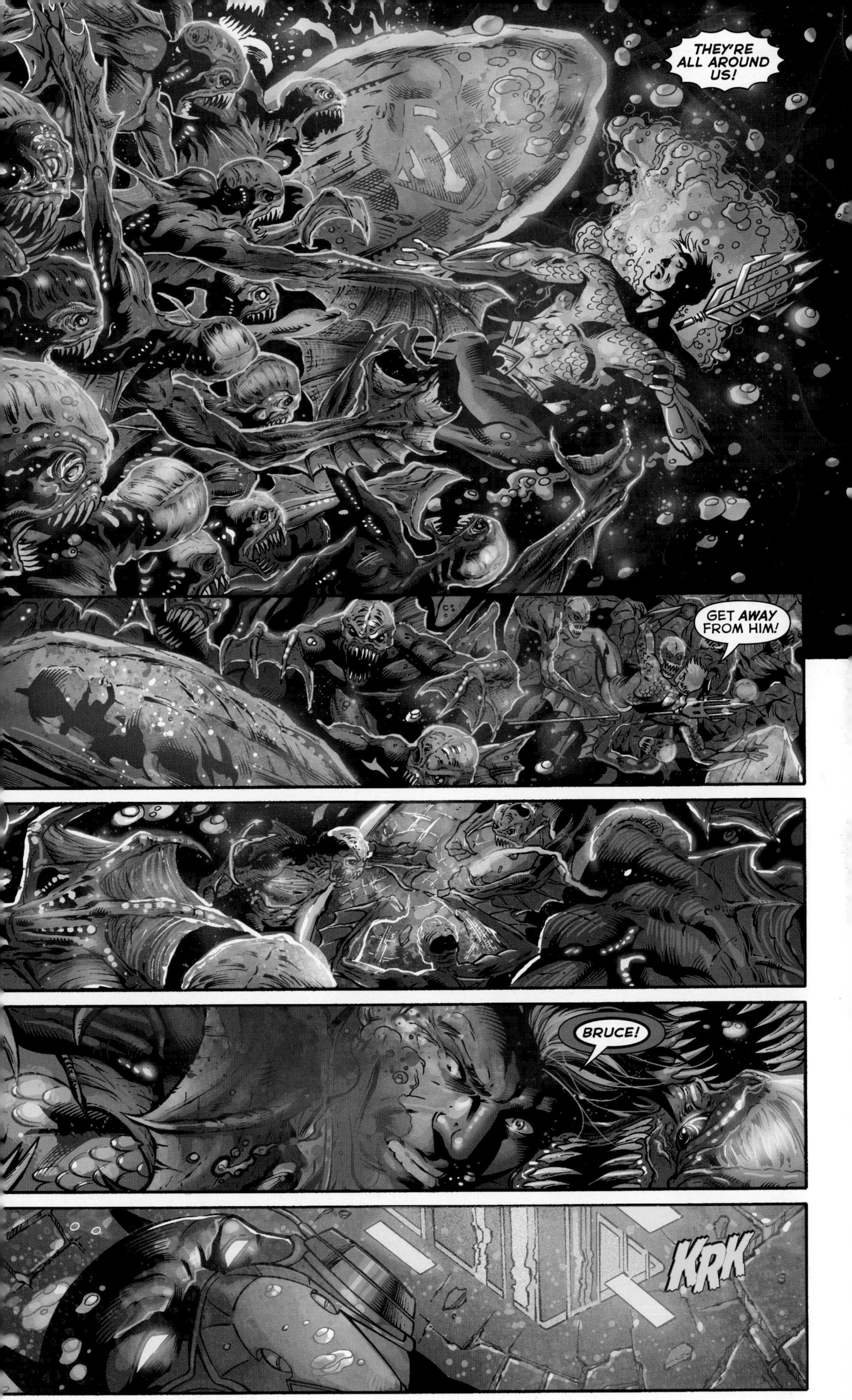
THEY'RE ALL AROUND US!
GET AWAY FROM HIM!
BRUCE!
KRK

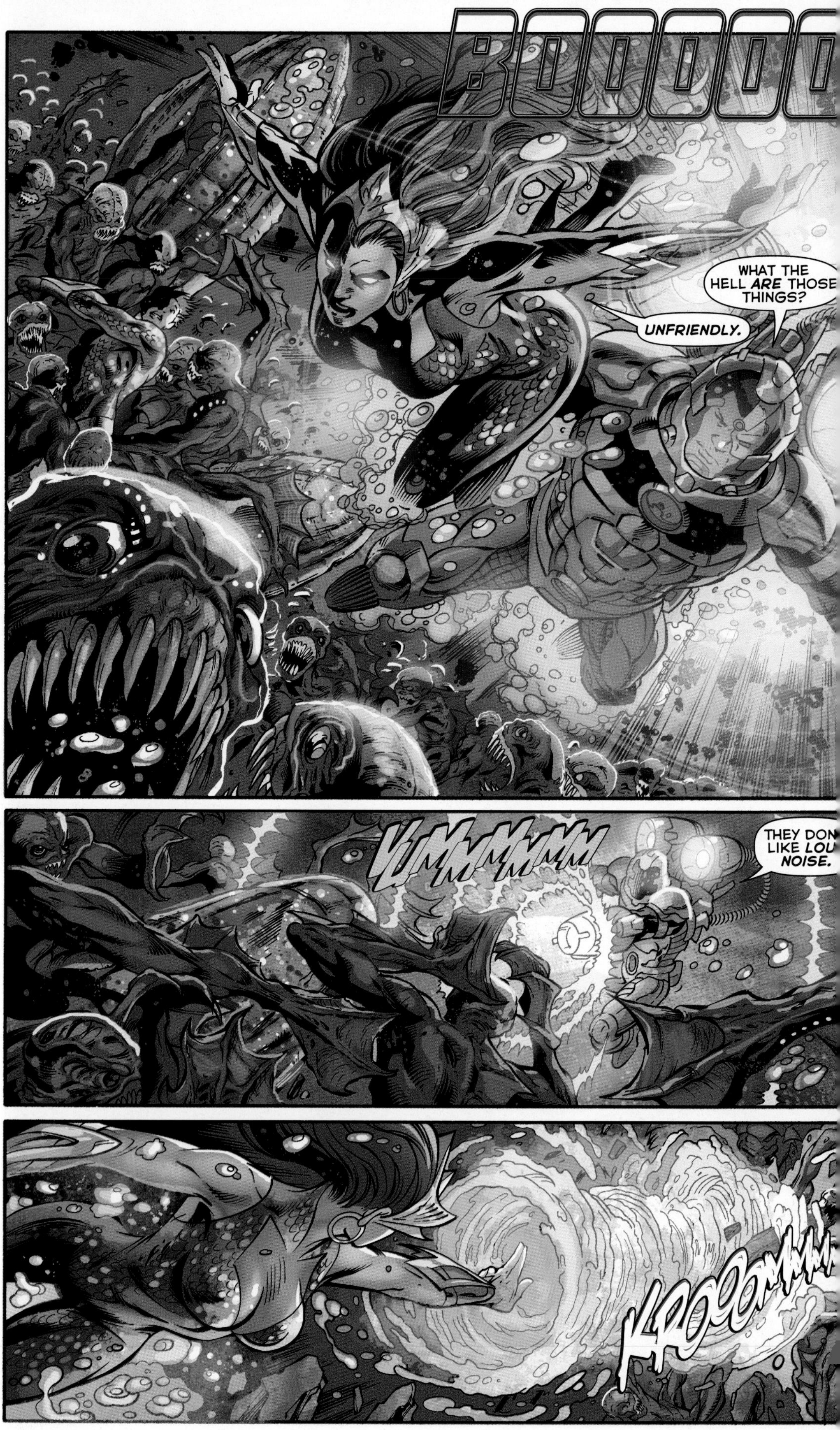
BOOOOOO
WHAT THE HELL ARE THOSE THINGS?
UNFRIENDLY.
VUMMMMMM
THEY DON
LIKE LOU
NOISE.
KROOOMMM

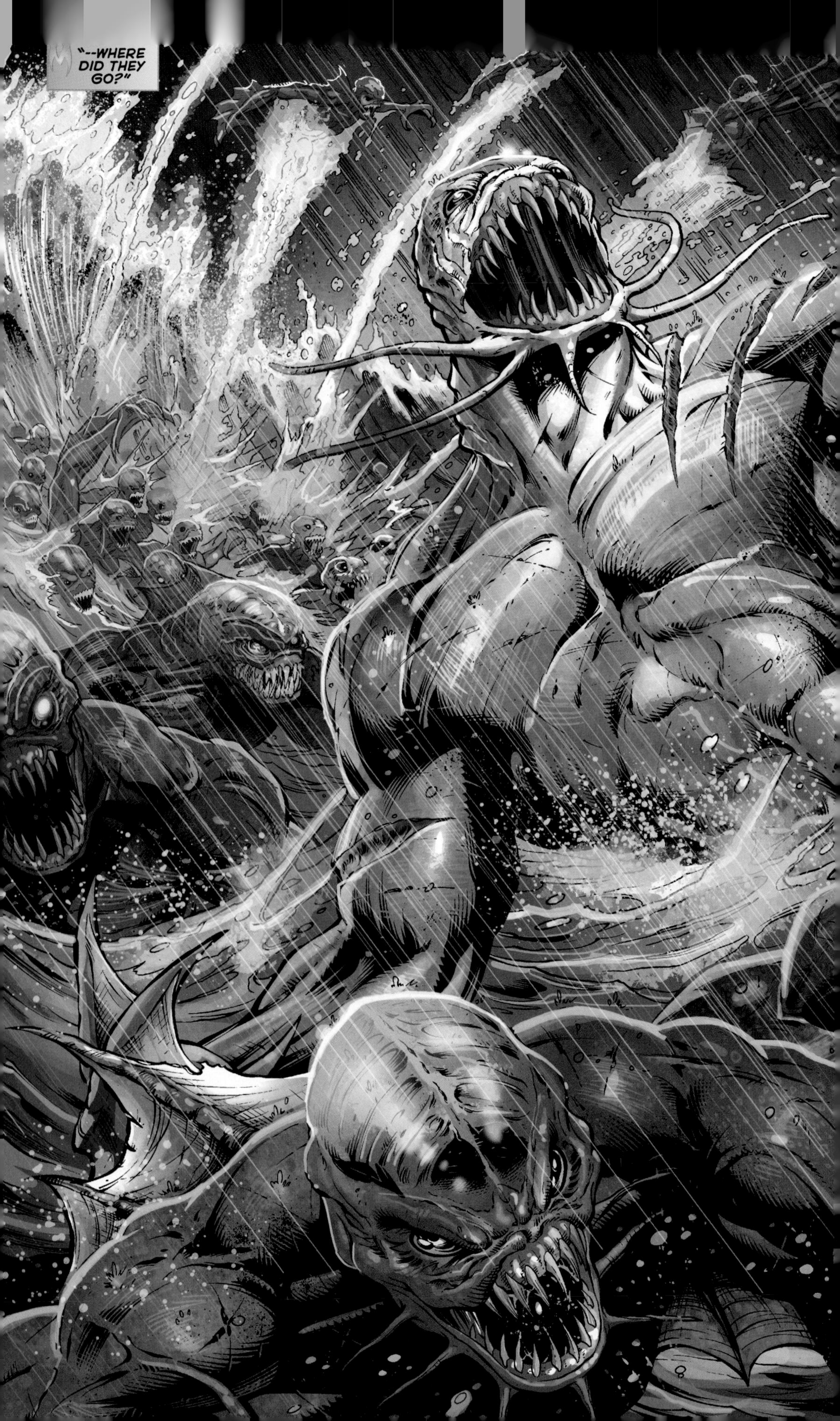
"--WHERE DID THEY GO?"

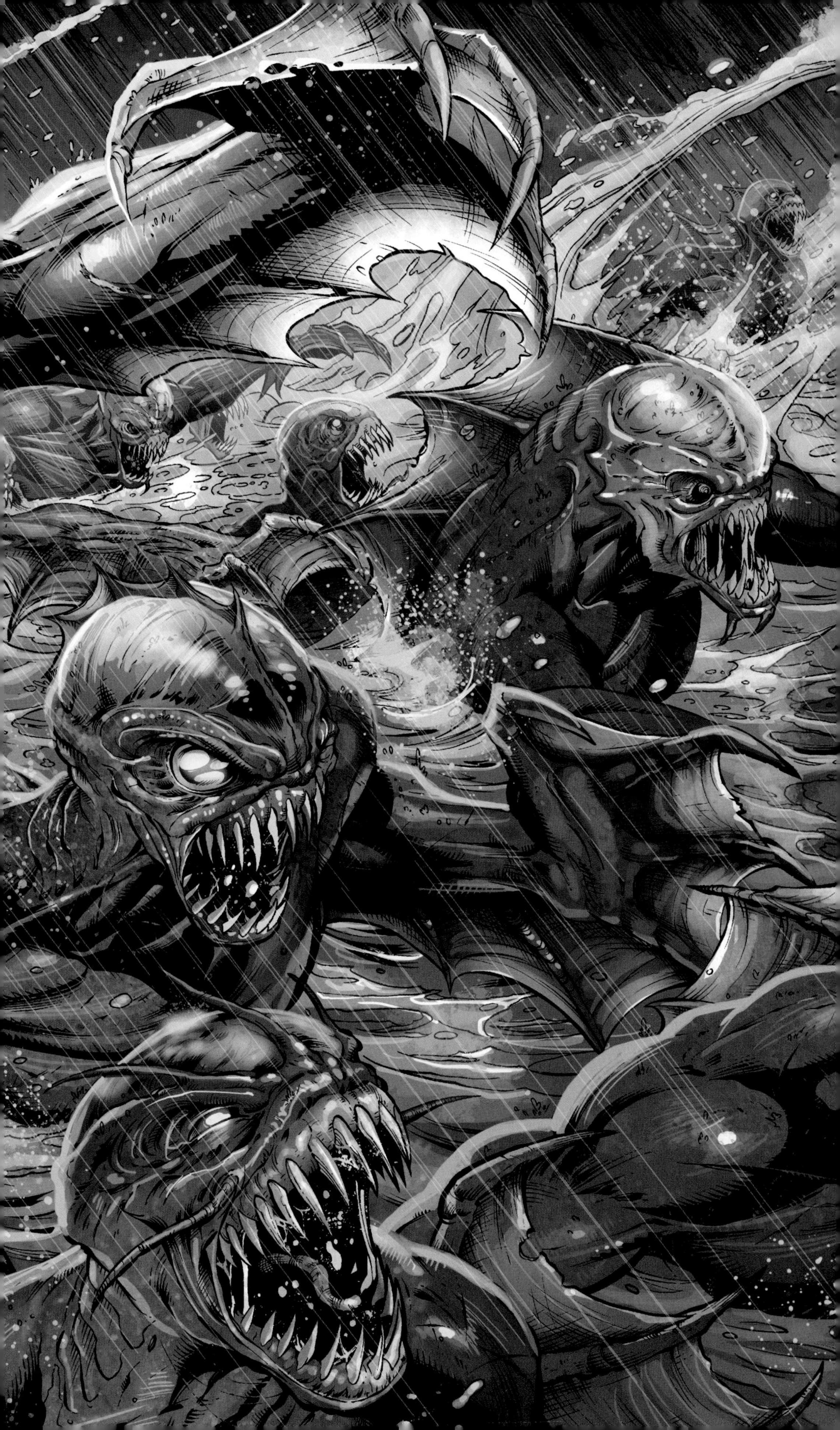

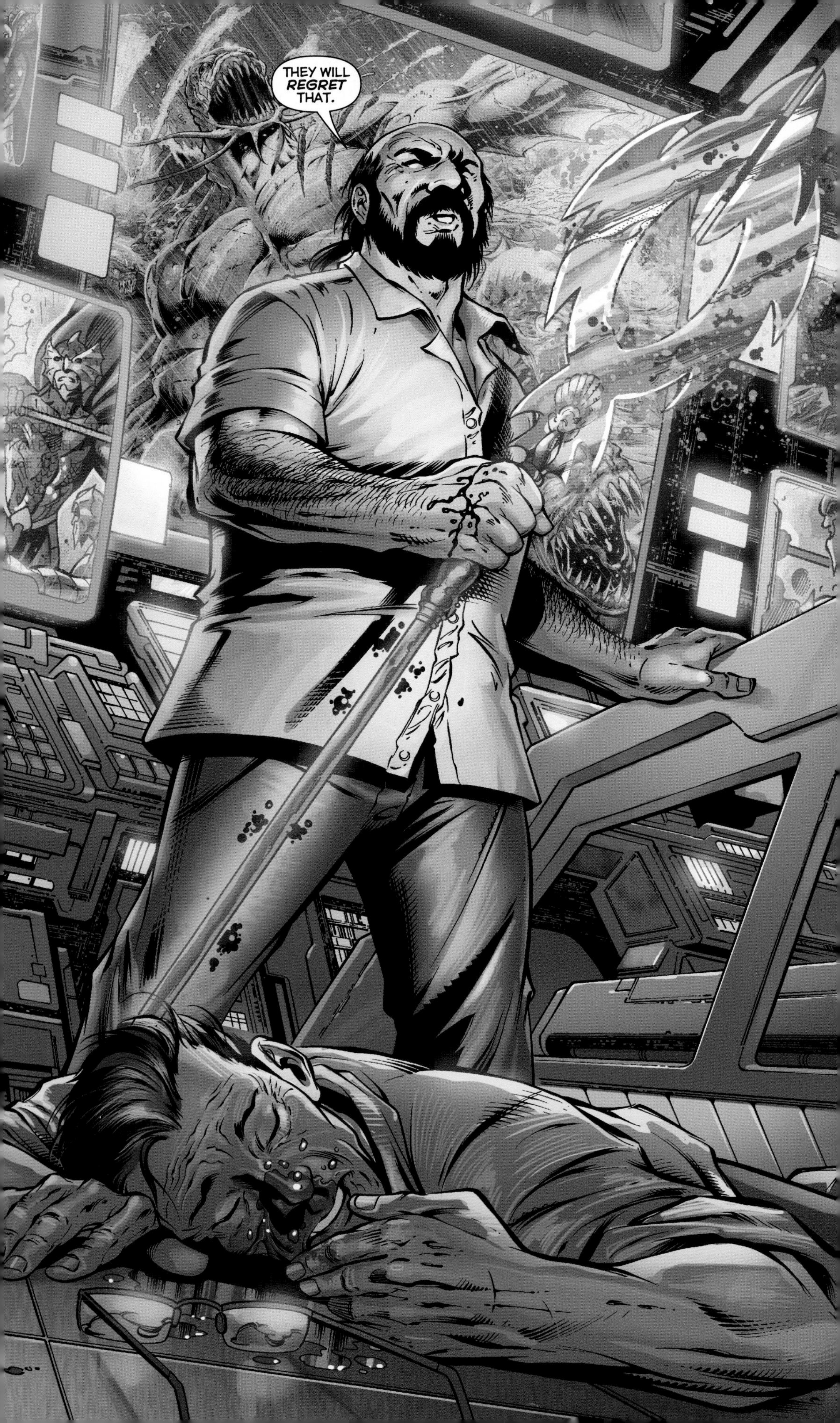
THEY WILL REGRET THAT.

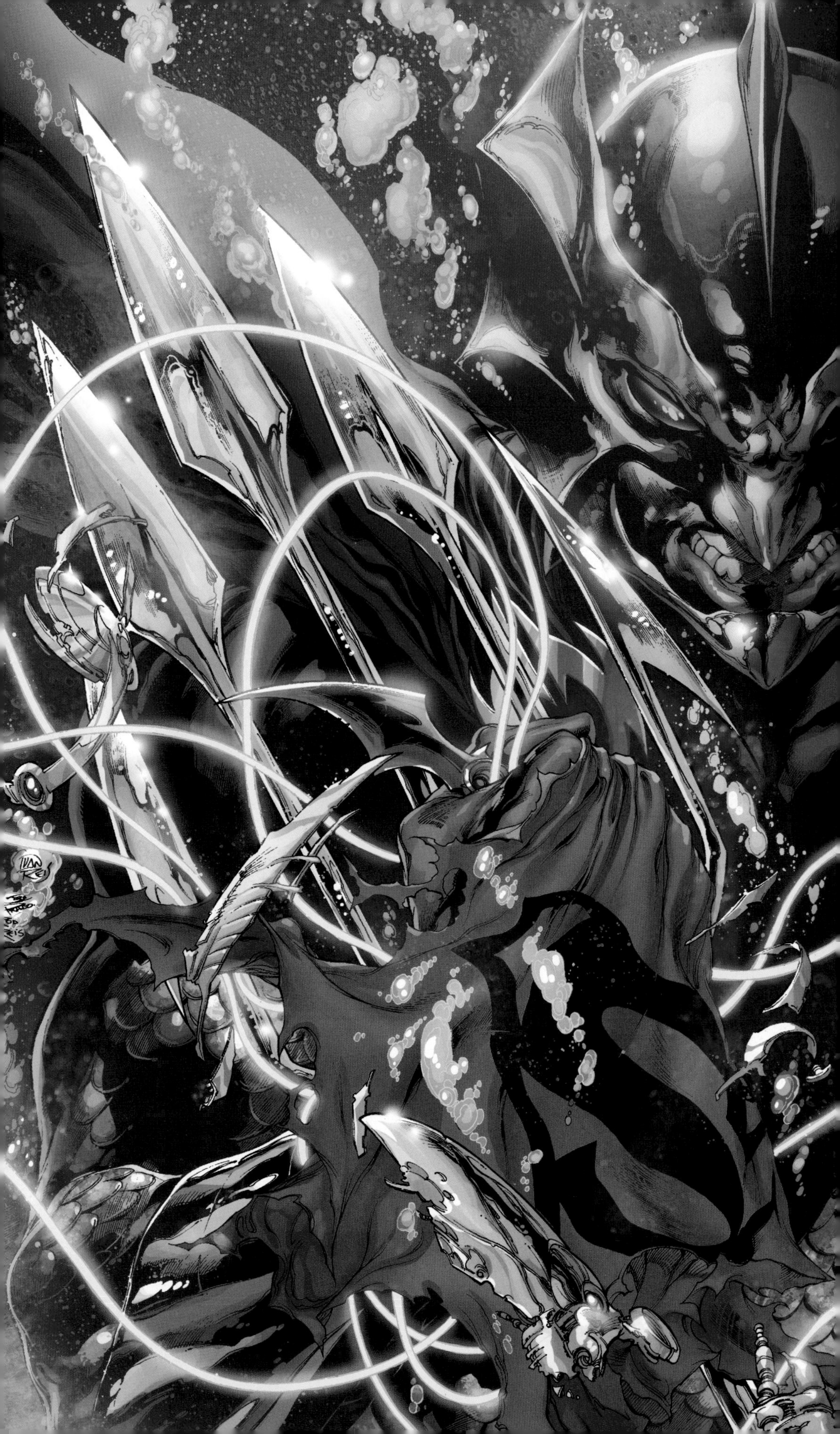

GEOFF JOHNS writer **IVAN REIS & PAUL PELLETIER** pencillers **JOE PRADO, OCLAIR ALBERT & SEAN PARSONS** inkers
cover by **IVAN REIS, JOE PRADO & ROD REIS**

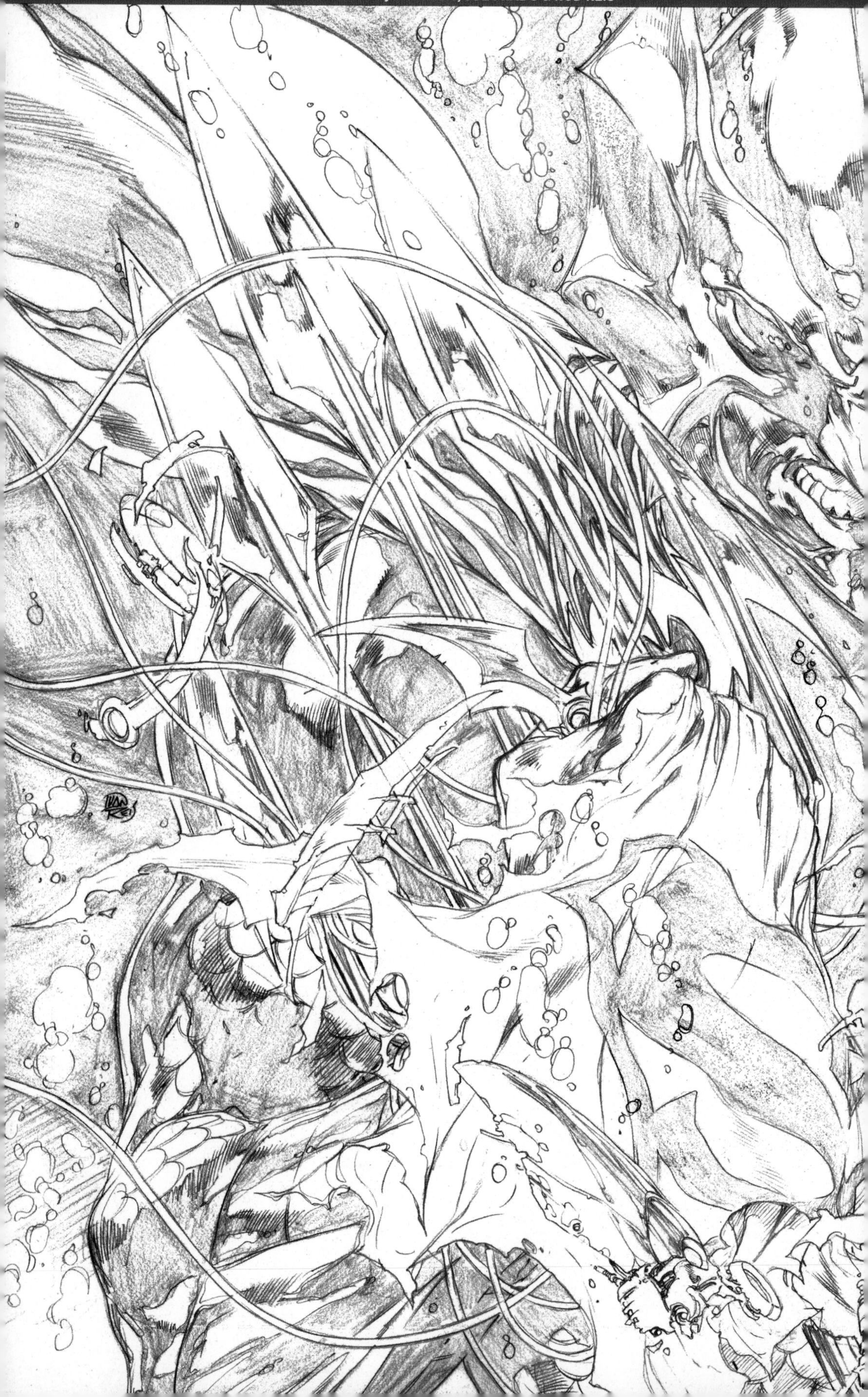

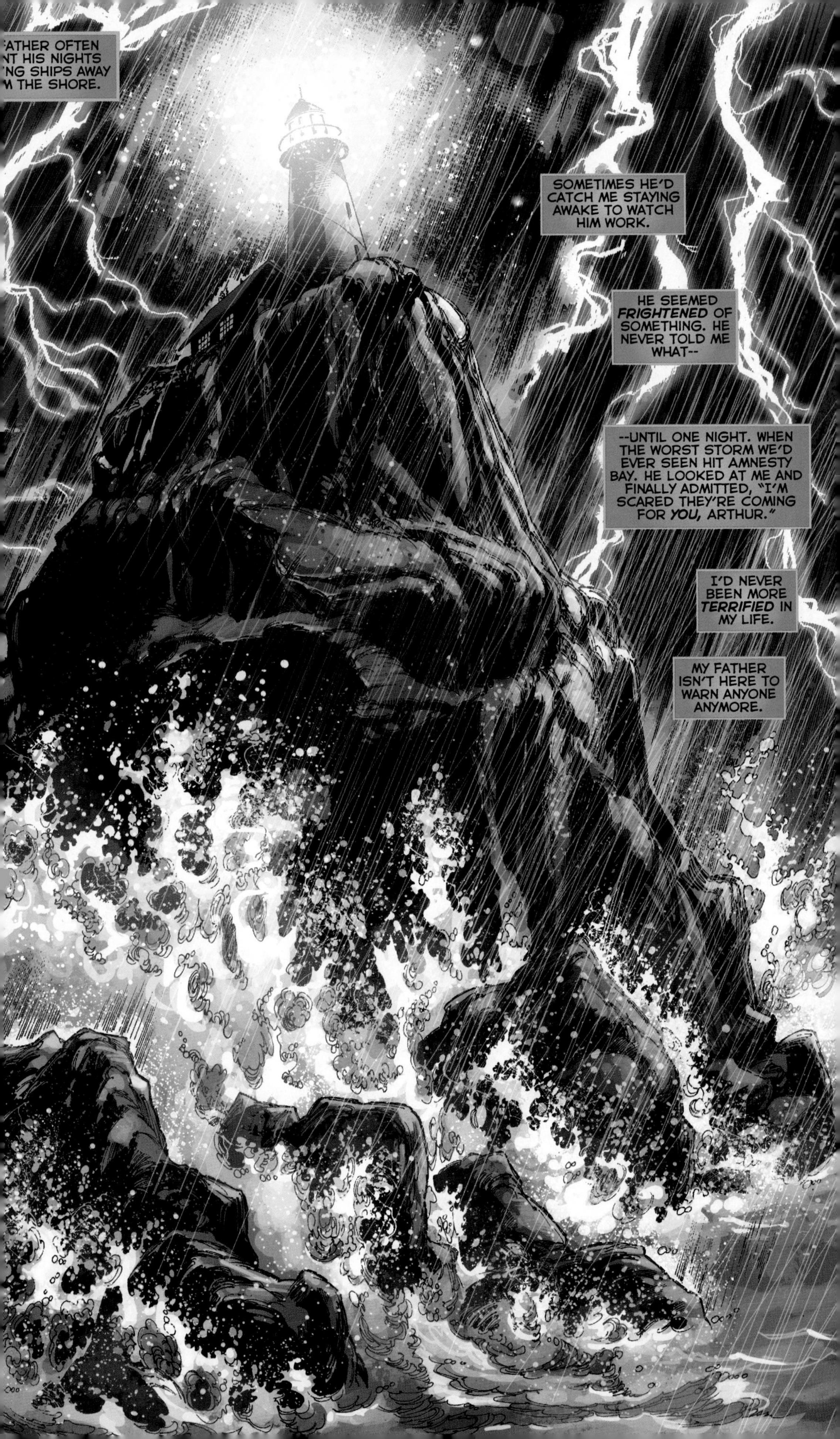
FATHER OFTEN NT HIS NIGHTS NG SHIPS AWAY M THE SHORE.
SOMETIMES HE'D CATCH ME STAYING AWAKE TO WATCH HIM WORK.
HE SEEMED *FRIGHTENED* OF SOMETHING. HE NEVER TOLD ME WHAT--
--UNTIL ONE NIGHT. WHEN THE WORST STORM WE'D EVER SEEN HIT AMNESTY BAY. HE LOOKED AT ME AND FINALLY ADMITTED, "I'M SCARED THEY'RE COMING FOR *YOU,* ARTHUR."
I'D NEVER BEEN MORE *TERRIFIED* IN MY LIFE.
MY FATHER ISN'T HERE TO WARN ANYONE ANYMORE.

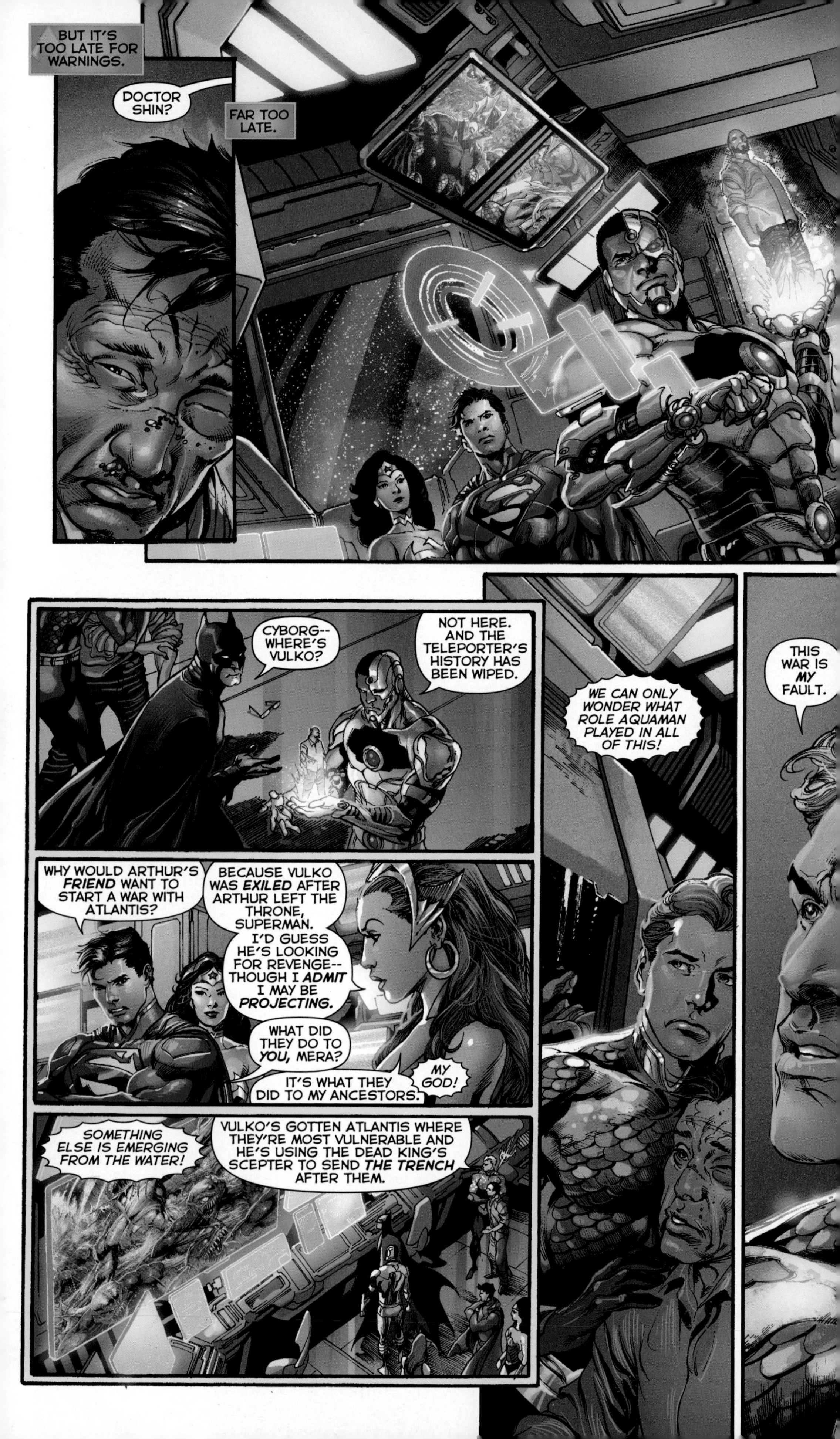

BUT IT'S TOO LATE FOR WARNINGS.
DOCTOR SHIN?
FAR TOO LATE.
CYBORG-- WHERE'S VULKO?
NOT HERE. AND THE TELEPORTER'S HISTORY HAS BEEN WIPED.
WHY WOULD ARTHUR'S FRIEND WANT TO START A WAR WITH ATLANTIS?
BECAUSE VULKO WAS EXILED AFTER ARTHUR LEFT THE THRONE, SUPERMAN.
I'D GUESS HE'S LOOKING FOR REVENGE-- THOUGH I ADMIT I MAY BE PROJECTING.
WHAT DID THEY DO TO YOU, MERA?
IT'S WHAT THEY DID TO MY ANCESTORS.
MY GOD!
SOMETHING ELSE IS EMERGING FROM THE WATER!
VULKO'S GOTTEN ATLANTIS WHERE THEY'RE MOST VULNERABLE AND HE'S USING THE DEAD KING'S SCEPTER TO SEND THE TRENCH AFTER THEM.
WE CAN ONLY WONDER WHAT ROLE AQUAMAN PLAYED IN ALL OF THIS!
THIS WAR IS MY FAULT.

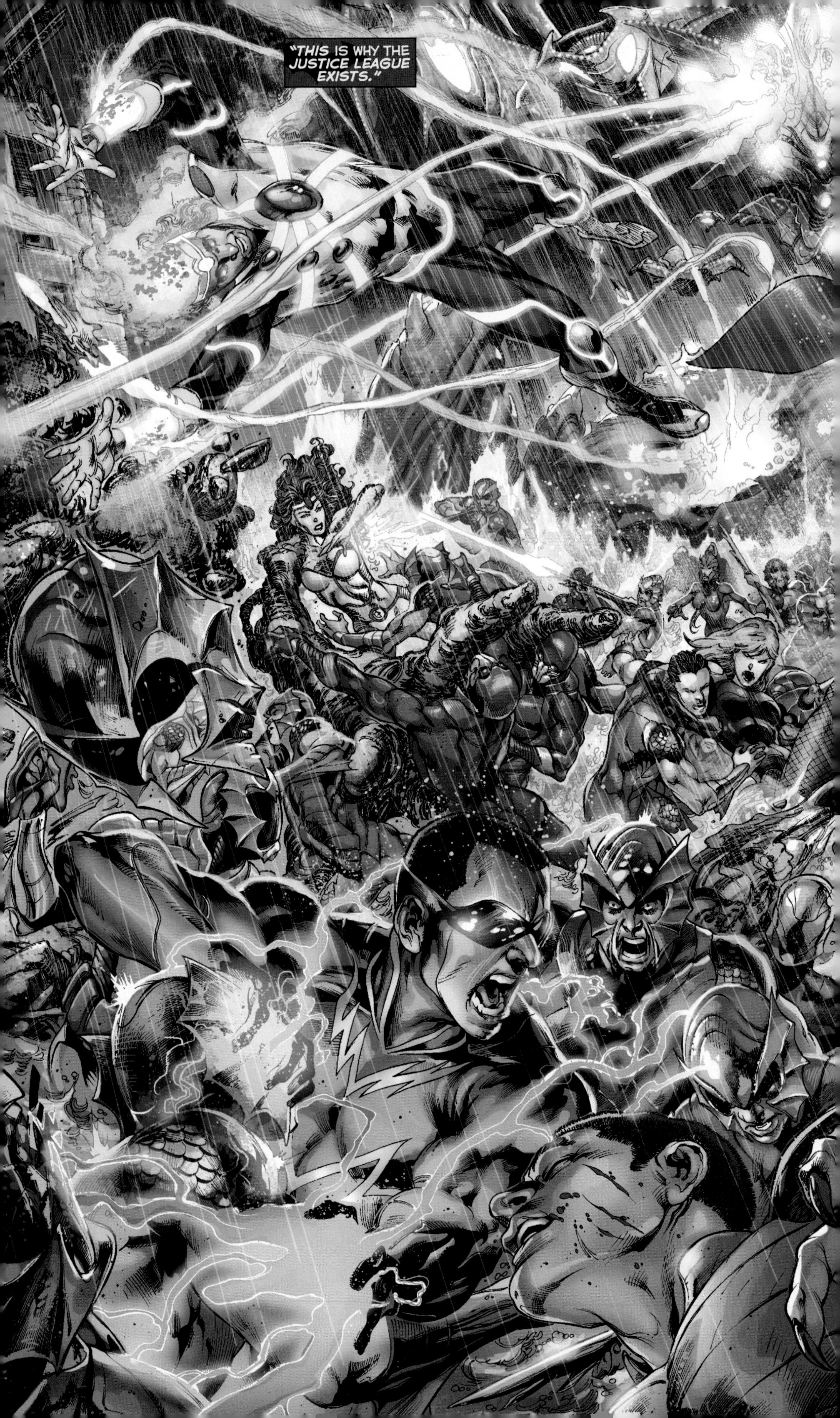
"THIS IS WHY THE JUSTICE LEAGUE EXISTS."

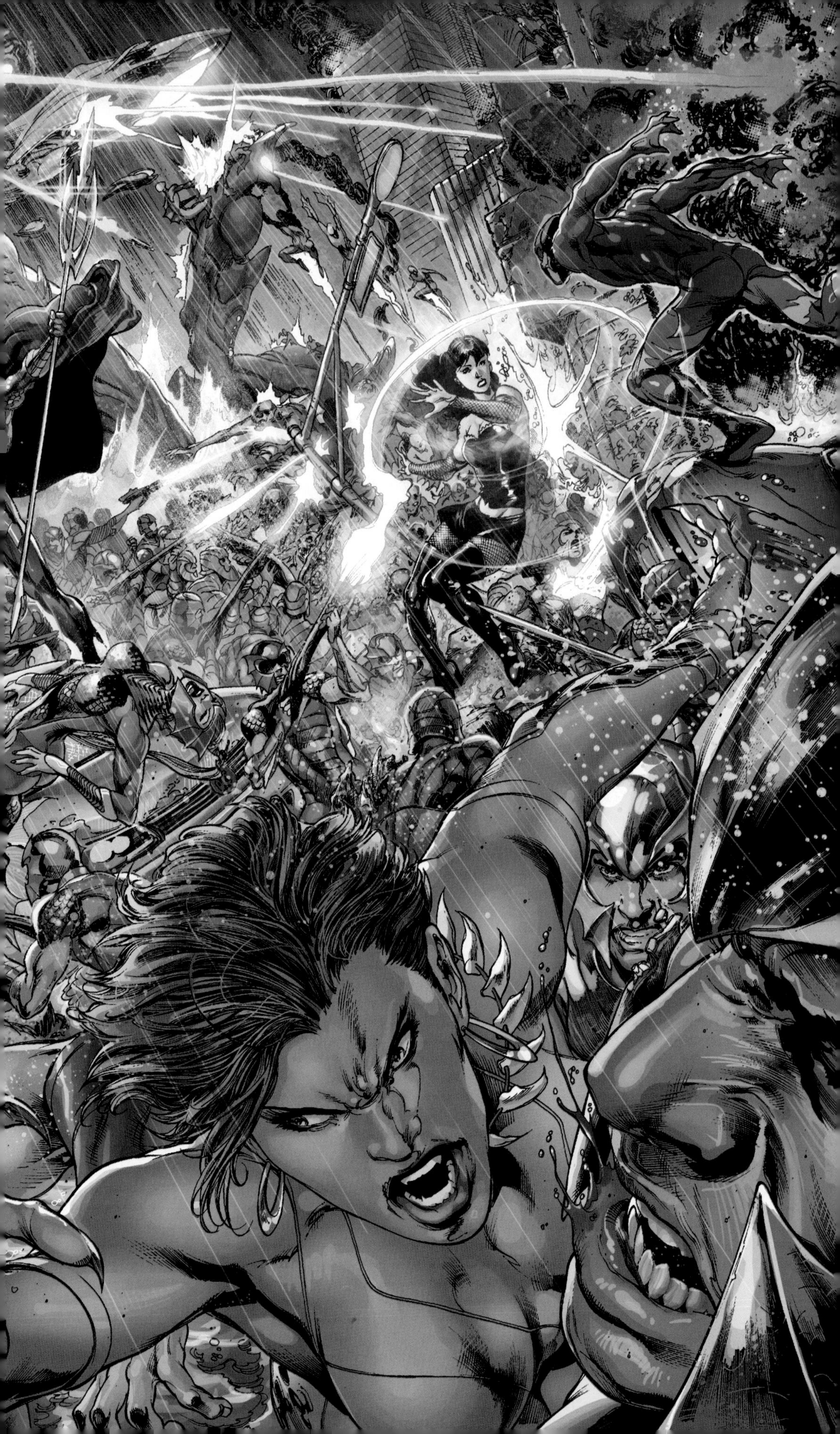

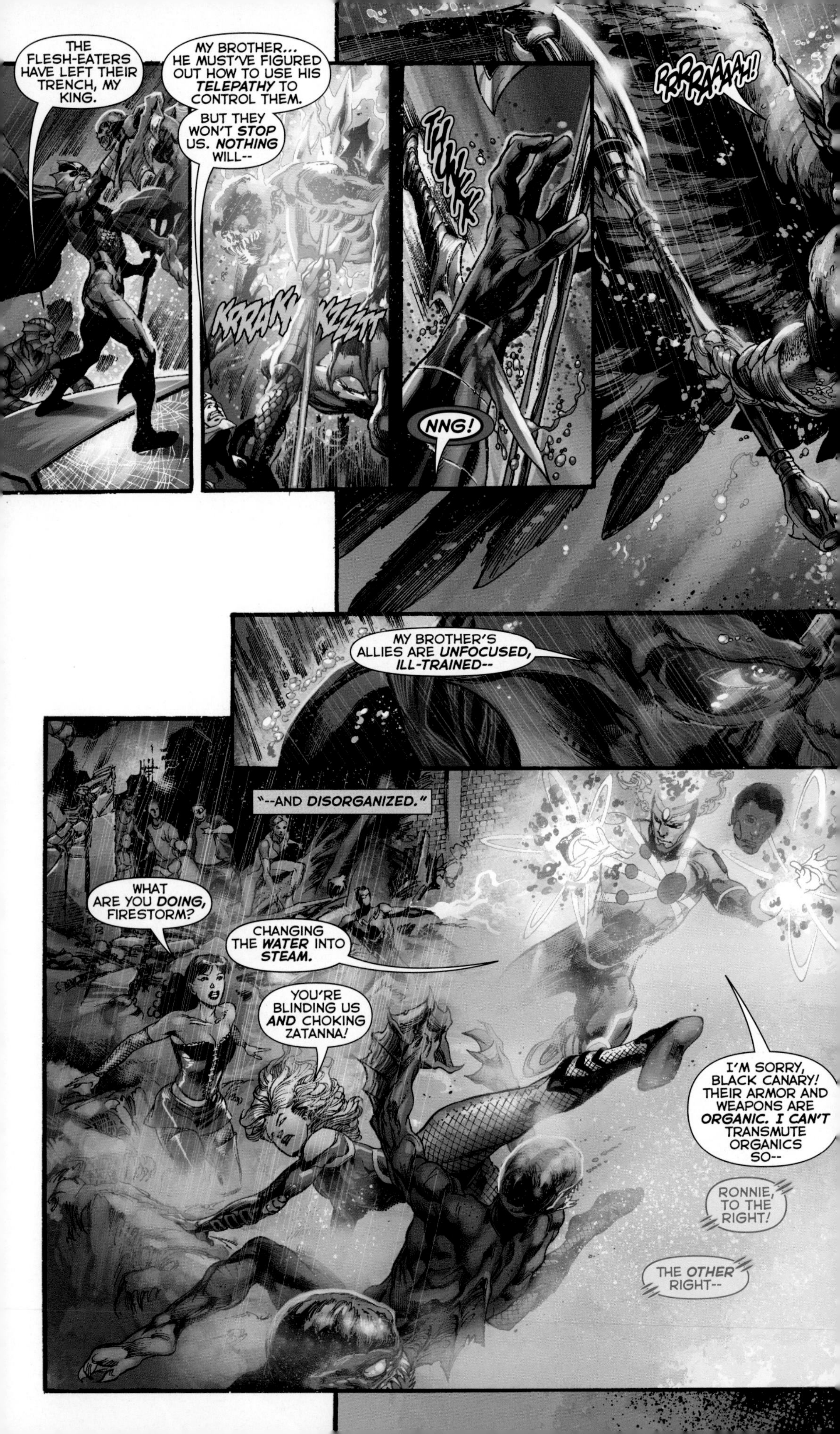

THE FLESH-EATERS HAVE LEFT THEIR TRENCH, MY KING.
MY BROTHER... HE MUST'VE FIGURED OUT HOW TO USE HIS TELEPATHY TO CONTROL THEM.
BUT THEY WON'T STOP US. NOTHING WILL--
KRRAK!
KZZZTT
THUNK
NNG!
RRRRAAAAH!
MY BROTHER'S ALLIES ARE UNFOCUSED, ILL-TRAINED--
"--AND DISORGANIZED."
WHAT ARE YOU DOING, FIRESTORM?
CHANGING THE WATER INTO STEAM.
YOU'RE BLINDING US AND CHOKING ZATANNA!
I'M SORRY, BLACK CANARY! THEIR ARMOR AND WEAPONS ARE ORGANIC. I CAN'T TRANSMUTE ORGANICS SO--
RONNIE, TO THE RIGHT!
THE OTHER RIGHT--

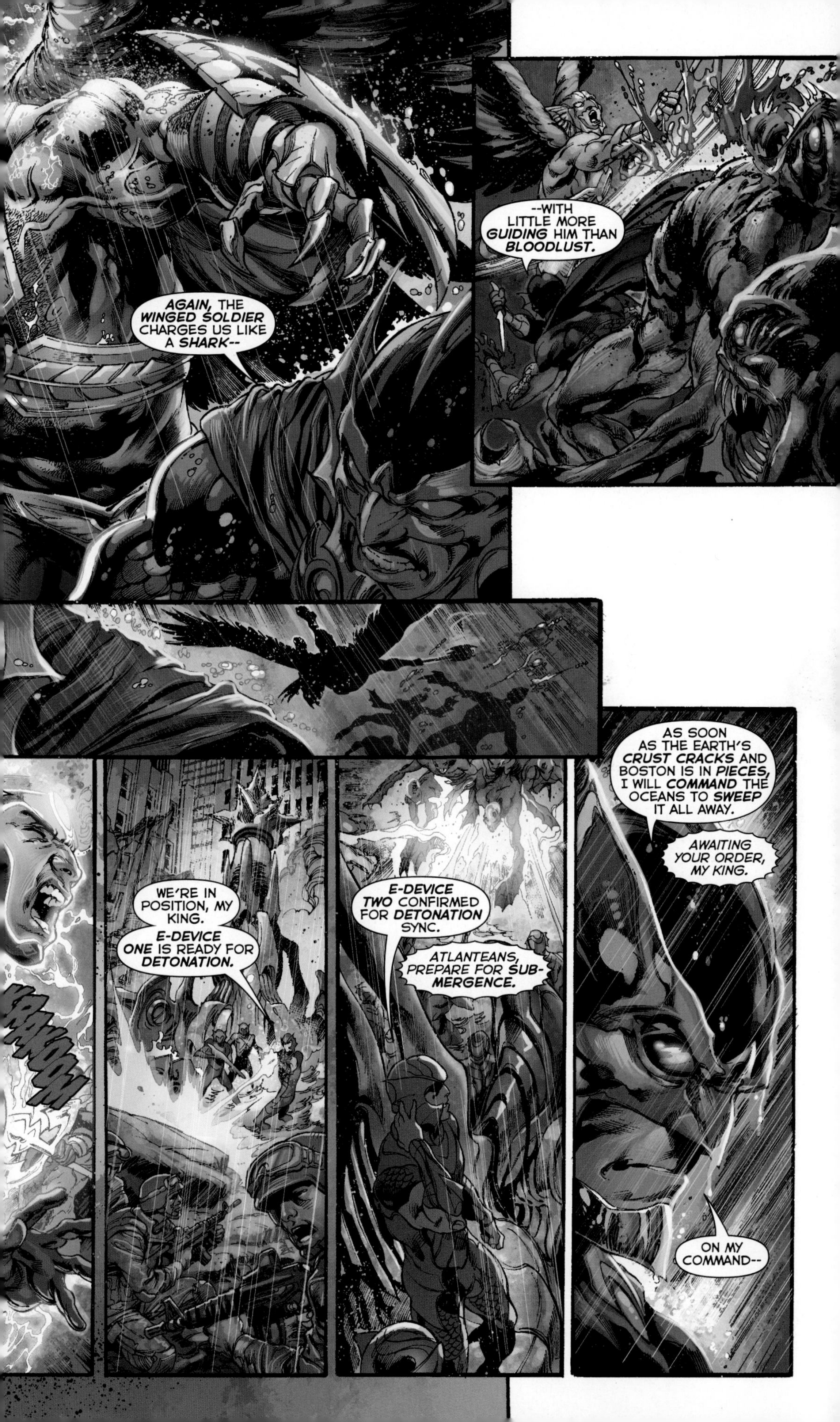
AGAIN, THE WINGED SOLDIER CHARGES US LIKE A SHARK--
--WITH LITTLE MORE GUIDING HIM THAN BLOODLUST.
WE'RE IN POSITION, MY KING.
E-DEVICE ONE IS READY FOR DETONATION.
E-DEVICE TWO CONFIRMED FOR DETONATION SYNC.
ATLANTEANS, PREPARE FOR SUB-MERGENCE.
AS SOON AS THE EARTH'S CRUST CRACKS AND BOSTON IS IN PIECES, I WILL COMMAND THE OCEANS TO SWEEP IT ALL AWAY.
AWAITING YOUR ORDER, MY KING.
ON MY COMMAND--

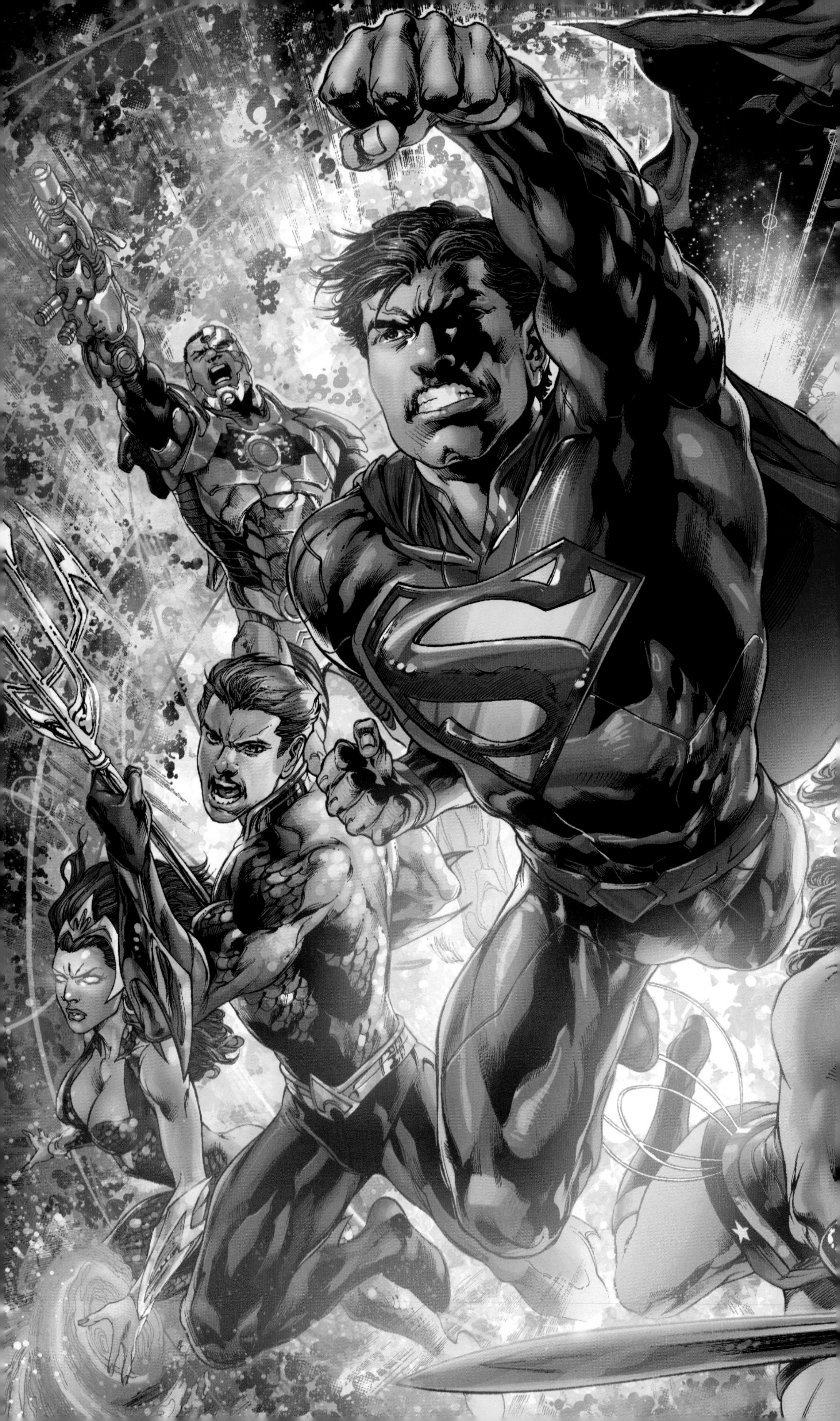

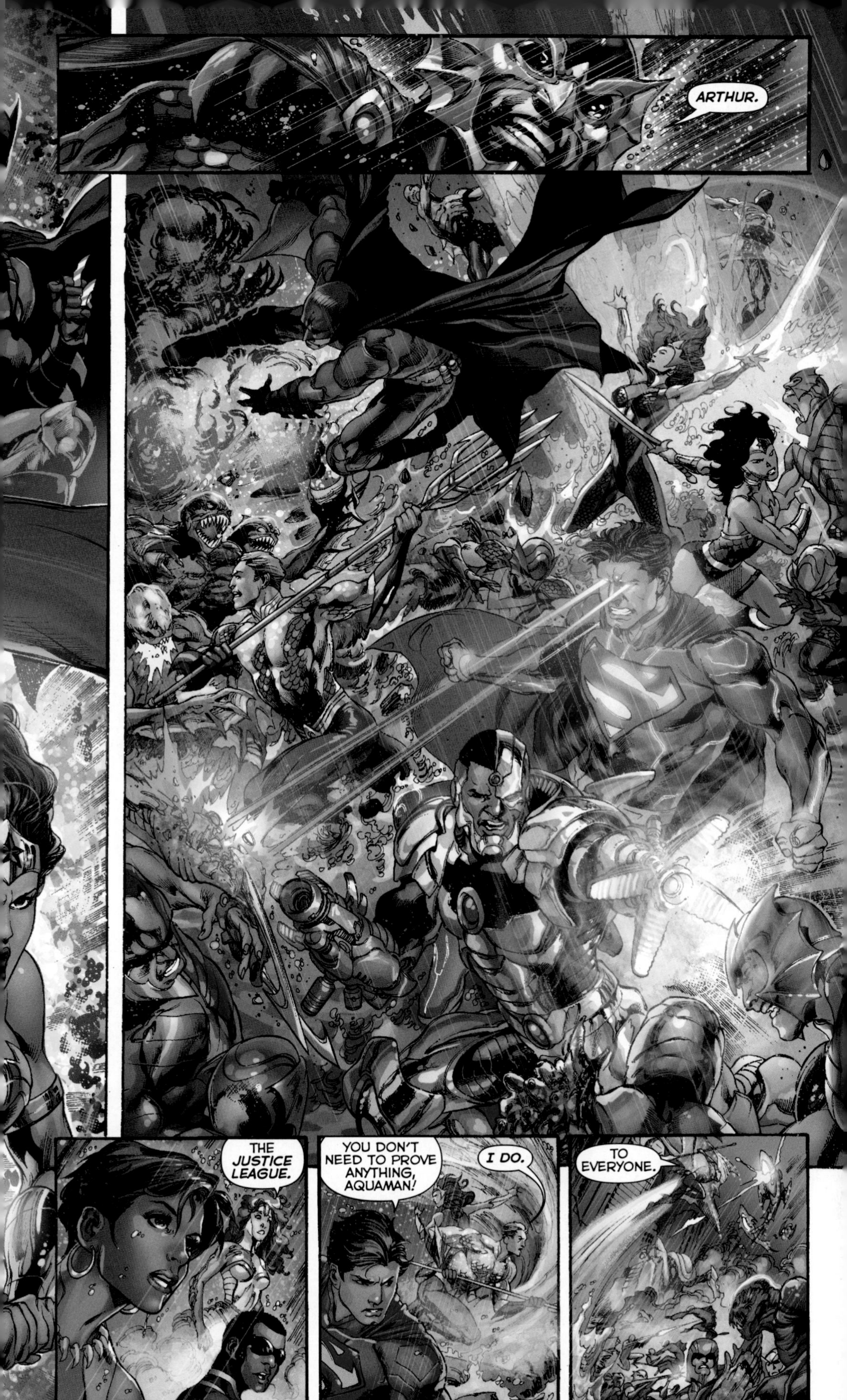
ARTHUR.
THE JUSTICE LEAGUE.
YOU DON'T NEED TO PROVE ANYTHING, AQUAMAN!
I DO.
TO EVERYONE.

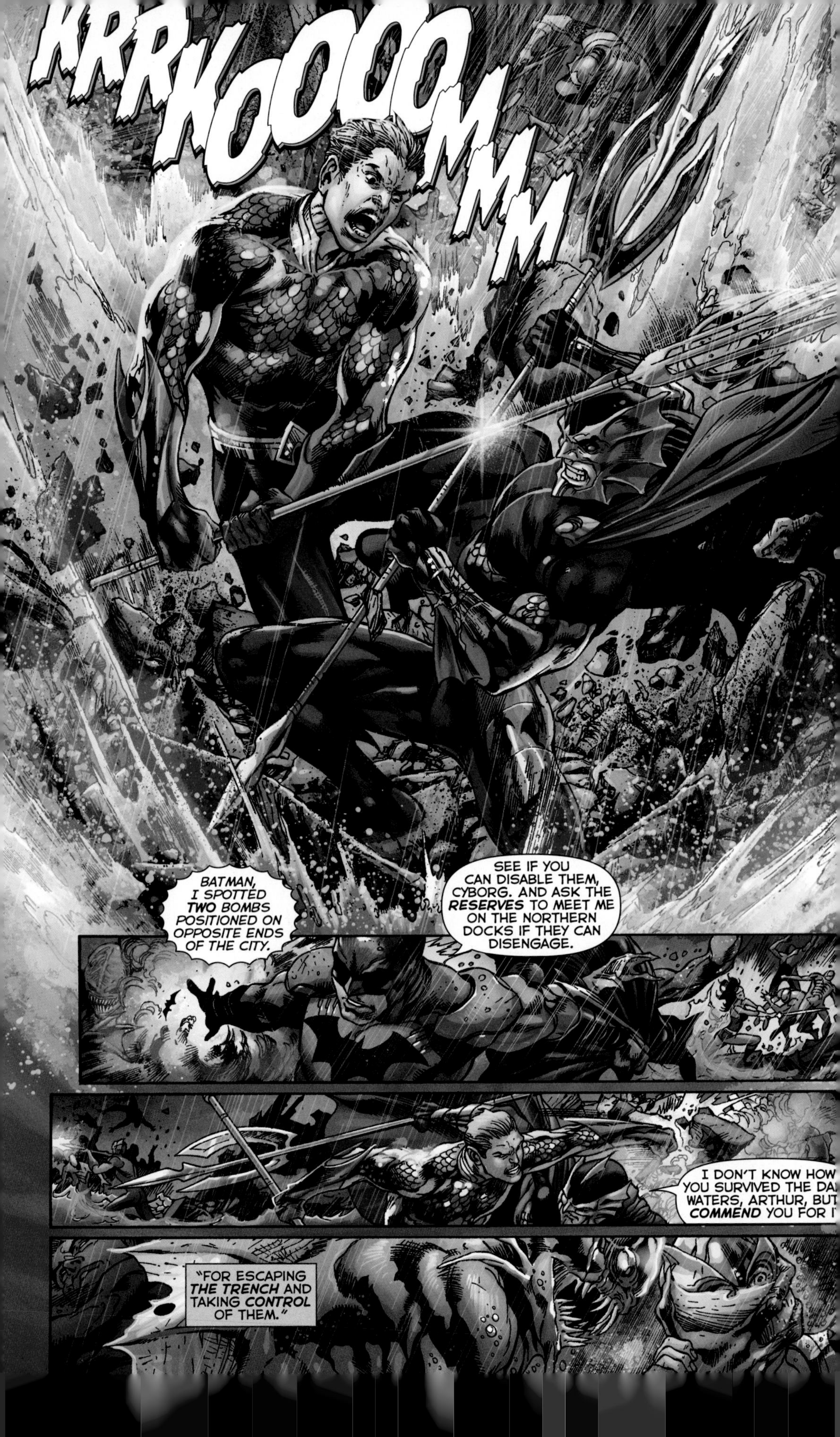
KRRKOOOOMMM
BATMAN, I SPOTTED TWO BOMBS POSITIONED ON OPPOSITE ENDS OF THE CITY.
SEE IF YOU CAN DISABLE THEM, CYBORG. AND ASK THE RESERVES TO MEET ME ON THE NORTHERN DOCKS IF THEY CAN DISENGAGE.
I DON'T KNOW HOW YOU SURVIVED THE DA WATERS, ARTHUR, BUT COMMEND YOU FOR I
"FOR ESCAPING THE TRENCH AND TAKING CONTROL OF THEM."

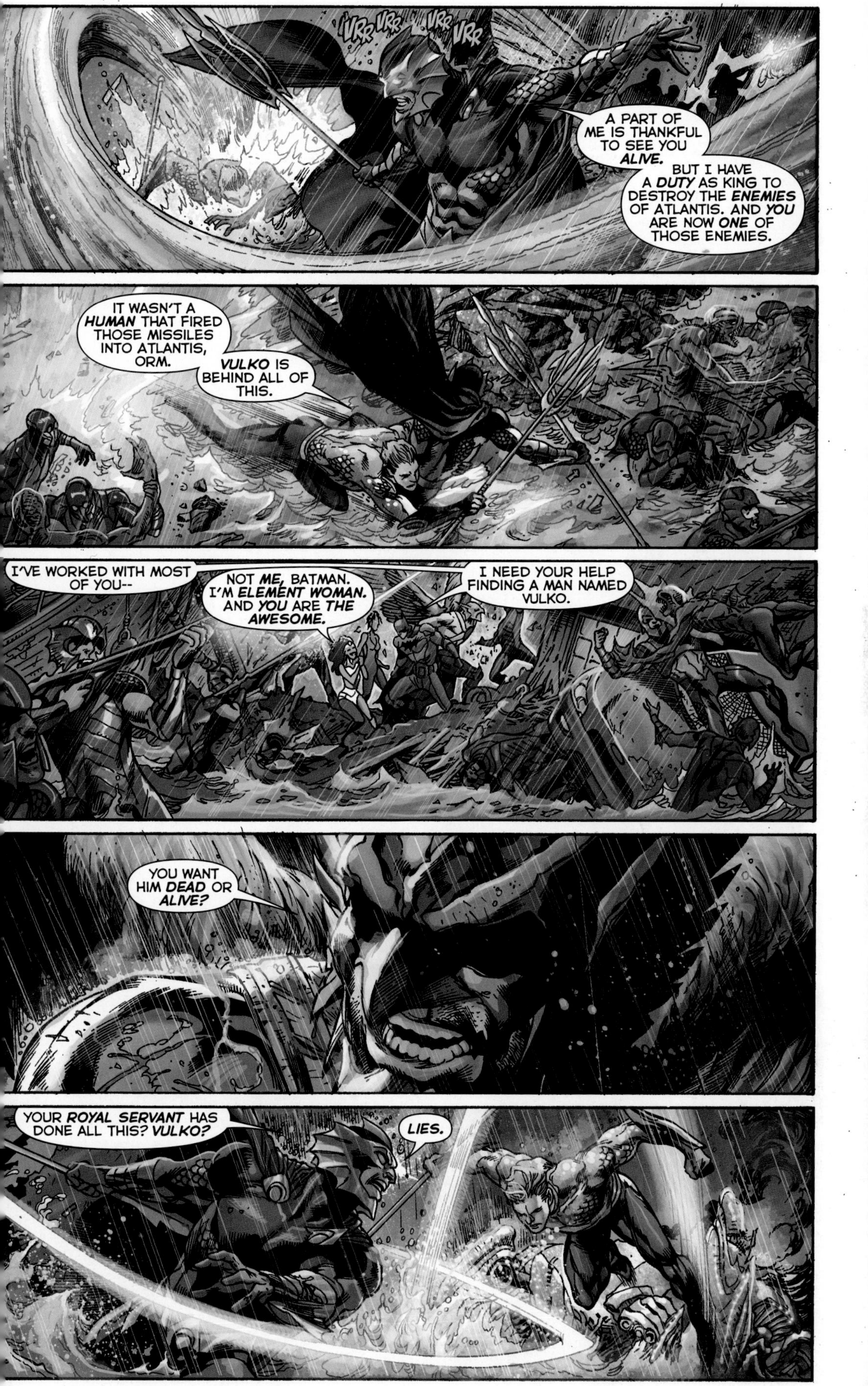
VRR VRR VRR VRR
A PART OF ME IS THANKFUL TO SEE YOU ALIVE.
BUT I HAVE A DUTY AS KING TO DESTROY THE ENEMIES OF ATLANTIS. AND YOU ARE NOW ONE OF THOSE ENEMIES.
IT WASN'T A HUMAN THAT FIRED THOSE MISSILES INTO ATLANTIS, ORM.
VULKO IS BEHIND ALL OF THIS.
I'VE WORKED WITH MOST OF YOU--
NOT ME, BATMAN. I'M ELEMENT WOMAN. AND YOU ARE THE AWESOME.
I NEED YOUR HELP FINDING A MAN NAMED VULKO.
YOU WANT HIM DEAD OR ALIVE?
YOUR ROYAL SERVANT HAS DONE ALL THIS? VULKO?
LIES.

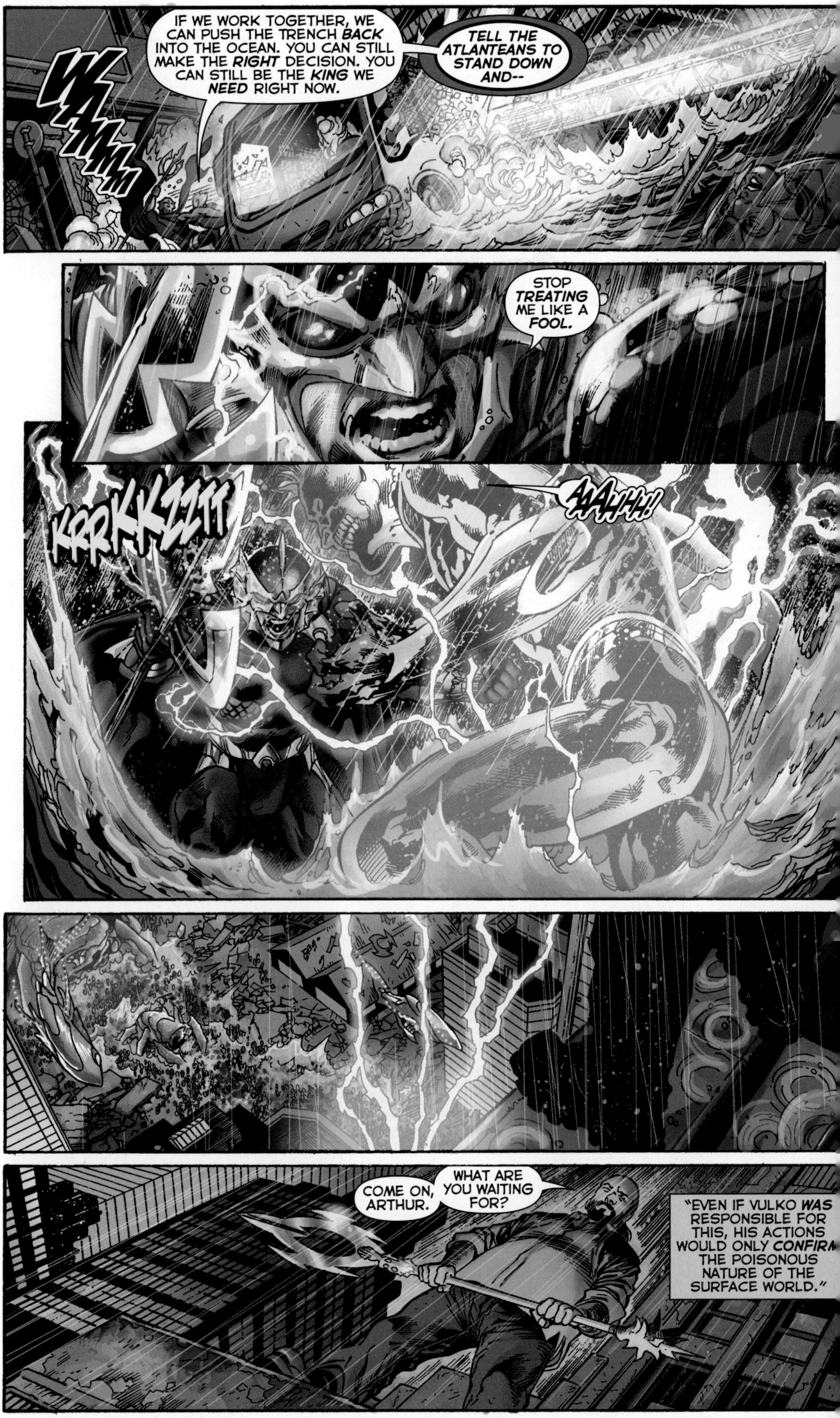

WHAAMM
IF WE WORK TOGETHER, WE CAN PUSH THE TRENCH *BACK* INTO THE OCEAN. YOU CAN STILL MAKE THE *RIGHT* DECISION. YOU CAN STILL BE THE *KING* WE *NEED* RIGHT NOW.
TELL THE ATLANTEANS TO STAND DOWN AND--
STOP *TREATING* ME LIKE A *FOOL.*
KRRKKZZTT
AAAHHH!
COME ON, ARTHUR.
WHAT ARE YOU WAITING FOR?
"EVEN IF VULKO *WAS* RESPONSIBLE FOR THIS, HIS ACTIONS WOULD ONLY *CONFIRM* THE POISONOUS NATURE OF THE SURFACE WORLD."

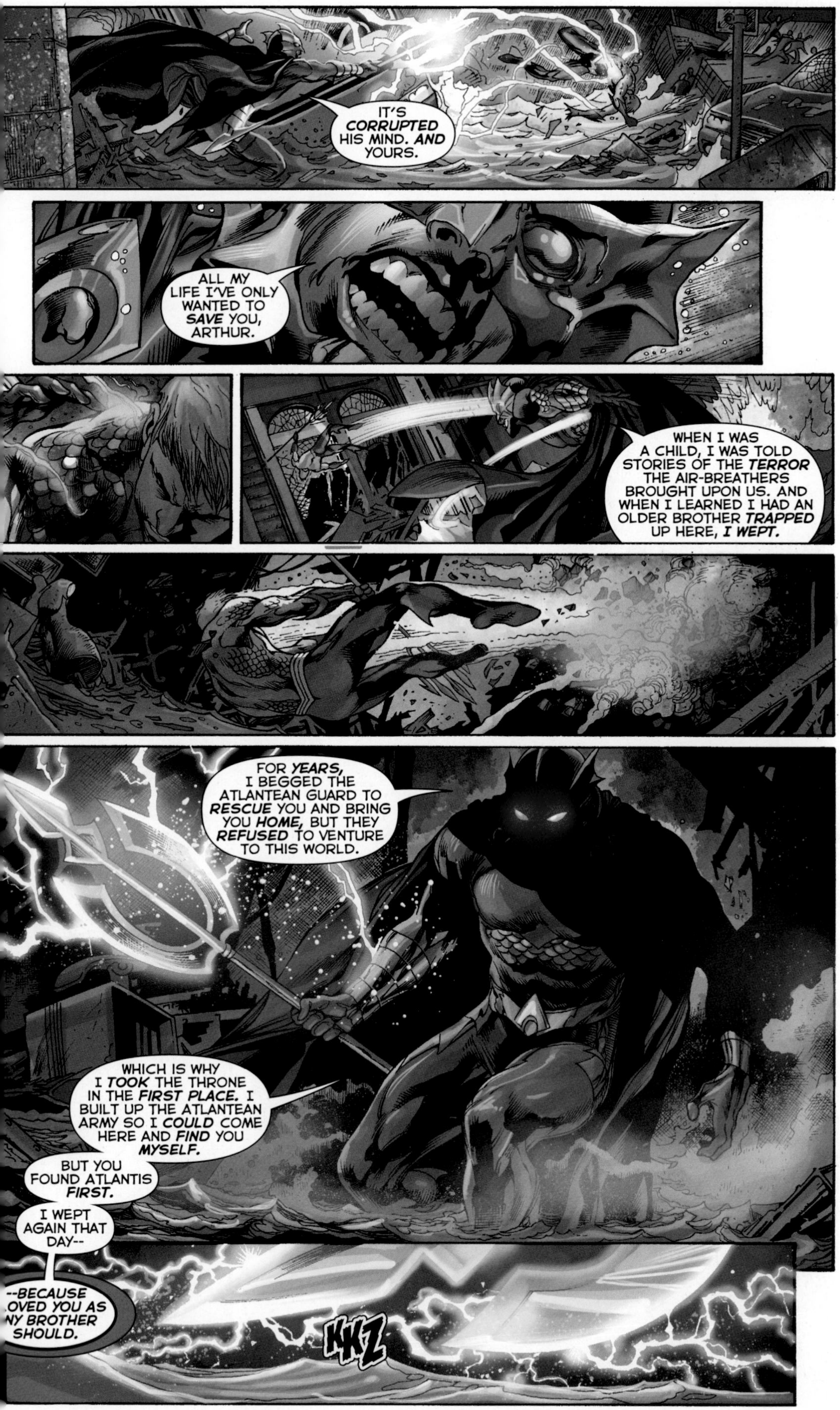
IT'S CORRUPTED HIS MIND. AND YOURS.
ALL MY LIFE I'VE ONLY WANTED TO SAVE YOU, ARTHUR.
WHEN I WAS A CHILD, I WAS TOLD STORIES OF THE TERROR THE AIR-BREATHERS BROUGHT UPON US. AND WHEN I LEARNED I HAD AN OLDER BROTHER TRAPPED UP HERE, I WEPT.
FOR YEARS, I BEGGED THE ATLANTEAN GUARD TO RESCUE YOU AND BRING YOU HOME, BUT THEY REFUSED TO VENTURE TO THIS WORLD.
WHICH IS WHY I TOOK THE THRONE IN THE FIRST PLACE. I BUILT UP THE ATLANTEAN ARMY SO I COULD COME HERE AND FIND YOU MYSELF.
BUT YOU FOUND ATLANTIS FIRST.
I WEPT AGAIN THAT DAY--
--BECAUSE OVED YOU AS NY BROTHER SHOULD.
KKZ

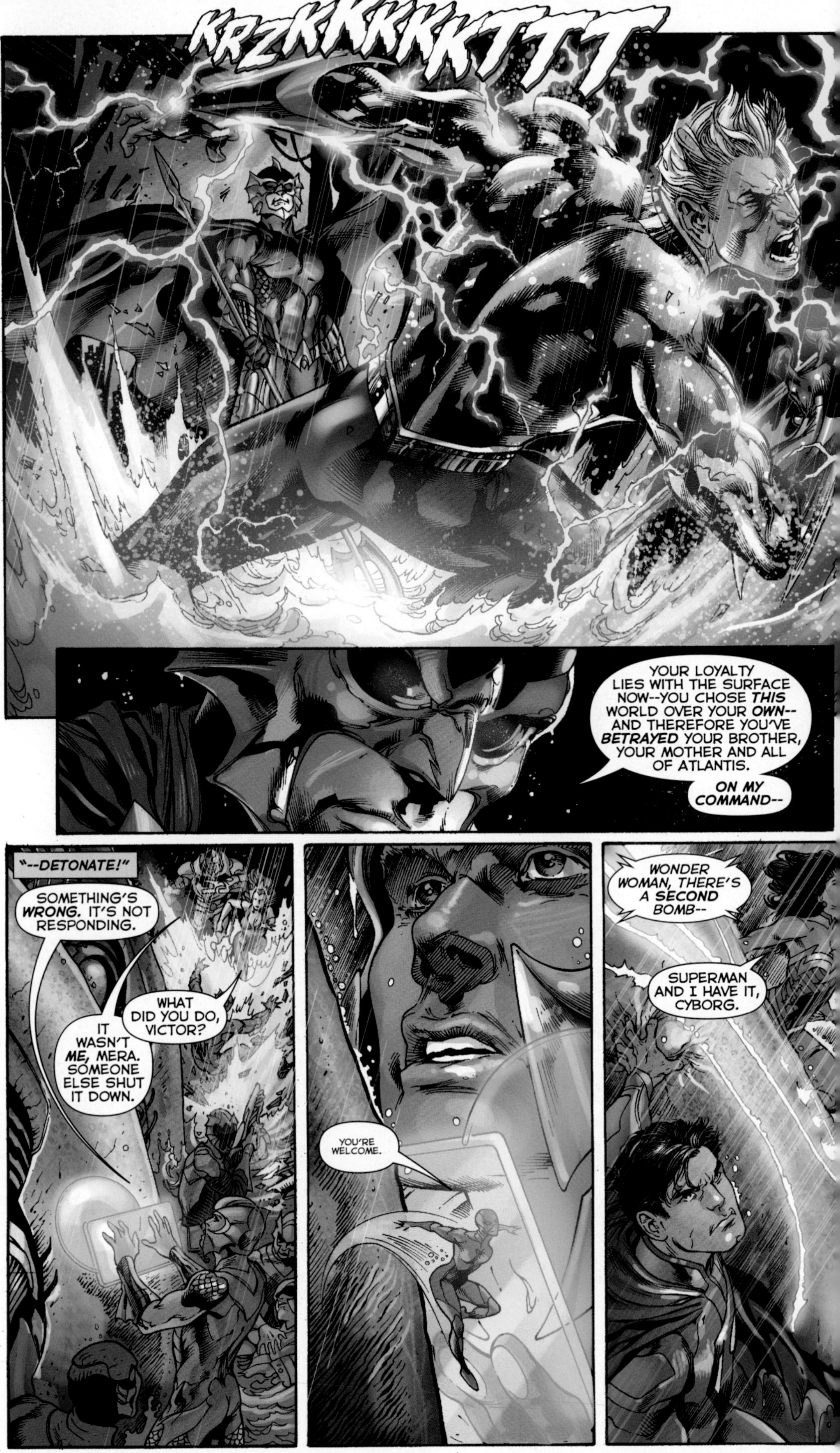
KRZKKKKKKTTTT
YOUR LOYALTY LIES WITH THE SURFACE NOW--YOU CHOSE THIS WORLD OVER YOUR OWN-- AND THEREFORE YOU'VE BETRAYED YOUR BROTHER, YOUR MOTHER AND ALL OF ATLANTIS.
ON MY COMMAND--
"--DETONATE!"
SOMETHING'S WRONG. IT'S NOT RESPONDING.
WHAT DID YOU DO, VICTOR?
IT WASN'T ME, MERA. SOMEONE ELSE SHUT IT DOWN.
YOU'RE WELCOME.
WONDER WOMAN, THERE'S A SECOND BOMB--
SUPERMAN AND I HAVE IT, CYBORG.

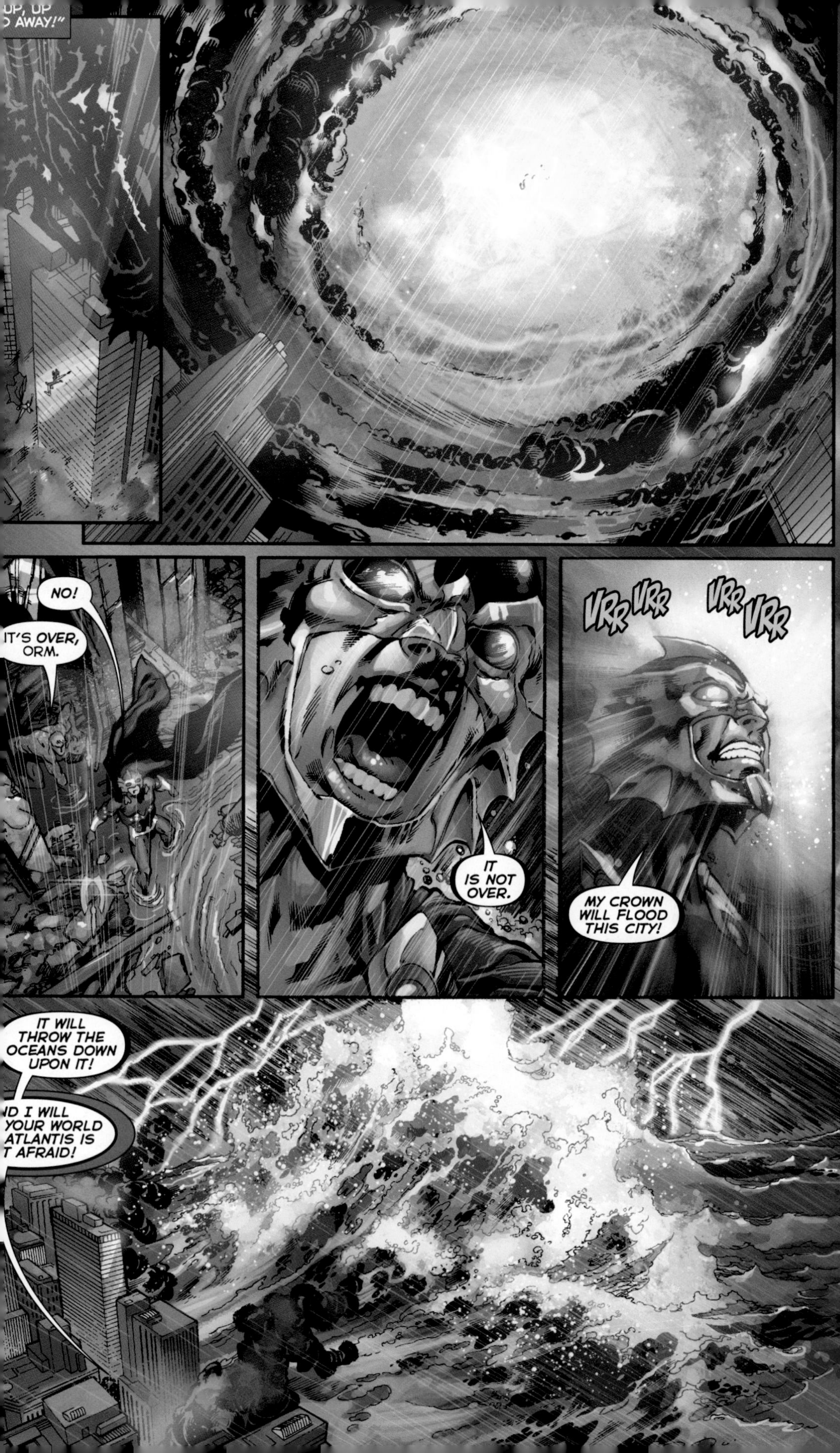
UP, UP
D AWAY!"
NO!
IT'S OVER, ORM.
IT IS NOT OVER.
VRR VRR VRR VRR
MY CROWN WILL FLOOD THIS CITY!
IT WILL THROW THE OCEANS DOWN UPON IT!
ND I WILL
YOUR WORLD
ATLANTIS IS
T AFRAID!

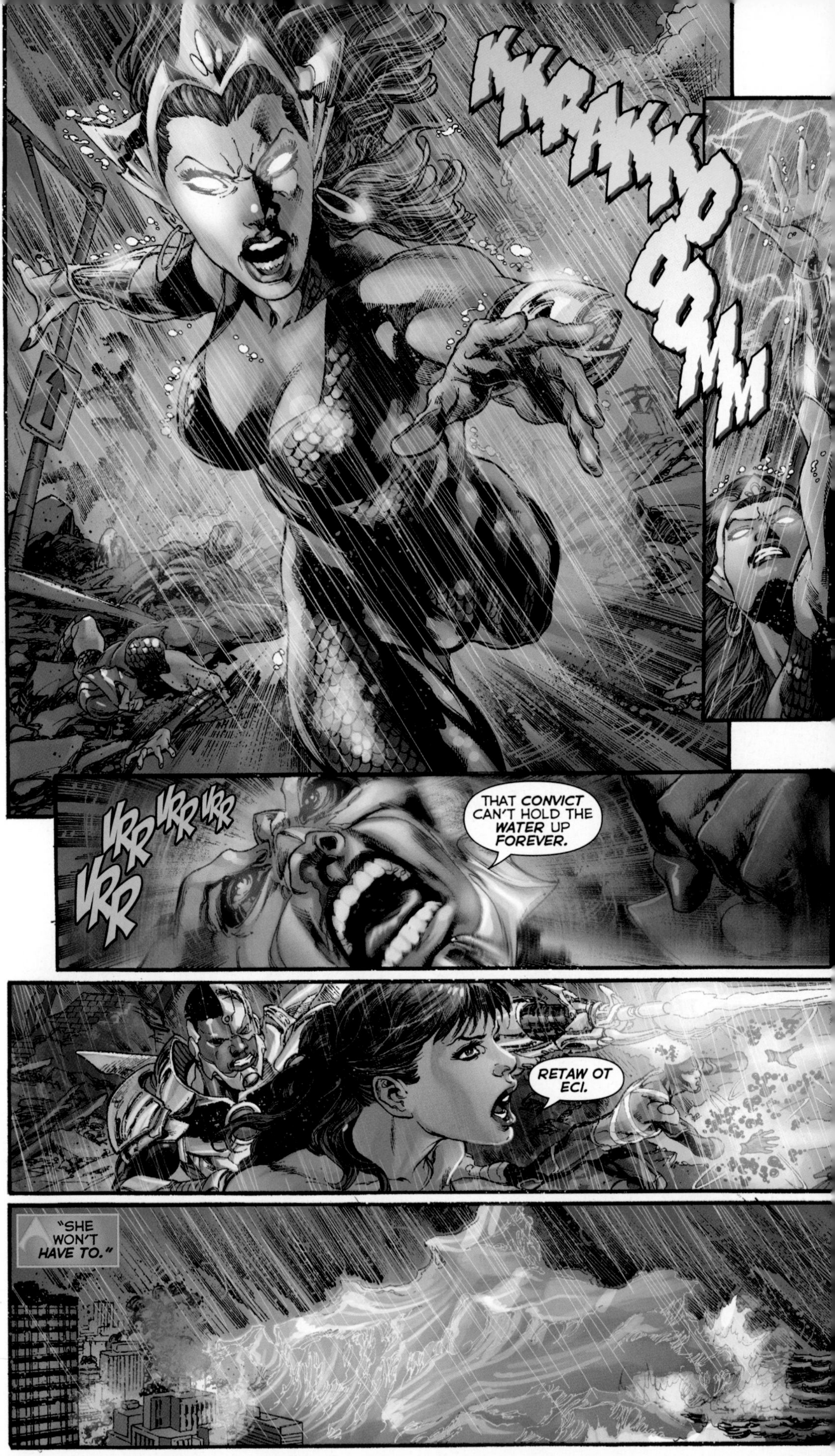
KKRAKKOOOOMM
URRR URRR URRR URRR
THAT CONVICT CAN'T HOLD THE WATER UP FOREVER.
RETAW OT ECI.
"SHE WON'T HAVE TO."

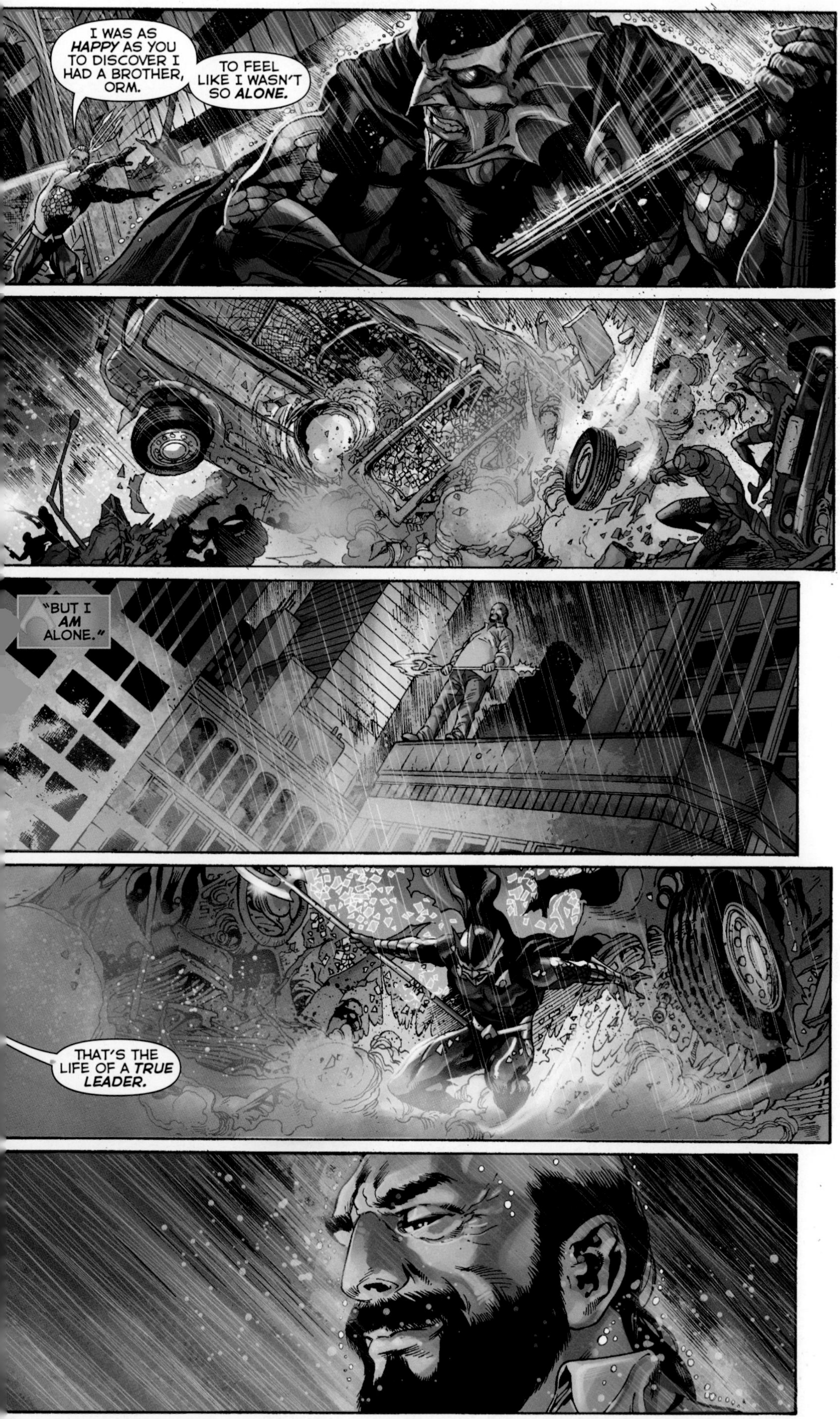
I WAS AS HAPPY AS YOU TO DISCOVER I HAD A BROTHER, ORM.
TO FEEL LIKE I WASN'T SO ALONE.
"BUT I AM ALONE."
THAT'S THE LIFE OF A TRUE LEADER.

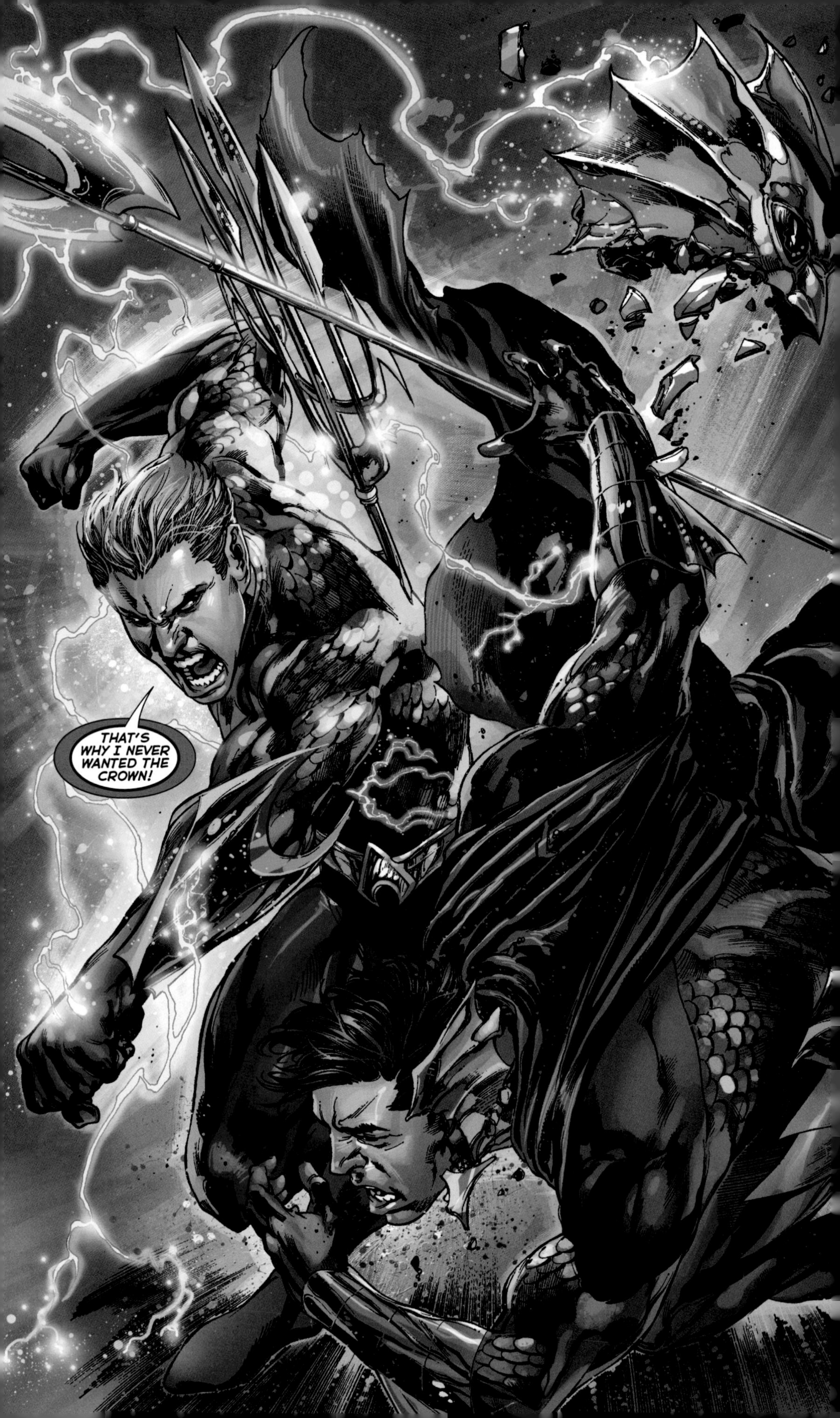
THAT'S WHY I NEVER WANTED THE CROWN!

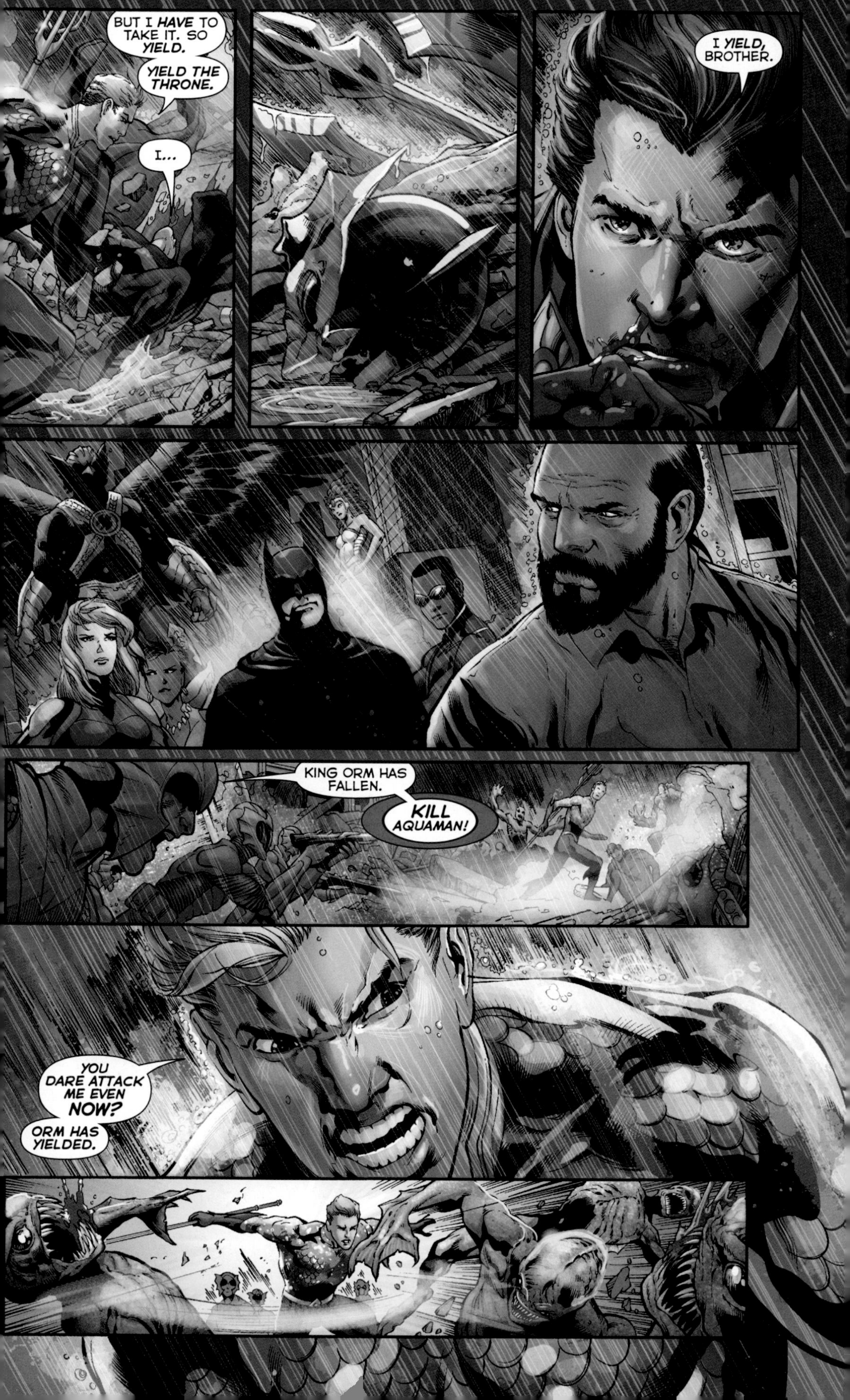
BUT I HAVE TO TAKE IT. SO YIELD.
YIELD THE THRONE.
I...
I YIELD, BROTHER.
KING ORM HAS FALLEN.
KILL AQUAMAN!
YOU DARE ATTACK ME EVEN NOW?
ORM HAS YIELDED.

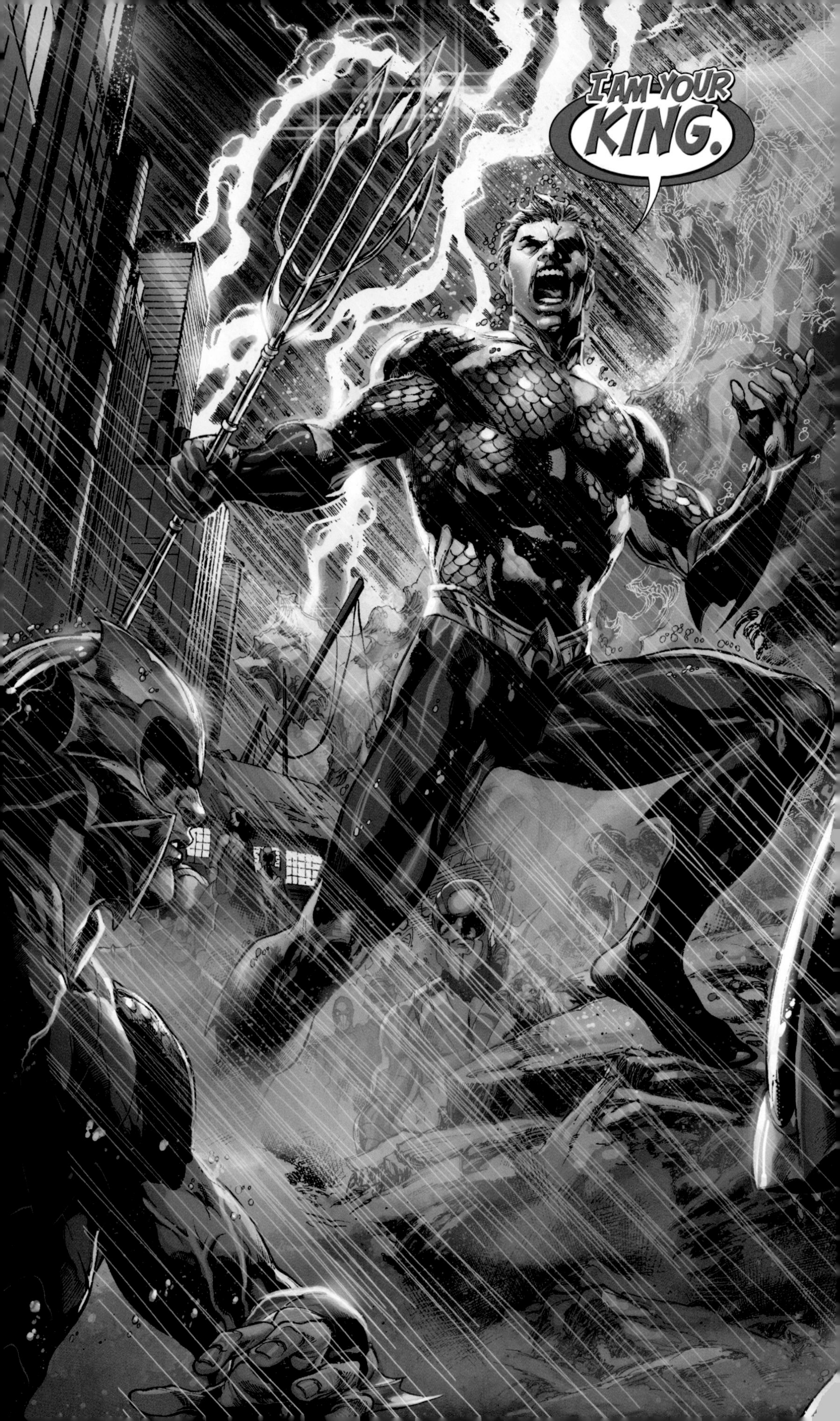
I AM YOUR KING.

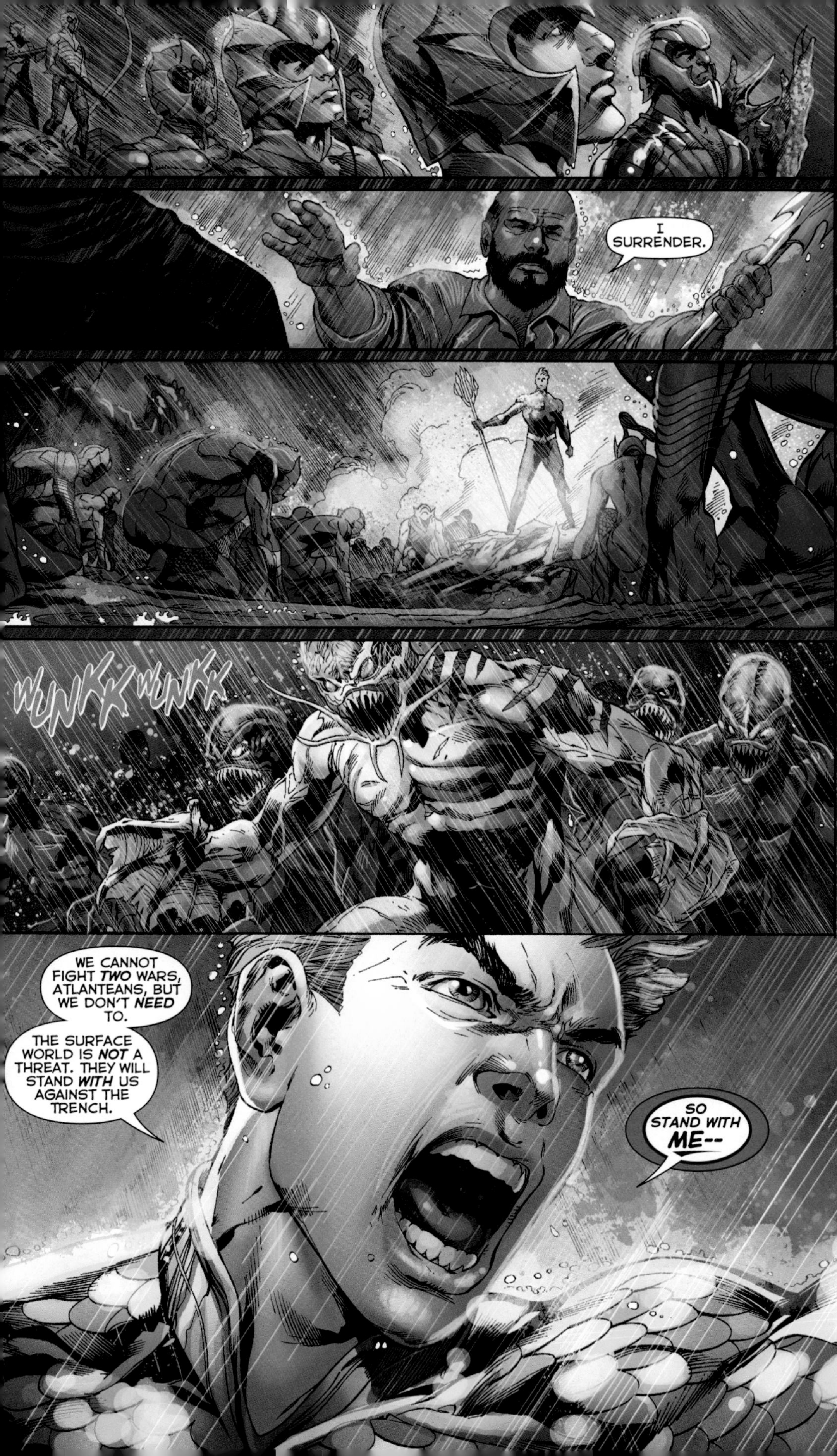
I SURRENDER.
WUNKK WUNKK
WE CANNOT FIGHT TWO WARS, ATLANTEANS, BUT WE DON'T NEED TO.
THE SURFACE WORLD IS NOT A THREAT. THEY WILL STAND WITH US AGAINST THE TRENCH.
SO STAND WITH ME--

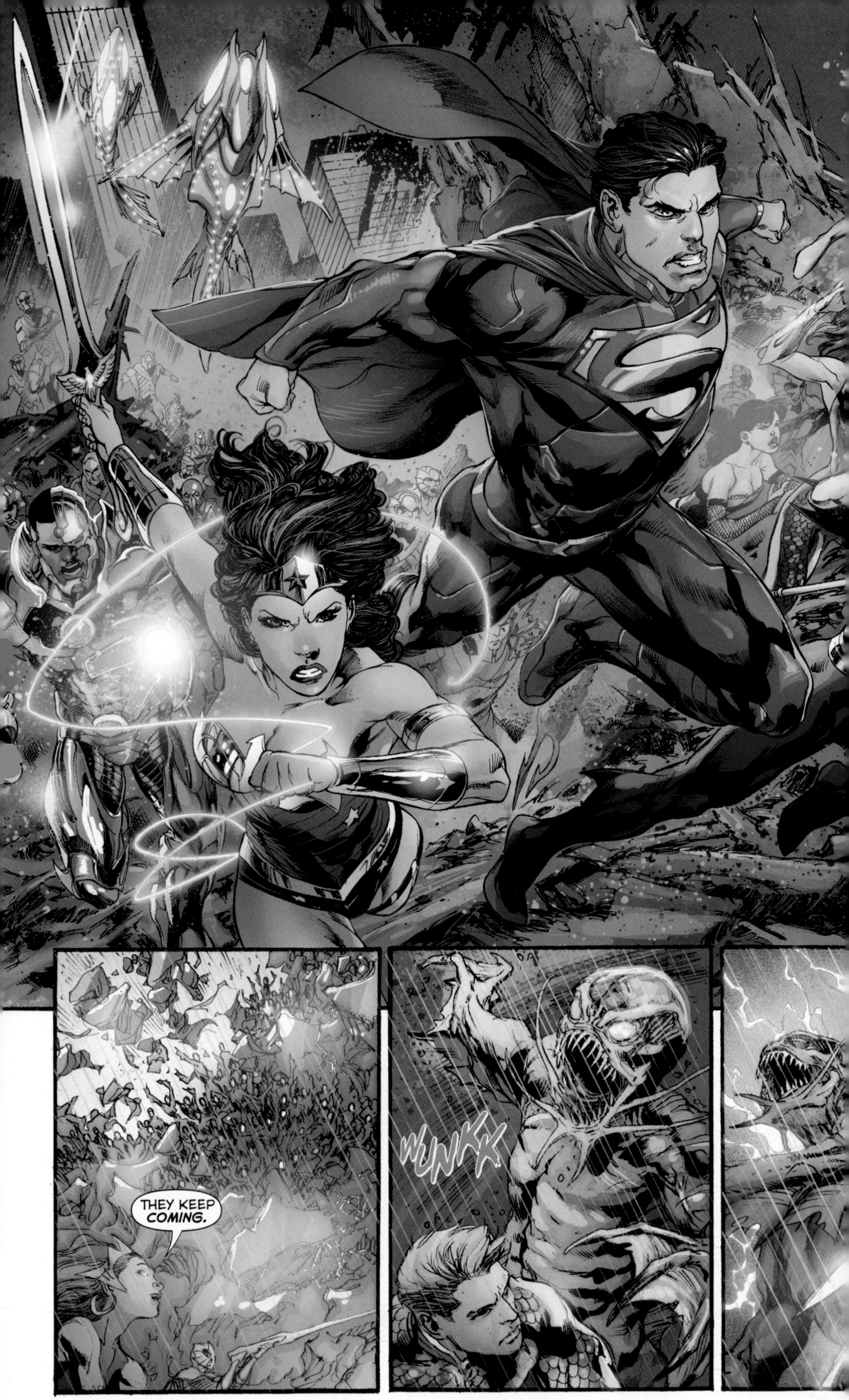
THEY KEEP COMING.
WUNKK

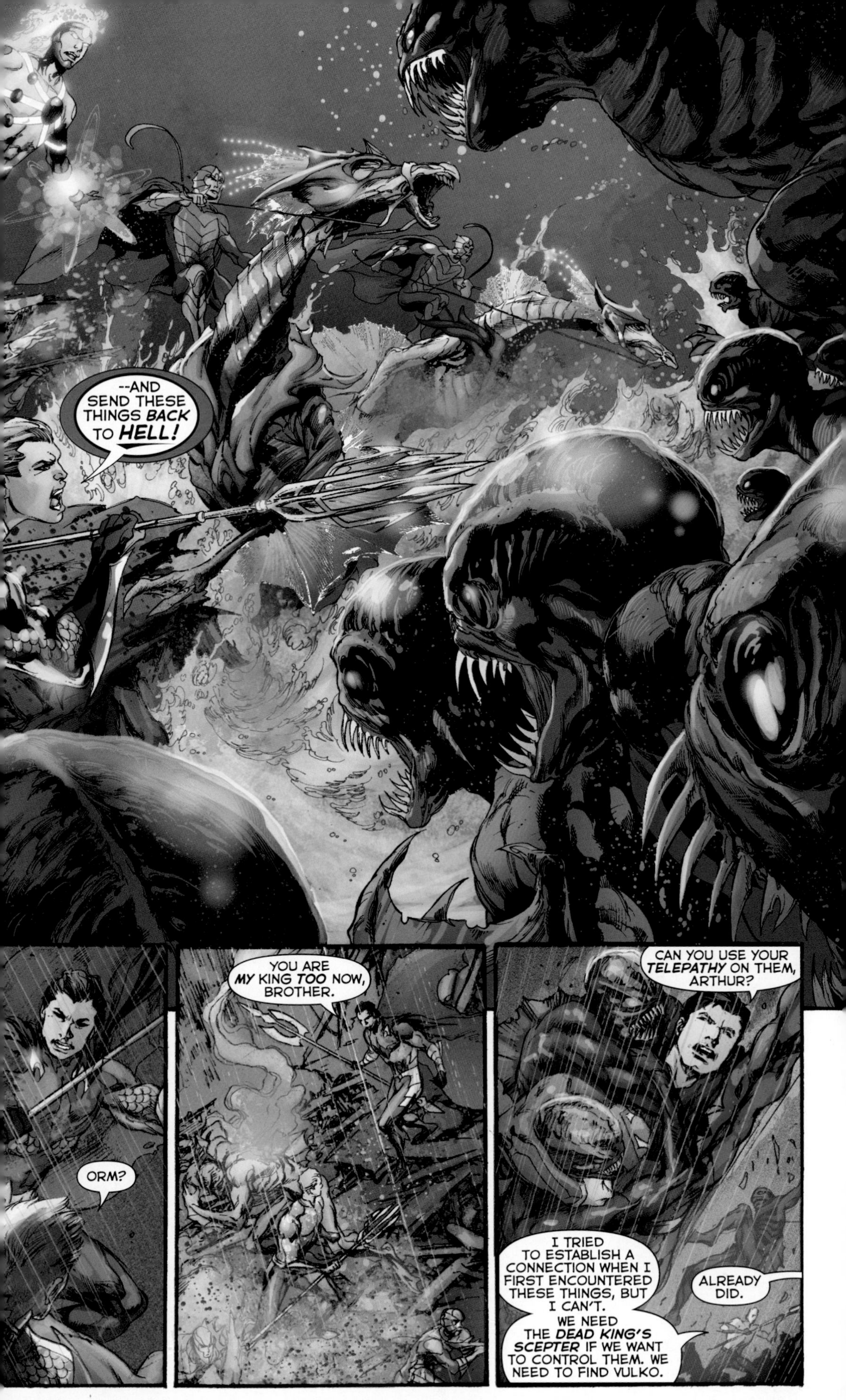
--AND SEND THESE THINGS BACK TO HELL!
ORM?
YOU ARE MY KING TOO NOW, BROTHER.
CAN YOU USE YOUR TELEPATHY ON THEM, ARTHUR?
ALREADY DID.
I TRIED TO ESTABLISH A CONNECTION WHEN I FIRST ENCOUNTERED THESE THINGS, BUT I CAN'T.
WE NEED THE DEAD KING'S SCEPTER IF WE WANT TO CONTROL THEM. WE NEED TO FIND VULKO.

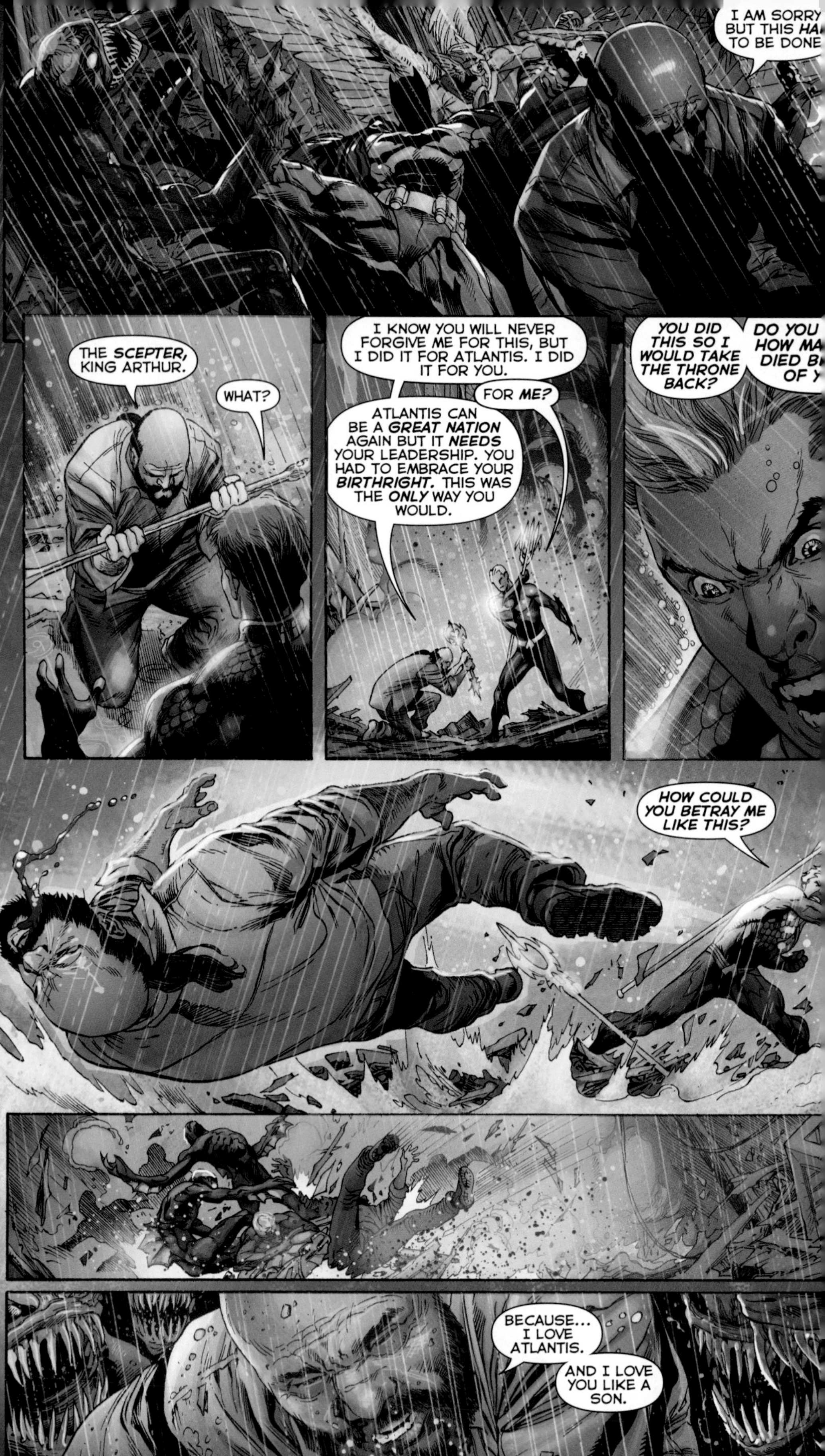
I AM SORRY BUT THIS HA
TO BE DONE
THE SCEPTER, KING ARTHUR.
WHAT?
I KNOW YOU WILL NEVER FORGIVE ME FOR THIS, BUT I DID IT FOR ATLANTIS. I DID IT FOR YOU.
FOR ME?
ATLANTIS CAN BE A GREAT NATION AGAIN BUT IT NEEDS YOUR LEADERSHIP. YOU HAD TO EMBRACE YOUR BIRTHRIGHT. THIS WAS THE ONLY WAY YOU WOULD.
YOU DID THIS SO I WOULD TAKE THE THRONE BACK?
DO YOU
HOW COULD YOU BETRAY ME LIKE THIS?
BECAUSE... I LOVE ATLANTIS.
AND I LOVE YOU LIKE A SON.

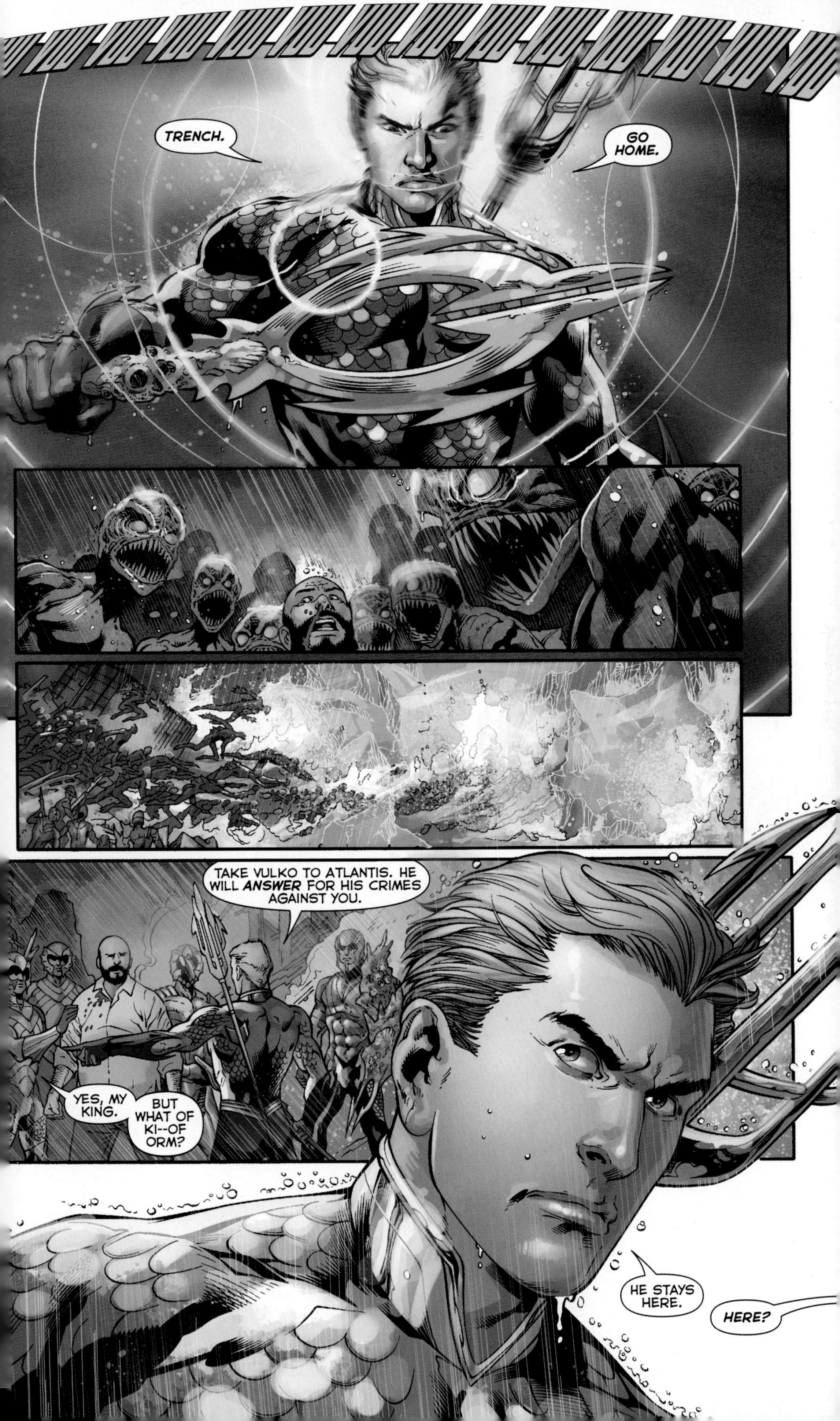
VOO-VOO-VOO-VOO-VOO-VOO-VOO-VOO-VOO-VOO-VOO-VOO-VOO-VOO-VOO-VOO
TRENCH.
GO HOME.
TAKE VULKO TO ATLANTIS. HE WILL ANSWER FOR HIS CRIMES AGAINST YOU.
YES, MY KING.
BUT WHAT OF KI--OF ORM?
HE STAYS HERE.
HERE?

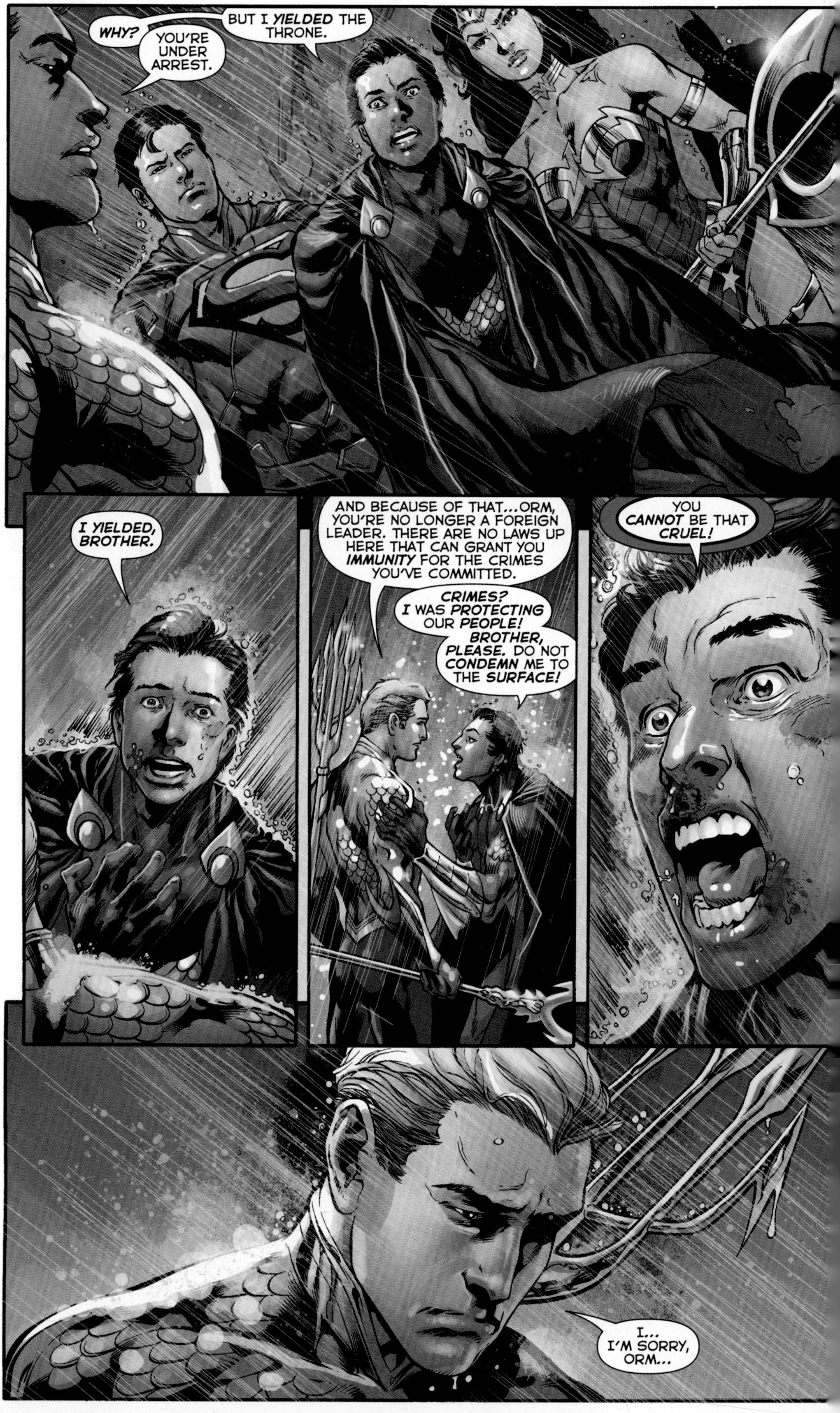
WHY?
YOU'RE UNDER ARREST.
BUT I YIELDED THE THRONE.
I YIELDED, BROTHER.
AND BECAUSE OF THAT...ORM, YOU'RE NO LONGER A FOREIGN LEADER. THERE ARE NO LAWS UP HERE THAT CAN GRANT YOU IMMUNITY FOR THE CRIMES YOU'VE COMMITTED.
CRIMES? I WAS PROTECTING OUR PEOPLE! BROTHER, PLEASE. DO NOT CONDEMN ME TO THE SURFACE!
YOU CANNOT BE THAT CRUEL!
I... I'M SORRY, ORM...

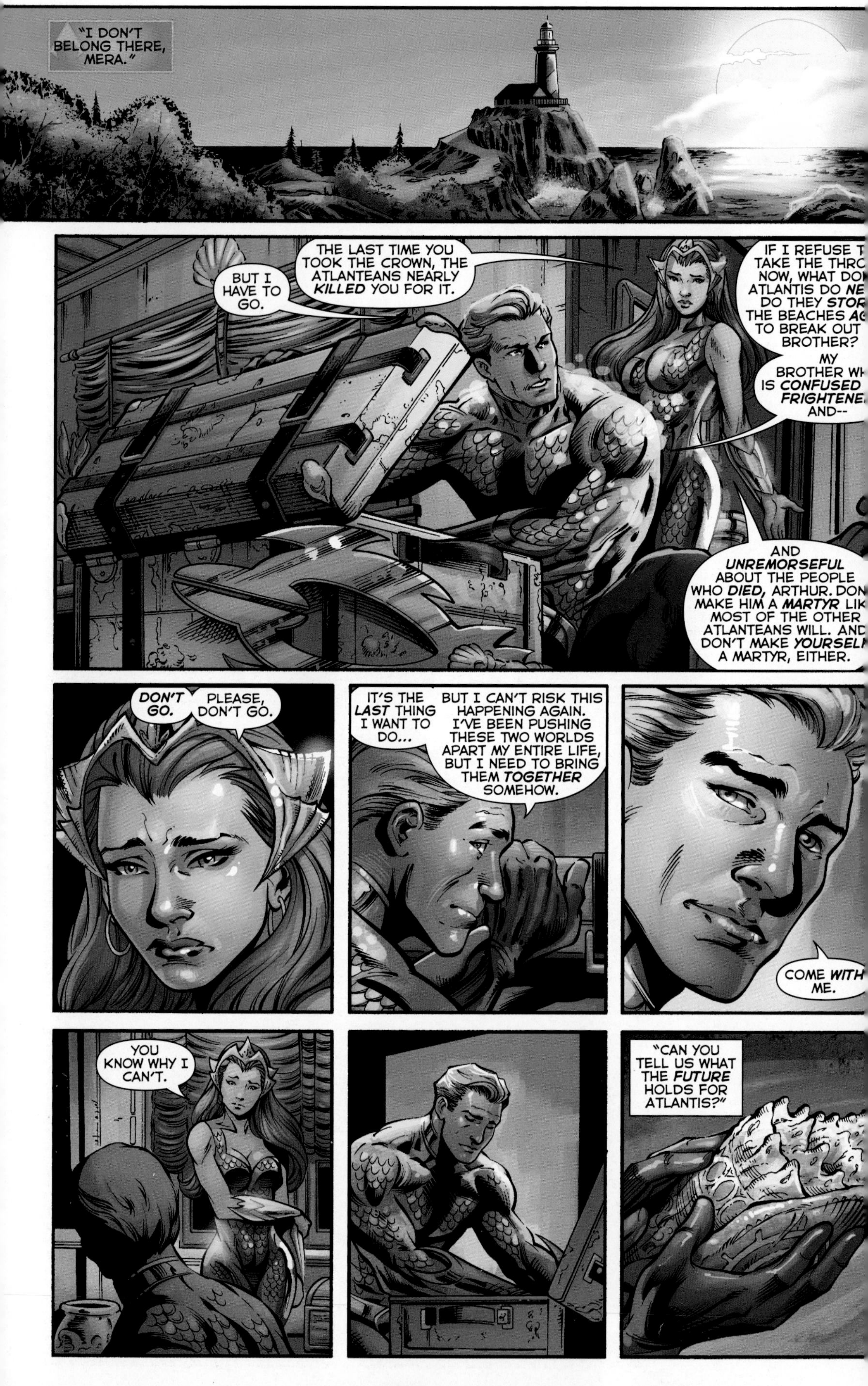

"I DON'T BELONG THERE, MERA."
BUT I HAVE TO GO.
THE LAST TIME YOU TOOK THE CROWN, THE ATLANTEANS NEARLY *KILLED* YOU FOR IT.
IF I REFUSE T TAKE THE THRO NOW, WHAT DO ATLANTIS DO *NE* DO THEY *STOR* THE BEACHES *AG* TO BREAK OUT BROTHER?
MY BROTHER WH IS *CONFUSED* *FRIGHTENE* AND--
AND *UNREMORSEFUL* ABOUT THE PEOPLE WHO *DIED*, ARTHUR. DON MAKE HIM A *MARTYR* LIK MOST OF THE OTHER ATLANTEANS WILL. AND DON'T MAKE *YOURSEL* A MARTYR, EITHER.
DON'T GO.
PLEASE, DON'T GO.
IT'S THE *LAST* THING I WANT TO DO...
BUT I CAN'T RISK THIS HAPPENING AGAIN. I'VE BEEN PUSHING THESE TWO WORLDS APART MY ENTIRE LIFE, BUT I NEED TO BRING THEM *TOGETHER* SOMEHOW.
COME *WITH* ME.
YOU KNOW WHY I CAN'T.
"CAN YOU TELL US WHAT THE *FUTURE* HOLDS FOR ATLANTIS?"

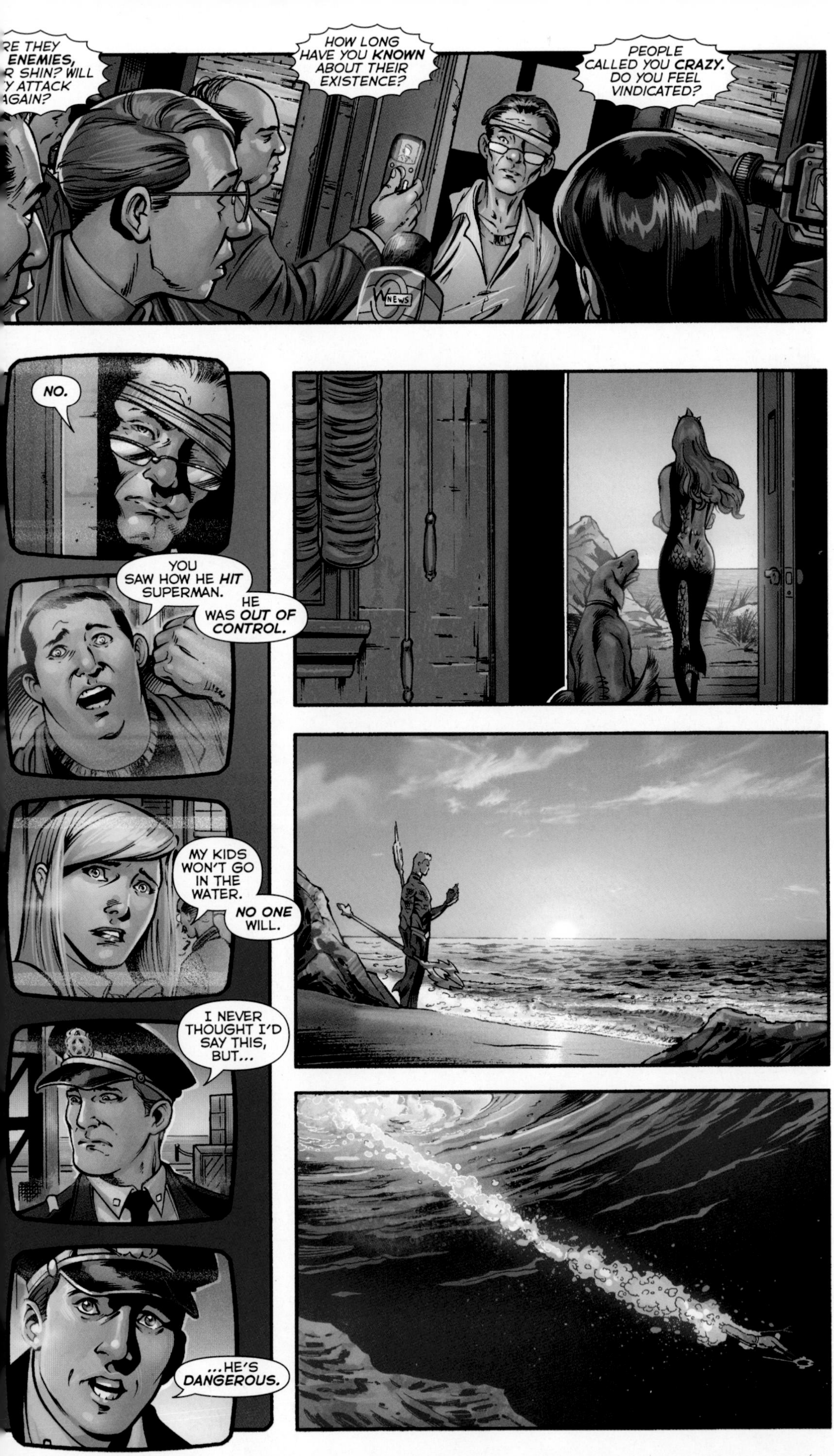
RE THEY ENEMIES, R SHIN? WILL Y ATTACK AGAIN?
HOW LONG HAVE YOU KNOWN ABOUT THEIR EXISTENCE?
PEOPLE CALLED YOU CRAZY. DO YOU FEEL VINDICATED?
NEWS
NO.
YOU SAW HOW HE HIT SUPERMAN.
HE WAS OUT OF CONTROL.
MY KIDS WON'T GO IN THE WATER.
NO ONE WILL.
I NEVER THOUGHT I'D SAY THIS, BUT...
...HE'S DANGEROUS.

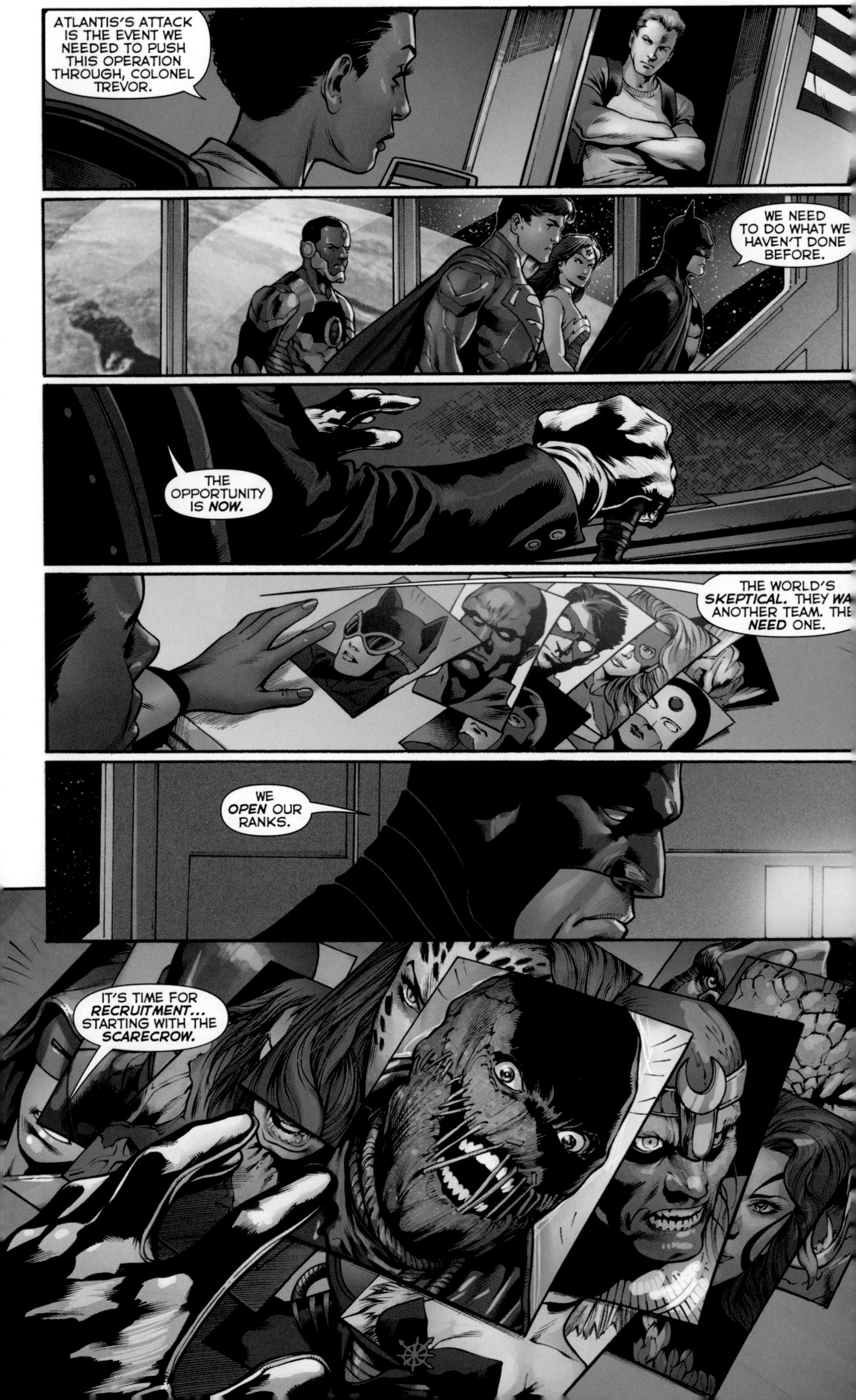
ATLANTIS'S ATTACK IS THE EVENT WE NEEDED TO PUSH THIS OPERATION THROUGH, COLONEL TREVOR.
WE NEED TO DO WHAT WE HAVEN'T DONE BEFORE.
THE OPPORTUNITY IS *NOW.*
THE WORLD'S *SKEPTICAL.* THEY *WA* ANOTHER TEAM. THE *NEED* ONE.
WE *OPEN* OUR RANKS.
IT'S TIME FOR *RECRUITMENT*... STARTING WITH THE *SCARECROW.*

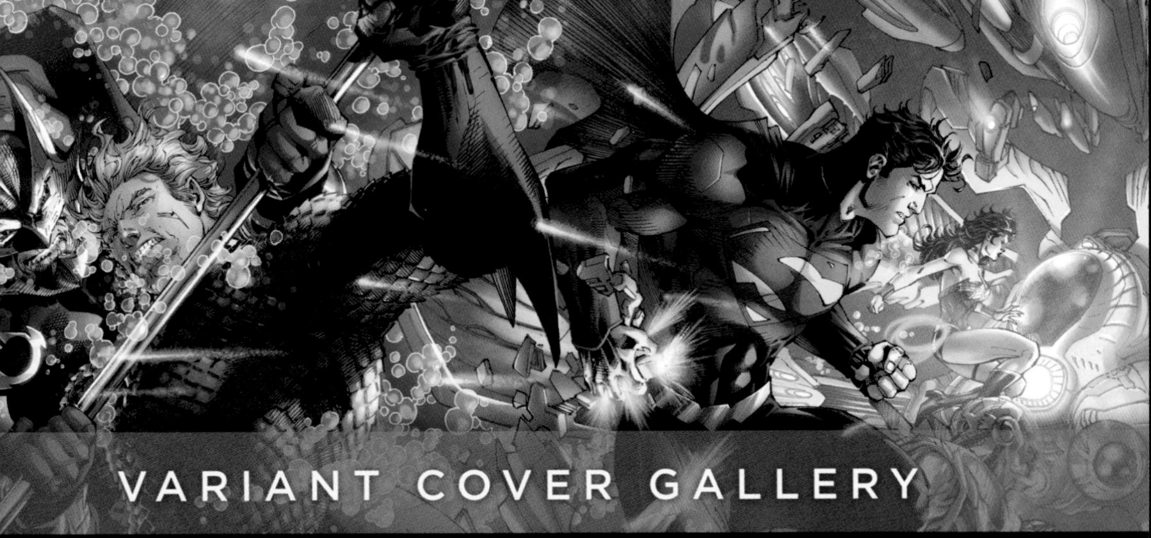
VARIANT COVER GALLERY

AQUAMAN 15
By Jim Lee, Scott Williams & Alex Sinclair

JUSTICE LEAGUE 15
By Jim Lee, Scott Williams & Alex Sinclair

JUSTICE LEAGUE 15
By Billy Tucci & Hi-Fi

JUSTICE LEAGUE 16
By Langdon Foss & Jose Villarrubia

JUSTICE LEAGUE 17
By Steve Skroce & Alex Sinclair

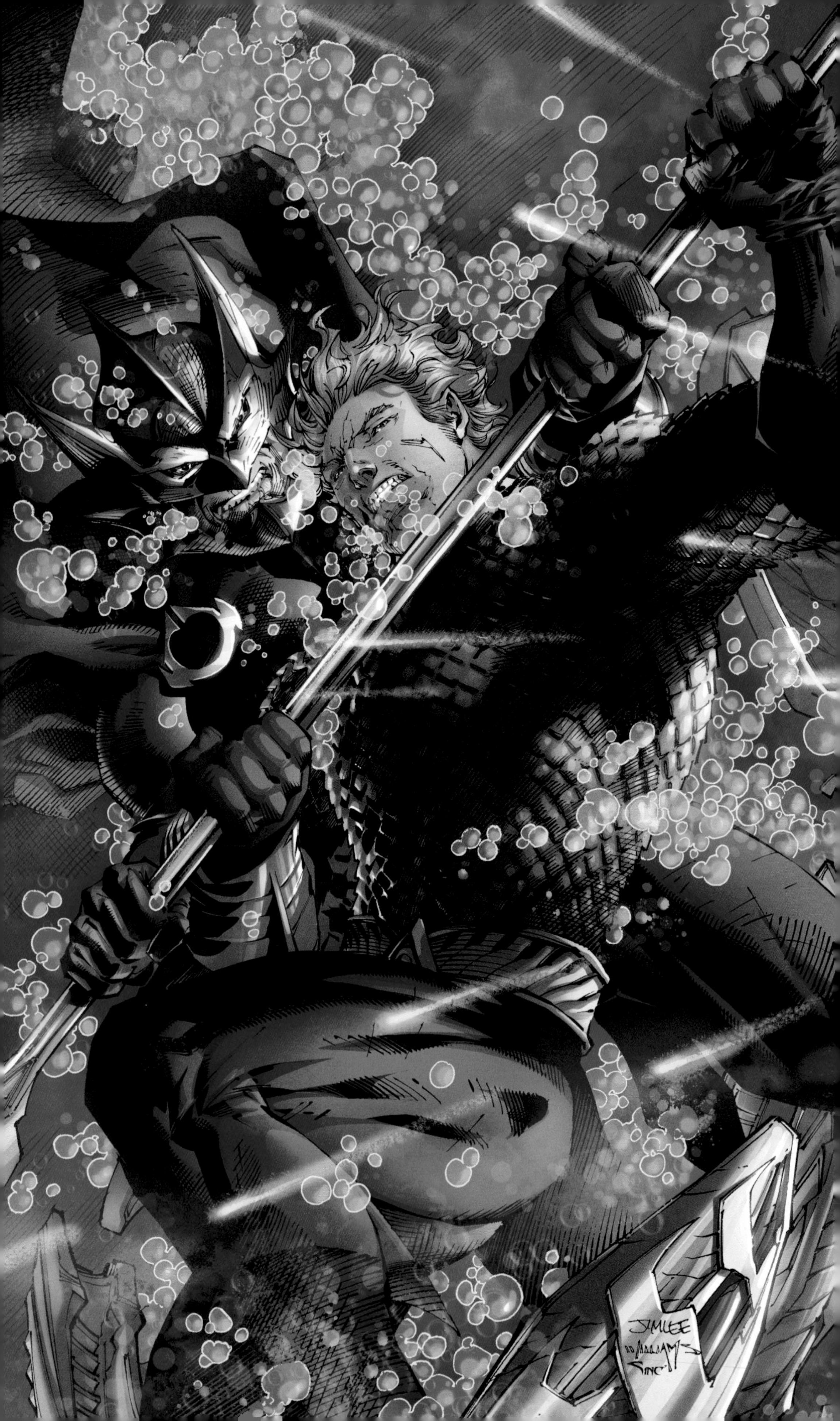
JIMLEE

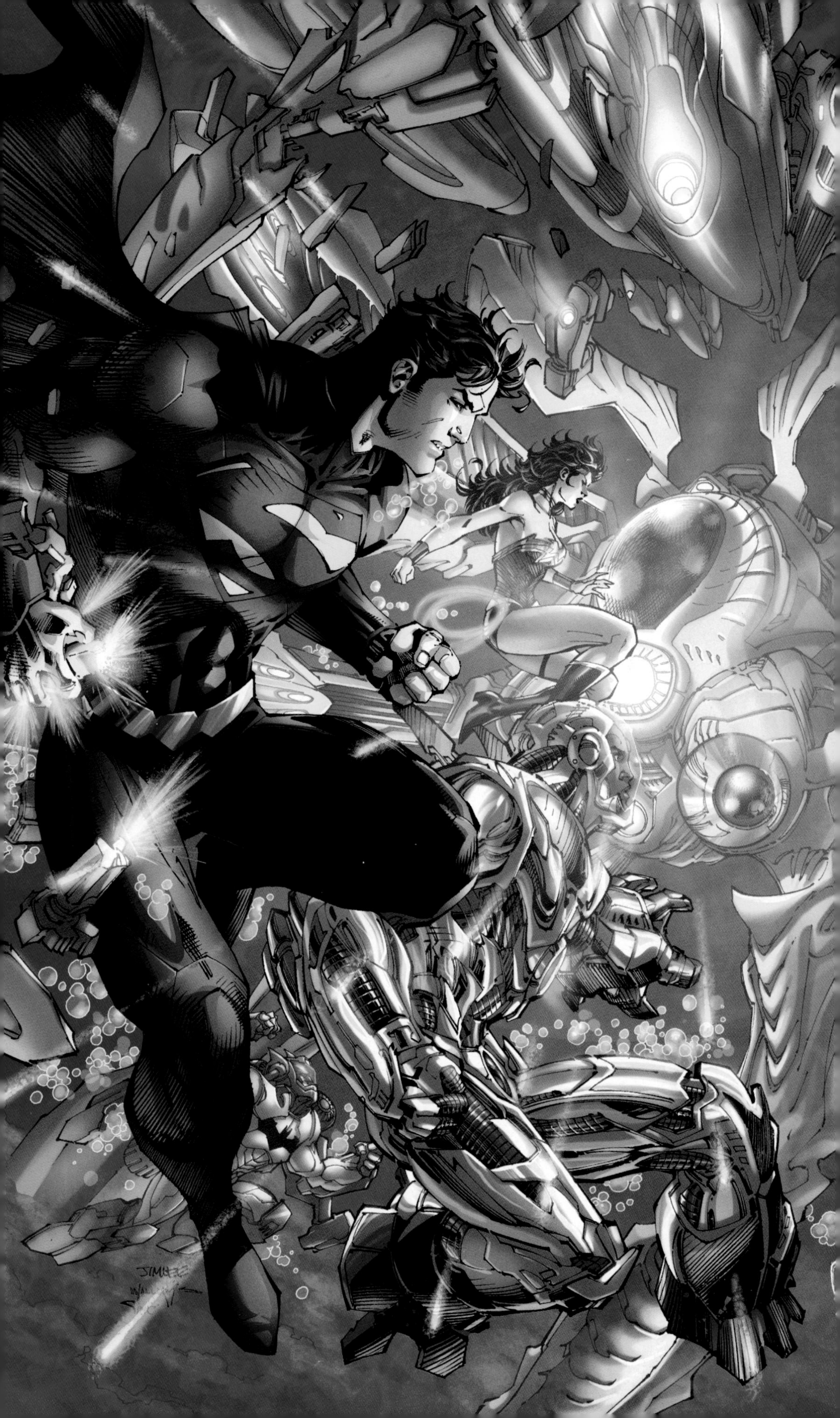

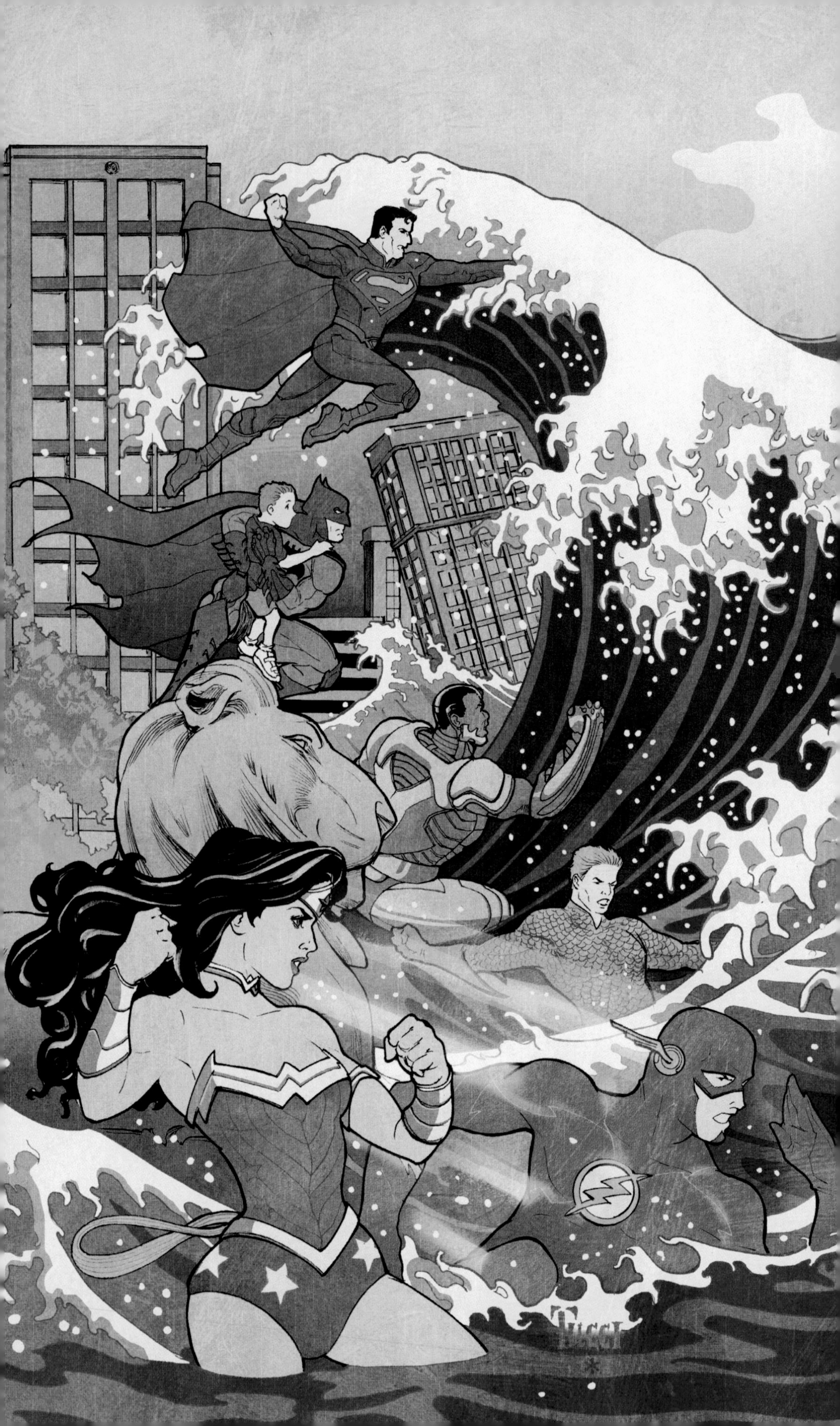
TUCCI

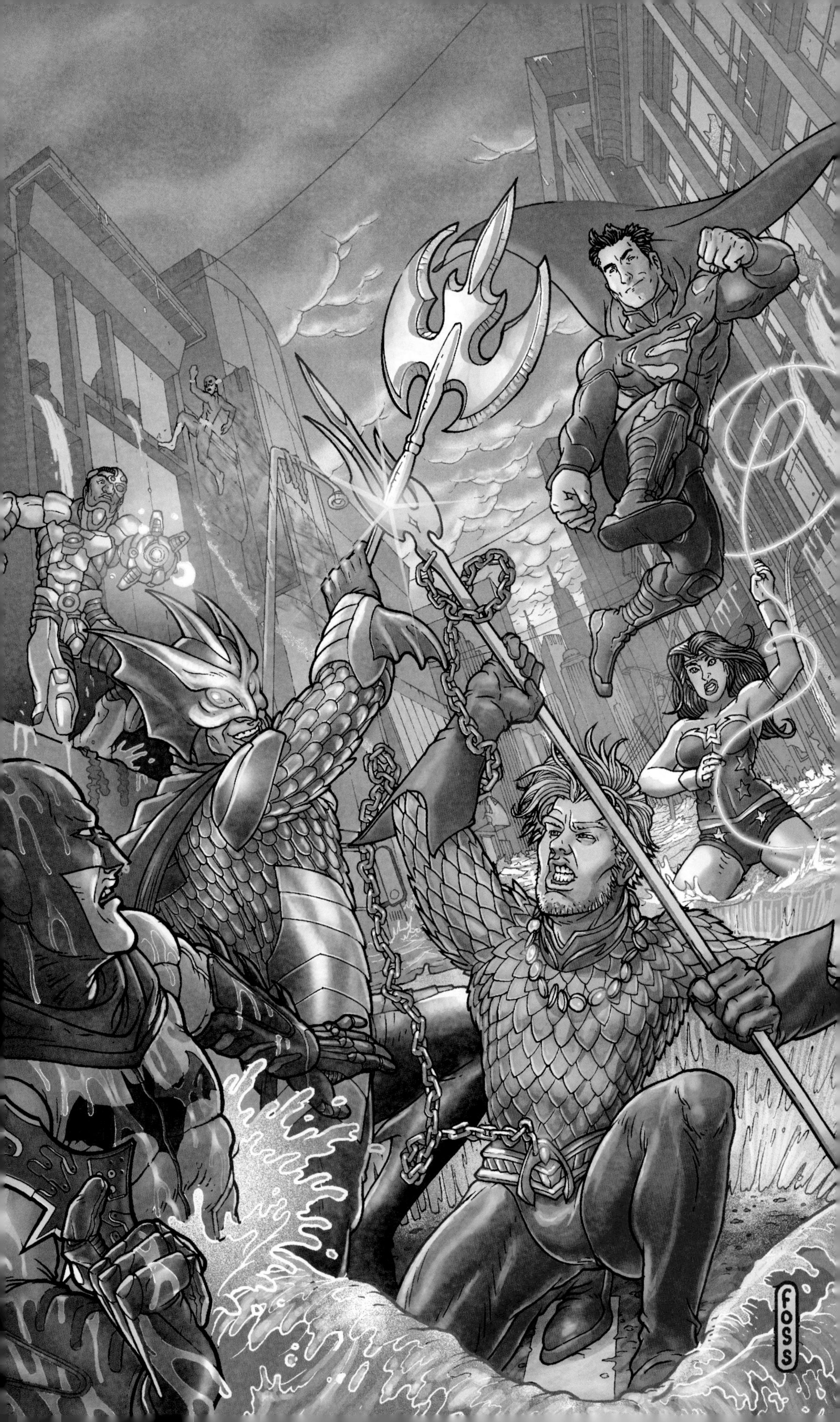
FOSS

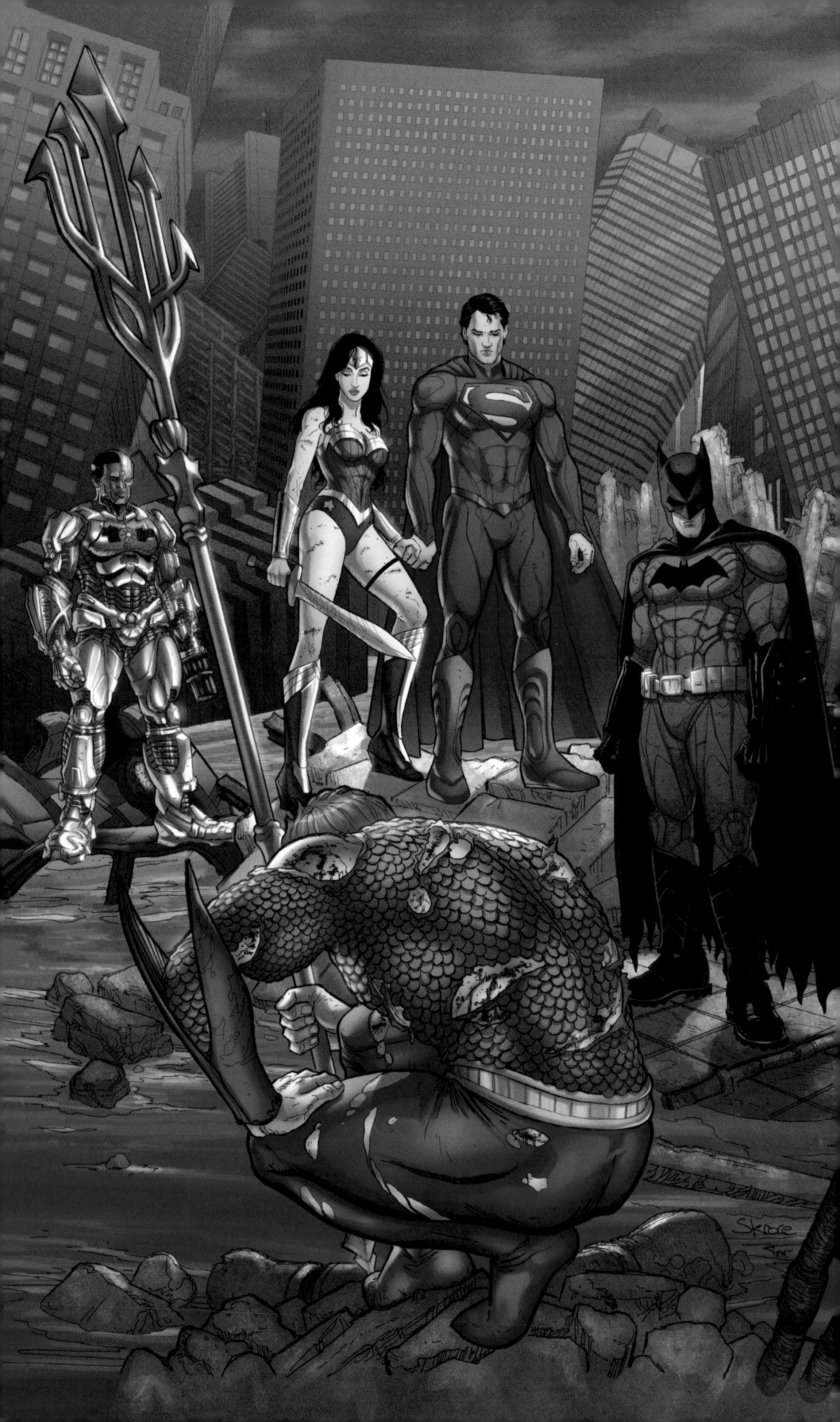

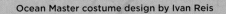

Ocean Master costume design by Ivan Reis

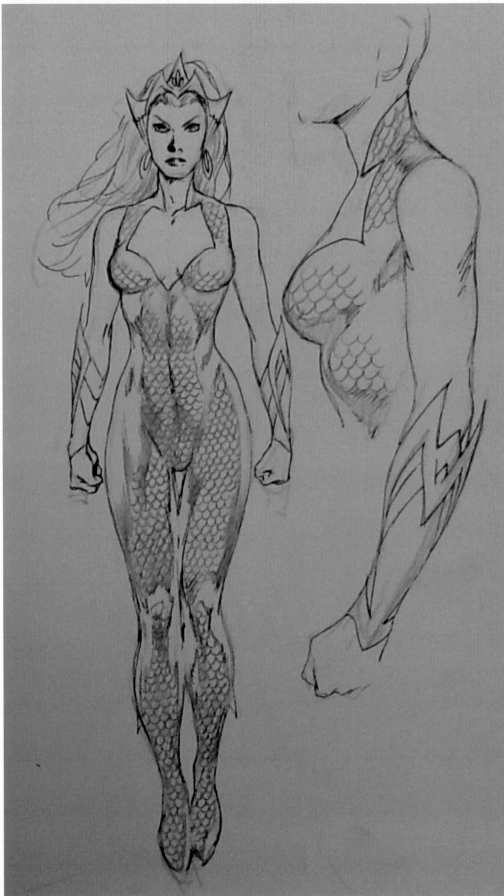

Mera costume update by Ivan Reis

-step progression of New York Comic Con AQUAMAN promo piece by Paul Pelletier, Art Thibert & Gabe Eltaeb.

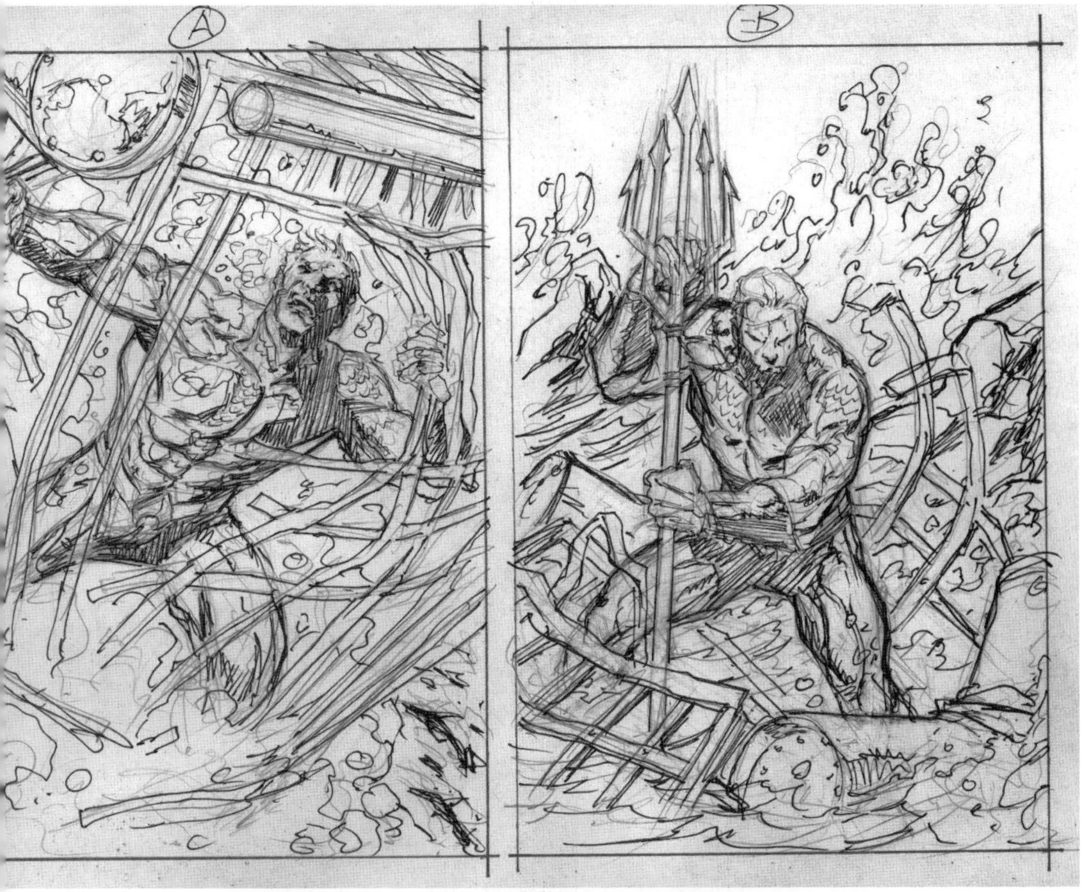
A
B

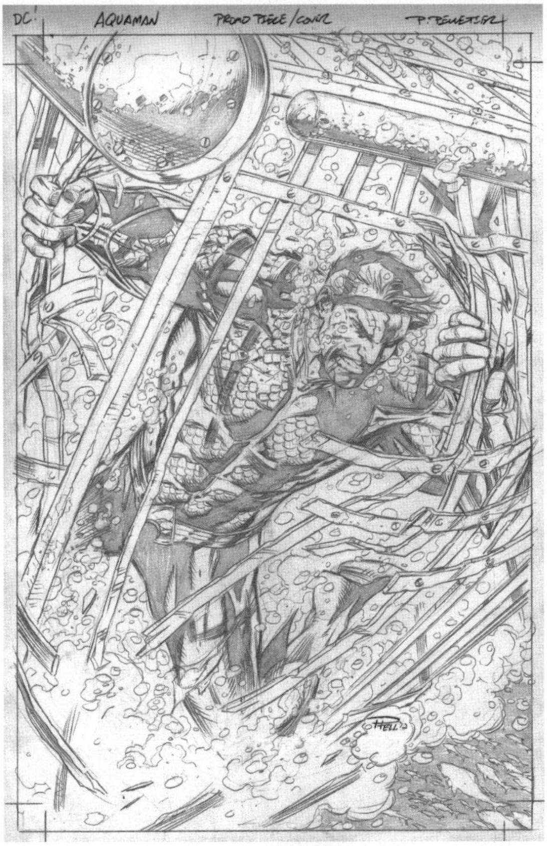
DC!
AQUAMAN
PROMO PIECE / COVER
P. PELLETIER

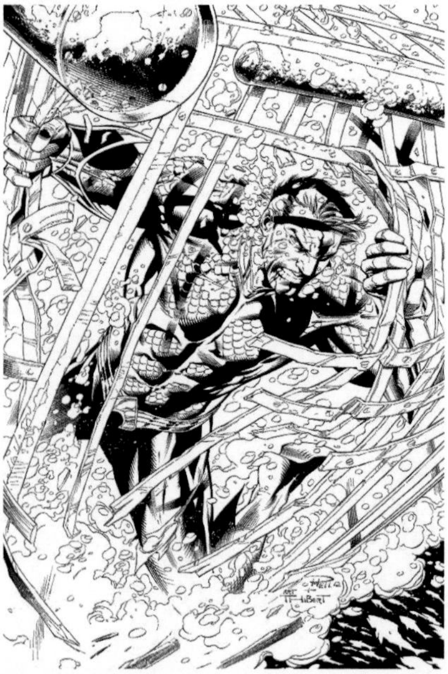

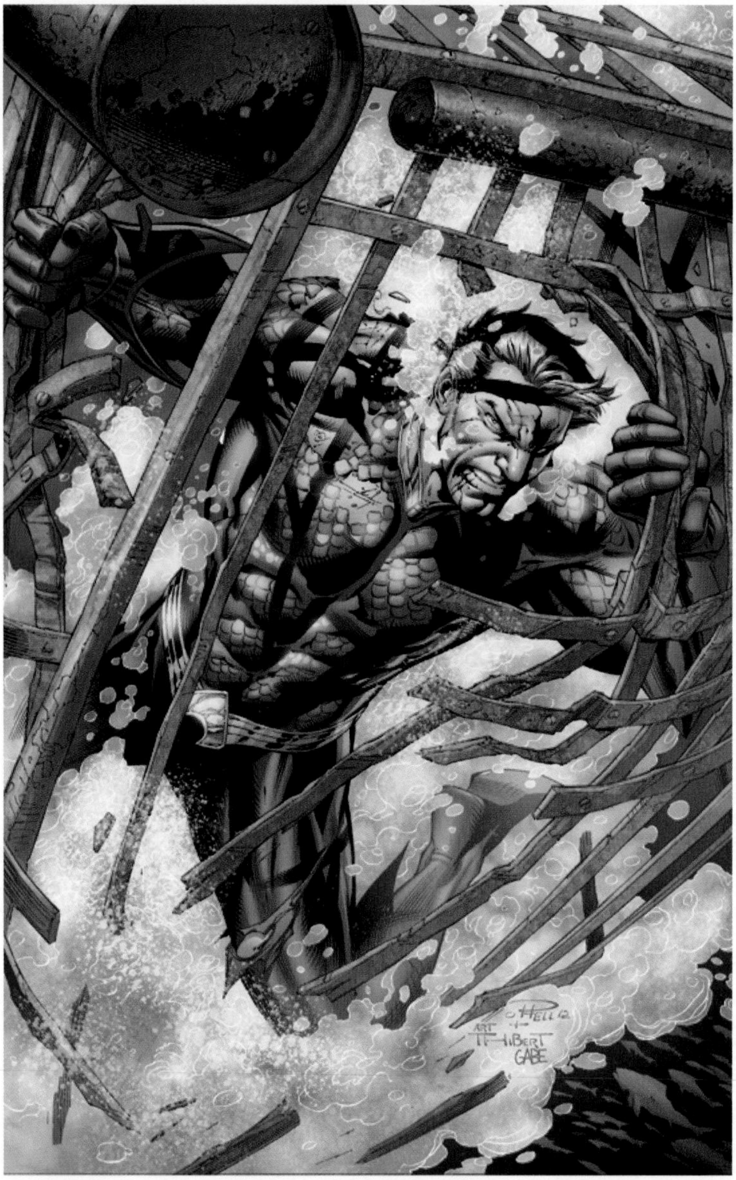

AMAN #15 cover sketches by Pete Woods

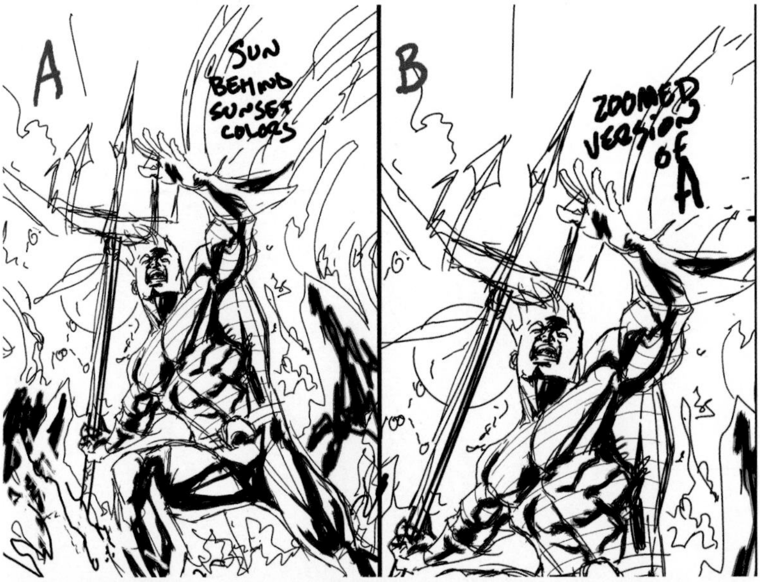
A
SUN
BEHIND
SUNSET
COLORS
B
ZOOMED
VERSION
OF
A

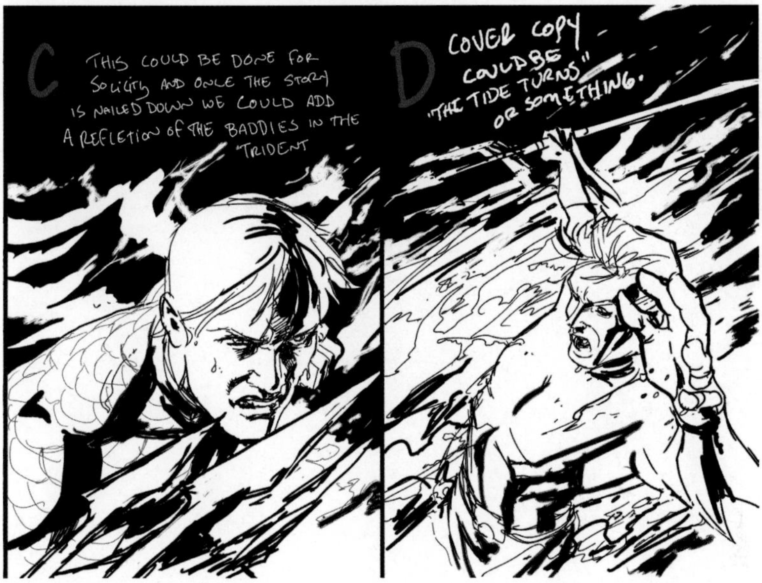
C
THIS COULD BE DONE FOR
SOLICITS AND ONCE THE STORY
IS NAILED DOWN WE COULD ADD
A REFLETION OF THE BADDIES IN THE
TRIDENT
D
COVER COPY
COULD BE
"THE TIDE TURNS"
OR SOMETHING.

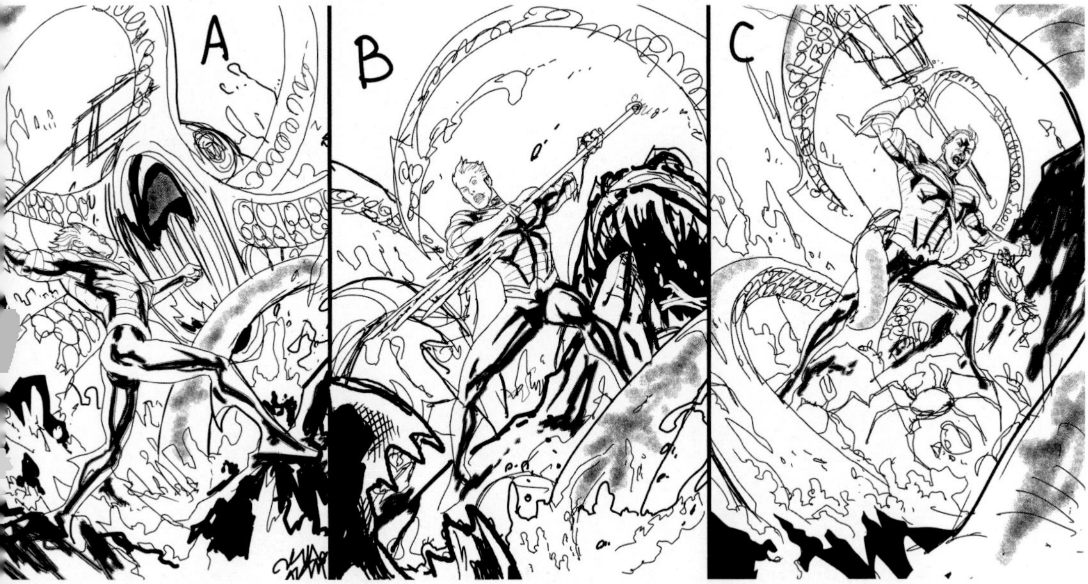
A
B
C

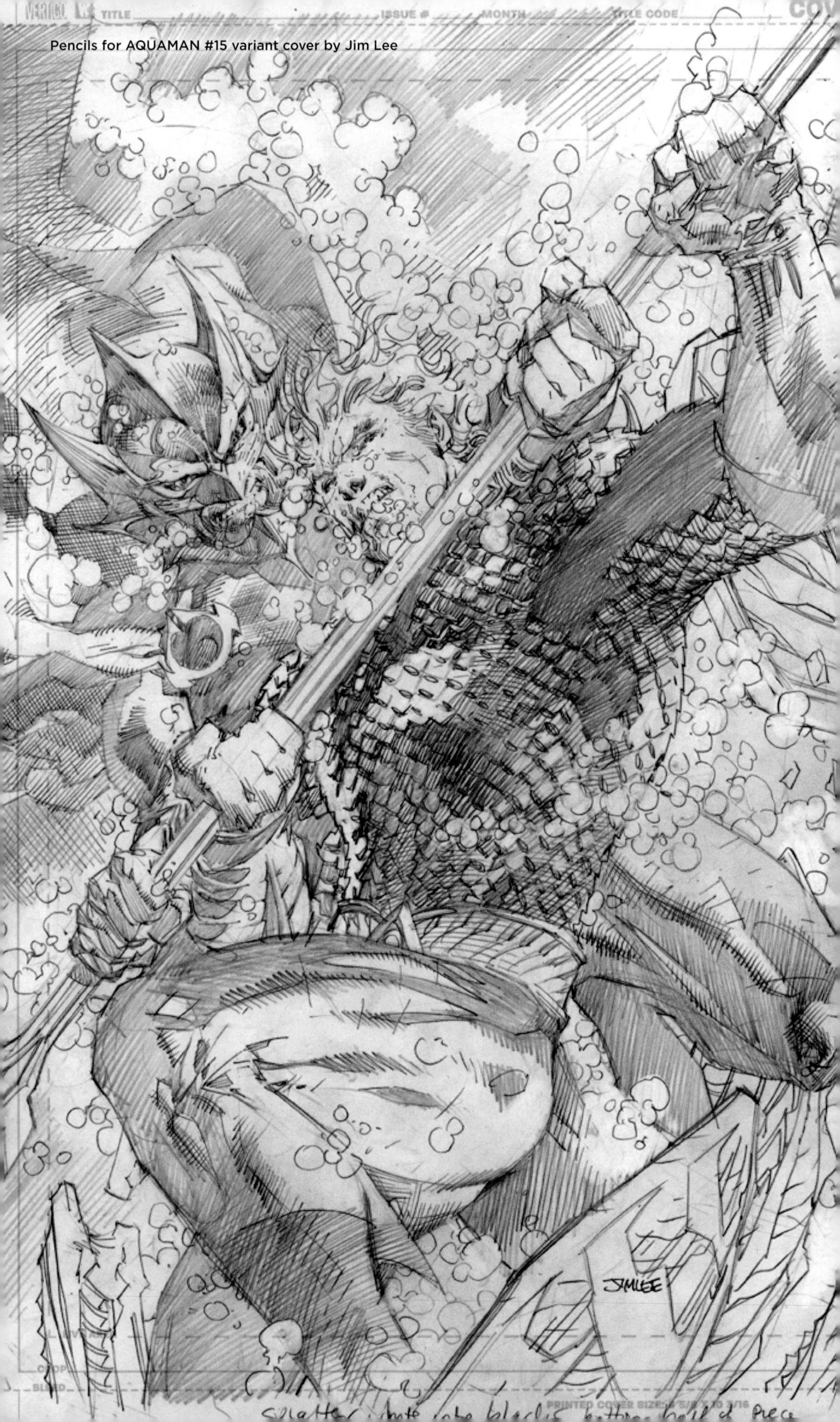
TITLE
ISSUE #
MONTH
TITLE CODE
JIMLEE
CROP
BLEED
Pencils for AQUAMAN #15 variant cover by Jim Lee

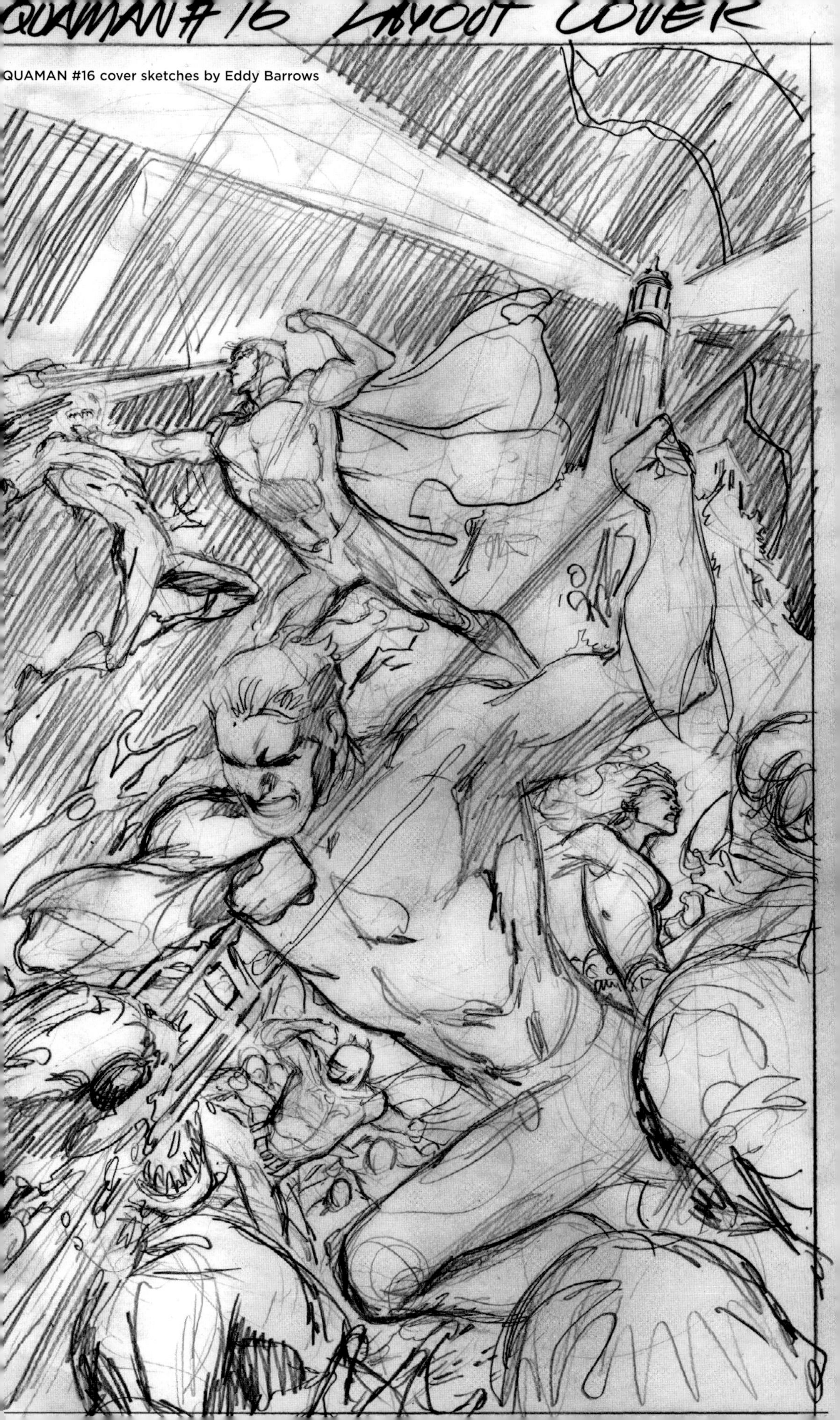
QUAMAN #16 LAYOUT COVER

QUAMAN #16 cover sketches by Eddy Barrows

AQUAMAN #16 LAYOUT COVER (

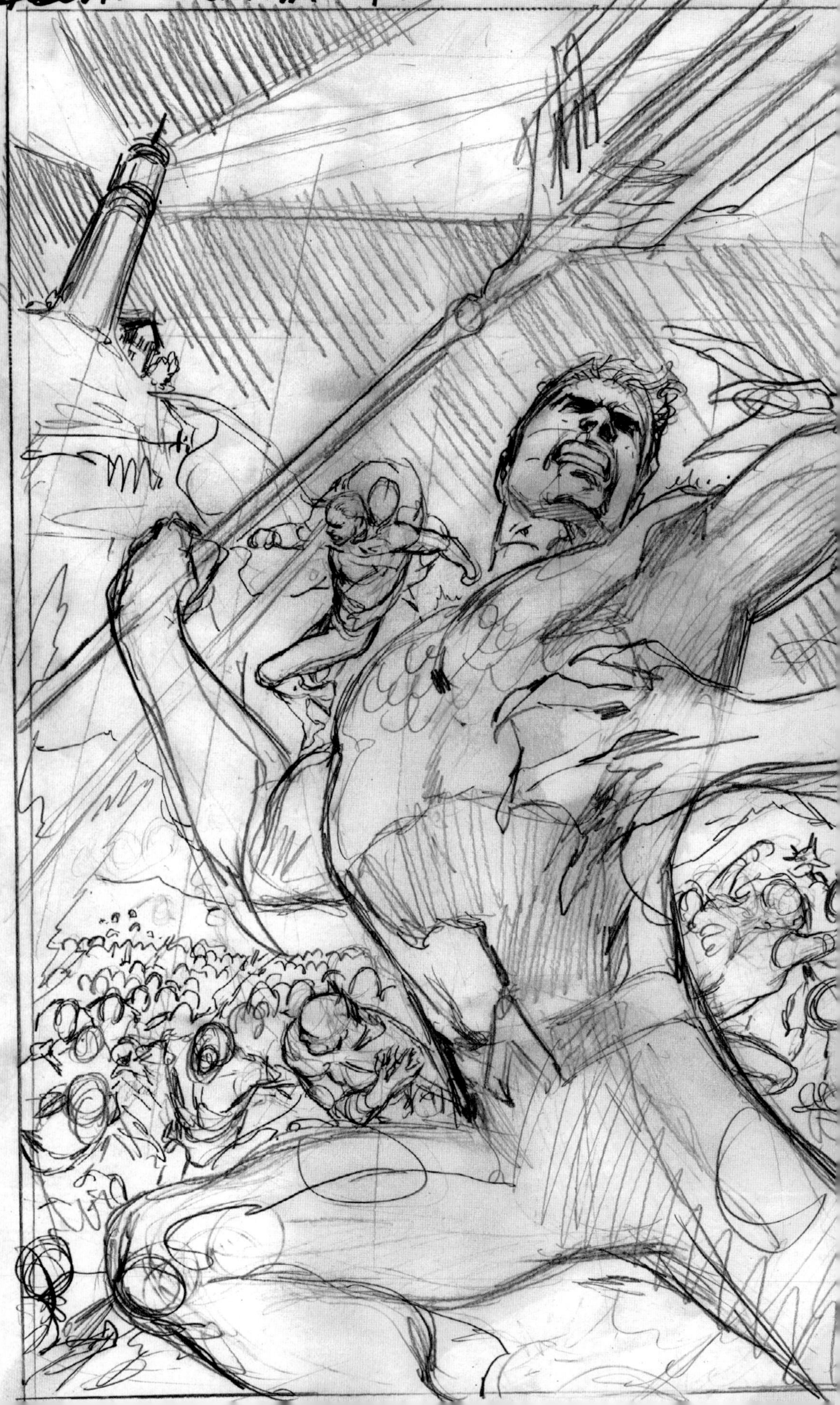

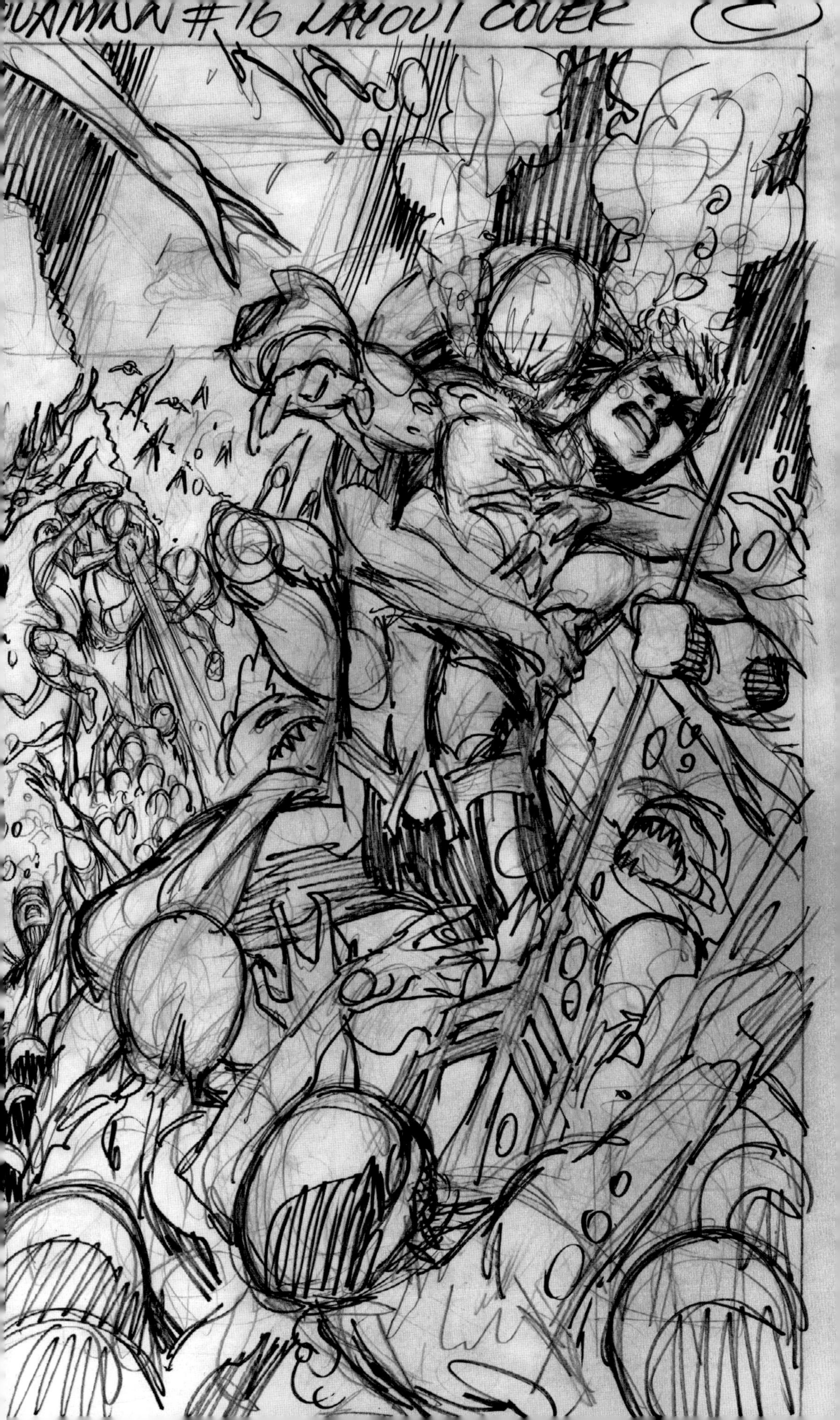
UAMAN #16 LAYOUT COVER
C

START AT THE BEGINNIN

JUSTICE LEAGU
VOLUME 1:ORIGI

**AQUAMAN
VOLUME 1:
THE TRENCH**

**THE SAVAGE
HAWKMAN VOLUME 1:
DARKNESS RISING**

**GREEN ARROW
VOLUME 1:
THE MIDAS TOUCH**

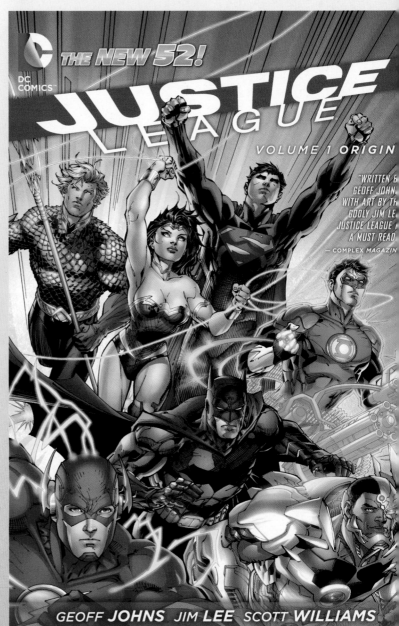

GEOFF *JOHNS* JIM *LEE* Scott *WILLIAMS*